HISTORICAL DICTIONARIES OF RELIGIONS, PHILOSOPHIES, AND MOVEMENTS
Edited by Jon Woronoff

1. *Buddhism,* by Charles S. Prebish, 1993
2. *Mormonism,* by Davis Bitton, 1994
3. *Ecumenical Christianity,* by Ans Joachim van der Bent, 1994
4. *Terrorism,* by Sean Anderson and Stephen Sloan, 1995
5. *Sikhism,* by W. H. McLeod, 1995
6. *Feminism,* by Janet K. Boles and Diane Long Hoeveler, 1995
7. *Olympic Movement,* by Ian Buchanan and Bill Mallon, 1995
8. *Methodism,* by Charles Yrigoyen Jr. and Susan E. Warrick, 1996
9. *Orthodox Church,* by Michael Prokurat, Alexander Golitzin, and Michael D. Peterson, 1996
10. *Organized Labor,* by James C. Docherty, 1996
11. *Civil Rights Movement,* by Ralph E. Luker, 1997
12. *Catholicism,* by William J. Collinge, 1997
13. *Hinduism,* by Bruce M. Sullivan, 1997
14. *North American Environmentalism,* by Edward R. Wells and Alan M. Schwartz, 1997
15. *Welfare State,* by Bent Greve, 1998
16. *Socialism,* by James C. Docherty, 1997
17. *Bahá'í Faith,* by Hugh C. Adamson and Philip Hainsworth, 1998
18. *Taoism,* by Julian F. Pas in cooperation with Man Kam Leung, 1998
19. *Judaism,* by Norman Solomon, 1998
20. *Green Movement,* by Elim Papadakis, 1998
21. *Nietzscheanism,* by Carol Diethe, 1999
22. *Gay Liberation Movement,* by Ronald J. Hunt, 1999
23. *Islamic Fundamentalist Movements in the Arab World, Iran, and Turkey,* by Ahmad S. Moussalli, 1999
24. *Reformed Churches,* by Robert Benedetto, Darrell L. Guder, and Donald K. McKim, 1999
25. *Baptists,* by William H. Brackney, 1999
26. *Cooperative Movement,* by Jack Shaffer, 1999
27. *Reformation and Counter-Reformation,* by Hans J. Hillerbrand, 2000
28. *Shakers,* by Holley Gene Duffield, 2000

Historical Dictionary of Mormonism

Second Edition

Davis Bitton

Historical Dictionaries of Religions,
Philosophies, and Movements, No. 32

The Scarecrow Press, Inc.
Lanham, Maryland, and London
2000

SCARECROW PRESS, INC.

Published in the United States of America
by Scarecrow Press, Inc.
4720 Boston Way, Lanham, Maryland 20706
www.scarecrowpress.com

4 Pleydell Gardens, Folkestone
Kent CT20 2DN, England

British Library Cataloguing in Publication Information Available

Library of Congress Cataloging-in-Publication Data

Bitton, Davis, 1930–
    Historical dictionary of Mormonism / Davis Bitton. — 2nd ed.
      p. cm. — (Historical dictionaries of religions, philosophies, and
movements ; no. 32)
    Includes bibliographical references.
    ISBN 0-8108-3797-8 (alk. paper)
    1. Mormon Church—Dictionaries. 2. Mormons—Dictionaries. I. Title.
II. Series.
BX8605.5 .B558 2000
289.3′03—dc21   00-061210

⊚™ The paper used in this publication meets the minimum requirements of
American National Standard for Information Sciences—Permanence of
Paper for Printed Library Materials, ANSI/NISO Z39.48-1992.
Manufactured in the United States of America.

Contents

Editor's Foreword

The Church of Jesus Christ of Latter-day Saints, or Mormonism, as it is widely known, is one of the younger religions. To the surprise and sometimes consternation of many outside the Church, it did not wither and die. To the contrary, it has grown at an exceptional pace, taking root in many different settings. Whether it will eventually join the select circle of "world religions," as many of its adherents hope, remains uncertain. At any rate, it is well on the way. And its increasing size and significance readily explain its inclusion in this series of historical dictionaries.

The story of Mormonism is frequently gripping, when you consider the efforts of its founders and leaders over the past century and a half. But it is just as important to consider the present to understand why the Church has retained its vitality and achieved record growth. For this, it is necessary to examine, in addition to Mormonism's religious precepts and practices, its social, economic, and cultural activities as well as its ability to adapt to changing circumstances and keep abreast of the times. All of this—the past and the present, the essential religious concepts, the work in many different fields and countries, and the role of both leaders and ordinary members—is described in this book. It is supported by a helpful chronology and a selective bibliography for those who want to do further reading.

The *Historical Dictionary of Mormonism* was written by Davis Bitton, professor of history at the University of Utah and author of numerous articles and books on Mormonism. Among the best known of these are *Guide to Mormon Diaries and Autobiographies*, *The Ritualization of Mormon History*, and (with Leonard Arrington) *The Mormon Experience* and *Mormons and Their Historians*. Having lectured and written so extensively on the subject, Dr. Bitton knows the material well and presents it compellingly. He knows what the questions are and gladly provides the answers, which is of particular importance to non-Mormons. But this book is also a very useful—and handy—guide for Mormons.

Jon Woronoff
Series Editor

Preface

From one point of view the Mormons are but one group, and, at that, not the largest group, within the contemporary religious spectrum. They see themselves as God's chosen people, as the "only true and living church," not unlike many other religious groups.

Since their formal organization in 1830, the Mormons have had a colorful, exciting history. In the 20th century, while melding into the larger society and achieving respectability in the eyes of most people, Mormonism continued to grow. That growth has been dramatic, especially during the past 30 or 40 years, which, not surprisingly, has evoked new opposition and denunciation. Mormonism is not a quiet, dull religion undifferentiated from the many Christian denominations.

Scarecrow Press has recognized that there is no handy guide to Mormonism written for the general public. Other references exist, but they are written for a Mormon audience or, in the case of older biographical and historical encyclopedias or the five-volume *Encyclopedia of Mormonism*, are library reference works rather than a handbook that can be easily carried and used. I have benefited from these other works and have supplied a bibliography for those who wish to read more. But the present dictionary should prove useful to those needing a preliminary orientation to Mormon history, beliefs, practices, and terminology.

We are all so familiar with encyclopedias that are arranged in the irrational but convenient alphabetical order that little explanation is required here. Part of the fun of using such a work is in random browsing. At the same time, however, readers new to the subject may wish to gain a quick overview of Mormon history. One way of doing this would be to read in the sequence listed the dictionary entries entitled New York Period, Ohio Period, Missouri Period, Illinois Period, Exodus, Utah Period, and Colonization. Alternatively, the biographical sketches provided of the Church presidents might be read in chronological sequence: Joseph Smith, Brigham Young, John Taylor, Wilford Woodruff, Lorenzo Snow, Joseph F. Smith, Heber Jeddy Grant, George Albert Smith, David Oman McKay, Joseph

Fielding Smith, Harold Bingham Lee, Spencer Woolley Kimball, Ezra Taft Benson, Howard William Hunter, and Gordon Bitner Hinckley. Other entries, as well, often include historical information.

Mormons still use the King James, or authorized, version of the Bible. All biblical quotations are drawn from that version, as republished in 1979, with explanatory notes and cross-references, by the Church of Jesus Christ of Latter-day Saints.

I wish to thank my wife, JoAn, who encouraged me in this project; three Church officials and two BYU professors, who read the manuscript and made helpful suggestions; several leaders of the general Relief Society, who reviewed the articles relating to women; Richard Jensen, of the Joseph Fielding Smith Institute for Latter-day Saint History, who also made helpful suggestions; and Marilyn R. Parks, whose efficiency as a secretary and computer specialist is unrivaled.

List of Abbreviations

AML	Association for Mormon Letters
BYU	Brigham Young University
CEBA	Centro Escolar Benemérito de las Americas
CPART	Center for the Preservation of Ancient Religious Texts
FARMS	Foundation for Ancient Research and Mormon Studies
JST	Joseph Smith Translation (of the Bible)
JWHA	John Whitmer Historical Association
LDS	Latter-day Saint. Often used as a substitute for Mormon or for Church of Jesus Christ of Latter-day Saints.
LDSSA	Latter-day Saint Students Association
MHA	Mormon History Association
MTC	Missionary Training Center
MYSC	Mormon Youth Symphony and Chorus
NCW	National Council of Women
NRI	Nauvoo Restoration, Inc.
NRM	New Religious Movement
RLDS	Reorganized Church of Jesus Christ of Latter Day Saints
YMMIA	Young Men's Mutual Improvement Association. Superseded by Young Men.
YWMIA	Young Women's Mutual Improvement Association. Superseded by Young Women.
ZCMI	Zion's Cooperative Mercantile Association

Chronology of Mormon History

1805

23 December   Joseph Smith Jr. was born in Sharon, Windsor County, Vermont.

1830

26 March   The Book of Mormon (second book of scripture after the Bible) was published in Palmyra, New York.

6 April   Joseph Smith organized the "Church of Christ" in Fayette, New York.

30 December   Church members were instructed to gather in Ohio (Doctrine and Covenants, section 37).

1831

2 August   Missouri was dedicated as the Land of Zion.

1833

20 July   A mob destroyed the Mormon printing office in Independence, Missouri.

November   Mormons left Jackson County, Missouri, because of mob opposition.

1834

8 May   A small "army" known as Zion's Camp began its march from Ohio to Missouri to assist beleaguered Mormons. The group dispersed on 30 June.

1835

14 February	Quorum of Twelve Apostles was organized.
28 February	First Council of the Seventy was organized.
17 August	A meeting was held, at which the contents to be included in the Doctrine and Covenants (which became the third book of scripture [the "standard works"]) were agreed on.
September	Doctrine and Covenants was published.
14 September	Emma Smith was appointed to select hymns.

1836

27 March	The Kirtland (Ohio) Temple was dedicated.

1837

13 June	Two Mormon apostles left Ohio on a mission to England, which was the first Mormon proselytizing outside of North America.
30 July	Nine persons were baptized in the River Ribble at Preston, England.

1838

6 July	Exodus of most Mormons from Kirtland, Ohio.
27 October	An order was given by Missouri Governor Lilburn W. Boggs to exterminate or expel the Mormons from the state.
30 October	Seventeen Mormons were killed at Haun's Mill in Missouri.

1839

January	The exodus of Mormons from Missouri began.
25 April	Land was purchased in Illinois at a site that was soon renamed Nauvoo.
8 August	John Taylor and Wilford Woodruff left for a mission to England.

1840

6 June	Forty-one converts set sail from England.

| 15 August | Baptism for the dead was officially announced. |
| 16 December | Nauvoo Charter was signed by the Illinois governor. |

1841

| 24 October | Palestine was dedicated for the return of the Jews by Apostle Orson Hyde. |

1842

| 1 March | Articles of Faith were written by Joseph Smith in a letter to John Wentworth and published in the Nauvoo newspaper. |
| 17 March | Female Relief Society was organized. |

1843

| 23 May | Missionaries left Nauvoo for the Pacific islands. |
| 12 July | Revelation on marriage was recorded, instituting the possibility of plural marriage, or polygamy. |

1844

| 27 June | Joseph and Hyrum Smith were killed by a mob in Carthage, Illinois. |
| 8 August | Leadership of the Church by the Twelve under Brigham Young was approved by a vote at a large meeting in Nauvoo. |

1846

4 February	Evacuation of Nauvoo began.
1 May	Nauvoo Temple was dedicated.
13 July	Volunteers began to enlist in the Mormon Battalion of the U.S. Army.

1847

| 22–24 July | Arrival in the Salt Lake Valley of the pioneer company under Brigham Young. |
| 5 December | First Presidency was reorganized, with Brigham Young the president of the Church. |

1848

June   Crops were saved when flocks of gulls devoured the crickets.

1849

6 October   Missionaries were called to preach in continental Europe.

1850

15 June   *Deseret News* began publication.
20 September   Brigham Young was appointed governor of the Utah Territory.

1851

11 July   Pearl of Great Price (fourth volume of scripture) was published as a pamphlet in England.

1852

28–29 August   Plural marriage was first publicly announced.

1857

24 July   News was received that a U.S. army had been ordered to Utah.
7–11 September   Mountain Meadows Massacre.

1858

11 June   Peace commissioners resolved dispute, bringing an end to the Utah War.

1859

10–17 July   Horace Greeley interviewed Brigham Young.

1860

24 August–
  10 September   English explorer Richard F. Burton visited Utah.

1861

18 October   Telegraph line reached Utah.

1869

10 May   The transcontinental railroad was completed.

1870

12–14 June   Debate between the Rev. J. P. Newman and Mormon apostle Orson Pratt on the question "Does the Bible sanction polygamy?"

1875

3 October   U.S. President Ulysses S. Grant began a visit to Utah.
16 October   Brigham Young Academy was founded in Provo, Utah.

1877

1 January   Dedication of St. George Temple.
29 August   Brigham Young died.
4 September   Twelve Apostles under President John Taylor presided over the Church.

1878

25 August   Aurelia Spencer Rogers founded the Primary organization for children.

1879

6 January   Reynolds Decision. The U.S. Supreme Court upheld the constitutionality of antipolygamy laws and confirmed the sentence of polygamist George Reynolds.
21 July   Joseph Standing, a Mormon missionary, was killed by a mob in Georgia.

1880

19 August   Mormon missionaries were arrested for preaching in Berlin and ordered out of Germany.

5–6 September	U.S. President Rutherford B. Hayes and party visited Utah.
10 October	Pearl of Great Price was officially accepted as a standard work. The first Presidency of the Church was reorganized, with John Taylor as president.

1882

22 March	The Edmunds Act came out against polygamy.

1887

3 March	The Edmunds-Tucker Act, intensifying penalties for polygamy, became law without presidential signature.
25 July	Church president John Taylor died. The Twelve Apostles presided over the Church.

1888

21 May	Manti Temple was dedicated.

1889

7 April	Wilford Woodruff was named as president of the Church.

1890

24 September	President Wilford Woodruff issued a manifesto.
6 October	The Manifesto was approved by vote in general conference.

1891

9 May	U.S. President Benjamin Harrison and party visited Salt Lake City.

1893

6 April	Salt Lake Temple was dedicated.
8 September	The Tabernacle Choir won second prize at the Chicago World's Fair (the Columbian Exposition).

1894

13 November   The Genealogical Society of Utah was organized.

1895

8 May   The Constitutional Convention completed its work in drafting a state constitution for Utah.

1896

4 January   Utah became a state.

1897

24 July   A great celebration was held, commemorating the 50th anniversary of the entrance of the Mormon pioneers into Salt Lake Valley.

November   *Improvement Era* began publication.

1898

2 September   Church president Wilford Woodruff died.

13 September   Lorenzo Snow was sustained by the apostles as president of the Church.

9 October   Lorenzo Snow and other authorities were sustained by vote of the general Church conference.

8 November   Brigham Henry Roberts was elected Utah's congressman (however, he was accused of polygamy and not allowed to take his seat).

1903

15 October   Brigham Young Academy became Brigham Young University.

1904

5 April   The "Second Manifesto" was issued, ending plural marriage.

1913

21 May   The Boy Scout program was officially adopted for the boys
                  of the Church.

1915

January   *Relief Society Magazine* for women began publication.

1929

15 July   The Tabernacle Choir started a weekly radio broadcast.

1930

6 April   Centennial of the organization of the Church.

1933

5 November   Chapel in Washington, D.C., was dedicated.

1936

7 April   The Welfare Program was introduced.

1937

July   The outdoor pageant, "America's Witness for Christ," began
                  at Hill Cumorah in New York.

1947

24 July   Centennial celebration of the arrival of Mormon pioneers in
                  the Salt Lake Valley.

1954

July   Indian Placement Program was inaugurated.
21 July   The Church College of Hawaii was announced.

1963

12 October   The Polynesian Cultural Center was dedicated in Laie, Hawaii.

1966

1 May   The first stake in South America was organized in São Paulo, Brazil.

1969

3–8 August   The World Conference on Records was held in Salt Lake City.

1970

15 March   The first stake in Asia was organized in Tokyo.
22 March   The first stake in Africa was organized in Transvaal, South Africa.

1971

January   New Church magazines began publication: *Ensign* (for adults), *The New Era* (for youth), and *The Friend* (for children).

1972

14 January   Establishment of the Historical Department of the Church was announced, replacing the Church Historian's Office.
27 February   J. Spencer Kinard succeeded Richard L. Evans as commentator for the Tabernacle Choir.

1974

1 September   The Church College of Hawaii was renamed Brigham Young University-Hawaii campus.

1975

19–21 June   An open house was held for the new 28-story Church Office building in Salt Lake City.

1976

25 June   Missouri Governor Christopher S. Bond rescinded the 1838 Mormon extermination order.

1978

9 June   The First Presidency announced that worthy men of all races would be eligible to receive the priesthood.
9 September   Missionary Training Center replaced Mission Home in Salt Lake City and Language Training Mission.

1979

29 September   A new edition of the King James version of the Bible was published.

1980

6 April   Sesquicentennial of the organization of the Church.

1981

26 September   New editions of Book of Mormon, Doctrine and Covenants, and Pearl of Great Price were issued.

1982

1 April   Church membership reached five million.
3 October   New subtitle was announced for Book of Mormon: "Another Testament of Jesus Christ."

1984

28 October   The 1,500th stake, the Ciudad Obregon, Mexico Yaqui Stake, was organized.

1985

27 January	Church members participated in a fast to raise funds ($11 million) for famine victims in Africa.
2 August	Revised hymnbook was published.
23 October	Family History Library was dedicated.
10 November	Ezra Taft Benson became the 13th president of the Church.

1988

12 November	Centennial of Ricks College, Rexburg, Idaho.

1989

16 May	Brigham Young University Jerusalem Center was dedicated.

1991

26 May	The 1,800th stake, the San Francisco de Macoris Dominican Republic Stake, was created.
31 May	Church membership reached eight million.
8–29 June	Tabernacle Choir toured eastern Europe.
December	Macmillan published the *Encyclopedia of Mormonism.*

1992

30 August	The 1,900th stake, the Orlando, Florida South Stake was created.
26 December	Tabernacle Choir began a tour of Israel.

1993

1 January	The India Bangalore Mission opened, with Gurcharan Singh Gill as president.
6 January	Tabernacle Choir concluded tour of Israel.
6 April	Centennial of the Salt Lake Temple was observed.

1994

5 June	Howard W. Hunter became the 14th president of the Church.

17 November	President Thomas S. Monson was honored by Catholic Community Services of Utah for humanitarian care.
3 December	More than 20,000 food packages were prepared for families in Bosnia, Croatia, and Albania.
11 December	2,000th stake in the Church was created in Mexico City.

1995

21 February	Gordon B. Hinckley was honored by the National Conference of Christians and Jews (Utah Region) for promoting high moral values.
March	President Howard W. Hunter died.
12 March	Gordon B. Hinckley became the 15th president of the Church.
1 April	The position of regional representative was replaced by the new position of area authority.
23 August	President Thomas S. Monson welcomed the king and queen of Sweden to the grounds of the Stockholm Temple.
23 September	Proclamation on the Family was issued by the First Presidency. See appendix 3.
18 December	Mike Wallace interviewed President Gordon B. Hinckley for the CBS television program *60 Minutes*.

1996

18 January	General Authorities announced withdrawal from boards of directors of business corporations.
28 February	More than half of the Church membership was living outside of the United States.
29 June	The American Academy of Achievement awarded President Gordon B. Hinckley the Golden Plate Award for exceptional accomplishment in public service.

1997

April	Organization of the Third, Fourth, and Fifth Quorums of Seventy was announced.
19–21 April	The Mormon Trail Wagon Train departed from Iowa and Nebraska to reenact the 1847 overland journey to the Salt Lake Valley.

28 May	A new, nine-story headquarters building for the *Deseret News* was dedicated in Salt Lake City, Utah.
9 July	The Smithsonian Institution's National Museum of American History in Washington, D.C., opened an exhibit on the Mormon Pioneer Trail.
24 July	The Mormon Trail Wagon Train, which for several weeks had reenacted the 1847 pioneer trek, arrived in Salt Lake City.
4 October	President Gordon B. Hinckley announced that "small" temples would be constructed in areas whose population would not justify larger ones.

1998

February	President Gordon B. Hinckley toured Nigeria, Ghana, Kenya, Zimbabwe, and South Africa and announced plans to construct a temple in Ghana.
26 April	President Gordon B. Hinckley addressed 20,000 people in Madison Square Garden in New York City.
7–10 June	Dedication of a temple in Preston, England, the site of the first English baptisms in 1837.
14 June–2 July	Tabernacle Choir toured England, Belgium, Switzerland, Italy, France, Spain, and Portugal.
28 June	The first meeting house in the Ukraine was dedicated at Donetsk.
8 September	President Gordon B. Hinckley was interviewed on *Larry King Live,* a network television show.

1999

9 February	Deseret Management Corporation, the Church's holding company for commercial entities, acquired Bookcraft, Inc.
11 February	Leonard J. Arrington, the Church's most prolific and respected historian, died.
1 April	The sesquicentennial of the organization of the Sunday School was celebrated.
1 April	The cemetery at Winter Quarters, Nebraska, was conveyed to Church ownership.
25 April	President Gordon B. Hinckley addressed a group of 57,500 in Santiago, Chile.

29–30 April	The Women's Conference at Brigham Young University was attended by 20,000 women.
13 May	President Gordon B. Hinckley addressed the Los Angeles World Affairs Council.
24 May	Free web site for genealogical research, www.familysearch.org, was launched.
11 September	A reconstructed monument honoring victims of the Mountain Meadows Massacre was dedicated.
25 September	The Relief Society declaration on the roles and values of women was announced.
26 November	"American Prophet: The Story of Joseph Smith," a television documentary, made its national debut on the Public Broadcasting System.
24 December	President Gordon B. Hinckley was interviewed on *Larry King Live*.

Introduction

As religions go, The Church of Jesus Christ of Latter-day Saints is not old. Just over 170 years ago it came into existence in upstate New York. Compared with the nearly 2,000 years that Christianity has been around, not to mention the older religions, such as Buddhism, it is a mere child, a toddler. The Church today (and for convenience, when I capitalize the word *Church* throughout the present work, it refers to this organization) stands in relation to its beginnings in 1830 as early Christian Fathers, such as Irenaeus, did to the beginnings of Christianity. No living Mormon remembers the beginning, but there are some in their advanced years whose parents or grandparents knew some of those who had been there at the beginning. Americans, who celebrated a bicentennial of the U.S. Constitution in 1987, are a good generation further away in time from the beginning of their country than Mormons are from the beginning of their Church, whose bicentennial they will commemorate in 2030.

Actually, what appears to be a short life span may not be so short after all. Many nations have come and gone in the last century or two, and the same is true with churches. More important, Mormonism did not, from the point of view of its believers, originate in the 19th century at all. It was rather a restoration of the same Church that Christ established, bringing back the same doctrine and same authority. Indeed, its basic principles and ordinances were given by the Lord at the beginning of human existence on earth. Although outsiders may not think in these terms, this is the way that Mormons see their Church—as a culmination of a series of divine dispensations stretching across several millennia.

Yet surviving even since 1830 is not bad for a religious organization. More than a few groups have come into existence only to disappear or fade into insignificance. Of the many religions founded in the 20th century, how many will still be around a generation or two from now? Contrary to the expectations—and wishes—of many who saw it as a seedling in the 1830s and 1840s, Mormonism survives.

It has been an exciting history. One can imagine a new religion making little commotion at all, melting readily into the existing landscape as its adherents go about their daily affairs with no obvious differences from anyone else. One can imagine a new religion remaining confined to a single locality at least for a generation or more. Such was not the case with Mormonism. From the beginning it was noticed—almost always negatively. Wherever the Latter-day Saints tried to settle, they ran into opposition. Grumbling turned into denunciation and then hounding and persecution. They were driven from place to place, strangers in the land, looking for "a city which hath foundations, whose builder and maker is God."[1]

From the beginning there was a bold range and sweep to the Mormon experience. Even though the new Church of Jesus Christ of Latter-day Saints (the official name) was organized in a private dwelling in Fayette, New York, it did not intend to stay there. In less than a year the headquarters had been moved to Ohio and another center established in Missouri. These are distances of several hundred miles. Travel was by riverboat, stage or wagon, or often simply by foot. Forced out of both Ohio and Missouri before the 1830s had run their course, the unpopular Mormons were soon establishing a new center on the banks of the Mississippi in western Illinois.

Five years later, on a dark night in June, amid the shrieks and yells of a militia turned into a lawless mob, their founder and leader fell dead in a hail of bullets while incarcerated in jail awaiting trial. Those who committed the deed saw it as a justifiable lynching, perfectly consistent with the traditions of 19th-century America. The Mormons, stunned and grief-stricken, saw it as a martyrdom.

In less than two years, still the victims of persecution, the Mormons were fleeing their city, crossing the river, and heading westward into Iowa Territory. A bird's-eye view during the next months would have seen wagon trains of refugees slowly moving westward, with camps established at intervals for rest and regrouping. It was another exodus. Fighting weather conditions, lacking supplies, and fearful of their persecutors, they were strung out over several hundred miles. After a halt for the next winter they pushed on to the Great Basin on the western slope of the Rocky Mountains. This was a journey that required several weeks of painful, persistent travel across a wilderness with no cities along the way to serve as supply stations.

The scope of the Mormon movement across the hemisphere was incredibly vast. There was not only the main group along the trail from Illinois to Utah. At the same time another company under Samuel Brannan was sailing from New York around the southern cape of South America and thence northward to Yerba Buena (later San Francisco) in California. And 500 Mormons were recruited into the U.S. Army and marched as an infantry battalion on a seemingly interminable journey to Kansas, New Mexico, across the dry wastes to the southern California coast, finally reaching San Diego.

Arriving in Utah, their new refuge, from different directions—the main route coming in from Wyoming, some coming eastward from California, converts from the South making their way by a southern route—the Mormons did not slink into a corner. Interrupted only briefly by a clash with federal troops in 1857 that miraculously escaped bloodshed, they embarked on an ambitious program of colonization, founding settlement after settlement throughout an immense empire. The pioneering so central to the American experience as part of the great westward movement was inescapably part of what it meant to be Mormon in the 19th century.

The range of Mormon activity also included missionaries who went forth to preach their gospel. Traveling singly or as time went on, increasingly in pairs, these fervent proselytizers typically carried only a small satchel and some pamphlets and copies of scripture. Relying on the hospitality of fellow believers or strangers who would spare a meal or a night's lodging, they crisscrossed the United States. As early as 1837 they were in England, and the 1840s saw these determined messengers showing up in France, Italy, India, and even Tahiti. In the latter half of the 19th century, the missionary fervor did not flicker but became more highly organized and more extensive.

As a counterflow to the missionaries going out, converts came to join their fellow believers in a movement of gathering. Starting on a small scale in Ohio, Missouri, and Illinois, this migration reached epic proportions as thousands, even tens of thousands, of Mormons from England and Scandinavia crossed the ocean in sailing ships and then, joining converts from the United States, made their way across the plains to their Zion in the West. The great flow of immigration to the New World, in other words, included Mormons who shared the hopes of their fellow immigrants, but also carried a vision derived from their religious faith.

Mormons were in the news. Objects of curiosity, often of pity or ridicule, they were described by newspaper reporters and travelers. The line drawings and cartoons of the periodicals often showed Mormons, who suffered from much the same stereotyping as other minorities. "I don't care what they say about me as long as they spell my name right." This quip, familiar to politicians and aspiring performers, might well have been the reaction of Church leaders. "I sit and laugh, and rejoice exceedingly when I see persecution," said Church president Brigham Young. "I care no more about it than I do about the whistling of the north wind, the croaking of the crane that flies over my head, or the crackling of the thorns under the pot. The Lord has all things in his hand."[2]

Part of the reason the Mormons made such interesting copy, indeed part of the reason for the persecution, was their practice of polygamy. For one man to have two or more wives was, to say the least, a departure from the norm. It was something one read about in *Arabian Nights*, not the prosaic monogamous marriage of Christian tradition. For several decades, polygamy was the publicist's "hook," the feature of the Mormon religion that could be counted on to attract interest. Books, newspaper articles, and cartoons conveyed the lip-smacking details of polygamy to an eager public. Lacking the stimulation of today's explicit television and movie fare, many let their imaginations run wild. Clucking tongues, shaking heads, people would pass on the latest about these people who were just too horrible for words. Those motivated by crusading zeal—it was an age caught up in abolitionism and the struggle for female suffrage—became militant, calling for the forcible repression of the religion in the West or, at the very least, a strict prohibition of the offensive marriage system. Even though it was officially discontinued more than a century ago, polygamy is still automatically associated with Mormonism in the minds of many people, who may know literally nothing else about the Church.

Other Mormon institutions were different from those of the typical U.S. city or state. The poverty of most converts, the opportunity to start with a clean slate in their new settlements, the necessity of cooperating in a hostile environment, and the idealistic egalitarianism remembered from primitive Christianity converged to produce a series of efforts among the Mormons to establish something close to the scriptural ideal of "all things in common" with "no poor among them." In the heyday of transcendentalism, in the wake of heady proposals from European and U.S. thinkers, other utopian communities appeared—Brook Farm was by no means the only example—but here was an entire people responding to ecclesiastical leaders whose teachings were accepted as God's will. While lacking the sensationalism of polygamy, the various Mormon "united orders" in the late 19th century attracted the attention of travelers and reporters, including Edward Bellamy, author of *Looking Backward*.

Historian Walter Prescott Webb once commented that Mormon history had everything: religious fervor, persecution, movements of people across space in immigration, exotic social practices, pioneering and settlement on the frontier. It also, he added, had a beginning, a middle, and an end. For Webb the end was the cessation of polygamy and the accommodation with the mores of the larger society at the end of the 19th century.

But more than half of Mormon history has occurred in the 20th century. By comparison with the dramatic struggles of the past the 20th-century history may appear dull. Sponsoring Boy Scout troops, emphasizing education, following an abstemious lifestyle, Mormons have succeeded in business, in politics, in law, even in entertainment. One survey showed them producing more scientists per capita than any comparable group. Patriotic, they supported the U.S. effort in both World War I and World War II. Articles in *Reader's Digest* and other publications portrayed them as exemplary citizens. Their Tabernacle Choir enjoyed unrivaled popularity for a group of its kind. Without question one dimension of Mormonism in the 20th century was increased respectability.

But settling down to a life of ease and stability, a denomination among denominations, was not to be the Mormon style. Earlier we said that, unlike some new religions, Mormonism survived. It did more than survive; it grew. There must have been some ironic satisfaction for the Church leaders as they observed the futility of the opposition. "Every time you kick Mormonism, you kick it up stairs," said Brigham Young in 1859. "You never kick it down stairs."[3] And indeed a combination of high birthrate, lower than average death rate, and especially the continuing conversions combined to produce a steady expansion.

Contrary to the expectations of some, the 20th century did not bring a leveling off. Relentlessly the numbers of Mormons increased past the middle of the century and then, in a way that could not have been predicted, a burst of missionary activity sent the numbers soaring. While continuing to work in the United States and western Europe, Mormon proselytizers moved out into South America, Asia, Africa, and eastern Europe. The number of these ardent missionaries, less than 5,000 at mid-century, escalated beyond 50,000. Church membership, barely a million at mid-century, soared past 10,000,000 and is still ascending.

It is this growth, almost certainly, that explains the hate movements that target Mormonism. Full of vitality, enthusiastic for their faith, Mormons may appear menacing. To combat them, modern opponents, successors of the anti-Mormon persecutors of the past century, have preached, written pamphlets and books, produced movies, and spoken on radio. While a calm statement of difference seems appropriate enough, all too often vitriolic Mormon-haters indulge in the smear tactics used by other hate movements. Such techniques have been condemned by the Anti-Defamation League of B'Nai B'rith and the American Council of Christians and Jews. In any case, once again we discover that Mormonism is not a religion easily ignored or dismissed with a yawn.

Which brings us to the question of point of view in the present work. It would serve no useful purpose in an introductory dictionary to engage in polemic. What can be done to good purpose, I think, is to explain what the Mormons have done, how they function, and what they believe (they themselves being the best authorities on that subject).

A multitude of titles, beliefs, and practices requires explanation if one is to avoid misunderstanding. What is a *ward* and a *stake*? Why does a *bishop* not wear the episcopal miter? Why do *elders* seem so young? What do Mormons mean when they talk about *testimony*? What is *Primary*? Why don't they use tobacco? Is it true what we hear about their *temples*? And on and on through the maze of terminology that requires explanation. The great majority of the following entries are informational, introducing the history, the leading personalities, the beliefs, and the practices of this extraordinary religion.

After all this time, after all the supposed accommodation and the middle-class respectability of many of them, Mormons continue to be a counter-culture. In a secular age they believe in God. In a cynical age they are idealistic. They scorn the values of the Hollywood elite and the mass media. Morality remains their commitment. While other conservative Christians and Jews, or other believers in natural law and traditional values, might find their presence uncomfortable, in Mormons they have allies on these basic matters. Resisting the spirit of the age, the Mormons will continue to advance their religion. Finding themselves at odds with the larger culture is not a new experience for them.

NOTES

1. Hebrews 11:10.
2. *Journal of Discourses* 2 (1855): 8.
3. *Journal of Discourses* 7 (1860): 144.

The Dictionary

-A-

AARONIC PRIESTHOOD. The lower of the two major divisions of Priesthood (q.v.), the other being the Melchizedek Priesthood (q.v.). As part of the restoration (q.v.), the Aaronic Priesthood was conferred upon Joseph Smith and Oliver Cowdery (qq.v.) by the resurrected John the Baptist (Doctrine and Covenants, section 13). The offices within the Aaronic Priesthood, from the bottom, are Deacon, Teacher, and Priest (qq.v.).

ABREA, ANGEL (1933–). General Authority. From Buenos Aires, Argentina. Baptized at age 10 after his mother and he read the Book of Mormon (q.v.) together, Abrea attended Primary (q.v.) classes. After graduating in accounting from the University of Buenos Aires, he became a certified public accountant. He served as secretary of the treasury for San Miguel, Argentina. He was called to church leadership positions: branch president, district president, mission president, stake (q.v.) president, and regional representative (q.v.). In 1981, at age 47, Abrea became a member of the First Quorum of the Seventy, the first Argentine General Authority (qq.v.). He also served as president of the Buenos Aires Temple.

ACTIVITY. Participation in church worship and callings (q.v.) or responsibilities. An "active" member, in the common usage, is one who faithfully attends meetings, pays a tithing (q.v.) and fast offerings (q.v.), follows the Word of Wisdom (q.v.), and in all respects tries to exemplify the standards of the Church. Obviously, there are degrees of activity. *See also* INACTIVITY.

AFRICA. At the end of 1997 there were about 112,000 Mormons in all of Africa, meaning sub-Saharan Africa, for the Muslim countries of North Africa have not proved congenial to Christian proselytizing.

South Africa contributed early converts. Then, after a 40-year hiatus, missionary (q.v.) proselytizing was resumed there in 1903. A temple (q.v.) was completed at Johannesburg in 1985. Since 1978 missionary work has been promulgated in other African countries where possible, with the greatest success in Nigeria, Ghana, and the Democratic Republic of the Congo (Zaire). The first Black African stake (q.v.) was created at Aba, Nigeria, in 1988. By late 1997 there were eight stakes in Nigeria, four in Ghana. Also considered part of the African Area for administrative purposes are Madagascar, Mauritius, and Reunion.

In 1998, President Gordon B. Hinckley (q.v.) visited Nigeria, Ghana, Kenya, Zimbabwe, and South Africa. In Ghana he met with the country's president, Jerry John Rawlings, and later that afternoon, before 6,500 members, announced that land had been purchased in Accra for the construction of Africa's second temple.

AMADO, CARLOS H. (1944–). Born in Guatemala City, Guatemala, Amado was 11 when his parents joined the Church. Carlos graduated from a technical college and then worked as a draftsman for four years. He served as a missionary (q.v.) in Peru. After marrying Mayavel Pineda, he served as branch president, bishop, seminary teacher (qq.v.), director for the Church Educational System in Central America, and president of the Guatemala City Mission. In 1989, he became a General Authority (q.v.) as member of the Second Quorum (q.v.) of the Seventy.

ANDERSON, RICHARD LLOYD (1926–). Missionary, lawyer, historian. Born in Salt Lake City on 9 May 1926, Anderson completed his early education in Utah, became a Navy radioman during World War II, and from 1946 to 1949 served as a missionary in the Northwestern states. The "Plan for Effective Missionary Work" he authored, known as the Anderson Plan, was widely used in many of the Church's missions in the early 1950s. After receiving a B.A. in history at Brigham Young University (q.v.) in 1951, Anderson attended Harvard Law School, earning the J.D. degree in 1954. After one year as a seminary and institute of religion (qq.v.) teacher he entered the graduate program in ancient history at the University of California at Berkeley, completing the Ph.D. in 1962.

At Brigham Young University, where he is professor of ancient scripture, Anderson was named honors professor of the year. Teacher of the New Testament, he nurtured a special interest in Paul, leading to a book, *Understanding Paul* (1983). His other area of expertise is Joseph Smith (q.v.) and early Mormonism. The acknowledged authority on the Witnesses of the Book of Mormon (q.v.), he published many valuable articles and in 1981 a book, *Investigating the Book of Mormon Witnesses.* He married Carma de Jong in 1951. They have four children.

ANTHON TRANSCRIPT. Characters from the original Book of Mormon (q.v.) plates shown by Martin Harris (q.v.) in February 1828 to Professor Charles Anthon, of Columbia College (later University) in New York City. According to Harris, Anthon first declared the characters legitimate but, when told of their miraculous origin, immediately recanted his authentication. Anthon later gave two contradictory accounts of the interview. Whatever was said, Harris was sufficiently convinced that he put up most of the funds for the publication of the first edition of the Book of Mormon in 1830. The characters of the transcript, as they survive in a handwritten version, have been ridiculed as clumsy scrawls, but parallels have been found in Demotic Egyptian, Old South Arabian, Old North Arabian, Micmac, and a script carved on Olmec baked clay seals.

ANTI-MORMONISM. Individual rejection of Mormonism's claims is not considered a manifestation of anti-Mormonism, but militant, repeated, and especially organized opposition is. The earliest examples occurred just before and soon after the inception of the Church in 1830 and led first to pamphlets and demonstrations and sometimes to looting and lynchings. Many of the publications about Mormons purveyed inaccuracies, oversimplification, and stereotyping typical of hate movements in general.

Although individual writings, films, and lectures against the Church can be found during every decade of Mormon history, anti-Mormonism has shown renewed vigor since the 1960s. At its worst, the anti-Mormon crusade is shamefully inaccurate and irresponsible, willing to use any means to accomplish its ends. At its best, anti-Mormons try to document their assertions but almost always with indifference to context and the question of typicality, and with a consistent determination to put Mormons and Mormonism in the worst possible light. In a similar vein, students of anti-Semitism have delineated all the key features of this mentality: scapegoating, obsession, stereotyping, caricaturing, overgeneralizing, and so on.

A key factor in provoking such opposition must be the success of Mormonism, which some would see as its expansionist thrust. A religion that was static or dwindling would more likely be ignored. Some anti-Mormons are ex-Mormons, whose motivations can be understood only by individual study. Although a few individual Mormons have written and spoken out in defense of their faith, the Church as such seldom responds to anti-Mormons, preferring to keep its attention on its positive goals.

APOCRYPHA. The 14 books included in Catholic Bibles (q.v.) but excluded from most Protestant versions. They were included in the original edition of the King James Version as a separate section but later removed. A larger definition of the term would include extra-canonical works produced by early Christians, for which the term *pseudepigrapha* is more commonly used. Since they do not believe in a closed canon, Mormons have been interested in these works. "There are many things contained therein that are true, and it is mostly translated correctly," wrote Joseph Smith of the Old Testament apocrypha. "There are many things contained therein that are not true, which are interpolations by the hands of men. . . . Therefore, whoso readeth it, let him understand, for the Spirit manifesteth truth" (Doctrine and Covenants, Section 91).

APOSTASY. Sometimes called the Great Apostasy. The falling away from the truths, principles, and authority of original Christianity. While its beginnings are discernible in the New Testament itself, the apostasy is thought to have reached the point, probably in the second century, where the Christian Church on earth no longer represented God's work.

Any digressions from the teachings of Jesus Christ (q.v.), whether theological under the influence of Greek philosophy or organizational under the influence of Roman law, are seen as manifestations of apostasy. Christians of the late Roman Empire and the Middle Ages were the victims of this process, not necessarily its perpetrators. Despite individual lives of sincerity and even faithfulness, the Church as an institution was devoid of divine authority. The changes in teachings and ordinances (q.v.) had not been minor but were fatal.

Protestants of the Reformation era had a similar view of Christian history, differing on their dating of the process and their prescription for a remedy. For Mormons the apostasy preceded the great church councils and creeds of the patristic era. Therefore they do not regard those doctrinal pronouncements as authoritative or as consistent with the New Testament norm. Most importantly, the loss of the true church in doctrine, organization, sacraments, (q.v.) and authority necessitated not a reformation but the restoration (q.v.) that began with God's call to Joseph Smith (q.v.).

APOSTATE. Someone who has abandoned the faith, especially one who has become belligerent. An "inactive" member, one who does not participate in the meetings and programs of the Church, is not so described, and more than a few Church members, after spending some months or even years in inactivity, resume participation. The apostasy *from* the Church of an apostate is not the same as the apostasy (q.v.) *of* the Church, or Great Apostasy. *See also* ACTIVITY; ANTI-MORMONISM; APOSTASY.

APOSTLE. *See* TWELVE APOSTLES, QUORUM OF THE.

AREA. Since 1984 the Church has been divided into geographical areas for administrative purposes. The presidency over an area is made up of three General Authorities (q.v.), members of the Quorums (q.v.) of the Seventy (q.v.). In April 1995 the new administrative position of area authority seventy was created while the position of regional representative (q.v.) was discontinued. This geographical division was a response to the growth of Church membership in different parts of the world and to the difficulty of coordinating everything from Church headquarters in Salt Lake City. Presidencies for areas outside the United States and Canada live in their areas, where they devote full time to planning, calling of leaders, training, and supervision.

Areas at the end of 1997 were Africa Southeast, Africa West, Asia, Philippines, Pacific Islands, Australia New Zealand, South America South, Chile, South America West, Brazil North, Brazil South, South America North, Central America, Mexico North, Mexico South, Europe West, Europe North, Europe East, North America Northwest, North America Southwest, North America West, North America Central, North America Northeast, North America East, North America Southeast, Utah North, and Utah South. Rather than having separate entries on each of these, the present dictionary groups them as follows: North America, Central America, South America, Europe, Africa, Asia, and the Pacific (qq.v.).

ARRINGTON, LEONARD J. (1917–1999). Historian, economist, intellectual leader. Born on a farm near Twin Falls, Idaho, Arrington received a B.A. at the University of Idaho, joined the U.S. Army during World

War II, serving in North Africa and Italy, and after the war earned a Ph.D. in economics at the University of North Carolina. His academic appointments were at Utah State University and Brigham Young University (q.v.). He had appointments as visiting professor at the University of Bologna and UCLA. Arrington has served as president of the Western History Association, the Agricultural History Society, and the Pacific Coast Branch of the American History Association. In 1986 he was named a Fellow of the Society of American Historians.

A leader among loyal Mormon intellectuals, Arrington was founding president of the Mormon History Association (q.v.) in 1965 and from 1966 was an advisory editor of *Dialogue: A Journal of Mormon Thought* (q.v.). In 1972 he was appointed Church Historian, serving until 1982 (with a change of title in 1987 to Director of History Division), and for 10 years supervised a team of professional historians who produced a remarkable sequence of books, articles, oral histories, and working papers. When this History Division was abolished in 1982, Arrington and his historians were transferred to the Joseph Fielding Smith Institute for Latter-day Saint History (q.v.) at Brigham Young University, which he directed until his retirement in 1987. After 12 more years of productivity, he died on 11 February 1999.

Enormously prolific, Arrington influenced a generation of historians working on the Mormon past. See his bibliography in Davis Bitton and Maureen Ursenbach Beecher, eds., *New Views of Mormon History: A Collection of Essays in Honor of Leonard J. Arrington* (1987).

ART. Not possessed of elaborate meetinghouses and with a worship service that is simple rather than highly symbolic or liturgical, the Church would not appear to be a likely patron of the arts. Mormon artists, like others, make their way by seeking commissions or selling their work in the private sector.

Still, in the visual arts there have been occasions when the Church has been a sponsor. First, architects have designed meetinghouses for wards and especially temples (qq.v.), some of which are architecturally significant.

Sculptors have produced works portraying sacred subjects that have been displayed on Temple Square (q.v.) or at historic monuments. A series of sculptures known as the Relief Society (q.v.) Monument to Women can be seen in a garden adjacent to the visitor center (q.v.) at Nauvoo, Illinois.

Paintings and murals have been important in the temples. At the end of the 19th century, some Mormon painters were sent to study in France in order to prepare them for this task. Other paintings hang in meeting-houses and visitor centers.

In 1984 the Museum of Church History and Art (q.v.) was dedicated in Salt Lake City. In addition to historical exhibits, it has both standing and temporary exhibits of Mormon art and intermittently holds Church-wide competitions. Hundreds of submissions of paintings, bas-reliefs, weaving, metalwork, and so on are submitted on Mormon religious subjects. Some of the most interesting of these come from areas of the world where the Mormon presence is relatively recent, such as Indonesia or Haiti, where native artistic traditions are employed to convey concepts of the Mormon religion. Besides such specifically religious work, of course, Mormon artists do portraits, landscapes, pottery, and the like.

Crafts have not had appreciable Church sponsorship, and conversions from a variety of ethnic and national backgrounds have precluded the creation of a single tradition. Almost since its beginning, however, the Relief Society (q.v.) has encouraged sewing, quilting, and other skills. *See also* LITERATURE; MUSIC.

ARTICLES OF FAITH. Thirteen statements of belief that appeared in an 1842 letter from Joseph Smith (q.v.) to John Wentworth, editor of *The Chicago Democrat*. The articles were also published in the Nauvoo newspaper *Times and Seasons* (q.v.). While similar listings had been drafted earlier by Orson Pratt (q.v.) and others, this 1842 version became authoritative, as it was later incorporated into the Pearl of Great Price (q.v.) and thus canonized. For many years Mormon children have memorized these statements as part of their Primary (q.v.) training. Often printed on small cards and distributed as a means of introducing Mormonism to interested parties, the Articles of Faith are technically not considered a creed.

1. We believe in God, the Eternal Father, and in His Son, Jesus Christ, and in the Holy Ghost.
2. We believe that men will be punished for their own sins, and not for Adam's transgression.
3. We believe that through the Atonement of Christ, all mankind may be saved, by obedience to the laws and ordinances of the Gospel.
4. We believe that the first principles and ordinances of the Gospel are: first, Faith in the Lord Jesus Christ; second, Repentance; third, Baptism by immersion for the remission of sins; fourth, Laying on of hands for the gift of the Holy Ghost.
5. We believe that a man must be called of God, by prophecy, and by the laying on of hands by those who are in authority, to preach the Gospel and administer in the ordinances thereof.

6. We believe in the same organization that existed in the Primitive Church, namely, apostles, prophets, pastors, teachers, evangelists, and so forth.
7. We believe in the gift of tongues, prophecy, revelation, visions, healing, interpretation of tongues, and so forth.
8. We believe the Bible to be the word of God as far as it is translated correctly; we also believe the Book of Mormon to be the word of God.
9. We believe all that God has revealed, all that He does now reveal, and we believe that He will yet reveal many great and important things pertaining to the Kingdom of God.
10. We believe in the literal gathering of Israel and in the restoration of the Ten Tribes; that Zion (the New Jerusalem) will be built upon the American continent; that Christ will reign personally upon the earth; and, that the earth will be renewed and receive its paradisiacal glory.
11. We claim the privilege of worshiping Almighty God according to the dictates of our own conscience, and allow all men the same privilege, let them worship how, where, or what they may.
12. We believe in being subject to kings, presidents, rulers, and magistrates, in obeying, honoring, and sustaining the law.
13. We believe in being honest, true, chaste, benevolent, virtuous, and in doing good to all men; indeed, we may say that we follow the admonition of Paul—We believe all things, we hope all things, we have endured many things, and hope to be able to endure all things. If there is anything virtuous, lovely, or of good report or praiseworthy, we seek after these things.

The name "Joseph Smith" appears as a signature at the bottom of these articles. While some important aspects of theology are not included, which is consistent with article 9, the Articles of Faith provide a good basis for understanding the Mormon position. Books discussing each of these statements in detail have been published by James E. Talmage and Bruce R. McConkie (qq.v.).

ASHTON, MARVIN JEREMY (1915–1994). Businessman and Apostle. Born in Salt Lake City on 6 May 1915, Marvin J. Ashton was the son of Marvin O. Ashton, who later became a counselor in the Presiding Bishopric (q.v.) of the Church. Raised in an active Latter-day Saint family, young Marvin received his primary and secondary education in Salt Lake

City and went on to graduate from the University of Utah in 1936 with a degree in business administration. For two years he then served as a missionary (q.v.) in Great Britain. Among his other assignments there he was associate editor of the *Millennial Star* (q.v.). After his mission he married Norma Bernston, a schoolteacher. They have four children.

In business, Ashton served on the boards of directors of several corporations. Elected to the Utah State Senate, he sponsored legislation for improved juvenile detention facilities. These experiences made him a natural choice as chairman of the Leisure Time Division of the White House Youth Conference for the State of Utah. As managing director of the Church's Unified Social Services Program, he supervised youth guidance, foster children, prisoners, adoptions, and Indian student placement. He was a member of the Utah State Alcohol and Drug Board.

For more than 21 years he served with the Church's youth program for Young Men (q.v.) either as a member of the board or in the presidency. He took a special interest in the All-Church athletic programs as well as Boy Scouts (q.v.), for which he was given the Silver Beaver and Silver Antelope awards. For many years he traveled frequently to address youth groups and train youth leaders.

Ashton was named an Assistant to the Twelve (q.v.) in 1969. At the end of 1971 he was named a member of the Quorum of the Twelve Apostles (q.v.). He has served on the State Board of Regents and the national advisory council of the University of Utah and has received several honorary degrees. He died in 1994. *See also* NATIVE AMERICANS.

ASIA. Although there were missionaries (q.v.) in India during the 1850s, virtually all progress in Asia has occurred since World War II. At the end of 1997, the Asia Area had 65,000 Mormons, with 12 stakes (q.v.). Taiwan had 24,000, five stakes, one temple (q.v.); Hong Kong had 19,000, five stakes. China is a major holdout, with only about 500 members. India, on the other hand, had about 2,000 members in 20 branches.

The Asia North administrative area (q.v.) is composed of Korea, Japan, and eastern Russia. Early missionary efforts under Heber J. Grant (q.v.) started in 1901 but had negligible results. After World War II, on the other hand, conversions were more numerous, reaching 211 by 1949. Continuing expansion led to the organization of stakes and in 1980 a temple was dedicated in Tokyo. Yoshihiko Kikuchi (q.v.) became a General Authority (q.v.) in 1977. By the end of 1997 Japan had 108,000 members in 26 stakes and 137 wards (q.v.).

Kim Ho Jik, studying for a doctorate at Cornell University, joined the Church in 1951 and, upon returning to South Korea, helped lay the foundations for missionary work in his country. In 1956 two missionaries were sent from Japan. Growing rapidly, the Church in South Korea had its first stake in 1973, with Rhee Ho Nam as president (q.v.). In 1985 a temple was dedicated at Seoul. Han In Sang became the first Korean General Authority. At the end of 1997 there were 69,000 Korean Mormons, divided into 16 stakes and 90 wards.

Perhaps the most striking Mormon success in Asia has taken place in the Philippines. The fact that most Filipinos were Christian and many spoke English facilitated proselytizing. The first mission was established in 1967, the first stake founded in 1973. In 1984 a temple was dedicated in Manila. At the end of 1997 there were 389,000 Mormons in 56 stakes and 336 wards. More than 80 percent of the missionaries in the Philippines are young Filipino men and women. After their missionary experience, they have been a major source of leadership for the Church in the Philippines. *See also* TEMPLES.

ASSISTANTS TO THE TWELVE. A small group of men, starting with five individuals in 1941, called as General Authorities (q.v.) to assist the Quorum of the Twelve Apostles (q.v.). Under the direction of the Twelve, they visited stake conferences (q.v.) and assisted in directing missionary (q.v.) activity. A number of them were later called into the Quorum of the Twelve Apostles. In 1976 this designation was terminated. The functions were assumed by the revived general quorums of the Seventy (q.v.).

ASSOCIATION OF MORMON LETTERS (AML). A private organization dedicated to the encouragement of Mormon literature (q.v.). Founded in 1976, the AML holds an annual meeting with papers critically examining Mormon literature, sponsors readings, and gives awards in fiction, poetry, essay, and criticism. Dues-paying members receive a quarterly magazine and an annual volume of academic papers.

AUDITORS. A committee of professional auditors examines church financial records each year and issues a formal statement attesting to the fact that proper procedures are followed and accountability maintained. Businesses owned or controlled by the Church are audited by the Church's internal auditors, independent professional auditing firms, or government regulatory agencies.

AUSTRALIA. *See* PACIFIC.

AUXILIARIES. Organizations within the Church with programs for specific age or gender groups. These developed in response to perceived needs, mostly in the latter half of the 19th century and have been modified as has been felt necessary in the 20th. In principle, the auxiliaries could be abolished, added to, or again modified, and the Church itself would go on. The principal auxiliary organizations as they now exist are: Relief Society, Primary, Sunday School, Young Men, and Young Women (qq.v.).

The Priesthood (q.v.) is not considered an auxiliary. Although the details of quorum organization and age-group divisions are subject to change as directed by General Authorities (q.v.), Priesthood authority is prerequisite to the Church itself.

-B-

BALLANTYNE, RICHARD (1817–1898). Credited with founding the first Sunday School (q.v.) in Utah at his home on 9 December 1849, Ballantyne was a convert from Scotland who emigrated to Nauvoo, Illinois, in 1843 and subsequently crossed the plains to Utah. In 1853–54 he preached Mormonism as a missionary (q.v.) in Calcutta, India. An astute businessman and supporter of education, Ballantyne lived in Ogden, Utah.

BALLARD, M. RUSSELL (1928–). Businessman and Apostle. Born in Salt Lake City on 8 October 1928, Ballard attended primary and secondary schools as well as the University of Utah. In the late 1940s he served in the British Mission, for a time as counselor in the mission presidency.

He married Barbara Bowen in 1951, and they went on to have seven children. He acquired interests in automotive, real estate, and investment businesses. Meanwhile his Church responsibilities included being a counselor (q.v.) in a bishopric, being bishop (q.v.), and serving in a stake high council (qq.v.).

In 1974 he became president (q.v.) of the Canada Toronto Mission. Two years later he was called to the First Quorum of the Seventy (q.v.), of which he was a member of the presidency from 1980 to 1985. In October 1985 he became a member of the Quorum of the Twelve Apostles.

In addition to the many other duties of a General Authority (q.v.), Ballard has served on several committees, including the Missionary Executive Council, Leadership Training, Personnel, and Information Communications Systems committees.

BAPTISM. Latter-day Saints regard baptism as an essential ordinance (q.v.) for entrance into the Kingdom of God, for membership in the Church, and as a condition for a remission of sins. Consistent with the original root meaning of the word and with the symbolism of death and rebirth, baptism is by complete immersion in water. Infants, incapable of exercising faith, are not baptized. Adult converts who decide to accept Mormonism are baptized. Children who are raised by Mormon parents and instructed are baptized at age eight, considered the age of accountability.

BAPTISM FOR THE DEAD. Baptism of a living person who serves as a proxy for a deceased person. The practice is referred to in 1 Cor. 15:19, where Paul cites it as evidence for the reality of the resurrection: "Else what shall they do which are baptized for the dead, if the dead rise not at all? Why are they then baptized for the dead?" Reinstituted by a revelation to Joseph Smith (q.v.) in 1840, baptism for the dead is carried out only in temples (q.v.).

The rationale underlying the practice rests on several propositions: that baptism is essential to salvation, that God would not be so unjust as to condemn someone for failing to accept a gospel never presented to him or her, that preaching and conversion go on in the spirit world, and that baptism, an earthly ordinance (q.v.), can be accomplished vicariously. It is not assumed that post-mortal spirits will be forced to accept, but for those who wish it, the means for satisfying all requirements is established. One result of belief in vicarious work for the dead has been much research in genealogy (q.v.) and the establishment of a notable Family History Library.

BATEMAN, MERRILL J. (1936–). Born in Lehi, Utah, Merrill Bateman served as a missionary (q.v.) in the British Mission. He received a bachelor's degree in economics from the University of Utah and a Ph.D. from the Massachusetts Institute of Technology. He was a visiting professor in Ghana. After three years on the faculty of the Air Force Academy, he accepted a position as professor of economics and director of the Center for Business and Economic Research at Brigham Young University (q.v.) in 1967. He was then hired by Mars Corporation as well as acting as consultant for the U.S. Departments of State and Commerce, the World Bank, and other agencies. He did much international travel, especially in Africa (q.v.). In 1975, he became dean of Brigham Young University's Graduate School of Management and College of Business. Bateman's Church callings (q.v.) included serving as bishop, stake president, and regional representative (qq.v.). He was called to the Second Quorum of the Seventy (q.v.) in 1992, as presiding bishop in 1994, and to the First Quorum of the Seventy in 1995 (qq.v.). That same year he was named president of Brigham Young University. He married Marilyn Scholes. The Batemans are the parents of seven children.

BEDNAR, DAVID A. (1952–). President of Ricks College (q.v.). Born in San Leandro, California, Bednar earned bachelor's and master's degrees from Brigham Young University (q.v.) and a Ph.D. from Purdue University. He has held faculty positions at Texas Tech University and the University of Arkansas at Fayetteville, Arkansas. Author of books on organizational behavior, he was named the College of Business Administration's outstanding teacher. He has served as a bishop, stake president, and Area Authority Seventy (qq.v.). He and his wife, Susan, have three sons.

BENNION, LOWELL LINDSAY (1908–1996). Educator and humanitarian. After growing up in the Salt Lake City area, Bennion graduated from the University of Utah in 1928. He married Merle Colton and one month later departed for a mission to Germany. After his mission, joined by his wife, he remained to study at Erlangen, Vienna, and Strasbourg, completing a doctoral dissertation under Maurice Halbwachs on the methodology of Max Weber.

Back in Utah, he briefly worked for the Civilian Conservation Corps—jobs were not plentiful in 1934—before accepting the assignment to be director of the institute of religion (q.v.) adjacent to the University of Utah. Until 1962 this was the main scene of his professional activity. Except for a two-year absence at Tucson, Arizona, where he founded an institute of religion, Bennion taught University of Utah students, ultimately thousands of them, on subjects ranging from Bible (q.v.) to Book of Mormon (q.v.) to courtship and marriage, always with a strong emphasis on practical ethics.

He authored many lesson manuals for use in seminary (q.v.) and institute classes, articles for Church magazines, a Sunday School (q.v.)

manual, and an introductory book for college students entitled *The Religion of the Latter-day Saints.* In 1962 he left the institute of religion and became assistant dean of students and professor of sociology at the University of Utah, positions he occupied for another 10 years. Lowell Bennion founded a boys ranch in Idaho that for many years provided a setting where urban youths could have a break from their stressful routine, learn to work in the outdoors, and come under the influence of a kindly mentor. After retiring from the university he became executive director of the private Community Services (q.v.) Council, which aided hundreds of indigent and senior citizens. His favorite passage of scripture—Micah 6:8: "What does the Lord require of thee? But to do justly, to love mercy, and to walk humbly with thy God."—was placed on his grave after his death in 1996.

BENSON, EZRA TAFT (1899–1994). Agriculture leader, cabinet member, Apostle, and Church president (q.v.). Born on a farm in Whitney, Idaho, Benson attended Utah State Agricultural College (now Utah State University), graduated from Brigham Young University (q.v.), and earned a master's degree in agricultural economics at Iowa State College. In 1926 he married Flora Amussen.

In addition to farming, Benson served as a county agricultural agent and was extension economist and marketing specialist for nine years in Boise with the University of Idaho.

President Benson's Church experience included service as a scoutmaster, a missionary (q.v.) in England, a counselor in the stake (q.v.) presidency, and from 1938 service as a stake president in Boise. When he became executive secretary of the National Council of Farmer Cooperatives in 1939, he moved to Washington, D.C., and soon was named president of the Washington, D.C., Stake.

In 1943 Benson was called to be a member of the Quorum of the Twelve Apostles (q.v.). After World War II he became president of the European Mission and supervised a massive distribution of welfare supplies.

He was a member of the national executive board of the Boy Scouts (q.v.) and received the Silver Beaver, Silver Antelope, and Silver Buffalo awards.

After the election of Dwight D. Eisenhower as president of the United States in 1952, Benson was named secretary of Agriculture. Under constant criticism, he stayed in office for Eisenhower's two terms, the first clergyman to serve in a cabinet position. During these years the Bensons' six children (four girls and two boys) grew, developed musical and other talents, and observed their father's dedication to family as well as church and state.

Back in his full-time Church service, Benson supervised work in Europe (1964–65) and Asia (1968–71). In 1973, he became president of the Quorum of the Twelve Apostles, where he demonstrated his administrative skills. He traveled widely, organized many stakes, and received more than a dozen honorary degrees. Themes especially common in his preaching were strengthening the family and preparation for emergency through food storage.

Ezra Taft Benson will long be remembered for his love of country, his repeated belief in the inspiration of the Constitution of the United States, (q.v.), and his conviction that there is a divine destiny for the United States. As Church president, however, he studiously avoided making narrow political pronouncements, instead emphasizing his love for all.

With experienced counselors Gordon B. Hinckley and Thomas S. Monson (qq.v.), Benson continued to emphasize missionary (q.v.) proselytizing and the simplification of programs through correlation (q.v.). Strongly urging Latter-day Saints to read the Book of Mormon (q.v.), he made special appeals to different groups: senior citizens, children, youth, women, and unmarried male adults. While not satisfying those who were looking for new standards or a new morality, he was loving and pastoral. "I love all our Father's children of every color, creed, and political persuasion. My only desire is to serve as the Lord would have me do." (*Ensign*, December 1985, 5.) Inactive members were urged to return, to "come unto Christ and be perfected in him."

BIBLE. One of the four scriptures (q.v.), or standard works, of the Church. The King James, or authorized version, is used in English-speaking countries. Other translations may be consulted for individual study and comparison.

Although sometimes charged with being untrue to the Bible, probably because they accept other works of scripture on the same level and consider the canon to be open, Mormons are quite traditional and even literal in their belief in the Bible as the word of God. They have not been enthusiastic about any criticism that would undermine the authority of the sacred text, although those who teach on the advanced level in Mormon universities are familiar with biblical scholarship. In the adult study course in Sunday School (q.v.), both the Old Testament and the New Testament are systematically read and discussed every four years. For non-English readers the Church decides on the best existing translation for its purpose.

During the early 1830s Joseph Smith (q.v.) prepared a revision of the Bible by going through a copy of the King James version and making hundreds of changes and additions. The resulting work was first published in the 1860s. The majoritarian Mormon Church has never regarded the JST (Joseph Smith Translation) as superseding the King James translation, but the latest English edition of the Bible sponsored by the Church, still the King James text, includes many of Smith's additions and emendations in footnotes and an appendix.

Mormons find themselves in an isolated position in that their approach to the Bible is too literal and traditional for most modern Bible scholars and mainstream Christian churches. Yet Protestant evangelicals, themselves literalist and conservative, find it impossible to accept the Mormon concepts of an open canon, continuing revelation, or "inspired" improvements of the sacred text.

BIRTH CONTROL. Based on the notion that preexistent spirits are waiting to be born into mortality, Mormon parents have historically had families larger than the U.S. average. Still, decisions about family size are left up to parents, who are expected to consider among other things the family's financial resources and the physical and mental health of both the father and mother.

BISHOP. The head of a congregation, or ward (q.v.), the bishop is closer to the level of a pastor or parish priest than to the bishops familiar to Catholics, Anglicans, and others. A layman called to preside over his congregation, the bishop is sustained by raised hand at a meeting of ward members. This call comes only to a male Latter-day Saint who has demonstrated faithfulness and who passes standards of worthiness (q.v.).

The bishop's responsibilities are numerous: calling members to fill the many lay positions in the ward, determining the worthiness of members for attending the temple (q.v.), visiting the sick, counseling as needed, and in general concerning himself with the spiritual and temporal welfare of ward members. He has the assistance of two counselors (q.v.), the three constituting a bishopric. Also assisting are an executive secretary, a ward clerk, and usually assistant clerks. Working in close conjunction with the bishop to meet the needs of ward members is the female president of the Relief Society (q.v.).

The bishop's assignment is temporary. Since the position pays no salary, he continues his regular vocation. Typically after a few years the bishop is released along with his two counselors, to be then replaced by another ward member called to this responsibility. *See also* CALLING; SUSTAINING.

BLACKS. In the 19th century, Mormons had little interaction with Blacks. Although identified with abolitionism to some extent, which contributed to their persecutions by proslavery Missourians, Mormons did not take a consistent antislavery position, and among those who settled Utah before the Civil War there were a few slaveholders. Blacks were eligible for baptism (q.v.) and membership in the Church but not for Priesthood (q.v.) and leadership. Only a few Blacks became Mormons during the first century and a half of the Church's history.

A great divide occurred in 1978, when President Spencer W. Kimball (q.v.) proclaimed that "every faithful, worthy man in the Church" (with no exclusion based on race) might hold the priesthood (Doctrine and Covenants, Official Declaration 2). Since then proselytizing has been carried out in several countries in Africa (q.v.). In the United States, Brazil, Democratic Republic of the Congo (Zaire), Nigeria, various European countries, and elsewhere, Blacks have joined the Church, served as missionaries (q.v.), and filled leadership positions. Since membership records do not indicate race, it is impossible to give the exact number of Mormon Blacks. *See also* GENESIS GROUP.

BLESSING OF INFANTS. An ordinance (q.v.) or ceremony in which the infant is brought to church by the parents and, during a Sunday meeting, given a name and a blessing. A group of Priesthood (q.v.) holders, including the father if he is present, form a circle, holding the baby, and a designated person, usually the father, formally declares the child's name and then pronounces words of blessing to be achieved in the child's future life on condition of faithfulness. Infants are not eligible for baptism (q.v.).

BONNEVILLE INTERNATIONAL CORPORATION. A corporation of Church-owned radio and television stations, including KSL in Salt Lake City. Other television and radio stations have been acquired and a production/advertising company created. As commercial enterprises, these all pay taxes. They do not proselytize directly but do broadcast public service announcements on basic family and community values.

BOOK OF COMMANDMENTS. First compilation of the revelations (q.v.) of Joseph Smith (q.v.) in published book form. A printing press had been established in Independence, Missouri, and in December 1832 the book was at press. Before the entire book could be printed, a mob stormed the printing office, destroying the press and type and scattering what had been printed. Some of the printed sheets were salvaged from the streets of Independence and later bound. Many of the revelations had already been published in *Evening and Morning Star*, a Church newspaper. In 1835, a larger collection of the revelations was published as Doctrine and Covenants (q.v.).

BOOK OF MORMON. One of the four canonical scriptures (q.v.), or standard works, of the Church. First published in 1830 in English, the Book of Mormon has since appeared in many editions, including translations into other languages (35 in its entirety, 44 others in an abbreviated version entitled *Selections*).

Although listed on the 1830 title page as "author," Joseph Smith (q.v.) consistently said that the work was a translation from ancient metal plates. Since these were in hieroglyphics ("reformed Egyptian"), which he made no pretense of understanding, the translation process was possible only "by the gift and power of God."

Recounting the experiences of an Israelite colony that migrated from Jerusalem around 600 B.C., the Book of Mormon tells of their settlement in the Western Hemisphere, their divisions, their wars, prophets, and religious teachings. After his death and resurrection in Jerusalem, Jesus Christ (q.v.) appeared to these "other sheep" and gave them a condensed version of his ministry as recounted in the Bible (q.v.). After a period of peace and harmony these people degenerated once again, participated in a series of bloody wars, and finally clashed in a struggle that saw one major group exterminated.

The survivors were among the ancestors of those later identified as the American Indians. One of the final prophets, Mormon (q.v.), abridged a vast quantity of earlier records; it is the abridger's proper name that gives the title to the book as a whole.

One of the "books" within the Book of Mormon also gives a highly compressed version of an earlier colony that had come to the Western Hemisphere as early as the third millennium B.C. On this historical framework, always presented as selective and "abridged" from more complete records, the book presents its religious message. At its heart is the repeated presentation, by anticipatory prophecy (q.v.) or later preaching, of Jesus Christ and his saving gospel as the divine means provided for human salvation. Looking forward to a future time, thought by Mormons to be the "dispensation" (q.v.) that started with Joseph Smith in the 19th century, the book also foretells the restoration of the Jews to Israel, the redemption of other tribes of Israel, and the restoration of the Christian gospel.

Naturally suspicious of the claims of ancient metal plates and translations, critics began to ridicule the Book of Mormon even before it was published and continued afterward. It was denounced as a patent forgery, full of references to 19th-century concerns. Its use of an English style borrowed from the authorized, or King James, version of the Bible, and its undisguised lengthy quotations from Isaiah and the Sermon on the Mount were pointed to as obvious giveaways. References to horses, elephants, and steel were trumpeted as anachronisms. Mark Twain, unimpressed, called it "chloroform in print." Two major obstacles prevented many modern people from taking the book seriously: those from Christian backgrounds, especially Protestants, considered the Bible to be unique as scripture and on the face of it could not accept the claims of an additional scripture, while those of a secular or skeptical bent, increasingly numerous, usually found it impossible to think in terms of prophets (q.v.), angels, and an intervening God.

Such obstacles notwithstanding, the Book of Mormon has a rather impressive record. Those who read it prayerfully and carefully testify in large numbers that it teaches them, inspires them, and speaks peace to their souls. Their conviction that it is true, they say, comes from the Holy Ghost. It continues to be taught in adult Sunday School (q.v.) classes of the Church on a regular basis along with the other standard works. Indeed, Church President Ezra Taft Benson (q.v.) advised members to give special attention to the Book of Mormon.

Non-Mormon reaction continues on the whole to be negative. Archaeologists and anthropologists find no support for a Hebrew population in the Western Hemisphere. Other critics continue to emphasize the environment of 19th-century New York as the formative matrix for the book.

Against this, Mormon scholars continue their work on several parallel paths, including (1) the Near Eastern setting of the first 40 pages of the Book of Mormon; (2) the possible geographical fit of the book's account with actual places in the Western Hemisphere; (3) refuting or explaining the claimed anachronisms; (4) studying the book's proper names against their alleged background; (5) discovering Hebraisms through analysis of the book's complex literary forms, including poetry, sermons, speeches, letters, typology, and others. Of particular interest has been the discovery of several outstanding examples of chiasmus (a parallel pattern of Near Eastern origins following the structure a-b-c-c-ba). These scholarly defenders of the Book of Mormon find it implausible that a 23-year-old of Joseph Smith's minimal educational background could have produced such a work. *See also* FOUNDATION FOR ANCIENT RESEARCH AND MORMON STUDIES; NATIVE AMERICANS.

BOOK OF REMEMBRANCE. The designation of a volume of family records containing genealogy (q.v.), patriarchal blessings (q.v.), and personal histories, biographies, or autobiographies. Encouraged by the Church to keep such records, members of the Church are also motivated by an interest in genealogy stimulated by baptism for the dead (q.v.) and other vicarious ordinances (q.v.) of the temples (q.v.).

BOY SCOUTS. In 1913, just a few years after the beginning of the scouting movement, the Church began sponsoring troops. Soon the percentage of participation by Mormon boys in scouting far exceeded the national average. In the United States Mormons are a prominent and respected facet of the Boy Scouts of America. In other countries, where possible, troops are sponsored in conjunction with the scouting organizations there.

BRANNAN, SAMUEL (1819–1889). Apostate (q.v.) Mormon who led a group to California, helping to found San Francisco. Born in Saco, Maine, Brannan was converted to Mormonism as a teenager and worked as a printer's apprentice in Kirtland, Ohio. In 1844 this early experience, which had been reinforced by work on newspapers, helped qualify him to assist in editing *The Prophet*, a Mormon newspaper in New York City. He got into trouble with Church authorities for an unauthorized and premature preaching of polygamy (q.v.). After being disfellowshipped, he was reinstated and assisted Parley P. Pratt (q.v.) in editing *The Messenger*.

In 1846, about the same time that Brigham Young (q.v.) was leading the main body of Mormons overland to the West, Brannan led 238 Mormons aboard the ship *Brooklyn*, which then sailed around Cape Horn. On 29 July the *Brooklyn* arrived at Yerba Buena (San Francisco). Brannan and his group proceeded to found a community, which they called New Hope. He published the first newspaper and preached the first sermon in the new settlement.

In June 1847 he finally received a letter from Brigham Young that stated the intention of the Church leaders to establish a settlement in the Great Basin, not in California. Brannan traveled overland to meet Young and try to convince him of the advantages of the coastal location. Unsuccessful, he returned and used his powers of persuasion on discharged members of the Mormon Battalion (q.v.), urging the great advantages of the beautiful California location over the rigors of the Rocky Mountains.

In 1849 Brannan became a promoter of gold mining, thus contributing to the great Gold Rush. Not through mining but by means of other investments, including hotels, shipping, and construction, he became California's first millionaire. When asked for a generous contribution to Young and the Church, he refused. Two years later he was excommunicated (q.v.) for un-Christianlike conduct and neglect of duty. Also cited as a cause of action was his active role in founding a vigilante committee in San Francisco.

In 1859 Brannan established a 2,000-acre ranch in Napa Valley. In addition to raising Merino sheep and beautiful horses he distilled brandy from the harvest of the extensive vineyards. The place was christened "Calistoga," and for a few years its owner seemed to prosper. But he appeared bent on self-destruction. In a property argument he was wounded in 1868. Then affairs provoked a divorce suit from his wife, which forced a liquidation of his property holdings. Brannan's alcoholism became more and more severe.

After an ambitious plan to colonize Sonora in northern Mexico failed, Brannan became impoverished and spent his final years partially paralyzed and suffering from arthritis. In 1889 he died a pauper.

BRIGHAM YOUNG UNIVERSITY (BYU). Founded at Provo, Utah, in 1875 as Brigham Young Academy, this institution was named a university in 1903. During the first half of the 20th century its growth was slow but steady. After World War II BYU experienced spectacular growth, from 1,500 students in 1945 to 25,000 by 1970. A cap was then established; enrollment should not exceed 27,000.

Like other universities, BYU publishes a catalogue that describes its many colleges: Biology and Agriculture; Education; Engineering and Technology; Family, Home, and Social Sciences; Fine Arts and Communications; Humanities; Nursing; Physical and Mathematical Sciences; and Physical Education. There is also a law school and a school of management. To judge from its public relations department and the periodical sent to subscribing alumni, BYU is proud of the caliber of its students and their performance as they go on to other institutions of higher learning or into professions. BYU is accredited by the Northwest Association of Schools and Colleges.

The uniqueness, or special aura, that sets BYU apart from most other universities is religious. Well over 90 percent of the student body and faculty are Mormon, and all are expected to adhere to an honor code that includes abstinence from tea, coffee, alcohol, and tobacco according to the Word of Wisdom (q.v.). Students are required to take classes in religion. In addition, student wards are organized for religious worship; they also function as support groups.

Given this mix, questions of academic freedom have arisen occasionally. One flurry occurred in 1910–11 over the modernist views of a few professors, three of whom were forced to resign. In the early 1990s sociologists and historians raised questions about the attitude of the university toward their research and participation in certain popular organizations. A statement of the university's position on academic freedom sought to allay fears. The great majority of subjects—mathematics, agriculture, nursing, chemistry, foreign languages, management, and others—raise no problems. As for the rest, both students and faculty are fully aware before going there of BYU's basic commitment to the sponsoring church. The university is committed to harmonizing learning by study and also by faith.

BRIGHAM YOUNG UNIVERSITY–HAWAII CAMPUS. Known for many years as the Church College of Hawaii, this institution at Laie on Oahu was renamed in 1974. Enrollment is about 2,000 students, half or more of whom are Polynesian (q.v.). Like those at Brigham Young University (q.v.) in Utah, students of whatever religion agree to follow a basic code of behavior. BYU–Hawaii is accredited by the Western Association of Schools and Colleges.

BRIGHAM YOUNG UNIVERSITY STUDIES. A refereed learned journal, or scholarly periodical, established at Brigham Young University (q.v.) in 1959 and published quarterly. This "voice for the community of LDS scholars" has included bibliographies, essays, poetry, occasional fiction, and articles from the various disciplines of the humanities and social sciences. Most prominent has been Mormon history, including primary documents. The fall 1991 issue contained a comprehensive index for volumes 1–31.

BROOKS, JUANITA (1898–1989). Mormon folklorist and historian. Born in Bunkerville, Nevada, Juanita Leavitt experienced the hardships of the frontier as well as the closeness to nature of her rural setting. She became a schoolteacher in Mesquite, an adjacent community, and married Ernest John Pulsipher in 1919. A son was born, but in early 1921 Ernest died.

After working for a period, Juanita attended Brigham Young University (q.v.), graduating in 1925. She took a position at Dixie Junior College in St. George, Utah, where for a generation she taught English and debate. Later she attended Columbia University and earned an M.A. degree. In 1933 she married a widower, Sheriff Will Brooks.

As president of the Relief Society in her stake (qq.v.), she supervised a project of typing early pioneer diaries for preservation. She also became a field representative for the Huntington Library and was a major force in building up a Mormon (q.v.) collection there. Meanwhile, she wrote poetry and fiction and embarked on several historical projects. Over a generation of productivity, often stealing time for writing from her household duties, she produced edited journals, biographies, a history of Jews in Utah, a memoir, and the definitive study of the Mountain Meadows Massacre (q.v.).

Juanita Brooks was a prominent figure in the Utah Historical Society. Among other honors she received an honorary doctorate from the University of Utah and a distinguished service award from the Utah Academy.

BROTHER AND SISTER. In addition to the usual biological meaning of these terms, Mormons use them as forms of address for other members of the Church, for example, "Brother Smith" or "Sister Hernandez." The term connotes a feeling of affection and closeness to fellow Church members. In the strict sense, as children of the one Heavenly Father, all humans are brothers and sisters. *See also* FORMS OF ADDRESS.

BROWN, HUGH B. (1883–1975). Lawyer, educator, Apostle, and member of the First Presidency (q.v.). Although born in Utah on 24 October 1883, Brown was essentially a Canadian, for his family moved to Alberta when he was only six years old. He married Zina Young Card in 1908 and became a major in the Canadian Army during World War I.

After studying law, Brown became a barrister and solicitor in Lethbridge, Alberta, as well as president (q.v.) of the Lethbridge Stake (q.v.). In 1927 he moved his family to Salt Lake City and joined a prominent law firm. Two years later he became president of the Granite Stake.

Politically, Brown was a Democrat. During the 1930s he served as state chairman of the Democratic Party and, after an unsuccessful bid for the U.S. Senate, was appointed chairman of the State Liquor Commission.

In 1937 he was called as president of the British Mission. He supervised the downsizing of the mission during World War II, served as coordinator of LDS servicemen, and resumed presidency of the mission after the war. In 1946 he took a position as professor of religion at Brigham Young University (q.v.). Known as an inspiring speaker, he influenced hundreds, if not thousands, of students in his classes. In 1953 he was called to be an Assistant to the Quorum of the Twelve (q.v.) Apostles, and in 1958 was named to the Twelve. In 1961 he became a counselor (q.v.) in the First Presidency. As a member of the First Presidency, he was an important participant in the expansion associated with the presidency of David O. McKay (q.v.). Brown repeatedly emphasized the Church position in favor of civil rights even though ordination of Blacks to the Priesthood (qq.v.) came only later.

BUSCHE, F. ENZIO (1930–). Born in Dortmund, Germany, Busche grew up during the Nazi era and World War II. He was drafted into the army in 1944 at age 14. Graduating in economics and management from the universities of Bonn and Freiburg, he pursued graduate studies in technical printing. He became a partner and chief executive officer of a printing and publishing business. After studying Mormonism for a year and a half, the Busches were baptized in 1958. He served as branch clerk, elders quorum president, branch president, district president, mission president, and regional representative (qq.v.). In 1977, he became a member of the First Quorum (q.v.) of the Seventy (q.v.). In 1987, he became president of the Frankfurt Germany Temple (q.v.).

BYBEE, ARIEL (1943–). Opera singer, mezzo-soprano. Born 9 January 1943 in Reno, Nevada, Bybee is a graduate of Brigham Young University (q.v.) and also studied at the University of Southern California. At the Metropolitan Opera in New York City, she has performed in a variety of roles.

-C-

CALLING. The basis of service in the Church, a lay organization relying on volunteers for its functioning. General Authority, stake president, bishop, Relief Society president, ward librarian, home teacher, missionary, scoutmaster, teacher of 10-year-olds in Primary (qq.v.)—all of these are callings. In practice, active Mormons can expect to fill many callings during the course of their lives. Although time consuming, the callings are to be performed conscientiously and willingly. Many members attest to the variety of growth and leadership experiences they otherwise would not have had, were it not for their participation in the callings.

Two characteristics of callings deserve explanation. First, they come from the top down. It is the bishop who must staff the many positions in his ward (q.v.) by issuing calls to ward members. Moving up the ladder, presidents of stakes and General Authorities staff positions in the areas of their assigned jurisdiction. One does not apply for a position or lobby for it. The tradition and expectation is that loyal Church members will respond affirmatively when asked to fulfill a specific responsibility.

Second, callings are temporary. With the exception of the 15 General Authorities who make up the First Presidency and the Quorum of the Twelve Apostles (qq.v.), callings are for a limited period of time. Full-time missionaries (q.v.) serve for 18 months, two years, or, in the case of mission presidents, three years. Other positions are more flexible in their duration. This conception of the calling occasions some adjustment for those who are accustomed to the upward mobility of business and government. In the Church, empire building is not welcomed. One who has been a bishop or stake president and thus very prominent can suddenly find that his calling is that of a choir director or Sunday School (q.v.) teacher (q.v.). In a year or more he may receive a call to serve as scoutmaster or to serve a mission.

Those who have seen Mormon missionaries in different locations may not be aware that missions too are callings. One may indicate a willingness to serve and must pass standards of worthiness (q.v.), but the call itself comes from Church headquarters, at which time one discovers where the missionary service will be. *See also* ARTICLES OF FAITH, 5; MISSIONARY PROGRAM.

CANADA. *See* NORTH AMERICA.

CANNON, ELAINE ANDERSON (1922–). Journalist, author, Young Women's (q.v.) leader. Born in Salt Lake City on 9 April 1922, Elaine Anderson grew up and attended school there. Starting as a teenager, she wrote a daily column for the *Deseret News* (q.v.) for many years and edited the women's section. In 1942 she married D. James Cannon and went on to become the mother of six children.

She became a radio artist for both NBC and CBS while locally hosting a TV talk show. A prolific author, she wrote many books and produced audiotapes. She wrote for national magazines like *Better Homes and Gardens* and *Seventeen*. From 1950 to 1954 she served on the President's White House Committee on Children and Youth. For the Church magazine *The Improvement Era* (q.v.) she coedited with Marion D. Hanks (q.v.) a section addressed to youth. In addition, she has written many self-help and inspirational books as well as one on a Mormon artist.

In 1960 she was named to the general board of Young Women (q.v.) and served as general president from 1978 to 1984. In the 1980s she served as vice president of the National Council of Women. A cheerful personality who relates easily to people of all ages, Elaine Cannon has devoted years of her life to promoting loyalty, high ideals, and positive self-image among Mormon youth.

CANNON, GEORGE QUAYLE (1827–1901). Journalist, missionary (q.v.), political leader, Apostle, and counselor (q.v.) to four presidents (q.v.) of the Church. Born in Liverpool, England, in 1827, Cannon was still a teenager in 1842 when his family was converted to Mormonism by his uncle John Taylor (q.v.). They emigrated to Nauvoo, Illinois. Left an orphan by the death of his mother during the journey and of his father shortly after their arrival, George was taken in by John Taylor and assisted him in editing the *Times and Seasons* (q.v.).

Young and strong, Cannon was sent to mine gold in California in 1849 and was called the following year as a missionary to Hawaii. He mastered the Hawaiian language and, with his fellow missionaries, succeeded in converting many natives to the Church. With assistance he translated the Book of Mormon (q.v.) into Hawaiian.

Returning to the mainland, he married Elizabeth Hoagland, published the Book of Mormon in Hawaiian at San Francisco, and for a brief period put out the *Western Standard*, a newspaper there. In 1858 he was named editor of the *Deseret News* (q.v.). Cannon seemed to be constantly on the move, a rolling stone. In 1858, he was assigned to provide information to newspaper editors and preside over Latter-day Saints in the eastern states. When he returned to Utah in 1860, he was ordained an Apostle and sent to England to preside over the European Mission, returning in 1864. In 1872 he was elected as delegate to Congress from Utah Territory.

A polygamist (five wives, 35 children), Cannon was expelled from Congress in 1882 for violating the new Edmunds Act. In 1888, he was imprisoned for unlawful cohabitation. Like other Mormons in the same situation, he saw himself as "a prisoner for conscience sake."

An astute businessman, Cannon owned a publishing company and was a director of several businesses, including the Bullion-Beck and Champion Mining Company. He served as a secretary to Brigham Young (q.v.) and then as a counselor to Presidents Brigham Young, John Taylor, Wilford Woodruff, and Lorenzo Snow (qq.v.).

Cannon was a diligent diarist. His journal has remained inaccessible in the Church archives, but in 1999 the first volume in a projected publication of most or all of this significant primary source appeared. His publications included, in addition to sermons and hundreds of editorials, *My First Mission* (1879) and *Life of Joseph Smith the Prophet* (1888).

CANNON, SYLVESTER Q. (1877–1943). Businessman, engineer, General Authority (q.v.). A son of George Q. Cannon (q.v.), Sylvester was born on 10 June 1877 in Salt Lake City. His early education and graduation from the University of Utah was followed by completion of an engineering degree at Massachusetts Institute of Technology. From 1899 to 1902 he served as a missionary (q.v.) in the Netherlands and Belgium. In 1904 he married Winifred Saville.

After directing a land and irrigation survey of Weber River, Cannon returned to Holland as mission president (q.v.) for two years. From 1912 to 1925 he was engineer for Salt Lake City. Among the projects he supervised was a major reservoir.

Sylvester Q. Cannon's Church service was extensive. He was counselor in a stake (q.v.) presidency and in 1917 became president of the Pioneer Stake. In 1925 he was named Presiding Bishop (q.v.) of the Church. In this capacity he was a key figure in the administration of Heber J. Grant (q.v.). Among many other construction projects he supervised plans for the construction of the Idaho Falls Temple (q.v.). In 1939 he joined the ranks of the Quorum of the Twelve Apostles (q.v.).

CARD, ORSON SCOTT (1951–). Writer. Born in Richland, Washington, Card served as a missionary (q.v.) in Brazil. He earned degrees at Brigham Young University (q.v.) and the University of Utah.

Best known for his science fiction, he received the Hugo and Nebula awards for best novel in 1986 and 1987. But Card is both prolific and highly versatile. A series of American fantasy, the Alvin Maker series, is set in a magical version of the American frontier and contains many parallels and echoes of the Prophet Joseph Smith (q.v.). Another series, the Homecoming Saga, retells Mormon scripture as science fiction. Another is an alternate history novel in which time travelers try to prevent Columbus from discovering America. Several contemporary novels emphasize character and moral dilemmas. Card's works have been translated into Catalan, Danish, Dutch, Finnish, French, Japanese, Polish, and other languages.

A novelized historical biography, *Saints*, touches upon many of the events of early Mormon history. The essays and speeches compiled in *A Storyteller in Zion* discuss the challenges of being a writer in the Mormon culture setting. Card and his wife, Kristine, live in Greensboro, North Carolina. They have five children.

CARMACK, JOHN K. (1931–). Lawyer, businessman, Church leader. Born in Winslow, Arizona, Carmack was a missionary (q.v.) in the West Central States Mission and served in the U.S. Army during the Korean War. He received a B.A. degree from Brigham Young University (q.v.) and a law degree from UCLA. He was a legislative assistant in the California Legislature, president of a Los Angeles law firm, and president of the Westwood Bar Association. In West Los Angeles he was chairman of the board of the Chamber of Commerce, a member of the executive council for Los Angeles council for the Boy Scouts (q.v.) of America. He was a bishop's counselor, high councilor, stake president, regional representative, and president of the Idaho Boise Mission (qq.v.). He became a member of the First Quorum of the Seventy (q.v.)

CATHOLICISM. On the personal level many examples exist of friendly relations between Mormons and Catholics. Although neither group accepts the ultimate authority claims of the other, they are similar in their insistence on the need for legal authority in the church, on the importance of sacraments or ordinances (qq.v.), and on some basic social values. Despite examples of cooperation and sometimes even mutual admiration, however, images on both sides have not always been positive.

The Mormon perception of Catholicism has sometimes been very critical for the following reasons: most converts to Mormonism came from Protestant backgrounds with a traditional anti-Catholic animus; and Catholic countries proved especially unreceptive to the Mormon message. Although related, these are not identical propositions; the first refers to the makeup of the Mormon population, the latter to the frustrations encountered by Mormon proselytizing. It was not entirely surprising, then, to find references in some early Mormon sermons and writings to the tyranny of the pope and the superstition of Catholics. Biblical expressions such as "whore of Babylon," which Protestants had long put to polemical purposes against the Catholic Church, were repeated by some Mormons along with counterparts in the Mormon scriptures such as "the great and abominable church." Some Mormon descriptions of the Great Apostasy (q.v.) were in effect indictments of historical Catholicism.

In the latter part of the 20th century the attitude toward Catholics has considerably softened. In 1958 a reference by a Mormon General Authority (q.v.) to the Catholic Church as "most abominable above all other churches" was removed in a revised edition of the book. Articles in Mormon magazines more carefully described the apostasy as occurring in the first and second centuries, thus exculpating later Catholics, who were victims, not villains. Some publications even began emphasizing the many basic points on which Mormons and Catholics agreed or at least shared similar positions.

Possibly contributing to the more lenient attitude are the following: (1) proselytizing successes in largely Catholic countries; (2) an awareness that an overwhelmingly secular world has created a situation in which Mormons and Catholics can make common cause; and (3) more sophisticated historical and theological scholarship has discouraged the demonizing of such a large part of Christianity.

As for Catholic views of Mormons, they remain negative. Rome sees Mormons as one of the nuisance "sects" or "cults" (q.v.), which a more neutral usage has labeled "new religious movements." Catholic works on Mormons are few and range from the irresponsible and inaccurate to a few works of history and sociology.

CELIBACY. Mormons do not believe in celibacy as a requirement for the Priesthood (q.v.). Indeed, the married state is considered to be on a higher level and essential to the highest degree of salvation. On the other hand, in the sense of abstinence from sexual intercourse as long as one is unmarried, celibacy is in fact an expectation.

CENTRAL AMERICA AND MEXICO. In 1875 the first Mormon missionaries (q.v.) entered Mexico and arranged for the publication of a pamphlet in Spanish. A few converts were made, but most of them were unsteady.

The next phase occurred with the colonization of northern Mexico by Anglo Mormons. Many of these settlers were driven out during the Mexican Revolution, but some of them returned. A few hundred native Mexicans rallied to the Mormon religion as well.

After World War II the Church grew rapidly. Many young Mexicans were instructed in Church-owned schools and served as missionaries. Stakes and wards (qq.v.) were organized. A temple (q.v.) was built in Mexico City in 1983. At the end of 1997 there were 783,000 Mexican Mormons in 162 stakes and 1,059 wards.

Not until 1947 did missionaries enter Guatemala. By the end of 1997 there were 164,000 members in 33 stakes and 198 wards. A temple was constructed in 1984.

The other Central American countries also saw a rather dramatic increase in Church membership (q.v.). By late 1997 membership totals were: El Salvador, 77,000, 16 stakes; Honduras, 82,000, 20 stakes; Nicaragua, 25,000; Costa Rica, 28,000, 4 stakes; and Panama, 32,000, 5 stakes.

CENTRO ESCOLAR BENEMERITO DE LAS AMERICAS (CEBA). Church-owned preparatory school on the northern outskirts of Mexico City founded in 1964 on the 90-acre site of the old Rancho Arbolilio. Starting with 15 teachers and 125 students, the school had 120 teachers and 2,100 students in 1999. Housing is provided for 1,065 students. Seminary (q.v.) classes are taken by all students. The library contains 90,000 volumes. In addition to basic college preparatory courses, many students participate in sports or artistic pursuits. Sponsored performing groups include the Banda de Guerra, Porristas, the Rondalla, the Symphony Orchestra, the Choir, and Ballet Folklorico. In 1994 the Agricultural Institute was established, a one-year program in horticulture. About 80 percent of the students continue their education on the university level. In addition to improving the lives of the students as they qualify themselves for careers, the school has made significant contributions to Mexico and to the Church.

CHAPLAINS. During World War I, Brigham H. Roberts (q.v.) served as a chaplain in the Utah National Guard and later as one of three with the U.S. troops in France. During World War II, 46 Mormon chaplains served, and ever since, Mormon chaplains have served with the U.S. military, holding general worship services, counseling with military personnel, and performing duties for Latter-day Saint members in the military. In 1995 Kay Schwendiman, former chaplain for the 96th Army Reserve Command, became chairman of the United States National Conference on Ministry to the Armed Forces, representing 250 faith groups in providing assistance to chaplains.

CHASTITY. A term little understood in the late 20th century, the law of chastity forbids sexual relations outside of marriage. Although violations inevitably occur, they are to be deplored, not laughed at or shrugged off. The proper response for a violator is repentance (q.v.).

"CHOOSE THE RIGHT." Title of a popular Mormon hymn, with words by Joseph L. Townsend and music by a Salt Lake City candy maker named Henry A. Tuckett. It was first printed in a 1909 songbook. The three words assumed greater prominence in the final generation of the 20th century when used in awards given to children in Primary (q.v.) and, even more, when the initials CTR were widely used as a logogram, even by adults, on pins, rings, and other examples of Mormon kitsch.

CHRISTENSEN, JOE J. (1929–). Missionary (q.v.), educator, Church leader. Christensen was born in Banida, a farming community in southeastern Idaho. As a young man, he served as a missionary in Mexico and Costa Rica. His college training was at Utah State University and Brigham Young University (q.v.). After a tour of duty in the U.S. Air Force and completion of his university degrees, he was employed as a seminary and institute teacher (qq.v.). Christensen with his wife and six children went to Mexico in 1970 to preside over the Mexico City Mission. Called the associate Church commissioner of education, he spent the next several years establishing seminary and institute programs in many countries. For four years he was president (q.v.) of the Missionary Training Center (q.v.) in Provo, Utah. In 1985, Christensen was appointed president of Ricks College (q.v.). In 1989, he became a General Authority (q.v.) as a member of the First Quorum of the Seventy (q.v.) and in 1993 was sustained a member of its presidency. In late 1999, attaining emeritus status, he became president of the San Diego California Temple (q.v.).

CHRISTIANITY. Mormons have an inclusive definition of Christianity, including within its boundaries Catholicism, Protestantism (qq.v.), and of course themselves. This does not mean they consider all equally valid or all ideas right. The term is not therefore a declaration of total approval but a simple way of designating those who accept Jesus Christ (q.v.) as Lord. On the other hand, some of their opponents have obstinately denied that Mormons are Christians on the ground that they do not accept the creeds of historic Christianity starting in the fourth century. By such a definition, some Mormons have responded, the original Christians of Bible (q.v.) times would be excluded.

Such terminological decisions depend entirely on definitions and may seem pointless, but behind them are serious efforts to defame and exclude. The use of terms like *sect* and *cult* (q.v.) has served a similar purpose. Whatever others may say, the Mormons declare their faith in Jesus Christ as Creator, Redeemer, Lord, and Master, now physically resurrected, a divine member of the Godhead. Some whose claim to Christian status has not been challenged believe far less about Christ. *See also* ANTI-MORMONISM.

CHRISTOFFERSON, D. TODD (1945–). Attorney, Church leader. Born in American Fork, Utah, Christofferson majored in English and international relations at Brigham Young University (q.v.). After serving as a missionary (q.v.) in Argentina from 1964 to 1966, he earned a juris doctorate from Duke University. A law clerk for U.S. District Court Judge John J. Sirica during the Watergate hearings, he then joined a Washington, D.C., law firm. Specializing in legal work for financial institutions, Christofferson with his wife, Kathy, and five children lived in Tennessee, Virginia, and North Carolina. Active in community service, he participated in interfaith organizations, received the Silver Beaver Award of the Boy Scouts (q.v.) of America, and served as chairman of the Middle Tennessee Literacy Coalition and chairman of Affordable Housing of Nashville. Simultaneously, accumulating a rich experience in Church leadership, he was a seminary teacher, high councilor, bishop, stake president, and regional representative (qq.v.). In 1993 he became a General Authority (q.v.) as a member of the First Quorum of the Seventy (q.v.).

CHURCH OF JESUS CHRIST OF LATTER-DAY SAINTS. Official name of the Church popularly known as the Mormon Church. Although its headquarters are in Salt Lake City, Utah, it is a world Church with members in all continents. When organized in 1830, the organization was known as the Church of Christ and for a brief period by some as the Church of the Latter-day Saints, but in 1838 the present name was given by revelation (q.v.) (Doctrine and Covenants 115:4): "For thus shall my church be called, even The Church of Jesus Christ of Latter-day Saints." Although long, the name admirably conveys important ideas. The definite article *the,* capitalized and included as part of the name, is significantly not the indefinite article *a.* Mormons see theirs as God's Church on earth, uniquely authorized and recognized by Him. Although such exclusivity appears arrogant and does not encourage ecumenism, Mormons answer that the designation is not their own but God's and that they fully acknowledge sincerity, goodness, and truth wherever found. The term *church* conveys the importance and value of organization. Mormons believe that Jesus Christ (q.v.) deliberately founded an organization, this both at the time of his earthly ministry in Palestine and at the time of the restoration (q.v.) in 1830. The desire of some to "go it alone" or do without institutional religion is incompatible with the human need for instruction, support, and especially the sacrament (q.v.) of the Lord's Supper and other ordinances (q.v.) of salvation, for all of which the Church is vital.

Of Jesus Christ—these words indicate the "ownership" of the Church, whose it is, the source of its authority. It is not the prerogative of human beings on their own to organize the Lord's Church. They can go through the motions, of course, even for the crass motive of obtaining a tax-exempt status, but without divine authorization a church is not His. Careless librarians and others who classify works on Mormonism as non-Christian, perhaps because of a surface similarity between "Mormon" and "Muslim," have probably paid little attention to the official name.

"Of Latter-day Saints" refers to the members of the Church. For many people, the word *saints* (q.v.) designates those canonized from Mary and the original Apostles to the person most recently elevated through the Catholic Church's procedures. As used in the New Testament, the word referred generally to members of the Church, as when Paul wrote to the saints at Corinth or Ephesus. To differentiate themselves from such original, or early-day, saints the Mormons call themselves Latter-day Saints.

While the Church derives its authority from above, it is here pronounced also to be "*of* the Latter-day Saints." It is *for* them, obviously, and is operated *by* them. As a lay organization each ward or stake (qq.v.) requires the services of many unpaid laborers. Those named to positions, from the president (q.v.) of the Church on down, receive the approval of the members by a sustaining vote. *See also* AREA; FIRST VISION; MISSION OF THE CHURCH.

CLARK, JOSHUA REUBEN (1871–1961). International lawyer, public servant, ambassador, and Church leader. Born in Grantsville, Utah, on 1 September 1871, J. Reuben Clark grew up in a small town environment. After early schooling and much personal reading, he attended Latter-day Saints' College in Salt Lake City and came under the influence of its president, James E. Talmage (q.v.). Then came the University of Utah, from which he graduated as valedictorian in 1898, and that same year he married Luacine Savage in the Salt Lake Temple (q.v.).

After some teaching in Utah, Clark moved east to attend Columbia Law School. An appointment as assistant solicitor in the U.S. State Department and as solicitor in 1910 led him to work on problems with Mexico. Although he left the State Department with the election of Woodrow Wilson, Clark continued, in addition to his private law practice, to accept government assignments: general counsel for the American-British Claims Commission, special assistant to the attorney general, executive officer to the judge advocate general, and special counsel for the U.S. negotiators at the Washington Arms Conference of 1921–22.

After returning to Utah for a period, J. Reuben Clark was again called into government service. From counsel to the U.S. commission pressing claims against Mexico he went on to become undersecretary of state and then special advisor to Dwight W. Morrow, U.S. ambassador to Mexico. From 1930 to 1933 Clark was U.S. ambassador to Mexico. Then, even though he had never held any high Church office, he was named a counselor (q.v.) to President Heber J. Grant (q.v.) in the Church's First Presidency (q.v.).

For 28 years Clark served as a counselor in the First Presidency—in sequence to Presidents Heber J. Grant, George Albert Smith, and David O. McKay (qq.v.). Because of his extensive experience and strong will, his was a major contribution to all of these presidents. But he was entirely loyal and when, from 1951 to 1959, he became second counselor instead of first counselor, his memorable statement was, "In the service of the Lord, it is not where you serve but how" (*Conference Reports*, April 1951, 154).

Among the matters Clark was intimately involved with were the introduction of the Welfare Program (q.v.), the evacuation of missionaries (q.v.) from Europe in 1939, the reopening of the missions after World War II, and the building of many chapels. A student of the scriptures (q.v.), he produced his own harmonization of the gospels (q.v.) and a series of radio lectures on the Great Apostasy (q.v.). After studying the implications of modern translations of the Bible (q.v.), he spoke out in favor of the Church's continued use of the King James Version. As the Church's educational system of seminaries and institutes of religion (qq.v.) expanded, he insisted that all teachers (q.v.) must adhere to belief in the atonement of Jesus Christ (q.v.), the divine calling of Joseph Smith (q.v.) as prophet (q.v.), and the continued legitimate leadership of the successive Church presidents.

A conservative Republican, Clark was less than enthusiastic about U.S. participation in World War II, deplored the use of the atomic bomb, warned against the power of the military-industrial elite, and lamented "our dwindling sovereignty." At the same time he acknowledged that these were personal opinions, not Church policies.

CLEGG, GAYLE MUHLESTEIN (1942–). Second counselor (q.v.) in the general Primary presidency from 1999. Born on 23 June 1942 in Glendale, California, she earned a B.A. degree in history at the University of Utah and a teaching certificate in early childhood, elementary, and secondary education. She married Calvin C. Clegg on 14 August 1964. They have five children. After living in Florida, Arizona, Washington, D.C., New Jersey, Brazil, and Argentina, the family returned to Salt Lake City, Utah. She taught elementary school from 1982 to 1996. Then, for three years, the Cleggs presided over the Portugal Lisbon North Mission.

CLERGY. In the usual sense, the Church has no clergy. It is a lay organization. With no divinity schools and no paid ministry, it does not follow the practice of other churches. No young Mormon looks forward to becoming a clergyman in the Church; the concept does not exist.

With the expansion of membership (q.v.), of course, there are those who are employed by the Church. These include teachers in the seminaries and institutes of religion (qq.v.), the editors of magazines, librarians, and many secretaries and other professionals in different departments. All of these are full-time positions and are regarded as employment, not callings (q.v.).

On the local level, in the ward (q.v.) congregation, all interaction is between fellow members, all amateurs or laity, although some occupy positions of responsibility. Visitors are sometimes surprised to find that the person standing at the pulpit and conducting a meeting is actually a barber or a grocer. In the Church, however, he may be the bishop (q.v.).

Missionaries serve full time during their two-year calling, but they are not paid for this. Their minimal support comes from their own savings, the support of their families, or, in some cases, donated missionary (q.v.) funds. Never do these young men and women (qq.v.) think of themselves as professional clergymen in the sense of having chosen a life's career. *See also* CALLING.

COLONIZATION. If colonization refers to the establishment of new settlements, Mormons have been in the forefront of colonization. Looking at the different phases of Mormon history, we discover the beginnings of such conscious establishment of settlements in Missouri. To some degree the same process was repeated in Illinois with the buildup at Nauvoo and the establishment of several settlements in the region.

But it was in the West that Mormon colonization moved into high gear. The initial establishment of Salt Lake City in the Great Salt Lake Valley (1847) was followed by the deliberate peopling of the region as pioneers were sent out to establish communities in designated locations. Dots appeared on the map, as it were, as new settlements were founded north and south of Salt Lake City. Ambitious plans for a far-flung empire led to Mormon communities as far away as the Salmon River in Idaho and San Bernardino, California, but the political and military pressures of the mid-1850s led to a pullback from these most distant outposts.

Partially because of the population pressure caused by a high birthrate and a steady flow of new immigrants, the settlement expansion continued. By the time of Brigham Young's (q.v.) death more than 300 settlements had been founded. (These are listed in Milton R. Hunter, *Brigham Young the Colonizer.*)

If the Mormon colonization was any different from that taking place all across the U.S. landscape, it was in its organization and advance planning. Sites were selected on the basis of preliminary reconnaissance that assured a supply of water and soil that was cultivable. A leader was named and people were called—or summoned—by Church leaders on the basis of needed skills. Madcap individualism was suppressed in favor of the community interest, as lots were assigned and work assignments handed out. Of course there was the initial phase of confronting an environment devoid of amenities or even minimal shelter. Living in tents or wagon boxes was followed by putting up simple shacks or cabins. If necessary, a wall to provide protection against Indians was built. Planting, irrigating, cultivating, and the initial harvest were always an arduous, suspenseful drama. The extreme hardship of the initial phase often led to premature deaths, sometimes to defections. As time went on, however, homes were gradually improved, the community became larger and more adequate in providing support, and civic pride manifested itself in parades and celebrations.

Although the completion of the transcontinental railroad in 1869 ended Utah's isolation in some respects, it did not mean the end of colonization. And those who left the more settled areas to strike out in their wagons for a new site several hundred miles away were pioneers as much as were those who first came to the Salt Lake Valley in 1847. Each place had its heroic leaders, its founding fathers and mothers. Some of the settlements and their dates follow: Little Colorado River in Arizona (1876), Bunkerville, Nevada (1877), Star Valley, Wyoming (1879), St. Johns, Arizona (1879), Rexburg, Idaho (1882), Colonia Juarez, Mexico (1885), Cardston, Alberta, Canada (1887). *See also* ILLINOIS PERIOD; MISSOURI PERIOD.

COMMANDMENTS. Mormons are often urged to "keep the commandments." This is meant to include not only the Ten Commandments (but not the detailed dietary proscriptions of the Mosaic law) and such commands from Jesus Christ (q.v.) as to preach the gospel unto all the world but also instructions from the Lord in modern revelation (q.v.). The Word of Wisdom (q.v.) has been construed as a commandment. The specific covenants of baptism and the temple (qq.v.)—generally to live a life of Christian service and unselfishness—also become obligations one should keep.

To those who see such an emphasis on adhering to a set of rules as "Judaizing," as a failure to understand the liberty with which Christ has made humans free, Mormons would respond that God has always provided such helps, that Jesus Christ himself said "if ye love me, keep my commandments" (John 14:15), and that his yoke is easy and his burden light (Matt. 11:30). They also fully recognize that without the grace of God their efforts would be meaningless.

COMMUNITY SERVICE. Church members are encouraged to participate in their communities, volunteering when possible to assist deserving programs. In addition to such individual activity, wards and stakes (qq.v.) often organize themselves to assist in community projects. The full-time missionaries (q.v.) throughout the world are also asked to assist the communities to which they are assigned on a regular basis. *See also* HUMANITARIAN AID; WELFARE PROGRAM.

CONFERENCE CENTER. Large assembly hall in Salt Lake City, first used in April 2000. The fan-shaped auditorium has a capacity of 21,000 and is used for conference sessions, pageants (q.v.), and other events. Also in the building are more than 60 translation booths, a theater with 900 upholstered seats, and underground parking for 1,300 vehicles. The roof is landscaped with fountains, waterfalls, trees, planters, and flowers. The center was constructed to meet the highest seismic standards.

CONFERENCES, GENERAL. Gatherings in April and October of each year at the Tabernacle (q.v.) in Salt Lake City, where members and officers listen to addresses from the General Authorities (q.v.) and sometimes women leaders of auxiliaries (q.v.). In addition a report by auditors (q.v.) is presented and the names of current General Authorities are read aloud for the sustaining (q.v.) vote of the congregation. Radio and television broadcasts, including the use of some 2,600 satellite dishes, reach a wide audience.

The proceedings of these conferences are published in the *Ensign* (q.v.) each May and November and also in a series entitled *Conference Reports*. These meetings and the published sermons from them are considered a basic channel by which Latter-day Saints receive guidance and instruction from the leaders they sustain as prophets (q.v.).

CONFERENCES, STAKE. Gatherings of members in a stake (q.v.) that occurred every three months until 1979, when they were reduced to two per year. Several meetings, or sessions, are held during a two-day period. Visiting General Authorities (q.v.) address the stake once every other year. The rest of the time the stake presidency is in charge. Authorities are sustained by vote, and instructional and inspirational addresses are given.

CONFIRMATION. A sacred ordinance (q.v.) following baptism (q.v.). Seated in a chair, the recipient has hands laid on his/her head by one or more individuals who hold the Melchizedek Priesthood (q.v.) authority. By the authority of that Priesthood (q.v.) and in the name of Jesus Christ (q.v.), the officiator confirms the recipient a member of the Church of Jesus Christ of Latter-day Saints, bestows the Holy Ghost, and adds additional words of blessing and advice.

CONSTITUTION OF THE UNITED STATES. This document is commonly referred to as "inspired." "And for this purpose have I established the Constitution of this land, by the hands of wise men whom I raised up unto this very purpose, and redeemed the land by the shedding of blood" (Doctrine and Covenants 101:80). The primary concern in the 19th century was protection in the free exercise of religion. From the public announcement of polygamy (q.v.) in 1852 through the next generation, Mormons claimed protection of the practice as part of their religion, but this claim was struck down by the Reynolds decision (1879), in which the Supreme Court made a distinction between protected belief and not-necessarily-protected action. A prophecy by Joseph Smith (q.v.) that the Constitution would be imperiled, hanging as it were by a thread, but would be saved by the elders (q.v.) of the Church has been cited by individuals and groups within the Church at different points in time in explanation of their political views.

CORRELATION. In 1960, building on earlier efforts, the First Presidency (q.v.) started a review of Church programs. Three coordinating committees were created, one each for children, youth, and adults. A permanent Correlation Department was established in 1972.

The purposes of correlation have been to (a) see to it that the family (q.v.) is the central focus and that auxiliaries (q.v.) and other Church programs function in their role to support the family rather than displace it; (b) maintain order among the different auxiliaries and programs; (c) ensure that lesson materials and other publications of the Church are doctrinally sound; (d) simplify Church programs and demands; and (e) bring all organizations under the direction of the Priesthood (q.v.).

The entire curriculum of the Church was reviewed, reorganized, and rewritten so that the gospel (q.v.) would be taught at the three stages of life—childhood, youth, and adulthood—in a coherent way, at the appropriate level, and with proper reinforcement and review. Care was exercised to avoid overemphasizing some points and leaving out others. This revised, systematic curriculum has been translated into many languages.

Also shaped by correlation have been Church magazines and weekly Family Home Evenings (q.v.). Meeting schedules were consolidated so that only one trip to church on Sunday would be required. Materials printed for use throughout the Church were reviewed by a committee to ensure accuracy and avoid unnecessary duplication. In short, the ongoing correlation program attempts to ensure that the Church will function with maximum efficiency in achieving its lofty purposes. *See also* MISSION OF THE CHURCH.

COUNCIL OF FIFTY. *See* FIFTY, COUNCIL OF.

COUNCIL OF TWELVE APOSTLES. *See* TWELVE APOSTLES, QUORUM OF THE.

COUNSELOR. An important, easily overlooked position in the functioning of the Church at all levels. Soon after the organization of the Church in 1830, Joseph Smith (q.v.) became president (q.v.) and had two counselors, the three making up the First Presidency (q.v.). In time the same kind of three-person executive body appeared on other levels: areas, stakes, wards, the auxiliaries (qq.v.). In fact, the principle of collective leadership by such an executive body appears up and down the Church organization.

The president of the Church has two counselors, as indicated. The Presiding Bishop (q.v.) has two counselors, thus the Presiding Bishopric. Presidents of the general Relief Society, Sunday School, Young Men, Young Women, and Primary (qq.v.) each have two counselors. Area presidencies, stake presidencies, and ward (qq.v.) bishoprics are similarly constituted, as are the presidencies of priesthood quorums and ward auxiliary (qq.v.) organizations. In each of the 267-plus missions there is a president who is assisted by two counselors.

The role of the counselor is always to be supportive and helpful to the president. At meetings of these three-person groups, decisions are made. Although the counselors do give advice, their role is not limited to this. Normally the duties of the leadership are divided among the three individuals, although it is the president (or bishop) who in the final analysis has responsibility.

This leadership principle—a triumvirate, or troika—helps to preclude the possibility of the single individual becoming too self-centered or isolated. The counselors function as sounding boards and sources of information. They also lighten the load of the president or bishop by willingly taking on whatever responsibilities are assigned to them.

The training and experience accumulated by counselors is enormous. Many who are called to the position of bishop or president, including women in Primary, Young Women, and Relief Society, had earlier served as counselors.

COWDERY, OLIVER (1806–1850). One of the witnesses of the Book of Mormon (q.v.) and in authority second only to Joseph Smith (q.v.) at the organization of the Church. Born at Wells, Vermont, on 3 October 1806, he remained there and no doubt received basic education. In 1826 he moved to New York to join his older brothers. He worked as a clerk in a store before taking a job as a schoolteacher in 1829. Boarding with Joseph Smith's (q.v.) parents, he found out about the translation of metal plates. After receiving a revelation (q.v.), he volunteered his services, working as scribe and copyist in 1829–30.

Cowdery participated in several miraculous experiences: the appearance of John the Baptist to restore the Aaronic Priesthood (q.v.); the appearance of Peter, James, and John to restore the Melchizedek Priesthood (q.v.); and as one of the "three witnesses," Oliver saw the plates of the Book of Mormon (q.v.) and an angel. (His testimony is printed in all editions of the book.)

At the Church's organization in 1830 Cowdery was known as "second elder." When a presidency was organized, he became an Associate President. He also had the title of Church Recorder in 1830–31 and 1835–37. Literate above the average, Cowdery assisted in preparing some of the early revelations for printing and wrote a series of letters that remain a basic primary source.

In 1838 Cowdery joined others in disputing some of the Church's organizational, economic, and political policies. He also became embroiled in problems having to do with polygamy (q.v.), this in the 1830s when the practice was still highly secretive. He was excommunicated (q.v.) along with some other dissidents.

For 10 years Cowdery was out of the Church. He studied law and practiced it in Kirtland, Ohio, before moving to Tiffin, Ohio, in 1840. His reputation was good. In 1847 he moved to Wisconsin and was defeated in a bid for the state legislature.

In 1848 he rejoined the Church at Council Bluffs, Iowa, reaffirming his earlier testimonies (q.v.). Failing in health and short of funds, he was unable to proceed directly to Utah but remained near relatives in Richmond, Missouri. There he died on 3 March 1850 at age 43.

COWLEY, MATTHEW (1897–1953). Apostle and missionary (q.v.) to the Polynesians (q.v.), especially the Maoris. Born on 2 August 1897 at Preston, Idaho, Matthew was the son of Apostle Matthias Cowley, who soon moved his family to Salt Lake City. After basic schooling Matthew left at age 17 on a mission to the New Zealand Maoris. During his five years there he learned the language, preached, translated scriptures (q.v.), and developed a great love for the people.

After graduating from the University of Utah he attended law school at George Washington University. He married Elva Taylor in 1922 after his first year at law school and worked in the office of Utah Senator Reed Smoot (q.v.). He practiced law in Salt Lake City, serving twice as county attorney.

In 1938 he was called to be mission president (q.v.) in New Zealand. Beloved by the Maori people as *Tumuaki* (leader or chief), Cowley knew them by name and often stayed in their homes. When the other U.S. missionaries returned to the United States because of the war, he remained in order to look after the Church members in New Zealand. In all, this mission lasted nearly eight years.

In 1945 he was called to the Quorum of the Twelve Apostles (q.v.). The next year he was made president of the Church's Pacific (q.v.) missions. Traveling by air, he visited not only New Zealand but also Samoa, Tonga, the Cook Islands, and Hawaii. In 1949 he also visited Japan and China, holding conferences and helping establish the Church. A down-to-earth man who related easily to people, he was a favorite speaker wherever he went. He died on 13 December 1953.

CREATION. Mormons are creationists in the sense that they believe the world is not a product of chance but of conscious creation by God. They do not insist on a limited time frame for the process, regarding the "days" spoken of in Genesis as creative periods of indefinite length. Nor do they consider creation to be ex nihilo, the bringing of the world into existence from nothing. Rather, reasoned Joseph Smith (q.v.) on the basis of the Hebrew verb, *creation* could mean causing the world to come into existence by assembling or organizing existing material elements into a new combination. The creation of humans could likewise mean the combining of physical bodies with an immortal spirit; this individual spirit was not created on earth but had existed in a pre-mortal state. As far as earth and the mortal phase of existence are concerned, the emphasis is not on the process but on the fact of God's intentionality and divine purpose. *See also* PLAN OF SALVATION.

CROSS. This symbol found throughout the Christian world is not used in Mormon worship or architecture. President Gordon B. Hinckley (q.v.) explained that "the cross is the symbol of the dying Christ, while our message is a declaration of the living Christ." Absence of the cross among Mormons by no means signifies denial of the atoning sacrifice of Jesus Christ (q.v.) through the suffering that began in Gethsemane and was completed on Golgotha.

CULT. Term used by some sociologists of religion to describe churches that are not part of "historical" or "orthodox" Catholicism or Protestantism (qq.v.) or that reject all or some of the historic Christian creeds. Although used dispassionately by Max Weber and others, *cult* is often used as a term of disparagement, even contempt, by those who see themselves as superior to upstart religions. Recognizing the unfortunate polemical uses of the term, some recent scholars have preferred the term *New Religious*

Movements (NRM) to describe groups of relatively recent origin. Objecting to being defamed by avowed enemies or to being excluded from Christianity (q.v.), some Mormon defenders have pointed out inconsistencies in use of the term and have argued that primitive Christianity itself possessed all the supposed criteria of a cult. *See also* ANTI-MORMONISM.

-D-

DAMIANI, ADHEMAR (1939–). Businessman, Church leader. Born in Brazil, Damiani was converted to Mormonism by Walkyria Bronze, who became his wife. He had a successful career in business, retiring as owner and partner in SEDA Tecnologia, which produced software for business applications. Church callings included bishop, high councilor, counselor in stake presidency, and mission president of the Brazil Curitiba Mission from 1995 to 1998, and Area Authority Seventy (qq.v.). In 1999, he became a General Authority (q.v.) as a member of the Second Quorum of the Seventy. He and his wife have two children and five grandchildren.

DANCE. Unlike some religions of a Puritan or Pietist tradition, Mormons have welcomed dancing as a legitimate form of recreation. Crossing the plains as they fled from Illinois, they would often rejuvenate themselves around the campfire in the evening by getting out the fiddles and kicking up their heels in reels and schottisches. In the West every community found that dances provided necessary recreational relief and were both popular and relatively easy to organize.

Social dancing has not been without some tension among the Mormons, for as new dance fashions were introduced they were often perceived as improper. Thus starting as early as the waltz in the late 19th century and continuing through the fox-trot and, after the middle of the 20th century, the jitterbug, the twist, and various styles associated with rock and roll, Mormon leaders have not welcomed the new dance styles in social events sponsored by the Church. First the new dance step would be forbidden and then often gradually accepted as long as certain guidelines were followed. Adult leaders supervising these social events have not wished to encourage behavior that seemed sexually provocative or tasteless, but at the same time they realized that a strict exclusion of current music and dance steps would render their sponsored activities unpopular, because they would be perceived as old-fashioned.

Throughout the Mormon communities of the West and in ward and stake (qq.v.) recreational activities, social dances—square, country, and ballroom dancing—have continued in the 20th century. For many years the Young Men and Young Women (qq.v.) sponsored dance instruction and put on a giant dance festival in the University of Utah stadium.

Ballet and modern dance, quite different arts for a few performers and many spectators, have never been sponsored by the Church, but Salt Lake City did prove congenial to them after World War II, when professional companies were established.

DANITES. 1. In the 1980s the discovery of early diaries and letters from the Missouri Period (q.v.) indicated the existence of a public Danite organization that assumed responsibility not only for the defense of the community but also for the construction of homes and for providing supplies.

2. A splinter of the larger group was a paramilitary organization. Apparently some members of the smaller group engaged in illegal activities against the Missourians, no doubt justified in their own minds by the persecution they were experiencing. To determine the extent of this violence requires sifting through contradictory accounts by participants in the events. On balance, however, it seems clear that the Mormons suffered far more than they inflicted. The best evidence indicates that the smaller group was unknown to Joseph Smith (q.v.) and was started privately by Sampson Avard.

3. In the Illinois Period and during the Exodus and the subsequent Utah Period (qq.v.), the Danite organization did not exist. But the legend took on a life of its own in 50 or more novels portraying the Danites as sinister night riders who intimidated and brutalized ordinary people. A highly negative stereotype of Mormonism was thus produced. *See also* ANTI-MORMONISM.

DEACON. An office in the Aaronic Priesthood (q.v.). At the age of 12, worthy males are ordained deacons. For two years they are given such assignments as passing the sacrament (q.v.) to Church members in sacrament meeting (q.v.), collecting fast offering (q.v.), and assisting in the maintenance of building and grounds.

Deacons are grouped into quorums (q.v.) of 12 or fewer members. A president, two counselors, (qq.v.) and a secretary are called. An adult adviser teaches and trains.

This is the first level or office of Priesthood (q.v.) service. At age 14 comes ordination to the office of a Teacher (q.v.)

DEAD SEA SCROLLS. Discovered in 1947, the Dead Sea Scrolls consist of materials copied and produced by the separatist Jewish settlement of Qumran between 200 B.C. and A.D. 70. The community was annihilated by the Romans, but these records had been placed in sealed earthenware jars. Because of their great significance for understanding the Judeo-Christian world of the first century, Mormons have been interested in them. Some popular speeches and publications were extravagant in claiming parallels, but serious Mormon scholars, while interested, have been appropriately cautious. In 1996 the Provo International Conference on the Dead Sea Scrolls brought scholars from many different countries to Brigham Young University (q.v.). The Foundation for Ancient Research and Mormon Studies (q.v.) produced a database on CD-ROM that contains a fully integrated and computerized collection of Dead Sea Scrolls texts.

DESERET. 1. A Book of Mormon (q.v.) term meaning "honeybee." 2. The first name chosen in 1849 for the new territory hoping to become a state in the West. It was rejected in favor of Utah but remained attached to several businesses and activities.

DESERET ALPHABET. A proposed phonetic alphabet promoted by Brigham Young (q.v.) and others in the 1850s. Partially modeled on Pitman shorthand, the new alphabet was supposed to be easier to learn by foreigners. A few books were published in the Deseret Alphabet, but because of the prohibitive cost of putting all publications of the territory into this new type, it was abandoned.

DESERET BOOK COMPANY. A book company owned by the Church's Deseret Management Corporation. Its publishing arm publishes many of the writings about and for Mormons. Its retail arm, consisting of stores in several Western states, sells its own publications, works by other publishers, and general trade books. In 1999 it produced a compact disc called GospeLink, which included hundreds of titles by General Authorities (q.v.) and others, conference addresses, and Church periodicals. The same year Deseret Book announced a merger with Bookcraft, another publisher of books for the Mormon market.

DESERET NEWS. Daily newspaper owned by the Church and published in Salt Lake City. Started in 1850 and taking its name from the Book of Mormon (q.v.) word meaning "honeybee" that had been proposed as the name of the territory, the *Deseret News* was originally a weekly. Later a semiweekly edition was produced and, in 1867, a daily.

Subscribing to national press services, the *Deseret News* has the sections found in other newspapers: news, editorials, comics, and classifieds. Editorially it has expressed a conservative to moderate position with special attention to moral values. Of special interest is the section entitled *Church News*, published weekly in the Saturday edition, which enables readers to keep current on news of the Mormon Church worldwide. On 28 May 1997, a new nine-story building to house the editorial and production departments was dedicated in Salt Lake City.

DEW, SHERRY L. (1953–). Editor, publisher, women's leader. Born in Ulysses, Kansas, Sherry Dew graduated from Brigham Young University (q.v.). An assistant editor with Bookcraft publisher, she then became editor and associate publisher of a magazine. Employed by Deseret Book Company (q.v.), she was associate editor, director of publishing, and then vice president of publishing. She wrote biographies of Ezra Taft Benson and Gordon B. Hinckley (qq.v.). She was a ward and stake Relief Society president before becoming a member of the Relief Society general board (qq.v.). In 1997, she became second counselor (q.v.) in the general Relief Society presidency.

DIALOGUE: A JOURNAL OF MORMON THOUGHT. Quarterly periodical started in 1966 by editors G. Eugene England Jr. (q.v.) and G. Wesley Johnson, then graduate students at Stanford University. *Dialogue* includes historical articles, essays, studies of theological and scriptural topics, fiction, poetry, photography, art, book reviews, and letters to the editor. *Dialogue* is not sponsored by the Church. Indeed, some articles have been perceived by some readers as so critical as to be anti-Mormon. *Dialogue* has served as an outlet for opinion and scholarship about Mormonism. Like other learned journals, it does not have a mass audience and does not necessarily reflect the views of the General Authorities (q.v.) or the entire membership of the Church. *See also* ANTI-MORMONISM.

DISPENSATION. Mormons have a view of salvation history that includes a series of dispensations, efforts by God to reach humankind through the divine saving gospel (q.v.). Each of these efforts, represented by such figures as Adam, Noah, Abraham, and Moses, was followed by a declension or apostasy (q.v.).

This dispensational pattern includes certain corollaries. For one thing, the gospel of Jesus Christ (q.v.) did not originate in first-century Palestine but instead goes back to the creation. Indeed, it had been spelled out and agreed to in the pre-mortal existence. The mission of Jesus Christ on earth included the unique, infinite atonement for the sins of all humans, but the Church he founded carried no guarantees of permanence. The warnings of a "falling away" were part of the teaching of both Jesus and the original apostles (2 Thess. 2:3). The Great Apostasy (q.v.) merely repeated a process that had occurred repeatedly before.

The restoration of the gospel by Joseph Smith (q.v.) was seen as the beginning of the final dispensation. Smith was a prophet (q.v.), not the only begotten Son of God, not the Christ, but the time had come in the divine economy for the final act, the dispensation of the fullness of times. By contrast, the Christian church of the first and second centuries represented the dispensation of the meridian of time.

All of this adds up to a view of human existence that is as vast as creation itself. If the geographical sweep of Mormonism included all the world, at least in the intention to carry the message to all peoples, the temporal sweep is equally extensive. In a sense, therefore, it is incorrect to see Mormonism as a new religion less than two centuries old. In the view of its adherents, it is the "eternal gospel" restored to earth in the culminating phase of human history. *See also* PLAN OF SALVATION.

DISSENT. In any group of human beings disagreement is bound to occur on some matters, and Mormons are no exception. If the disagreement is peripheral, it can be managed; if it is central, the individual person's identification with the group becomes tenuous or ceases altogether. Either the individual person becomes "inactive" or the organization expels recalcitrant, obstreperous persons who are no longer loyal and are not contributing to the purposes of the group.

Such general statements are applicable to all groups in one sense or another. In the history of Mormonism a series of persons, having rejected the position of the Church leadership on specific issues, either simply departed quietly or, in some cases, established rival organizations.

After the death of Joseph Smith (q.v.), many of those who did not accept the leadership of Brigham Young (q.v.) eventually formed themselves into the Reorganized Church of Jesus Christ of Latter Day Saints (q.v.), while others rallied behind other claimants to the succession (q.v.).

Technically schisms, these divisions nevertheless reflect matters on which dissent within the majoritarian Church was impossible. Each new organization would then confront the same inevitable question: To what extent is disagreement allowable?

Another issue arose at the end of the 19th century with the official abandonment of polygamy (q.v.). Those few who refused to follow the Church's prohibition of new polygamous marriages were excommunicated. Such dissent could not be allowed within the organization.

On the other hand, the Church has not wished to insist on some kind of uniformity that denies human nature, the natural process of growing in knowledge, or legitimate differences of opinion. Excommunication (q.v.) is more often for behavior than belief. But belief is not a matter of indifference, especially if one is teaching or influencing others. A member of the First Presidency, Joshua Reuben Clark (qq.v.), declared that those who taught in Church classes must accept three things: the divinity of Jesus Christ (q.v.), the status of Joseph Smith as a prophet (q.v.), and the present head of the Church as Smith's legitimate successor. A teacher (q.v.) in the Church setting who took issue with any of these fundamentals would be testing the limits of dissent and would be corrected or otherwise disciplined. How, one might ask, could a person presume to teach as a representative of the Church while rejecting and undermining its basic positions? The important distinction here is that between teachers or officials and Church members who are not serving in such a capacity. *See also* ACTIVITY; POLITICS.

DISTRIBUTION CENTERS. Church-owned stores throughout the world that sell authorized literature (q.v.) and curricular materials in many languages. Included are scriptures, (q.v.) lesson manuals, handbooks, forms, audiovisual materials, hymnbooks, and video and cassette tapes. Using order forms printed in the *Ensign* (q.v.), people may order such material by mail.

DIVORCE. Although regarded as an evil, divorce is permitted by the Church. The rate of divorce among Mormons is slightly lower than that in the general U.S. population. Those who marry in the temples (q.v.), because of a shared religious commitment, have far fewer divorces. When these temple marriages fail, the parties may, after a civil divorce, request from Church authorities a "cancellation of sealing," which has the effect of rescinding the relationship after death.

DOCTRINE AND COVENANTS. One of the four standard works or scriptures (q.v.) of the Church. Mostly made up of revelations (q.v.) issued by Joseph Smith (q.v.), the work also contains prayers, letters, and official declarations. Although the subject matter has to do with specific problems that arose in the early years, the principles are broadly applicable to Latter-day Saints. The work is divided into 138 sections, equivalent to chapters, which in turn are subdivided into verses.

Examples of the subject matter include: the atonement of Jesus Christ (q.v.) (section 19), baptism (q.v.) (section 22), Sabbath (q.v.) day (section 59), the three levels or glories that await humans after death (section 76), Priesthood (q.v.) (sections 84, 107, 121), the code of health known as the Word of Wisdom (q.v.) (section 89), the manifesto officially ending polygamy (q.v.) in 1890 (official declaration 1), and the granting in 1978 of the Priesthood to all worthy males of whatever race (official declaration 2).

The revelations issued by Joseph Smith first circulated in handwritten copies or were printed in Church newspapers. As early as 1833 an effort was made to compile them into a work entitled *Book of Commandments* (q.v.), but its printing was stopped by mob action in Missouri and very few copies were salvaged. In 1835 the first edition of Doctrine and Covenants included the revelations from the ill-fated earlier work and others received since. The most important later editions, edited and expanded, appeared in 1844, 1876, 1921, and 1981. Twenty or more editions in translation have appeared.

The Doctrine and Covenants is systematically studied in adult Sunday School (q.v.) classes every four years.

-E-

EDUCATION WEEK. Each year thousands of people gather at Brigham Young University (q.v.) for a week of educational and religious lectures by prominent speakers, including some General Authorities (q.v.). Classes are offered in self-improvement, family relations, religious education, history, science, youth interests, health, and literature (q.v.). Originally called Leadership Week, the first meeting, intended for those holding leadership positions in the Church, took place in the winter of 1922 with 2,046 in attendance. It was soon opened up to all interested members 14 years of age and older. During and immediately after World War

II, Education Week was canceled five different times, but otherwise attendance has steadily increased each year. Education week is now held annually in August. The 1999 Education Week hosted 29,775 registrants. Selected lectures were telecast over the Church satellite system. In 1998, Ricks College (q.v.) began sponsoring its own Education Week, starting with 300 classes offered by 45 instructors to about 2,000 people.

EIGHT WITNESSES. *See* WITNESSES OF THE BOOK OF MORMON.

ELDER. An office in the Melchizedek Priesthood (q.v.). Male Church members who pass standards of worthiness (q.v.) are ordained elders at the age of 18. Adult male converts are ordained as soon as possible after their baptism (q.v.).

Elders possess authority to perform all the functions of the lesser, Aaronic Priesthood (q.v.), including baptism and passing of the sacrament (q.v.). In addition, they have the necessary authority to confer the gift of the Holy Ghost in the ordinance (q.v.) of confirmation (q.v.). Elders fill many positions in the Church. Male missionaries (q.v.), with the exception of older persons who may be high priests (q.v.), are ordained elders.

Elders are organized into quorums (q.v.) of as many as 96 persons with a president, two counselors (qq.v.), and a secretary. They meet weekly for instruction and for the planning and reporting of service projects.

As a form of address (q.v.) the term *elder* is appropriate for all holders of the Melchizedek Priesthood, including General Authorities (q.v.).

EMERITUS. Status of General Authorities, specifically the First Quorum of the Seventy (qq.v.), who have been honorably released at the age of 70. Members of the First Presidency and Quorum of the Twelve Apostles (qq.v.) have lifetime tenure and thus, to the present at least, are never emeriti. Members of the other quorums of the Seventy serve for a five-year term and are then released but are not considered to have emeritus status.

ENDOWMENT. *See* TEMPLES.

ENGLAND, G. EUGENE JR. (1933–). English professor, essayist, poet, and founder of private Mormon intellectual organizations. Born in Logan, Utah, on 22 July 1933, Eugene England received the usual primary and secondary education. He married Charlotte Hawkins, and the two of them served as missionaries (q.v.) in Samoa from 1954 to 1956. They went on to have six children.

After graduating from the University of Utah in 1958, England attended Massachusetts Institute of Technology for one year and then entered the graduate program in English at Stanford University, receiving his M.A. in 1969 and a Ph.D. in 1974.

His professional career has taken him to St. Olaf College in Minnesota and, since 1977, to Brigham Young University (q.v.), where he won several coveted teaching awards. Retiring from Brigham Young University, he continued teaching at Utah Valley State College. England belongs to the Shakespeare Association of America. His total publication record includes books, edited works, poetry, and essays.

England (along with G. Wesley Johnson) was founding editor of *Dialogue: A Journal of Mormon Thought* (q.v.) in 1965. He promoted Mormon creative writing through his own poetry and essays, through critical reviews and anthologies, and through the Association of Mormon Letters (q.v.), which he cofounded in 1977.

England's extensive Church experience includes serving in four bishoprics and as branch president, bishop, and high councilor (qq.v.).

ENSIGN. Official magazine of the Church, published monthly beginning in January 1971. The *Ensign* includes editorials, nonfiction articles in history and doctrine, fiction, poetry, news of events in the Church, letters to the editor, and even some humor. Especially important are the May and November issues, which publish the proceedings of the April and October general conferences (q.v.).

EUROPE. The first preaching of Mormonism in Europe began with the mission to Great Britain in 1837. The *Millennial Star* (q.v.), which started publication in 1840, is filled with the details of conversion and emigration. Perhaps as many as 100,000 English converts migrated, first to Nauvoo, then to the Great Basin in the West.

Around the middle of the century missionaries (q.v.) preached in various parts of the continent. Except for scattered individual conversions, the area of success was limited to Scandinavia, which contributed tens of thousands to the companies of immigrants bound for Zion (q.v.) in the U.S. West. By 1900, close to 100,000 European Mormons had emigrated.

Proselytizing continued in the 20th century. Added to England and Scandinavia as places where there were Mormon congregations were France, the Netherlands, and Germany. A preliminary effort leading to a few converts was made in Czechoslovakia. All of this was interrupted by World War II.

When missionaries returned to Europe after the war, they looked up the scattered surviving members and added to their number by conversions. Success increased in the 1960s and after. Where numbers were sufficient, wards and stakes (qq.v.) were established. Local members were called to positions of responsibility. Temples (q.v.) were constructed. It was a generation of growth and maturation.

Long kept out of eastern Europe by the conditions of the Cold War, Mormon missionaries began to gain access during the 1980s. Missions have been established in Czechoslovakia, Poland, Yugoslavia, Bulgaria, Greece, Ukraine, and Russia.

At the end of 1997 membership for the different European countries stood as follows:

country	members	stakes	wards	temples
Austria	3,800	2	12	
Belgium	5,700	2	10	
Bulgaria	1,100			
Czech Republic	1,500			
Finland	4,400	2	13	
France	30,000	7	39	
Germany	36,000	14	90	2
Greece	300			
Hungary	2,800			
Iceland	200			
Italy	18,000	3	16	
Netherlands	7,500	3	16	
Norway	4,100	1	7	
Poland	900			
Portugal	35,000	5	23	
Romania	1,100			
Russia	8,000			
Spain	29,000	6	30	1
Sweden	8,400	4	19	1
Switzerland	6,800	3	17	1
United Kingdom	173,000	45	268	2
Ukraine	5,000			

Although the percentage growth in Europe was not so rapid as in South America or Asia (qq.v.), it has been steady. Second-generation Mormon families have demonstrated tenacity. Many young members study in seminary and institute of religion (qq.v.) classes, after which they serve full-time missions. Experienced leadership has been built up. General Authorities (q.v.) of European origin have included F. Enzio Busche and Dieter F. Uchtdorf (qq.v.) (Germany), Charles A. Didier (Belgium), Derek A. Cuthbert (England), Jacob de Jager (Netherlands), and Hans B. Ringger (Switzerland).

EVANS, RICHARD LOUIS (1906–1971). Radio announcer, "voice" of the Tabernacle Choir (q.v.), civic leader, Apostle. Born in Salt Lake City, Evans served as a missionary in England as a young man and gained experience as an assistant editor of the *Millennial Star* (q.v.). In 1928 he became an announcer for KSL radio in Salt Lake City and the following year began announcing for the weekly broadcast of the Tabernacle Choir. "Once more we welcome you within these walls, with music and the spoken word, from the Crossroads of the West." "May peace be with you, this day and always." Such expressions became readily recognized throughout the country. His short talks, or "sermonettes," were widely appreciated. Many of them were published in books, including *This Day and Always*. He also wrote a newspaper column for King Features.

In 1937 Evans began a long career as managing editor and later senior editor of *The Improvement Era* (q.v.). The next year, only 32 years old, he became a General Authority (q.v.) as one of the seven presidents of the First Council of Seventy (qq.v.). In 1947 he was appointed director of Temple Square (q.v.). In 1953, at age 47, he became an Apostle.

Active in the community, Richard Evans was president of the Utah Alumni Association, president of a Knife and Fork Club, and in 1949 president of the Salt Lake Rotary Club. He became president of Rotary International.

EXCOMMUNICATION. A formal action that deprives a person of Church membership. Careful procedures are described in the *General Handbook of Instructions* (q.v.). Grounds for such an action vary from flagrant moral infractions to the deliberate teaching of false doctrine or belonging to apostate (q.v.) groups. Exercising considerable latitude in addressing such problems, bishops (q.v.) also have the option of imposing lesser penalties of disfellowshipment or a temporary suspension of some privileges.

When excommunication proceedings are instituted, standards of fairness are followed. The person charged is allowed the opportunity for a hearing, records are kept, and appeals are allowed. Except where the membership needs to be warned, these proceedings are kept confidential.

While attempting to maintain the integrity of the Church and its purposes, bishops are urged to be solicitous and kindly in order, where possible, to bring the offender back into fully participating membership.

EXODUS. The great migration of the Mormons, forced from Nauvoo, as they made their way westward over many months and hundreds of miles, finally to find their refuge in the Salt Lake Valley and elsewhere in the Great Basin.

After the prophet Joseph Smith (qq.v.) was assassinated on 27 June 1844, the Mormons accepted the leadership of Brigham Young (q.v.) and the Quorum of the Twelve Apostles (q.v.) in August. The attempt to remain in Nauvoo, Illinois, signaled by continued in-migration and construction on the temple (q.v.) and other structures, had to be given up under the increasingly insistent, sometimes violent pressure of anti-Mormonism (q.v.). On 4 February 1846 the Mormon wagons began moving out from the city, across the Mississippi River, and to the plains of Iowa. By fall the city was virtually empty of inhabitants.

It was the task of Brigham Young to organize these 10,000 or so refugees into companies, provide protection and nourishment during whatever period of time they would be en route, determine a place of ultimate settlement, get the people to that destination in good order, and establish them there in such a way that an ugly competition for property claims would be avoided. Of some help was the recruitment of 500 males into the Mormon Battalion (q.v.), which, although it seemed oppressive to many at the time, did get one group to the West under government direction and provided a payroll to aid the others.

By the late fall and early winter of 1846, the Mormons were strung out in various encampments through Iowa. Along the banks of the Missouri River near present-day Omaha, Nebraska, they built temporary settlements for the winter, which remained inhabited for several years as a mustering and jumping-off place for the westward migrants. On 14 January 1847 Brigham Young issued a set of instructions called "The Word and Will of the Lord" (Doctrine and Covenants, Section 136). Organized into companies, the people were to cooperate in helping one another, raising crops and building houses, and were to send "pioneers" (q.v.) on ahead to move westward and put in crops.

The pioneer company of 143 men, 3 women, and 2 children set out in mid-April. In their number were Brigham Young and seven other Apostles (q.v.). Diarists William Clayton and Thomas Bullock kept a detailed account f the journey, carefully recording the distance traveled each day, as calculated by a mechanical odometer constructed for the purpose and attached to a wagon wheel. Their destination was already known, Young and his colleagues having studied a map made by John C. Frémont and regarding this move as fulfillment of earlier plans and prophecies of Joseph Smith. One effort to dissuade them was reportedly made by Jim Bridger. Another was made by Samuel Brannan (q.v.), who came from California in a vain effort to persuade Young to settle there. But the decision had been made.

On 21 July advance scouts entered the Salt Lake Valley. When Brigham Young, suffering from mountain fever, entered with the remainder of the company, some crops had already been planted. He pronounced it as indeed the right place. For the next few weeks members of the advance company explored, surveyed, established simple shelters, coaxed water from the stream onto the dry soil, and planted crops. Then many returned eastward to get their families.

This original exodus consisted of more than just one small exploring company. Joining the advance company in a kind of convergence were Mississippi converts, one contingent that had been detached from the Mormon Battalion because of poor health, and soon from the west, other discharged battalioneers. Behind the advance company other groups had been moving westward and over several weeks entered the valley company after company. By December 1847 something close to 2,000 people were trying to establish themselves in their promised land. By the 1850 census 11,380 people inhabited the new Great Salt Lake City and the small settlements in the immediate vicinity. Others making their way westward, or temporarily halted at the Missouri, were still experiencing their own "exodus."

The comparison with the children of Israel led by Moses from Egypt to their promised land could not be avoided. In January 1847 Brigham Young in a revelation had proclaimed, "I [God] am he who led the children of Israel out of the land of Egypt; and my arm is stretched out in the last days, to save my people Israel." (Doctrine and Covenants 136:22.) Although pioneering and colonization (q.v.) did not stop with the original westward thrust, the initial exodus had saved the destitute Mormons and established them in their land of refuge. See also ILLINOIS PERIOD; PIONEER(S); SUCCESSION; "THIS IS THE PLACE" MONUMENT.

EYRING, HENRY (1901–1981). Scientist, educator. Born on 20 February 1901 of Mormon parents in Colonia Juarez, Mexico, Henry moved with his family to Arizona. Along with the usual rough and tumble of boyhood in rural America, Henry did well in his schooling, graduating from Gila Academy in Thatcher.

When he went off to attend the University of Arizona at Tucson on scholarship, as Eyring often recounted in later years, his father told him that his religion did not require him to believe anything untrue. Graduating with a bachelor's degree and completing a master's degree the following year, he pursued his doctorate at the University of California at Berkeley, receiving his Ph.D. in 1927.

After a year as an instructor at the University of Wisconsin, a year in Europe (q.v.) working with Michael Polanyi and others, and a one-year lectureship at Berkeley, Eyring accepted an appointment at Princeton University. He advanced to the rank of full professor and became director of the Textile Research Institute.

In 1946 Eyring became professor of chemistry and dean of the graduate school at the University of Utah, his professional home for the remainder of his life. A prolific scholar, he produced more than 350 publications, including four books.

Professional associations he belonged to included the American Chemical Society, which he served as president, the National Science Board, and the American Association for the Advancement of Science. Recipient of the National Medal of Science, the Joseph Priestley Celebration Award, the Berzelins Gold Medal from the Swedish Academy of Science, and the Wolf Prize in Chemistry from the Wolf Foundation in Israel, Eyring also received honorary degrees from 15 different universities.

His contributions to science were many. One colleague listed the following as disciplines to which he was a contributor: mining engineering, metallurgy, ceramics, fuels, explosives, geology, plastics, fibers, lubricants, organic chemistry, molecular biology, analytical chemistry, radiation chemistry, electrolytic chemistry, quantum chemistry, and statistical mechanics. Perhaps his most basic discovery was the absolute rate theory of treating chemical reaction kinetics and other rate processes.

Always a devout member of the Church, Eyring served on the general board of the Sunday School (q.v.) for many years. In addition to articles in Church magazines, he wrote *The Faith of a Scientist* (Salt Lake City: Bookcraft, 1967).

He and his wife, Mildred Bennion Eyring, had three sons: Edward M., Henry B. (q.v.), and Harden. Mildred died in 1969. In 1971 Eyring married Winifred Brennan. Until nearly the end of his life he participated in an annual 50-yard dash with his graduate students.

EYRING, HENRY B. (1933–). Businessman, educator, Church leader. Second son of the eminent scientist Henry Eyring (q.v.), Henry B. Eyring received a bachelor's degree in physics from the University of Utah. After serving as an officer in the U.S. Air Force, he attended the Harvard Graduate School of Business, receiving his MBA and a doctorate in business administration. He married Kathleen Johnson. Accepting a position at the Stanford Graduate School of Business, he taught but also entered the business world as founder and director of a computer manufacturing company. In 1971 he was named president of Ricks College (q.v.). Eyring served as bishop, regional representative, member of the Sunday School general board (qq.v.), and commissioner of the Church Educational System. In 1985, he became a General Authority (q.v.) as first counselor in the presiding bishopric, in 1992 a member of the First Quorum of the Seventy, and in 1995 a member of the Quorum of the Twelve Apostles (qq.v.).

-F-

FAMILY. Much of Mormon life revolves around the family. In an age of family breakdown, Mormons are among those fighting to preserve the nuclear family as the best assurance of fulfillment for individuals and the best protection against social disintegration.

Not immune from the problems of the larger society, Mormons have their share of dysfunctional families, divorce, and other signs of tension. To combat these, principles are taught in all of the auxiliary (q.v.) organizations as well as seminaries and institutes of religion (qq.v.). Church members are encouraged to participate in weekly Family Home Evenings (q.v.). Each ward provides support through home teaching and visiting teaching (qq.v.) The resources of the Welfare Program (q.v.), including LDS (q.v.) Social Services, can be called upon. In addition to whatever assistance might be available from the community, the Church is striving to strengthen and reinforce its families.

As part of their belief in the ordinances of the temples (qq.v.), Mormons have faith in the possibility that the family unit will endure beyond the grave. "Families can be together forever"—these words begin the chorus of one of their hymns. Such an eternal union of husband and wife, parents and children, is dependent on receiving the sealing (q.v.) ordinances of the temples either in this life or, if one has not had the opportunity, vicariously after death; and living in faithful obedience to the commandments (q.v.).

On 23 September 1995 the First Presidency (q.v.) issued a Proclamation on the Family, reaffirming traditional values (*see* appendix 3).

FAMILY HISTORY. *See* GENEALOGY.

FAMILY HOME EVENING. A regularly scheduled time once a week in which families enjoy recreation and some form of instruction or spiritual enhancement.

To some extent such activities occurred naturally within families, but the urbanization and intensified pace of life in the 20th century combined with evidence of family breakdown to increase concern among Church leaders. In 1965 the program as it now exists was instituted. Manuals were produced containing lessons and suggested activities. Monday was designated as an evening in which there would be no Church meetings so that time for the family home evening was ensured. Since then a resource book and videos have been produced. Responding to interest from others, the Church has publicized the family home evening program broadly and has readily shared its resource materials.

FARNSWORTH, PHILO (1906–1971). Father of television. Born near Beaver, Utah, Farnsworth early showed an aptitude for mathematics and technology. As early as age 13, he won a national contest with an invention related to automobiles.

Living in Idaho at the time, interested in electricity and radio, he drew for his teacher, Justin Tolman, an "image dissector." Tolman copied the drawings in his notebook, which later turned out to be crucial evidence in a battle over the television patent.

In 1921, the Farnsworths moved to Provo, Utah, where Philo attended Brigham Young University (q.v.), married Elma "Pem" Gardner, and aroused the enthusiasm of a few collaborators for his television scheme. In 1926, he moved to San Francisco to work on the project.

Overcoming obstacles one at a time, Farnsworth and his friends finally produced an electronically transmitted image. "In 1927 when I first saw a television image transmitted without any moving parts," he said, "I believe I felt the greatest thrill of my lifetime before or since, and I have had quite a lot of them."

When a Russian scientist named Vladimir Zworykin showed up at the laboratory and claimed to represent Westinghouse, Farnsworth showed him everything. Later Zworykin, who actually worked for RCA, fought Farnsworth for the patent rights. Examining the evidence, including Tolman's earlier notebooks, the U.S. Patent Office upheld Farnsworth's claims.

Farnsworth died on 11 March 1971. About 20 years later, a statue of Farnsworth was placed in the rotunda of the nation's capitol, joining Brigham Young's to represent the state of Utah.

FAST OFFERING. A donation to the Church on the first Sunday of each month, the equivalent of the value of the meals one has abstained from. These funds are specifically designated for helping the poor and needy.

Increased poverty and the expansion of the Church into areas of the world where many people live close to the subsistence level have increased the need for assistance. Church president Spencer W. Kimball (q.v.) urged members to donate not merely the cost of two meals but substantially more when possible. Unlike many relief programs, the fast offering program results in 100 percent of the donation going to the assistance of the needy.

FASTING. Abstaining from food and drink. Combined with prayer (q.v.), fasting contributes to feeling close to God. Often this is done by persons requesting special blessings or inspiration in making personal decisions. In addition to such individual occasions, Church members are urged to fast from two meals on the first Sunday of each month and to pay a fast offering (q.v.) to the Church. On this day a meeting is devoted to the expression of personal testimony (q.v.).

FAUST, JAMES E. (1920–). Attorney, legislator, Church leader. Born on 31 July 1920 in Delta, Utah, James E. Faust attended school in Salt Lake City. Although he started at the University of Utah, his college attendance was interrupted when he served as a missionary (q.v.) in Brazil and afterward entered the U.S. Air Force, reaching the rank of first lieutenant. He married Ruth Wright. The Fausts have five children, all married.

After World War II, he entered law school at the University of Utah and received the J.D. degree in 1948. Practicing law, Faust was president of the Utah Bar Association in 1962–63. He was elected to the state legislature from 1949 to 1951. President John F. Kennedy appointed him to the Lawyers Committee for Civil Rights and Racial Unrest.

In the Church he served as bishop, high councilor, stake president, and regional representative (qq.v.). In 1972 he became an Assistant to the Twelve and area (qq.v.) supervisor in South America (q.v.). In 1976 he was named one of the presidency of the First Quorum of the Seventy, and in 1978 became a member of the Quorum of the Twelve Apostles (qq.v.). As president of the International Mission, with responsibility for members and investigators (q.v.) in parts of the world without organized missions, he traveled widely, displaying a special ability to relate to people of all races and nationalities. In 1995 he became second counselor in the First Presidency (q.v.).

FEMINISM. As the term was understood in the past century, Mormons (q.v.) were feminists. Mormon women were among the first to vote and participated in the national movement for female suffrage. Basic spiritual equality between women and men has always been assumed: both may achieve salvation in the fullest sense of the word. In the Relief Society and other auxiliary (qq.v.) organizations women have played a prominent role from nearly the beginning of the Church.

The current women's liberation movement led to some complications as militant feminists disparaged the role of wife and mother, some going so far as to advocate abolition or restructuring of the family (q.v.). Mormon women adhere to more traditional values. A few Mormon women were caught up in the rhetoric and assumptions of national and world feminism in its extreme form. Other Mormon feminists, less extreme, have expressed concern about such issues as education and employment, child care, and occasions of male abuse of power.

Church leaders, including the women leaders in the Relief Society, have tried to show sensitivity to legitimate concerns. That education and professional accomplishment are valued is evident from the women selected to serve in leadership positions. The number of young women (q.v.) called to serve as full-time missionaries increased sharply before leveling off. At the same time Church leaders have insisted on the value and importance of the family. Rather than putting males and females into opposition, they pursue a partnership on the general Church level, in the stakes and wards (qq.v.) and in the family. *See also* MISSIONARY PROGRAM; WOMEN, ROLES OF.

FIFTY, COUNCIL OF. A council formed by Joseph Smith (q.v.) in the spring of 1844. At its origin this body appeared to be intended as the basis for establishing the political Kingdom of God on earth as part of the onset of the Millennium (q.v.). Three nonmembers of the Church were included. In practical terms the Fifty (whose membership overlapped with the Quorum of the Twelve Apostles [q.v.]) helped organize Joseph Smith's presidential campaign in 1844, supervised the migration to the West, and in territorial Utah met at infrequent intervals for a few years. Since it was not an essential body of government in church or state, it quite naturally lapsed.

FIRESIDE SERVICE. A Church-sponsored meeting outside the regular scheduled meetings of the Church. Sometimes held in private homes, more often in a ward (q.v.) building or stake (q.v.) center, firesides often invite all the youth of a stake to hear a musical presentation or a talk that will be of special interest to them. In a fireside service, there is greater latitude in choice of subject matter than in a sacrament meeting (q.v.).

FIRST PRESIDENCY. The president of the Church and his two counselors (q.v.). Upon the death of the president, the First Presidency is dissolved, the two counselors resuming their place in the Quorum of the Twelve Apostles (q.v.). The committee-of-three pattern is found throughout the administration of the Church. As with all of these units, the First Presidency functions with perfect unity, and the counselors, besides acting as advisers, perform many of the necessary functions.

Historically, the first First Presidency was organized in 1832 with Joseph Smith (q.v.) as president. Although on different occasions additional counselors or assistants were added to the First Presidency, the standard pattern was that of three individuals: the president and two counselors. Counselors who have been especially influential in the First Presidency, not including those who became president of the Church, are Sidney Rigdon, Hyrum Smith, George Q. Cannon, J. Reuben Clark, Hugh B. Brown, N. Eldon Tanner, and Thomas S. Monson (qq.v.). *See also* COUNSELOR.

FIRST PRINCIPLES. Faith in Jesus Christ, repentance, baptism (qq.v.), and laying on of hands for the gift of the Holy Ghost. Based on Acts 2:37–38, with the assumption of faith on the part of those addressed, these are the basics taught throughout the Mormon scriptures (q.v.). This is not a salvation-by-faith-alone doctrine, although faith is given priority. It is not an individual approach to salvation that disparages organized religion, for the ordinances (q.v.) of baptism and confirmation (q.v.) require the authority of Priesthood (q.v.).

Although not usually listed as one of the "first principles," enduring to the end has been suggested as implicitly the fifth principle. Without continued faithfulness, the whole process is frustrated.

The first principles and ordinances are not the whole of the gospel (q.v.). To them are added other covenants and ordinances, such as those of the temples (q.v.). But the first principles are foundational. And they are never superseded. One's entire life is to be one of faith and repentance and enduring; the commitments made at baptism and confirmation are to be renewed by partaking of the sacrament (q.v.) throughout life.

FIRST VISION. The first revelation received by Joseph Smith (qq.v.). The setting was upper New York State, where competition between the different Christian denominations was intense. Some members of the Smith family became Presbyterians. Young Joseph, not yet 15, was confused by the "war of words and tumult of opinions" (Pearl of Great Price, Joseph Smith History 1:10). A reading of James 1:5 prompted him to take his dilemma directly to God in prayer, which he did in the spring of 1820.

After an evil power tried to stop his effort, a great vision came: a pillar of light and two divine beings, one of them referring to the other as his Son. Joseph was told that his sins were forgiven, that he should join none of the existing churches, and that in the future, if faithful, he might be the means of bringing back the true Christian faith. Local ministers reacted to Joseph's experience with ridicule and persecution. Such things may have happened in the days of the Bible (q.v.), they said, but not now.

In the 20th century, some historians have attempted to undermine the First Vision by challenging the claim that there were any religious revivals in Palmyra, New York, in the year 1820, but historian Milton Backman has discovered several examples of such activity in the immediate area, which is all Joseph Smith said. For Mormons the First Vision is foundational—God's declaration, unequivocally and utterly authoritative, of the results of the Great Apostasy (q.v.) and the need for a restoration (q.v.).

Joseph Smith was only 14 years of age at the time. Not for another 10 years would the time be ripe to establish the Church.

FOLKLORE. Like all peoples, Mormons convey stories orally. Many of the stories told and passed on from generation to generation have to do with miracles of healing or dreams. The modernization usually associated with the 20th century has perhaps modified Mormon popular storytelling, but it still occurs in the form of "urban folklore" (folklorist

Jan Harold Brunvaand). One recurring tale in the Mormon oral tradition recounts appearances of "the Three Nephites," characters from the Book of Mormon (q.v.) who were promised that they could remain on earth and not taste of death.

Prominent in the study of Mormon folklore have been folklorists Hector Lee, Austin and Alta Fife, Thomas E. Cheney, and William A. Wilson (q.v.). Others, such as Jan Harold Brunvaand, have supervised the collection of and published articles on Mormon folklore.

FORMS OF ADDRESS. In any culture proper forms of address must be learned. Do you refer to the monarch as "King" or "Your Majesty"? Is the local parish priest properly addressed as "Reverend" or "Father"? Mormons are no exception, having their own standard usage. The following is descriptive—not attempting to lay down rules, in other words, but to describe how Mormons do it.

The most widely used titles are "Brother" and "Sister," (q.v.) used to address other adult Church members of the male and female gender, respectively. Children and nonmembers are not addressed in this way. Although occasionally heard in isolation, these words usually accompany the last name, as "Brother Smith" or "Sister Martinez."

A bishop and two counselors preside over a ward (qq.v.). The bishop is referred to as "Bishop Swallow" or often simply "Bishop," whereas the counselors are "Brother Clifford" or "Brother Muir." Among the General Authorities there is a Presiding Bishop (qq.v.). He is known as "Bishop Hales."

The term *president* applies most importantly to the president of the Church, who is properly addressed or referred to as President Ezra Taft Benson (q.v.) or President Benson. His two counselors have the same title: President Thomas S. Monson and President Gordon B. Hinckley (qq.v.). Note that the term *bishop* is not attached to the counselors (except counselors in the Presiding Bishopric), but the term *president* is.

There are many "presidents" in the Church. On the stake (q.v.) level the presiding triumvirate is a stake presidency, all three of whom are addressed and referred to as "president." There are also presidents of general, stake, and ward auxiliary organizations (qq.v.), and of the many priesthood quorums (qq.v.) throughout the Church. While it is not improper to address all of these by that title, the common usage is to employ the terms *Brother* or *Sister*.

Another term often used is *Elder* (q.v.). Within the Melchizedek Priesthood (q.v.) "Elders" are one of the levels. All worthy male members are thus ordained at the age of 18 or 19. Yet all such "Elders" are not addressed in this way. Those who are properly so addressed are (1) all General Authorities with the exception of the First Presidency and Presiding Bishop; and (2) all male missionaries (q.v.) during their two-year missions. Female missionaries are called "Sister."

Examples of well meant but awkward and improper usage include: Prophet Benson (although sustained as "prophet, seer, revelator" and referred to in the third person as "the Prophet," he is not given the title as a form of address); Apostle Oaks (although those in the Quorum of the Twelve Apostles are apostles, the term is not used as a form of address); and Mr. Benson (which comes across as lacking in respect).

First names are used by Mormons like everyone else, but they are considered inappropriate for General Authorities and for missionaries during their missions. In formal settings, as conferences (q.v.) or other Church meetings, even individuals who are close friends carefully use the appropriate titles. *See also* COUNSELOR.

FOUNDATION FOR ANCIENT RESEARCH AND MORMON STUDIES (FARMS). An independent research and service organization established in 1979 as a nonprofit, tax-exempt, educational corporation. Dedicated to scholarly research having to do with the history, culture, language, geography, politics, and law of the Book of Mormon (q.v.) and other ancient scriptures (q.v.), FARMS publishes a widely circulated newsletter, the *FARMS Review of Books* (formerly titled *Review of Books on the Book of Mormon*), a semiannual *Journal of Book of Mormon Studies*, and other books and research papers. In 1999 FARMS established the Center for the Preservation of Ancient Religious Texts (CPART), which sponsored an electronic Dead Sea Scrolls (q.v.) database and a series of Islamic texts. Supported by private donations, FARMS has contributed significantly to research in its stated areas of interest.

FRIEND, THE. A monthly magazine published for the children of the Church since January 1971. In addition to stories and puzzles, *The Friend* publishes accounts of children's activities and achievements from throughout the Church. Instruction about leaders, history, and religious teachings are pitched at a simple level. Its predecessor magazine was entitled *The Children's Friend.*

FUNDAMENTALISTS. 1. In general, those who are seeking to return to the "fundamentals" of something, as with the Protestant fundamentalists of the early 20th century. Martin Marty and other scholars have applied the term more widely as they study "fundamentalisms" not only in Christianity but also Islam and other world religions. Just how Mormonism fits into this terminology is not simply stated, for in their own conception Mormons have returned to the basics of primitive Christianity, while in the eyes of their detractors they are rather a deviation from the norms of historic Christianity.

2. In common discourse in areas with large Mormon population, fundamentalists are those Mormons who still cling to the practice of polygamy (q.v.). They are excommunicated (q.v.) from the Church when discovered and thus are not technically Mormons, although until inculpated they often pass themselves off as loyal Mormons. Several fundamentalist groups exist more or less clandestinely. Estimates of their numbers vary from 20,000 to 200,000. Prosecutions in the courts of this illegal activity are few, partially because of the practical problem of providing for the children if parents are imprisoned or deprived of income, and partially because of a changed climate of opinion that tolerates many kinds of behavior by consenting adults.

-G-

GARMENTS. White underwear worn by adult Mormons after receiving their endowments in the temples (qq.v.). This conservative underclothing has simple, unobtrusive markings symbolic of gospel (q.v.) ideals. Garments are not available in the general retail market but are purchased through Church distribution centers.

GATHERING. The "gathering of Israel" included not only the return of the Jews to the Holy Land but the concentration of Church members in a location in the Western Hemisphere where they would build a temple (q.v.) to God. Originally this was to be in Jackson County, Missouri.

Early gathering places in Ohio, Missouri, and Illinois attracted converts. As they joined the Church in other parts of the United States, they would, where possible, migrate to the current gathering place. After the exodus (q.v.) to the West, it was the Salt Lake Valley that drew members in by the thousands, year after year through the second half of the 19th century.

Because of population pressures, limited job opportunities, and a desire to build up the Church in many parts of the world, the gathering slowed down in the 20th century. Church leaders urged members to remain where they were. But longing for the opportunities that drew other immigrants to the United States, many Mormons continued to move there if possible. Desirous of living in the midst of fellow believers, they still moved to Utah and other intermountain states, although at a slower rate. It was a time of transition.

After World War II, especially since the 1960s, the pattern of growth through missionary (q.v.) proselytizing has greatly increased Mormon members and chapels, stakes and wards, and temples (qq.v.) in all of the 50 states and in Europe, Central America and Mexico, South America, Asia, and Africa (qq.v.). On 1 December 1999, the First Presidency (q.v.) repeated "the long-standing counsel to remain in their homelands rather than immigrate to the United States." Individuals are considered gathered into the Church and Kingdom of God when they are baptized (q.v.). *See also* ARTICLES OF FAITH, 10; ZION.

GENEALOGY. The discipline or activity of searching ancestry, including the preparation of pedigree charts and family (q.v.) reconstitution, or family group, sheets. Motivated by the doctrine of baptism for the dead (q.v.), Mormons have been diligent genealogists since the 1840s. The vicarious ordinance work performed in the temples (qq.v.) was based upon the genealogical research that allowed members to perform proxy service for their deceased ancestors.

On 13 November 1894 a genealogical society was organized. As an official designation, the name was changed to Family History Department in 1987, although the previous term is still used for some of the activities. From the 1930s, and especially after World War II, an ambitious microfilming project was launched. In many countries of the world, wherever permission could be obtained, ecclesiastical records and vital statistics were filmed. This formidable operation continues.

The Family History Library in Salt Lake City houses a vast collection of volumes and, most importantly, microfilm and microfiche records from many countries of the world. Through more than 3,200 branch libraries these materials are available to researchers in more than 40 countries.

Making its accumulated resources and finding aids as widely available as possible, the Family History Library offered for purchase on compact disk such databases as the British 1881 census. On 24 May 1999, in a dramatic move, it offered online access to many of its holdings through Family Search Internet Genealogy Service (www.familysearch.org). Sources initially available included Ancestral File, the International Genealogical Index, and the Family History Library catalogue. During a two-month trial more than 200 million hits were recorded at the web site.

GENERAL AUTHORITIES. Leaders of the Church on the general as opposed to the local level. Not including general officers, the General Authorities (the term is used in preference to hierarchy) include the First Presidency, the Quorum of the Twelve Apostles, the Presiding Bishopric, and the First and Second Quorums of the Seventy (qq.v.).

When the Church was organized in 1830, the organization was simple: Joseph Smith was first elder, and Oliver Cowdery was second elder (qq.v.). Soon, however, Smith became president, he and his counselors constituting a First Presidency of three. In 1835 a Quorum of the Twelve Apostles was organized. When a Quorum of Seventy was created, its seven leaders were known as the First Council of the Seventy. A Presiding Bishopric was appointed very early, and, finally, a Patriarch (q.v.) to the entire Church was designated. From the 1830s to the recent past these have been the Mormon General Authorities: First Presidency, Twelve Apostles, First Council of Seventy, Presiding Bishopric, and Patriarch.

During the past generation this basic structure has been adjusted according to needs. In 1941, in order to visit the increasing number of stakes (q.v.), Assistants to the Twelve (q.v.) were appointed. In 1967 Regional Representatives (q.v.) were established—not considered General Authorities—as a kind of intermediate supervisory level. In 1976 the First Council of the Seventy and the Assistants to the Twelve were released and called to the new First Quorum of the Seventy. In 1989 a Second Quorum of the Seventy was established, appointments to which were for a five-year term. These Seventies are all General Authorities and, among other responsibilities, are typically assigned to the presidencies of specific geographical areas (q.v.).

On the grounds that his functions were now adequately performed by stake patriarchs, the general Church Patriarch was declared emeritus (q.v.) in 1979 and the position left unfilled.

The total number of General Authorities thus has greatly enlarged: First Presidency (3), Quorum of the Twelve Apostles (12), First Quorum of Seventy (42), Second Quorum of Seventy (43), Presiding Bishopric (3). The First Presidency and the Apostles, who remain the final governing authority and court of appeal and have lifetime tenure, are not young men but tend to be in their 60s, 70s, and 80s. The Seventy tend to be in their 50s and 60s. Moreover, some national diversity has been introduced with the appointment to the Seventy of individuals from England, Belgium, Germany, Korea, Brazil, Argentina, Chile, Guatemala, Mexico, and Hong Kong.

GENERAL HANDBOOK OF INSTRUCTIONS. Official guide of procedures containing instructions for local leaders such as stake presidents and bishops (qq.v.). Given the lay nature of the Church organization, such guidance is helpful in answering questions ranging from the keeping of records to the care of buildings. Although local leaders still exercise judgment on details and the varying circumstances that arise, the handbook helps ensure a minimum standardization and uniformity. Not available in bookstores, the handbook is distributed to the Church officials it is intended to assist.

GENESIS GROUP. In the early 1970s, three Black Latter-day Saint men met together to discuss common needs and issues. As a result of those meetings, the senior leaders of the Church were contacted and three junior Apostles–Gordon B. Hinckley, Thomas S. Monson, and Boyd K. Packer (qq.v.)—were assigned to meet with the three Black men. As a result of those meetings, it was decided by the First Presidency and the Twelve Apostles (qq.v.) that an organization should be established as a support group for Black Latter-day Saints. The outcome of that decision was a dependent branch, organized in October 1971. The name *Genesis* was arrived at by the Black members to represent a beginning. The president was Ruffin Bridgeforth; first counselor, Darius Gray; and second counselor, Eugene Orr. After the death of Bridgeforth in 1997, Darius Gray became president. Membership is approximately 60 percent non-White–African-Americans, Africans (q.v.), African-Carribean, Latinos, Polynesians (q.v.) and 40 percent White, including parents of adopted Black children and several biracial couples. Members of Genesis maintain membership in their home wards (q.v.). Meetings are held monthly and do not conflict with regularly scheduled church meetings. *See also* BLACKS.

GENTILE. 1. Generally, in Jewish usage, non-Jews. 2. In informal Mormon usage, non-Mormons. It has been humorously remarked that Salt Lake City is the only place where a Jew is a Gentile.

GLOSSOLALIA. The gift of speaking in tongues, one of the spiritual gifts identified in the New Testament church (1 Cor. 12), glossolalia is usually identified with pentecostalism, although there are other Protestant and even Catholic examples. In the Mormon historic experience such speaking in tongues occurred and was seen as a heavenly manifestation. Although there are still reports of such activity, the more usual form of the gift of tongues is ease in learning, or ability to speak and understand, a foreign language in a missionary (q.v.) setting. Mormons are not given to extravagant display. Speaking in tongues or other dramatic signs of spiritual power are not characteristic of their meetings.

GODHEAD. God the Eternal Father, his son Jesus Christ (q.v.), and the Holy Ghost. Mormons prefer the term *Godhead* to Trinity because of the creedal terminology associated with the latter. For Mormons the three divine beings are separate individuals whose unity is one of purpose and intent. When Jesus was baptized by John the Baptist, the Father's voice was heard from heaven, and the Holy Ghost descended like a dove (Matt. 3:16). When Jesus was in Gethsemane, he prayed to his Father, not to himself. When Joseph Smith received the First Vision (qq.v.) in answer to prayer, two beings appeared to him, God the Father and God the Son. Jesus Christ, the Son, has a glorified, resurrected body of flesh and bones, as does the Father, while the Holy Ghost is a personage of spirit (Doctrine and Covenants, section 130). *See also* JESUS CHRIST.

GOSPEL. The good news of Christ and the atonement wrought by him that brings immortality and, on condition of repentance (q.v.), saves humans from their sins. As Mormons use this word, it almost always refers to the *restored* gospel, or the *fullness* of the gospel, as taught in the scriptures and by the prophets from Joseph Smith (qq.v.) to the present. Thus a more complete view of the "good news" is embodied in the plan of salvation (q.v.), which explains life and its meaning, including the blessings that are in store for those who love God and keep his commandments (q.v.). Basic essentials are the First Principles (q.v.) of faith in the Lord Jesus Christ (q.v.), repentance, baptism (q.v.), and the gift of the Holy Ghost, which along with resurrection (q.v.) and judgment are sometimes collectively defined in the scriptures as the gospel. Indispensable to achieving the fullness of salvation, according to the gospel plan, is the priesthood (q.v.), the power to administer the saving ordinances (q.v.).

GRANT, HEBER JEDDY (1856–1945). Businessman, Apostle, and seventh president (q.v.) of the Church. Born in 1856, the son of Jedediah Grant, a counselor (q.v.) in the First Presidency (q.v.) of the Church, who died when the boy was still an infant, Heber was raised by his mother,

Rachel Ivins Grant. His upbringing included a good basic education, considering frontier conditions, and activity in study groups and the Young Men's Mutual Improvement Association. Tall and lanky, he learned to throw a baseball by persistent practice against a barn door and later went on to play on a team that won the territorial championship.

Grant's was a life story ideal for Horatio Alger Jr. He learned to write a beautiful Spencerian hand, sold insurance, took a job as a bank cashier, saved his money and bought the Ogden Vinegar Works. The future seemed auspicious.

But he also faced difficulties. After he married Lucy Stringham, she developed serious health problems, which led to her death 12 years later. When he became a stake (q.v.) president at the young age of 23, the travel and worry so sapped his strength that he suffered from extreme depression. The decline of his business income and the loss of his Ogden factory to a fire did not help.

Despite these reverses, he was called to the Quorum of the Twelve Apostles (q.v.) in 1882. He was assigned to work with the Sunday School and the Young Men's Mutual Improvement Association (qq.v.). Like other Apostles, he traveled, especially to Arizona and Mexico, where he labored strenuously among the Yaqui Indians. He also remained active in private business: a bank, insurance, a newspaper, a livery stable, and retail companies. He was also prominent as one of the owners of the Salt Lake Theater and the Utah Sugar Company. He considered these activities permissible, as he used his profits to further the community and dispensed private charity.

Another crisis came in 1893 with the national depression that led to the loss of his business empire. Still, he was able to negotiate loans and assisted the Church to survive its financial plight.

He took two additional wives, both of whom had been schoolteachers. Twelve children came from these marriages. Despite his frequent absences from his family, surviving letters give every indication of tender, supportive, and respectful relationships.

Since he had become an Apostle at the relatively young age of 26, it was not surprising that he outlived his colleagues and became president of the Twelve and, in 1918, president of the Church.

Grant's presidency, from 1918 to 1945, included the post–World War I years, the Great Depression, and World War II. An outgoing, generous man, Grant traveled and made speeches. Serving on the board of directors of national corporations, he promoted goodwill for the Church. He was influential, for example, in promoting and assisting two Hollywood movie productions, *Union Pacific* and *Brigham Young*. Not given to heavy theological discourse, he advocated faithfulness and loyalty and obedience to the commandments (q.v.). He was especially emphatic in urging adherence to the Word of Wisdom (q.v.). He sprinkled his sermons with quotations from popular poet Edgar A. Guest and the essayist David Starr Jordan.

The Church was challenged by the moral laxity of the 1920s and by the economic crisis of the 1930s (which for many Mormon farmers was just a further burden added to the agricultural depression they had been experiencing ever since the war). Responding to the former, Grant stressed the old time virtues, which he exemplified. Although a Democrat, he was not a New Dealer. The widespread unemployment following the Crash prompted Grant to introduce the Welfare Program (q.v.) and call a young stake president, Harold B. Lee (q.v.), to administer it.

The Church grew steadily—not the later sharp increases of the 1960s and 1970s, perhaps, but growth nonetheless. Hundreds of chapels were constructed. Temples (q.v.) were built in Hawaii, Canada, and Arizona. An imposing chapel, still standing although no longer owned by the Church, went up in Washington, D.C. Missionary (q.v.) work continued. In 1937 he traveled to England to attend meetings commemorating the first missionaries' arrival there one century earlier.

As always with presidencies, his counselors shared the responsibility. Anthon H. Lund, Charles W. Penrose, and Anthony W. Ivins played this role through the 1920s. For the remainder of Grant's presidency his counselors, vigorous and able, were Joshua Reuben Clark Jr. and David O. McKay (qq.v.).

With the coming of World War II, Grant recognized that national loyalty would lead many young Mormons into military service. A committee was organized to supervise the calling (q.v.) of chaplains (q.v.) and the preparation of a miniature newspaper and special editions of Mormon books for servicemen. Not bellicose, President Grant expressed reservations about the war and recognized that Mormons in other countries would rightfully serve in their armed forces.

GREAT APOSTASY. *See* APOSTASY.

-H-

HAIGHT, DAVID BRUCE (1906–). Businessman, civic leader, Church leader. Born on 2 September 1906 in Oakley, Idaho, David B. Haight was the son of Bishop (q.v.) Hector C. and Clara Haight. Prominent not only in the Church, Hector was also a business leader in the community and state senator. He died suddenly of a heart attack in 1916.

Young David, encouraged by his mother, studied violin, participated in the Boy Scouts (q.v.), and completed high school. He then attended the state normal school at Albion and Utah Agricultural College at Logan. Taking a job at a retail store in Salt Lake City, he impressed his employers sufficiently that they assigned him to be general manager of a store in Berkeley, California. Before leaving for his new location he married his fiancée, Ruby Olson.

In Berkeley he joined the Retail Association, the Lions Club, and the Chamber of Commerce. As a successful manager he was in demand. An offer of a better position took him to Illinois and then, one year later, another offer came from ZCMI in Salt Lake City. After four years there he accepted employment with Montgomery Ward, living successively in San Diego, Pomona, and Santa Barbara, California. Finally in 1940 he became regional merchandise manager over 90 stores. The Haights moved to Palo Alto.

During World War II David Haight entered the Navy as a lieutenant, later becoming a lieutenant commander and finally commander.

Returning to Montgomery Ward, Haight was made a regional manager of the Chicago region, including nine states. The experience was valuable, but in 1950 he moved back to California and purchased a hardware store in Palo Alto. Again he participated in community affairs, joining the Chamber of Commerce and Rotary. Elected to the city council, he later was chosen by the council as mayor.

He also served in the Church. After a stint on the high council, he became stake president (qq.v.) in 1951. During 12 busy years he supervised a growing flock, trained bishops, divided wards (q.v.) when necessary, and oversaw the construction of new chapels. Then, quite suddenly, another call came from the Church, and in early 1963 he and his wife left for Scotland, where he became mission president for three years, supervising missionaries (q.v.), instructing local leaders, and directing the construction of some 15 new chapels.

Back in the United States after being released from the mission assignment in 1966, the Haights lived for a time in Provo, Utah, where he played a central role in fund-raising for Brigham Young University (q.v.). In 1967 he became a regional representative with responsibility for supervising several California stakes.

In 1970 he became a General Authority of the Church as an Assistant to the Twelve (qq.v.). Six years later he became a member of the Quo-

rum of the Twelve Apostles (q.v.). With a wealth of administrative experience and a track record of accomplishment in family (q.v.), business,
civic, and church affairs, Haight would spend the next decades of his life
in a variety of challenging assignments. Teacher and leadership development was a special concern. Traveling to South America, to Europe,
and elsewhere, he organized new stakes and called leaders (qq.v.). *See
also* REGION.

HALES, ROBERT D. (1932–). Businessman, Apostle. Born in New York
City, Robert D. Hales earned a bachelor's degree from the University of
Utah and a master of business administration degree from Harvard University. He was a jet fighter pilot in the U.S. Air Force. Then he became
an executive with four major national companies. His Church callings
(q.v.) include counselor in the stake presidency, regional representative,
president of the England London Mission, first counselor in the general
presidency of the Sunday School, assistant to the Twelve, First Quorum
of the Seventy, and presiding bishop (qq.v.). Hales was ordained an
Apostle in April 1994. He and his wife, Mary, have two sons.

HANDCART PIONEERS. Immigrants from England who crossed the
plains not in the standard covered wagons but by walking, carrying their
belongings in small two-wheeled carts that were either pushed or pulled.
Nearly 3,000 made the journey in this way between 1856 and 1860.

Of the 250 deaths that occurred in transit among the handcart pioneers,
most happened in two companies—led by James G. Willie and Edward
Martin—in 1856. A combination of late departure from Florence, Nebraska, and an unusually early winter led to tragedy. In Wyoming, both
of these companies were caught in bitter weather, including icy winds
and blizzards. Running out of food, they huddled in camps while waiting for help. Fortunately relief had been organized. Wagon trains found
the destitute immigrants, brought food and warm clothing and bedding,
and helped carry the survivors for the final lap of the journey.

While the poor judgment behind the late departure was obvious, it was
the courage and heroism of the handcart pioneers and their rescuers that
came to be emphasized. A statue by Torlief Knaphus on Temple Square
(q.v.) commemorates "The Handcart Family."

HANKS, MARION DUFF (1921–). Educator, community leader, and
General Authority (q.v.). Born on 13 October 1921 in Salt Lake City,
Hanks was raised and educated there. From 1942 to 1944 he was a mis-
sionary (q.v.) in the Northern States Mission and then enlisted in the U.S.

Navy, serving duty aboard a submarine chaser. He married Maxine Christensen, and they went on to have five children.

Hanks taught in the seminary and institute system (qq.v.). In 1953 he became a General Authority as a member of the First Council of Seventy (q.v.). He continued to teach institute classes when possible until 1970. From 1962 to 1964 he was president (q.v.) of the British Mission.

An effective communicator with youth (q.v.), Hanks was a frequent speaker to youth groups. In Boy Scouting (q.v.) he was a member of the National Executive Board and served on many committees, which led to such awards as the Silver Beaver, the Silver Antelope, and the Silver Buffalo. Along with Elaine A. Cannon (q.v.) he edited a section entitled "Era of Youth" for the Church magazine *The Improvement Era* (q.v.). For five years he was managing director of the LDS (q.v.) Student Association for college students.

Few have contributed so much in community service. For five administrations he was on the President's Council on Physical Fitness and Sports. He was president of the Salt Lake City Rotary Club and in 1977–78, district governor; first chairman of the Utah Committee on Children and Youth; chairman of the Salt Lake Cancer Society; chairman of the Mental Health Board; and president of the Community Service Board. He has been on the governing boards of Brigham Young University (q.v.), Weber State College, Southern Utah State College, and Snow College.

Hanks has played a significant role in Europe, Asia, and Africa (qq.v.). After presiding over the British Mission from 1962 to 1964, he was area (q.v.) supervisor for Southeast Asia/Hawaii. From 1980 to 1982 he was executive administrator of the Southeast Asia/Philippines Area, living in Hong Kong. He initiated a pioneering effort working with refugees. He chairs the board of the Ouelessebougou Mali-Utah Alliance, which since 1985 has assisted with sanitation, agriculture, and literacy in a consortium of 22 villages in Mali.

From 1982 to 1985 Marion D. Hanks was president of the Salt Lake Temple (q.v.). Then, after serving as executive director of the Priesthood (q.v.) Department of the Church, he was given emeritus (q.v.) status in October 1992.

HARRIS, FRANKLIN STEWART (1884–1960). Agronomist, educator, university president. Born in Benjamin, Utah, on 29 August 1884, young Franklin moved with his parents and siblings to Juárez, Mexico, in 1889. There, in a rural setting, he grew up. He attended the Juárez Stake Academy, graduating in 1903. He was ready for college.

During his first year at Brigham Young University (q.v.) his family (q.v.) moved from Mexico to Cardston, Alberta, Canada. Franklin continued pursuing his studies, working as a teaching assistant to John A. Widtsoe (q.v.) in soil chemistry, and in 1907 graduated with a B.S. degree. He married Estella Spilsbury in 1908.

After gaining admission to the graduate program at Cornell University and working as a teaching assistant he completed work for his Ph.D. Then, in 1912, he became a professor of agronomy at Utah Agricultural College, director of the school of agricultural engineering and mechanical arts, and in 1916, director of the experiment station. There he became an acknowledged authority, publishing *The Principles of Agronomy* (1915), *Sugar Beets in America* (1918), and *Soil Alkali* (1920).

In 1921 Harris became president of Brigham Young University. At the time the BYU faculty consisted of 78 persons, only 10 of whom had doctorates. His was the guiding hand that helped to raise the institution to a higher level by building a program, attracting qualified faculty, and in general maintaining high standards.

During these same years, the 1920s and 1930s, he was appointed to government missions: U.S. representative to the Pan Pacific Science Congress in Tokyo in 1926; chairman of a commission to check on conditions among Jews in the USSR in 1929; chairman of the agriculture section of a scientific congress in Mexico City in 1935; and member of an agricultural mission to Iran in 1939 (where later he helped set up the Point Four program).

In 1945 Harris resigned as president of BYU to become president of Utah State University, where for five years he provided effective leadership. At both of these institutions he was highly regarded by students, faculty, other administrators, and trustees. He retired in 1950 and died in 1960.

HARRIS, MARTIN (1783–1875). One of the Three Witnesses who testified to the divine origin of the Book of Mormon (q.v.). Born in 1783 in Easton, New York, Harris married Lucy Harris (a distant cousin) and the couple had at least six children. A veteran of the War of 1812, he gained a farm of 320 acres near Palmyra, New York. A person of substance, he was elected road overseer for seven years. Religiously he was unaffiliated but looked for a restoration of original Christianity (q.v.).

Sometime after 1824 he heard of Joseph Smith (q.v.) and the metal plates. Obviously believing what he heard, Harris helped Smith move to Harmony, Pennsylvania, for safety. In 1828 Harris took a transcription of characters from the plates to two scholars, Charles Anthon and Samuel L. Mitchill, for verification. Whatever took place in the interviews—and there were later embarrassed, contradictory accounts by Anthon—Harris came away convinced that a prophecy (q.v.) in Isaiah 29 had been fulfilled.

For a short period Harris assisted Smith as scribe, but when he borrowed and then lost the first 116 pages of the manuscript, he was reprimanded and removed from that position. He pled for forgiveness and, despite the disgust and departure of his wife, continued to support the project. His testimony of seeing the plates and an angel, signed along with Oliver Cowdery and David Whitmer (qq.v.), appeared in the front of the Book of Mormon (q.v.) when it was published in early 1830. Perhaps the only early follower with sufficient means, Harris mortgaged part of his farm as security for the printing of the book and later sold part of it to pay the bill.

Harris was baptized the day the Church was organized, 6 April 1830. A year later he moved to Kirtland, Ohio, traveled with Smith to Missouri, and preached Mormonism as a missionary (q.v.). He was a member of the first high council (q.v.) at Kirtland. After traveling again to Missouri as a member of Zion's Camp (q.v.), a relief expedition, he returned to Ohio and, with his two fellow Book of Mormon witnesses, selected the first Quorum of the Twelve Apostles (q.v.). His first marriage having failed, he married a niece of Brigham Young (q.v.).

From 1837 on he became more or less disaffected from the Church. Except for one missionary trip to England, he lived in Kirtland and showed the Kirtland Temple to visitors. His wife and children moved to Utah in 1856, but not until 1870 did Harris himself move there and rejoin the Church. Many times he bore his testimony of the Book of Mormon, reaffirming what he had written for the original 1830 publication. He died in Clarkston, Utah, on 10 July 1875. *See also* ANTHON TRANSCRIPT; COWDERY, OLIVER; WHITMER, DAVID; WITNESSES OF THE BOOK OF MORMON.

HIERARCHY. *See* GENERAL AUTHORITIES.

HIGH COUNCIL. A body of 12 men, high priests in the Melchizedek Priesthood (qq.v.) who assist a stake (q.v.) president (q.v.). Holding regular meetings, a stake high council advises the stake president on matters he presents to it, including the selection of individuals for specific callings (q.v.) in the stake. In serious disciplinary actions, the high council discusses and evaluates the evidence along with the stake presidency and ratifies the decision of the stake president (Doctrine and Covenants, sec. 102).

Individual high councilors, not to be confused with counselors (q.v.), are given different supervisory and training assignments. They represent the stake presidency by speaking in ward sacrament meetings (qq.v.). *See also* EXCOMMUNICATION.

HIGH PRIEST. An office in the Melchizedek Priesthood (q.v.). Those who are called to serve in bishoprics, stake presidencies, high councils, or as General Authorities (qq.v.) are first ordained high priests. For reasons of age compatibility, as well, elders (q.v.) who have served faithfully in other callings (q.v.) are often advanced to the high priest office.

All of the high priests in a stake (q.v.) constitute the stake high priest quorum. Those in a ward (q.v.) are a group and meet each Sunday for instruction. The prophet and president (qq.v.) of the Church is the presiding high priest in the Church; the stake president, the presiding high priest in the stake; the bishop (q.v.), the presiding high priest in the ward.

High priest is not used as a form of address (q.v.). Instead, these men are referred to as, for example, "Brother" (q.v.) or "Elder" Johnson.

HILL CUMORAH. Near Palmyra, New York, a hill (drumlin) where Mormons believe an ancient prophet (q.v.) buried the inscribed plates later translated and published as the Book of Mormon (q.v.). The precise location of the buried plates is unknown. In 1928, the Church purchased the hill and erected a large monument on the site. Since 1937 the hill has annually been the site of the popular Hill Cumorah Pageant (q.v.).

HILLAM, HAROLD G. (1934–). Orthodontist, Church leader. Born in Sugar City, Idaho, Hillam served as a missionary (q.v.) in Brazil, graduated from Brigham Young University (q.v.), and attended dental school at Northwestern University, where he later returned for an advanced degree in orthodontics. He practiced his profession in Idaho Falls, Idaho, and was president of the Rocky Mountain Society of Orthodontists. He was a bishop's counselor, high councilor, stake president, and regional representative (qq.v.). Then he served as mission president in Portugal. In 1990 he became a member of the Second Quorum of the Seventy (q.v.), in 1991 a member of the First Quorum of the Seventy, and in 1995 a member of its presidency. He served as general president of the Sunday School (q.v.). He and his wife, Carol, have seven children.

HINCKLEY, GORDON BITNER (1910–). Journalist, public relations specialist, Apostle, 15th Church president (q.v.). Born in Salt Lake City, Hinckley went through the schools there and graduated from the University of Utah in 1932. He was a missionary (q.v.) in Great Britain for two years.

Employed by the Church as executive secretary of its Radio, Publicity, and Mission Literature Committee, he became executive secretary of the General Missionary Committee in 1951, managing the entire missionary program. He was president of the East Mill Creek Stake.

In 1958 Hinckley was called as an Assistant to the Twelve and three years later became a member of the Quorum of the Twelve Apostles (qq.v.). His assignments have been numerous, including serving or chairing committees on missionaries, temples, correlation, and welfare (qq.v.). He has served on the Church Board of Education and the Board of Trustees of Brigham Young University and Ricks College (qq.v.).

Since 1981 he served in the First Presidency (q.v.), as second counselor to President Spencer W. Kimball and from 1985 as first counselor to President Ezra Taft Benson (qq.v.). Because of the fragile health of these Church presidents, Hinckley carried much of the burden of leadership.

Among his special interests were Asia and temples (qq.v.). He traveled in Asia after World War II and played a key role in establishing the Church and calling leaders in the Philippines, Taiwan, Hong Kong, Japan, and Korea. With the beginning of a major program of constructing temples in many different countries, it was Hinckley more than anyone else who was assigned to travel to the different locations and dedicate the new sacred edifices.

On 12 March 1995 he became the 15th president of the Church. Two of the keynotes of his administration were public relations and continued temple construction. Experienced in dealing with the media, he launched initiatives to improve the image of the Church, encouraged community service (q.v.), and with grace and good humor responded to the questions of Mike Wallace, Larry King, and other interviewers. Temple construction had already been going on, as indicated, but in 1998 he announced a goal of 100 temples, which was made realizable by scaling back on their size. In addition, more than any of his predecessors President Hinckley traveled widely, including trips to China, South America, and Africa, (q.v.) to encourage Church members. He and his wife, Marjorie Pay Hinckley, have five children.

HISTORIC SITES. The following historic sites and visitor centers (q.v.) are staffed by missionaries (q.v.). Beehive House, Salt Lake City; Book of Mormon Historic Publication Site, Palmyra, New York; Brigham Young Winter Home, St. George, Utah; Carthage Jail, Carthage, Illinois; Cove Fort, Utah; Hill Cumorah, Manchester Township, New York; Independence Visitors' Center, Independence, Missouri; Jacob Hamblin Home, Santa Clara, Utah; John Johnson Farmhouse, Hiram, Ohio; Joseph Smith Memorial, Sharon, Vermont; Joseph Smith Sr. Farm, Manchester Township, New York; Liberty Jail, Liberty, Missouri; Mormon Battalion Visitors' Center, San Diego, California; Mormon Handcart Visitors' Center, Alcova, Wyoming; Mormon Trail Center at Historic Winter Quarters, Omaha, Nebraska; Nauvoo Historic District and Visitors' Center, Nauvoo, Illinois; Newel K. Whitney Store and Home, Kirtland, Ohio; Peter Whitmer Farm, Fayette Township, New York; St. George Tabernacle, St. George, Utah; and Temple Square, Salt Lake City, Utah. There are, of course, many other sites of historic interest. In addition, visitor centers are located at temples in Mesa, Arizona; Laie, Hawaii; Idaho Falls, Idaho; Los Angeles and Oakland, California; St. George, Utah; and Washington, D.C.; Mexico City, Mexico; and Hamilton, New Zealand.

HISTORICAL DEPARTMENT OF THE CHURCH. As part of a reorganization of several departments, what had been the Church Historian's Office was renamed the Historical Department of the Church on 14 January 1972. Originally subdivided into Library Division, Archives Division, and Historian's Division, it was later slightly reorganized into Library-Archives, Arts and Sites, and History Divisions, and still later into Library, Archives, and Museum.

The stated mission of the Historical Department of the Church is to acquire, organize, preserve, and oversee the use of records, publications, photographs, artifacts, and other materials having to do with the history of the Church (q.v.).

The History Division, under the direction of Leonard J. Arrington (q.v.), was a group of about a dozen professional historians who from 1972 prepared bibliographies, established an oral history program, and produced many books and articles on Church history. In 1982 this group was transferred to Brigham Young University and designated the Joseph Fielding Smith Institute for Church History (qq.v.).

HISTORY OF THE CHURCH. Articles in the present volume treating Mormon history include: New York Period, Ohio Period, Missouri Period, Illinois Period, Exodus, and Utah Period (q.v.). Also historical are such topics as Colonization, Polygamy, Mountain Meadows Massacre, and Gathering (q.v.).

The biographical articles naturally relate to different periods of the Church's history. One recommendation would be to read in sequence the sketches of the presidents (qq.v.) of the Church from the beginning to the present: Joseph Smith, Brigham Young, John Taylor, Wilford Woodruff, Lorenzo Snow, Joseph F. Smith, Heber J. Grant, George Albert Smith, David O. McKay, Joseph Fielding Smith, Harold B. Lee, Spencer W. Kimball, Ezra Taft Benson, Howard W. Hunter, and Gordon B. Hinckley (qq.v.). Articles treating different geographical areas are also in part a historical overview.

HOLLAND, JEFFREY R. (1940–). Educator, president of Brigham Young University, and General Authority (qq.v.). Born in St. George, Utah, on 3 December 1940, Holland was educated in southern Utah before serving as a missionary (q.v.) in the United Kingdom from 1960 to 1962. Returning, he earned a B.A. and an M.A. from Brigham Young University (q.v.) and married Patricia Terry. He became an instructor in the system of institutes of religion (q.v.), teaching and directing programs at Hayward, California, Seattle, Washington, and New Haven, Connecticut.

At New Haven, Holland gained admittance to Yale University's graduate program in American studies and earned an M.A. and Ph.D. He returned to Brigham Young University and in 1973 became dean of religious education. Three years later, only 36 years old, Holland became Church Commissioner of Education. Although relatively young, Jeffrey Holland had accumulated much experience in Church service: bishop, counselor in stake presidencies, high councilor, regional representative (qq.v.). For two years he was chairman of the Church-wide young adult committee.

Named president of Brigham Young University in 1980, Holland presided during a decade of expansion and increased visibility of BYU in both athletics and scholarship. A vigorous, personable administrator, he was a champion of the institution and an effective communicator with the students. He worked in close cooperation with his wife, Pat; in fact, a typical address to student assemblies by the couple became known as "the Pat and Jeff Show."

In 1989 he became a member of the First Quorum of the Seventy (q.v.). In 1994, at age 53, he was sustained to the Quorum of the Twelve Apostles (q.v.).

HOME TEACHING. Program of the Church that sends Priesthood (q.v.) holders as visitors into the home of every member at least once a month. Standard procedure is for the teachers (q.v.) to go as a pair, a mature man with a youth (q.v.) or, in special circumstances, a husband and wife. The Church is brought into the lives of the people on the ground level, as it were. A message of inspiration and instruction is delivered, special needs are ascertained, and friendships are formed. The home teachers are instructed to do more than make a mechanical call; they are to become acquainted with the needs of each family (q.v.) or individual and prayerfully seek to be of assistance.

The program has been readjusted from time to time, but the original impetus goes back to the organization of the Church and the instruction (Doctrine and Covenants, section 20) that teachers are to "visit the house of each member and exhort them to pray vocally and in secret and attend to all family duties." *See also* VISITING TEACHING.

HOMOSEXUALITY. Sexual relations between persons of the same gender are considered sinful. One must not act on this orientation but, like all unmarried people, should refrain from sexual intercourse. Sexual intercourse outside of marriage is a sin, say the Church leaders, and it is not up to humans to change the law of God.

HUMANITARIAN AID. To assist those in need or victims of disasters, a variety of channels are used by Mormons. They can volunteer or donate to relief programs of their choice. In the payment of Fast Offering (q.v.) on a monthly basis they create a fund that can be drawn upon by bishops (q.v.) to meet needs. In Salt Lake City at the end of the 1990s a program was organized in which Church-service missionaries (q.v.) were assigned to low-income areas of the central city to work with individuals and families to give career counseling, budgeting advice, and other forms of assistance.

On the standard form used for donations to the Church one designated category is "humanitarian." These funds are used throughout the world according to need, and none of them are used for administrative expenses. An extensive Sort Center in Salt Lake City gathers, sorts, and bundles used clothing, bedding, medical equipment, and other material, sending them to areas of the world where they can be most effectively used. In responding to floods, tornadoes, and other disasters, Mormons are not alone of course. They cooperate with others in extending relief. But the record of quick and effective response is impressive.

In a 1997 address to Rotary International, President Thomas S. Monson (q.v.) revealed that during the previous 12 years Church humanitarian efforts included 2,340 projects in 137 countries. Food (9,800 tons), clothing (20,798 tons), medical equipment (894 tons), and educational material (794 tons) had been distributed. Relief had been provided for 76 major disasters.

HUMOR. Their conservative lifestyle—no smoking, no drinking, no sex outside of marriage—and the characteristically sober presentation of their religious beliefs combine to create the impression among some that the Mormons are humorless. It is thus important to state that in this respect they are about the same as other people, sharing the humor of their society, differing individually on the extent to which this is an important feature of their lives.

In the 19th century Mormons were frequently the butt of ridicule and jokes. In turn, they had their own humor, as in the short-lived periodical *Keep-a-Pitchinin'*. The harsh environment with its exacting challenges led to some humor as a form of release, as in the handwritten newspaper *Veprecula*, put out by a group of young people in the 1860s. From 1892, one of the General Authorities, Jonathan Golden Kimball (qq.v.), a tall, skinny man with a high-pitched voice, became a popular preacher, combining serious moral injunction with an eccentric, individualistic tendency to poke fun at pomposity and self-importance.

In the late 20th century examples of Mormon humor include a good deal of self-ridicule in the form of cartoons (Pat Bagley, Calvin Grondahl) and mock-serious definitions (Orson Scott Card). Not all Mormons enjoy this kind of material, but obviously some do. In literature (q.v.) two humorous, even picaresque, novels are *Heaven Knows Why* by Samuel W. Taylor and *The Backslider* by Levi Peterson. Books of humorous essays have been published by Louise Plummer and Tom Plummer.

Most Mormons would not appreciate the raw, sexually explicit subject matter or the taunting ridicule of religion sometimes expressed by stand-up comedians. In other areas, however, Mormons are probably laughing at the same cartoons, movies, and comedians as everyone else.

HUNTER, HOWARD WILLIAM (1907–1995). Lawyer, businessman, Church leader, 14th Church president (q.v.). Born in Boise, Idaho, on 14 November 1907, Howard Hunter was raised and received his early education there. He became an Eagle Scout. In 1928 he moved to California, married Clara May Jeffs, and went on to receive a Juris Doctor degree cum laude from Southwestern University Law School. During the strenuous period when he was in law school, three sons were born, one of whom died in infancy.

Admitted to the California State Bar, he became a leading corporate attorney. In the Church he served as bishop, stake high councilor, and president (qq.v.) of the Pasadena Stake. While stake president he also served as chairman of the Southern California Welfare Region and Los Angeles Welfare Region. He was on the temple (q.v.) committee during the construction of the Los Angeles Temple.

In 1959, at age 51, he became a member of the Quorum of the Twelve Apostles (q.v.). He served on the board of directors of several corporations, including First Security Corporation and the New World Archaeological Foundation. He has been president of the Polynesian Cultural Center (q.v.), the Genealogical Society, and the West European Mission. In 1985 he became acting president and in 1988 president of the Quorum of the Twelve Apostles.

Clara, his wife of many years, died in 1983. Their two sons, both lawyers, lived in California. In 1990 he married Inis Bernice Egan. He became 14th president of the Church on 5 June 1994 at age 86 but died in March 1995. *See also* GENEALOGY.

HUNTSMAN, JON (1937–). Businessman, billionaire, philanthropist. Born on 21 May 1937 in Blackfoot, Idaho, Jon Meade Huntsman Sr. grew up in poverty and worked after-school jobs to help support his family. After earning an undergraduate degree at the Wharton School of Business at the University of Pennsylvania, Huntsman earned an MBA degree from the University of Southern California. President of the Huntsman Corporation, the largest privately held chemical company in the nation, he served as special assistant to the president under Richard Nixon and vice president of the U.S. Chamber of Commerce. Huntsman has given $40 million to his alma mater, the Wharton School, and pledged $100 million to create the Huntsman Cancer Institute at the University of Utah. He has also sponsored programs for the homeless and shelters for abused women. He has served as a stake president and Area Authority Seventy (qq.v.). Huntsman is married to Karen Haight Huntsman. They are the parents of nine children.

HYDE, ORSON (1805–1878). Missionary (q.v.), pioneer, Apostle. Hyde was born on 8 January 1805 in Oxford, Connecticut. Left an orphan at age 12, he was raised by neighbors. They moved to Kirtland, Ohio, in 1819. There Hyde took different jobs, including work as a clerk in the Gilbert-Whitney store. He joined the Methodists in 1827, but when he heard the preaching of Sidney Rigdon (q.v.), Hyde joined his congregation. When the first Mormon missionaries (q.v.) arrived in the fall of 1830, Rigdon accepted the new religion and Hyde soon followed in early 1831.

Immediately Hyde began preaching Mormonism as a missionary. Ohio, Missouri, Pennsylvania, New York, Canada, and Indiana were some of the scenes of his proselytizing. In 1834 he married Marinda Nancy Johnson. After returning from the strenuous expedition of Zion's Camp (q.v.), he became a member of the original Quorum of the Twelve Apostles (q.v.) in 1835. He was one of the original bearers of the message of Mormonism to England in 1837.

In Missouri during the height of the persecutions there, Hyde briefly defected and was excommunicated (q.v.). When he expressed his strong desire to return six months later, he was reinstated as a member and as an Apostle. He had no sooner moved to Nauvoo and established his family there than he was called on a special mission to Palestine. Taking months to make the long journey, he arrived in Jerusalem and on 24 October 1841 dedicated Palestine for the future return of the Jews.

Back in Nauvoo during the final year of the Illinois Period (q.v.), he was introduced to polygamy (q.v.) and, after soul-searching, took two wives. He would later add three additional wives. He fathered a total of 32 children. In the spring of 1844, Hyde became a member of the Council of Fifty (q.v.).

During 1846, the year in which the Exodus (q.v.) began, he was sent on another mission to England. Returning, he settled in Utah. As a loyal follower and pioneer (q.v.), he led a group to colonize Fort Supply in Wyoming. In 1855 he led a group to settle Carson Valley, Nevada, serving as a probate judge there. In 1858 he was called to lead the Mormon settlements in south-central Utah. He built a home in Spring City and for the final 20 years of his life was the Church leader in the area. Hyde also served on the territorial supreme court and in the legislature. *See also* COLONIZATION; MISSOURI PERIOD.

-I-

ILLINOIS PERIOD. Western Illinois was the main center of Mormonism from 1839 to 1846. Fleeing from Missouri after the extermination
order issued by Governor Lilburn W. Boggs, Mormon refugees were received and cared for in Quincy and other Illinois towns. While Joseph
Smith (q.v.) and other leaders languished in jail in Liberty, Missouri, he
sent out encouraging and inspiring instructions (Doctrine and Covenants,
sections 121 through 123). By spring of 1839, Smith having rejoined his
family and people, a site for settlement was selected at Commerce, on
the east side of a bend in the Mississippi River, a few miles north of
Quincy. Rechristened Nauvoo (based on a Hebrew word for "comely,"
or "beautiful"), this became the new gathering place and the Mormon
center.

Another boomtown, Nauvoo grew rapidly, eventually reaching a population of some 12,000. (Estimates vary, depending on the year and
whether or not the surrounding area is included.) A charter granting the
city extraordinary powers of self-government was granted by the Illinois
legislature. The Nauvoo Legion was organized as a militia for defense.
Two newspapers began publication. A Masonic lodge was formed. Even
a university was started, although it was one in little more than name.

In a bold stroke, when the Church and its people seemed to be in the
depths of persecution and despair, Joseph Smith sent most of the Twelve
Apostles (q.v.) to England, where they arrived in 1840. A preliminary
proselytizing mission there in 1837 had already started making converts.
Nearly 5,000 of these English converts immigrated to Nauvoo. With other
converts from the United States, the future of Mormonism in Illinois
seemed assured even with some loss by attrition.

Some of the houses erected in the new city were impressive two-story
brick structures. Joseph Smith moved his family into a new "mansion
house." Funds were raised and construction started on a hotel, the Nauvoo
House. A Masonic building served as a cultural hall. Although it is easy
to exaggerate the "refinement" of a community still close to its original
poverty, obviously this was a town on the rise. The people tried to raise
their sights as best they could. Included in the entertainment were din-
ner parties and balls, circuses, parades, and theater.

In addition to retailing food and clothing, much of the economic life
of Nauvoo revolved around the construction of roads, houses, and public buildings. Naturally there was trade with the surrounding area. Lo-

cated on the banks of the Mississippi, Nauvoo seemed a natural port for whatever trade the river could generate. A manufacturing and agriculture society was established. Plans were put forth for industry and a dam in the river that would greatly enhance its navigability. What was needed to undergird such development was capital, always in short supply.

The Mormon religion experienced important further development during this period. Concepts such as eternal progression, the potential deification of humans, and the eternal duration of family (q.v.) relationships were enunciated. Baptism for the dead (q.v.) was introduced. Polygamy (q.v.), which had been adumbrated even earlier, was announced to the inner circle of leaders by a revelation (q.v.) in 1843 and began to be practiced by a few of the leading families. The Kirtland Temple had been abandoned, and the temple (q.v.) announced for Independence, Missouri, had been thwarted by persecution and expulsion. Now a new temple, a sacred place for the ordinances (q.v.) of endowment and eternal marriage, began to rise, an imposing white edifice on the highest elevation of the city.

Organizationally, wards (q.v.) were established as the congregational unit. In 1842 the Relief Society (q.v.) was founded as the organization for women. A Council of Fifty (q.v.) with ambitious plans for colonization and government was initiated. Most importantly, perhaps, the Quorum of the Twelve Apostles (q.v.), seasoned after directing the migration from Missouri and by their missionary responsibility in England, came to occupy the most important administrative role next to the First Presidency (q.v.).

Repeating the pattern of the Ohio Period (q.v.), all of this doctrinal and institutional creativity did not preclude, indeed to some extent even caused, opposition. Nearby communities felt threatened by economic competition. As Mormons became numerous, they were a political force, a swing vote if not the dominant vote in the county. Other Illinois Masons were alarmed by the sudden emergence of a large lodge among the Mormons. Rumors of imperialistic designs and of the new marriage practices began to circulate, sometimes with a kernel of accuracy but exaggerated and distorted. For a variety of reasons some Mormons defected. Persecution raised its head once again as anti-Mormons formed vigilante groups.

Aware of opponents within and fierce enemies without, Joseph Smith did several things simultaneously. He pushed for the continued growth of Nauvoo, especially the completion of the Nauvoo House and the temple, this in the face of the revocation of the city's charter. He initiated an exploring expedition to find an alternative place of settlement in the West. The actual departure of this party was deferred until after the election of 1844. He assigned an Apostle, Lyman Wight (q.v.), to lead a company to find a place of settlement in Texas. He gave increased responsibility to the Twelve Apostles, declaring that they now had all the authority he had. He ran as an independent for president of the United States, sending out the Apostles and others to campaign for him.

By late spring of 1844 the opposition mounted in a deafening crescendo. Anti-Mormon newspapers were calling for the use of violence if necessary. Mobs were burning out Mormon farms and outlying settlements, sending their frightened inhabitants fleeing into Nauvoo for safety. The state of Missouri was demanding that Joseph Smith return for trial. When an opposition newspaper, *The Nauvoo Expositor*, appeared in Nauvoo itself, denouncing Smith and describing polygamy in intemperate terms, it was declared a public nuisance by the city council and its press destroyed. This simply fanned the flames.

Promised protection by the governor, Joseph and Hyrum Smith (q.v.) were imprisoned in Carthage, Illinois, where they were assassinated. The era of Mormonism's first prophet (q.v.) had come to an end, the Church just 14 years old. The big question, of course, was survival. Some newspapers expressed confidence that, deprived of their charismatic leader, the Mormons would quickly disperse. Sidney Rigdon (q.v.), who along with Joseph and Hyrum Smith had been a member of the First Presidency, put in a bid for the leadership. But at a large gathering of the members at Nauvoo on 8 August 1844 the vote was decisively in favor of the Twelve Apostles assuming the leadership, with Brigham Young (q.v.) as president.

For another year and a half Nauvoo survived. Young and his colleagues provided leadership, continuing the doctrines and policies of Joseph Smith. Construction of houses continued. The temple construction continued and was finally completed at the beginning of 1846. Although conversion and disaffection continued simultaneously, as almost always, the balance seemed in favor of continued growth, especially with dramatic successes in England. During 1845, however, anti-Mormon violence in the area combined with demands that the Mormons leave Illinois, which Young and the other leaders agreed to do, hoping first to sell their properties and to have adequate time for preparing wagons and supplies.

By winter of 1845–46 the writing was on the wall. The capstone of the temple having been laid, more than 6,000 Mormons received their temple ordinances in January and February. With the hoof beats of marauding mobsters' horses raising panic and forcing people to hasten into Nauvoo from the surrounding settlements, and with violence on both sides, the Mormon leaders agreed to depart. Starting in February 1846 refugees moved from the city and across the river—first on ice, then by barge—and continued on into Iowa. Those who required more time continued to be harassed. By the fall of 1846 the Mormons who recognized the leadership of Brigham Young had practically all departed.

Schism and apostasy (q.v.) had occurred as early as the 1830s when some refused to follow new revelations and policies of Joseph Smith that had not been part of the religion at its beginning. But such dissidents had always been relatively few. Now a larger group, although still a minority, refused to embark on the arduous journey to the distant Great Basin. Eventually some of these rallied to form the Reorganized Church of Jesus Christ of Latter Day Saints (q.v.).

In the 20th century, as a result of renewed proselytizing and growth mostly after the middle of the century, there were 45,000 Illinois Mormons at the end of 1997, divided into 12 stakes and 80 wards (qq.v.). A temple in a suburb of Chicago was completed and dedicated in 1985. *See also* ANTI-MORMONISM; EXODUS; MISSOURI PERIOD; NAUVOO RESTORATION, INC.; TEMPLES.

IMPROVEMENT ERA, THE. Magazine published monthly from 1897 to 1970. At first the official organ of the Young Men's Mutual Improvement Association, it enlarged its scope and was effectively the magazine for adults in the Church.

Contents included editorials, recipes, historical articles, short stories, poetry, and advertisements. Instructions for priesthood (q.v.) leaders and messages to be delivered by ward teachers, now called home teachers (q.v.), were included. The "Spoken Word" of Richard L. Evans (q.v.) was a regular feature. For many years John A. Widtsoe (q.v.) published answers to questions under the column title "Evidences and Reconciliations." Addresses at general conference (q.v.) by General Authorities (q.v.) were printed, selectively for many years and completely from 1942 on. A special section entitled "The Era of Youth," edited by Elaine A. Cannon and Marion D. Hanks (qq.v.), appeared from 1960 on. When the final issue of *The Improvement Era* appeared in December 1970, its circulation was 275,000. Its successor, the *Ensign* (q.v.), started publication in January 1971.

INACTIVITY. Inactive Mormons are those who do not attend Church, those sometimes called "nonpracticing" in other traditions. Other indications of this status include failure to observe the Word of Wisdom and failure to pay tithing (qq.v.). Obviously there are degrees of inactivity, ranging from the bitter apostate (q.v.), who resents the Church and wants nothing more to do with it, to the person who is still committed and believing but for a variety of reasons fails to attend the regular meetings. To recognize this variety and to avoid stereotyping, Mormon leaders now prefer the designation "less active."

INDIANS. *See* NATIVE AMERICANS.

INSTITUTES OF RELIGION. Programs of study in religion for college students. The first of these institutes was established in 1926 at the University of Idaho. When there are sufficient Mormon students, an institute building is usually constructed near a university campus. Courses are offered on the scriptures (q.v.), Church history, world religions, and marriage and family (q.v.). Recreational activities, social functions, and worship meetings provide opportunities for Mormon students to interact. Most institute instructors hold the doctorate or a Master's degree.

With the expanding Church population and the limited capacity of Brigham Young University (q.v.), institutes have become increasingly important. In 1993, the institute program was made available not only to college and university students but to all young adults between 18 and 30. In 1997, enrollment was 231,752.

INTERNATIONAL MAGAZINES. Magazines published in eighteen different languages, with different titles for each magazine: *l'Etoile*, *Der Stern*, *la Stella*, *Tambuli*, and so on. Many articles are translated and printed from English-language publications, but other articles are produced by people from the different nations or areas. Eight pages of each issue are filled with news from the country or area served. Produced monthly, bimonthly, or quarterly, depending on readership, the international magazines, like the *Ensign*, *New Era*, and *The Friend* (qq.v.), are designed "to strengthen the faith of members; to promulgate the truths of the restored gospel; to keep members informed of current and vital Church policies, programs, and events; and to entertain and enrich the lives of Church members" (*Ensign*, September 1986).

INTERNET. The rapid rise of the Internet as a means of communication and a source of information in the 1990s has brought a variety of sites about Mormonism. The official Church web site is www.lds.org. A published guide is Lauramaery Gold, *Mormons on the Internet* (Rocklin, Calif.: Prima Publishing, 1997). *See also* GENEALOGY.

INVESTIGATOR. Not a private eye in Mormon usage but someone who is seriously studying the Mormon religion with a view to possible conversion and baptism (q.v.). When missionaries (q.v.) find persons who are thus willing to study and consider, they teach them the gospel (q.v.) and its requirements in a series of lessons. *See also* REFERRAL.

-J-

JACK, ELAINE LOW (1928–). Leader of Young Women and Relief Society (q.v.). After growing up in Cardston, Alberta, Canada, Elaine Low attended the University of Utah for two years. Marrying medical student Joseph E. Jack in 1948, she moved with him to New York City. His medical training and practice as a surgeon took them to Boston, Alaska, and finally Salt Lake City. The Jacks have four sons.

Elaine Jack has done community service (q.v.) work for the American Cancer Society and served in medical and auxiliary positions. Her Church assignments included being ward Relief Society president, ward Young Women president, stake Relief Society president's counselor, Relief Society general board member, and counselor to Ardeth Kapp (qq.v.) in the Young Women general presidency. From 1990 to 1997 Elaine Jack served as general president of the Relief Society. Her two counselors were Chieko Okazaki and Aileen H. Clyde.

JACK-MORMON. Colloquial term for someone who is a member of the Church in name only or who never, or hardly ever, attends meetings. (The original usage of the term in the 1840s referred to non-Mormons who were friendly to the Church, but that meaning has lost its currency.) Heard only infrequently now, "Jack-Mormon" has been replaced for most purposes by "inactive" or "less active." *See also* ACTIVITY; INACTIVITY.

JACOBSEN, FLORENCE SMITH (1913–). Youth leader, art curator, historic preservationist. Born on 7 April 1913, Florence Smith was raised in Salt Lake City. She earned a bachelor's degree in interior design at the University of Utah and in 1935 married Theodore C. Jacobsen. They have three sons.

On the ward and stake (qq.v.) level she worked with the Primary, the Boy Scouts, and the Young Women (qq.v.). In 1955 the Jacobsens moved to New York City to preside over the Eastern States Mission. Upon their return in 1959, Florence was named to the general board of the Young Women, then known as the Young Women's Mutual Improvement Association. Two years later she became general president of the organization, serving from 1961 to 1972.

During these years, in addition to leading the many programs of the Young Women, she directed an ambitious centennial celebration in 1969, which included an original movie, *Pioneers and Petticoats*. She played a central role in the production of the musical *Promised Valley* and, growing out of its orchestra and chorus, the establishment of the Mormon Youth Symphony and Mormon Youth Chorus, which have become permanent performing groups. Her training in design and historic costume was also called upon when she was assigned to supervise the restoration of the Joseph Smith (q.v.) home in Palmyra, New York, and then Brigham Young's (q.v.) Lion House in Salt Lake City.

Jacobsen was a member of the National Council of Women (NCW) and the International Council of Women. In addition to serving on committees and attending conventions, she served as a vice president of the NCW.

In 1973 she was appointed Church Curator, a position of the Historical Department of the Church (q.v.). With a reorganization she became director of Historic Arts and Sites, serving until 1986. Building a staff of professionals, she was given responsibility over the many historic sites (q.v.) throughout the United States. Artifacts and works of art, which had been poorly displayed or stored in closets and attics, were catalogued and restored. Most importantly, a Museum of Church History and Art (q.v.) was constructed in order to provide a suitable facility for exhibiting examples of the Church's artistic heritage.

JENSEN, MARLIN K. (1942–). Attorney, Church leader. Born in Ogden, Utah, Jensen served as a missionary (q.v.) in Germany, graduated in German at Brigham Young University (q.v.), and earned the juris doctorate from the University of Utah. Specializing in estate planning with an Ogden law firm, he was also a partner in the Jensen Family Middle Fork Ranch, a 600-head beef operation. After serving as bishop, stake president, mission president, and regional representative, he was named to the First Quorum of the Seventy (qq.v.) in 1989. He and his wife, Kathleen, are the parents of eight children.

JENSEN, VIRGINIA URRY (1940–). Born in Salt Lake City, Utah, Virginia Urry studied history and drama at the University of Utah. She married J. Rees Jensen, president of a shopping center development company. They are the parents of four children. She was secretary of the Utah Alumni Association and counselor in the ward presidency of Primary, Young Women, and Relief Society (qq.v.). She was director of Church Building Hosting when called as first counselor (q.v.) in the general Relief Society presidency in 1997.

JERUSALEM CENTER. Brigham Young University's (q.v.) Jerusalem Center for Near Eastern Studies, on Mount Scopus, was dedicated in 1989. Public protests by ultraorthodox Jews had attempted to stop construction, but an official ruling that all legal requirements had been met allowed the structure to be completed.

Its seven levels and 120,000 square feet include classrooms, a library, a multipurpose room, a cafeteria and dining rooms, two auditoriums, and dormitory rooms. It was designed by Franklin T. Ferguson, a Salt Lake City architect, in cooperation with David Reznik, a Jerusalem architect.

Selected from applicants, 169 university students study the Bible (q.v.), the history and culture of Islam, Palestine, postbiblical Judaism, and languages. Weekly fieldtrips take students to sites of historical and cultural significance.

The 320-seat auditorium serves as a concert hall for performances on a 3,000-pipe organ and for groups and individual artists from the community.

JESSOP, CRAIG D. (1949–). Director of the Mormon Tabernacle Choir (q.v.). Born in Millville, Utah, Jessop received a bachelor's degree in music from Utah State University, an M.A. degree from Brigham Young University (q.v.), and a doctorate of musical arts from Stanford University. As a lieutenant colonel in the U.S. Air Force, he was director of the Singing Sergeants, 1980–87, conductor of the Band of the United States Air Forces in Europe, 1987–91, and conductor of the Air Combat Command Heartland of America Band, 1991–95. He also served as musical director of the Maryland Choral Society, the Rhineland-Pfalz International Choir of Germany, and the Omaha Symphonic Chorus. A baritone vocalist, Jessop performed in the Merola Opera Training Program of the San Francisco Opera. He was a member of the Robert Shaw Festival Singers. An associate director of the Tabernacle Choir since 1995, he became director in 1999. He and his wife, RaNae, have four children.

JESUS CHRIST. The Savior and Redeemer of the world. Born in Bethlehem, Jesus performed miracles, called Apostles, founded a Church, was betrayed, crucified, and resurrected. The second member of the Godhead (q.v.) (Articles of Faith, 1), by commission the Creator of the earth (John 1:3), Jesus Christ is the "author and finisher of our salvation" (Hebrews 12:2; Moroni 6:4)

The Church is named after him; baptized Mormons take upon themselves his name; his sacrifice is memorialized weekly in sacrament meetings (q.v.). Not feeling any need for an elaborate Christology, Mormons accept the virgin birth; that is, the infant was miraculously conceived by Mary. Of a divine Father as well as a human mother, Jesus had both divine and human attributes. Literally, he is the Only Begotten Son of God.

To suggest that Mormons do not believe in Christ is not a harmless misunderstanding but a gross misrepresentation. One among many passages in the Book of Mormon (q.v.) states: "We talk of Christ, we rejoice in Christ, we preach of Christ, we prophesy of Christ, and we write according to our prophecies, that our children may know to what source they may look for a remission of their sins" (2 Nephi 25:26). *See also* CHRISTIANITY.

JOHN WHITMER HISTORICAL ASSOCIATION (JWHA). Officially organized in 1973, by historians and others from the Reorganized Church of Jesus Christ of Latter Day Saints (q.v.), the JWHA has always included people from different religious and secular backgrounds. It now consists of several hundred members.

Its area of interest, according to its brochure, is "the study of early Mormonism, the history of the Reorganized Church of Jesus Christ of Latter Day Saints, and LDS (q.v.) factions located in the Midwestern United States."

JWHA distributes a newsletter, sponsors an annual meeting, cosponsors (with Graceland College) a spring lecture series, and publishes an annual journal. *See also* MORMON HISTORY ASSOCIATION.

JOSEPH FIELDING SMITH INSTITUTE FOR LATTER-DAY SAINT HISTORY. A group of historians at Brigham Young University (q.v.) whose primary assignment is the research and writing of the history of the Church (q.v.). Established in 1982 by the transfer and renaming of the group previously attached to the Historical Department of the Church (q.v.), the institute edits and publishes primary sources, such as the writings of Joseph Smith (q.v.), and works on a variety of individual projects. Some of these historians have appointments in academic departments at the university and teach some courses. The first director of the institute was Leonard J. Arrington (q.v.), who was replaced on his retirement by Ronald K. Esplin. Ronald W. Walker is director of research.

JOSEPH SMITH MEMORIAL BUILDING. A building in downtown Salt Lake City, Utah, known as the Hotel Utah since its completion in 1911. After major restoration and renovation, the building was dedicated in 1993 and given its new name. Open to the public are a magnificent lobby, a family (q.v.) history area with computers and assistants, a 500-seat theater, two top-floor scenic outlooks and restaurants. Office buildings of different Church departments occupy eight floors. On the mezzanine level are a chapel and teaching and leadership rooms. In the basement can be found a distribution center and an outlet for the purchase of temple (q.v.) clothing.

JOURNAL OF DISCOURSES. A 26-volume work published in Liverpool, England, between 1854 and 1884. Based on the shorthand reporting of George D. Watt and others, the *Journal of Discourses* includes many sermons by Mormon leaders of the latter 19th century. Since these were not canonized, they are something less than an official statement of Mormon doctrine. Nevertheless, since the Mormon homiletic style was informal, the sermons touch on many topics and constitute a valuable primary source for historians.

A five-volume addendum made up of sermons delivered by Mormon leaders from 1886 to 1898 has been published by Brian H. Stuy under the title *Collected Discourses* (1987–92).

-K-

KAPP, ARDETH GREENE (1931–). Leader of Young Women (q.v.). Born on 19 March 1931 in Glenwood, Alberta, Canada, Ardeth Greene had a small town upbringing. Attending Brigham Young University (q.v.), she began dating Heber Kapp, whom she married in 1950.

Living in Utah and California, the Kapps built a series of seven homes. Ardeth worked for the telephone company for 10 years. Later she earned a bachelor's degree in elementary education at the University of Utah, followed by an M.S. in curriculum development from Brigham Young University.

In addition to teaching school and supervising student teachers for Brigham Young University, Ardeth Kapp worked as a writer and consultant. She authored several books, articles, and instructional manuals.

In the Church she had experiences ranging from Primary and Sunday School teacher to board member of the Relief Society (qq.v.). Having served as Young Women president (q.v.) in three wards (q.v.), she was called to the Church's youth correlation (q.v.) committee and then the curriculum development committee.

In 1972 she became a counselor (q.v.) in the general presidency of the Young Women and from 1984 to 1992 served as general president of the Young Women. She placed emphasis on the training of leaders and promoted a theme for the Young Women that included this affirmation: "We will stand as witnesses of God at all times and in all things, and in all places" (from Book of Mormon, Mosiah 18:9).

Ardeth Kapp's community service has included membership on a citizens planning commission, on the board of trustees for several businesses, and on the National Coalition against Pornography.

She was released as president of the Young Women when Heber Kapp was called as president of the Canada Vancouver Mission. Since then she has continued to lecture and publish for the Latter-day Saint audience.

KENNEDY, DAVID MATTHEW (1905–1996). Banker, political leader, and Church leader. Born in Randolph, Utah, on 21 July 1905, David Kennedy lived in this small rural town and learned all the chores common to ranches. Later his family (q.v.) moved to Ogden. After his earlier schooling he attended high school at Weber Academy (later Weber College). At the youthful age of 20 he married Lenora Bingham, age 19. Within two months, having been called on a mission by the Church, he was on his way to Great Britain. During his mission he was influenced by two presidents, James E. Talmage and John A. Widtsoe (qq.v.).

Returning to Utah in 1928, he completed studies at Weber College. Then the couple went east to Washington, D.C. David found employment as a clerk with the Federal Reserve Board. He graduated from the George Washington University Law School in 1935 and continued working for the Federal Reserve. As children arrived, four daughters in all, the

Kennedys became well established in Washington and participated fully in the Church activities there. Among their Church associates were Senator Reed Smoot, Ezra Taft Benson, and J. Willard Marriott (qq.v.). In 1942 David became a member of a ward (q.v.) bishopric and in 1944 was made the bishop (q.v.).

Still employed by the Federal Reserve Board, he completed a degree at the Rutgers University Graduate School of Banking. In 1946 he accepted a position with the Continental Illinois National Bank and Trust Company of Chicago. He ascended to become president and then chairman. For 22 years the Kennedys were contributors to the Chicago community. In the Church he served for 15 years as a counselor in the stake presidency (qq.v.).

While at Chicago he was on the board of Nauvoo Restoration, Inc. (q.v.) He contributed to many civic programs: chairman of the mayor's committee for economic development, head of the Citizen's Bond Committee, on the board of trustees for the University of Chicago, and on the board of trustees for the Brookings Institution. He chaired a commission that made recommendations on improving the organization of the federal budget.

In early 1969 Kennedy became U.S. secretary of the Treasury in the Nixon administration. In less than two years he resigned but remained ambassador at large, traveling to many countries and negotiating on economic matters. He also became U.S. ambassador to NATO. In 1973 he resigned from government.

Kennedy then received another call from the Church. He was asked to be an ambassador to the world. Traveling to different countries, meeting with high government officials, he was remarkably successful in achieving goodwill and often official recognition of the Church. His "retirement" years thus continued to be of service, his role a key one in the worldwide expansion of Mormonism in the generation following 1973.

KIKUCHI, YOSHIHIKO (1941–). Church leader. First native-born Japanese to serve as a General Authority (q.v.). Born in Hokkaido, Japan, Kikuchi graduated from Asia University of Tokyo and became sales manager and then president of businesses. Converted to the Church in 1955, he served as a missionary and later as stake (qq.v.) president in Tokyo. He served as president of the Hawaii Honolulu Mission and president of the temple (q.v.) in Tokyo before his call as a member of the First Quorum of the Seventy (q.v.) in 1977. He and his wife, Toshiko, have four children.

KIMBALL, JONATHAN GOLDEN (1853–1938). General Authority (q.v.) and beloved preacher known for his humor and distinctive style. Born in Salt Lake City on 26 June 1853, J. Golden Kimball was the son of prominent leader Heber C. Kimball, close friend of Brigham Young and counselor in the First Presidency (q.v.) of the Church. Golden's mother, Christeen Golden, was a plural wife. Only 15 when his father died, Golden became a mule driver. In addition to making some money and acquiring a skill, he acquired the habit of swearing. "You can't drive mules if you can't swear," he said. (Thomas E. Cheney, *The Golden Legacy*, 18.) At the time he did not participate in Church activities.

In the 1870s Golden and his mother joined other family (q.v.) members in pioneering the Bear Lake area. Hard work was required for survival. Kimball was still not a church goer. Then he happened to attend a meeting addressed by Karl G. Maeser (q.v.). In 1881, at the age of 28, Golden moved to Provo with his brother to attend Brigham Young Academy. Inspired by Maeser's teaching, he raised his sights. Two years later he accepted a call to serve a mission in the southern states. It was a time of hostility toward Mormons. Yet Kimball served courageously and because of his down-to-earth way of expressing himself, he was able to communicate with ordinary people. He also worked as an assistant to Brigham H. Roberts (q.v.).

Back home after his mission, he married Jennie Knowlton. Business undertakings failed with the changing national economy, and Kimball was sent back to the southern states, this time as mission president. While still there, in 1892, Kimball was named as one of the First Council of the Seventy (q.v.). For the nearly half-century of his life that remained he would associate with other Church leaders, travel throughout the stakes and wards, and speak at general conferences (qq.v.).

A tall, lanky man, J. Golden Kimball spoke with a high-pitched voice. He was a distinctive personality. He tried but found it almost impossible to abandon the swearing habit. The words, he said, were left over "from a much larger vocabulary" (Cheney, 37). The people, even while realizing that they should try to control their own language, loved him for it.

"A lot of people in the Church believe that men are called to leadership in the Church by revelation and some do not," he said. "But I'll tell you, when the Lord calls an old mule skinner like me to be a General Authority, there's got to be revelation." (Cheney, 100.)

As stories by and about J. Golden Kimball were passed from person to person, they assumed a life of their own. Some were embellished. Others were invented. He had become a subject of Mormon folklore (q.v.). He died in a car accident in 1938. *See also* ANTI-MORMONISM; PERSECUTION.

KIMBALL, SPENCER WOOLLEY (1895–1985). Arizona businessman, civic leader, Apostle, and 12th president (q.v.) of the Church, especially known for the revelation (q.v.) extending the Priesthood (q.v.) to males of all races.

Born in Salt Lake City on 28 March 1895, Spencer Kimball moved with his family (q.v.) to southeastern Arizona at the age of three. Raised in Thatcher, where his father was stake (q.v.) president, he went through the local schools and from 1914 to 1916 preached Mormonism as a missionary in the Central States Mission. After one semester of study at the University of Arizona he was inducted into the army. He married Camilla Eyring and, when his army service was deferred, took a job at a bank.

By 1927 he had had enough of bank employment and started his own insurance agency in Safford, Arizona. During the next several years, despite depression conditions, he succeeded and was prominent in local politics and community service. In 1936 he became president of the Arizona Rotary Club. He also continued to be active in Church callings (q.v.). From 1924 he was a counselor in the stake presidency (qq.v.), and in 1938 he became president of the new Mount Graham Stake.

In 1943 he was called to the Quorum of the Twelve Apostles (q.v.) and moved to Salt Lake City. In addition to the usual travels to stake conferences throughout the Church, Kimball was given special responsibilities over missionary work and assisting Native Americans (q.v.). In both capacities he traveled extensively. Under his direction a program of placement for Indian children was established that would take those whose parents voluntarily signed up into temporary foster homes during the months of the school year in order to improve their educational opportunities. Kimball repeatedly preached against racial prejudice.

Although hard working, Kimball suffered from health problems, some serious. After throat cancer he was able to speak only with hoarseness, a magnified whisper, but he persisted and the people loved him for it.

It was a surprise when at age 78 he succeeded to the presidency of the Church. Harold B. Lee (q.v.) had died unexpectedly. At the most, people assumed Kimball would preside very briefly and because of his age would not do much. To the contrary, however, his administration of 12 years from 1973 to 1985 became the most animated in the history of the Church (q.v.). He greatly expanded the number of missionaries (q.v.). Countries hitherto unexposed to Mormonism were opened up to proselytizing. Temples (q.v.) were erected in many parts of the world, increasing from 15 to 31. Area (q.v.) conferences were held throughout the world, enabling members in Chile and Finland, Korea and Tonga, and many other places, to see President Kimball personally along with other General Authorities (q.v.) and in exciting Saturday programs demonstrate some of the costumes, songs, and dances of their own culture. Administrative changes, notably the organization of the First Quorum of the Seventy (q.v.), were made to cope with the rapid growth of membership (q.v.).

A great sense of vigor infused the Church under Kimball's leadership. "Lengthen your stride," he urged the members (*Ensign*, November 1974, 117). His own motto was "Do it."

In 1978 a long-standing policy of not ordaining Blacks to the Priesthood [qq.v.] (although some had been baptized as members) was reversed. The announcement, which was presented as the will of the Lord, was quickly followed by proselytizing in Nigeria, Ghana, and other parts of Africa (q.v.).

Following a cerebral hemorrhage, a third round of brain surgery in 1981 left him so weak that for the last three or four years of his life most of the routine business of administration was carried on by his two counselors (q.v.).

Supporting Kimball throughout his life was his wife, Camilla Eyring Kimball, a vivacious woman of obvious high intelligence. They had four children. *See also* PROPHET.

KNIGHT, GLADYS (1944–). Celebrated performing artist. Born in Georgia, Gladys sang as a soloist with the local church choir. At age eight, she won the Ted Mack *Original Amateur Hour* contest. With her cousins, she formed the group Gladys Knight and the Pips, producing such hits as "I Heard It through the Grapevine" and "Midnight Train to Georgia." She won Grammy awards, platinum and gold records, a Clio, a Cable Ace award, American Music Awards, and a place in both the Rock and Roll Hall of Fame and the Rhythm and Blues Hall of Fame.

When her daughter, Kenya, and her son, Jimmy, joined the Church of Jesus Christ of Latter-day Saints, Knight did not immediately show a personal interest. After several years, she agreed to take the missionary (q.v.) lessons. Convinced and obtaining a testimony (q.v.), she was baptized and has since been an active, enthusiastic Latter-day Saint. In 1999 she addressed the annual Women's Conference.

-L-

LAMANITE. (The first vowel is the long *a*—thus "layman-ite.") One of the large groupings in the Book of Mormon (q.v.) account, named after Laman, a member of the original colony that left Jerusalem. A superficial reading sometimes leaves the impression of a long struggle between "good guys" and Lamanite "bad guys," but the history was much more complex than this, as intermingling occurred and either group showed the ability at different points to achieve a high level of Christian living or descend to an abysmal depravity.

Since the Lamanites were the survivors at the end of the Book of Mormon narrative, they are considered to be among the ancestors of the Native Americans (q.v.), sometimes called Lamanites—a usage sometimes extended to include Polynesians (q.v.). A student performing group from Brigham Young University (q.v.) called "The Lamanite Generation" put on a lively show of song and dance that drew from both Native American and Polynesian cultures.

Those employing the term with reference to modern peoples intend to emphasize the promised "flowering," the glorious future, of the scriptural references. But non-Mormon Native Americans do not understand the designation. Even some Mormon Native Americans do not appreciate what they perceive as its frequently negative connotations in the Book of Mormon and, at the very least, find it unnecessary baggage requiring elaborate explanation.

LARSEN, SHARON G. (1939–). Schoolteacher, youth (q.v.) leader, women's leader. Born in Glenwood, Alberta, Canada, Sharon Greene went on to receive a bachelor's degree in elementary education from Brigham Young University (q.v.). She married Ralph T. Larsen, who became a dentist. An elementary school teacher in Utah and Missouri, she also served as president of the PTA. Her experiences in Church service were varied: organist, seminary teacher, ward Relief Society president, stake Young Women president, stake Relief Society president, member of Young Women general board, president of Lambda Delta Sigma (qq.v.). In 1997, she became a counselor (q.v.) in the general Young Women presidency. The Larsens have two children.

LATTER-DAY SAINT STUDENTS ASSOCIATION (LDSSA). Organization for Mormon college students. At colleges and universities where there are sufficient numbers of Mormons the LDSSA sponsors social activities and represents the interests of its student members on campus. Its officers are students, but it has a faculty adviser, usually an instructor from the institute of religion (q.v.).

LDS. Latter-day Saint, or Saints. In English-speaking settings, Church members often use LDS instead of Mormon.

LEE, HAROLD BINGHAM (1899–1973). Civic leader, Apostle, president (q.v.) of the Church in 1972–73. Born in Clifton, Idaho, in 1899, Lee had a boyhood of farmwork, schooling, and the usual Church activity. Precocious, he attended the state normal school and became a school principal at age 17. At age 21, he served a mission in Denver, Colorado, preaching, baptizing, and gaining administrative experience. After his mission he became principal of a school in Salt Lake City, Utah, and married Fern Lucinda Tanner. They had two daughters.

After a series of responsibilities on the ward and stake (qq.v.) level, Harold became president of the Pioneer Stake in 1930. He was also first appointed and then elected to the city commission. To help his stake members face the hardships of the depression, he began welfare and work projects. In 1935, after resigning from his city job and being released as stake president, he was appointed full-time organizer and administrator for a Church-wide welfare program (q.v.).

Named to the Quorum of the Twelve Apostles (q.v.) in 1941, Lee became thoroughly experienced with the Church by traveling to stake conferences and participating in the discussions of the Twelve Apostles. He had different administrative responsibilities. Especially important was his effort in the 1960s to promote correlation (q.v.), a simplification of programs.

The deaths of his wife, Fern, of a cerebral hemorrhage in 1962 and his daughter Maureen from a lung embolus in 1965 were personal tragedies for him. In 1963 he married Freda Joan Jensen, who often accompanied him on his assignments.

In 1970 he became a counselor (q.v.) in the First Presidency (q.v.), retaining his presidency of the Twelve Apostles. Thus he was thoroughly prepared when in 1972 he became president of the Church. Vigorous and forthright, President Lee traveled to area (q.v.) conferences throughout the world. It was a surprise when he suddenly died of heart failure on 26 December 1973.

LEE, REX E. (1935–1996). Attorney, educator, university president. Born and raised in St. Johns, Arizona, Rex Lee started as a student at Brigham Young University (q.v.) in 1953, served as a missionary (q.v.) in Mexico, and returned to graduate with a bachelor's degree. In 1959 he married Janet Griffin. After graduating from BYU and completing law school at the University of Chicago in 1963, Lee became a law clerk for U.S. Supreme Court Justice Byron R. White. Then for eight years he practiced with a law firm in Phoenix, Arizona.

In 1972 he became founding dean of the new J. Reuben Clark Law School at Brigham Young University. His job of building a reputable professional school was interrupted by government service in 1975 when he became assistant U.S. attorney general and in 1981 when he became U.S. solicitor general. Representing the government, he argued many cases before the Supreme Court.

In 1989 he was appointed president of Brigham Young University. Although fighting a battle with cancer, diagnosed in 1987, Lee functioned with energy, effectiveness, and good humor until 1995, when he resigned because of failing health. In 1996 he died. Father of seven children, Lee was a bishop, stake president, and member of the Young Men's (q.v.) general board.

LITERATURE. Most writing produced by Mormons from the beginning to the time of Brigham Young's (q.v.) death in 1877 is lacking in the literary qualities that would give it lasting interest. This does not mean there was a total lack of literary production, however. The Book of Mormon (q.v.), a work of over 500 pages, at the outset signaled a religion for people who were literate, as did the other scriptures (q.v.) and early periodicals. But it was not for their literary qualities that believers valued these writings or the pamphlets written in defense of the new religion.

The hymnal compiled by Emma Hale Smith (q.v.) in 1835 included borrowings, adaptations, and original hymns appropriate for the new faith; it was revised and expanded in later editions throughout the century. Some poetry, mostly doggerel, appeared in the early periodicals, but poets of greater than average ability, like Eliza R. Snow and John Lyon (qq.v.), were also expressing themselves. Two professors of English, Richard Cracroft and Neal Lambert, later compiled an anthology entitled *A Believing People*, in which they show examples of the early poetry. The anthology also demonstrates that the literary forte, if there was one for the early Mormons, was probably such personal writings as letters and, more importantly, diaries and autobiographies. A memorable example is the *Autobiography of Parley P. Pratt*.

During the final quarter of the 19th century the existence of auxiliary organizations for Young Men and Young Women (qq.v.) and the establishment of a periodical, *The Juvenile Instructor*, for the Sunday School (q.v.) provided outlets for some stories and poems. A poet of ambition, Orson F. Whitney, produced an epic entitled *Elias*. The fiction, highly didactic and moralistic, included a serialized novel based on the Book of Mormon, *Corianton*, by Brigham H. Roberts (q.v.), stories and novels by Susa Young Gates, and Nephi Anderson's *Added Upon* (1898), which traces the life of its characters from the pre-mortal existence through this life and on into their continued interaction after death.

In the early 20th century Anderson and others continued to write fiction in the genre known as "home literature." Similar patent moralism characterized the fiction in Church magazines. The *Relief Society Magazine* (q.v.) did much to stimulate literary interests through courses in literary history and appreciation and by publishing many stories and poems.

Around mid-20th century, several works by expatriate Mormons appeared. Vardis Fisher published his Harper Prize novel *Children of God: An American Epic* (1939). Maureen Whipple's *Giant Joshua* (1941) is still considered by some the finest, most distinctively Mormon novel. Virginia E. Sorenson (q.v.) was publishing her Mormon novels, and Samuel W. Taylor struck a humorous chord in *Heaven Knows Why* (1948).

In the second half of the 20th century, especially since the 1960s, various circumstances combined to create a renaissance of Mormon literature. The enlarged membership (q.v.) meant a larger audience. Church magazines like *Ensign, New Era,* and *The Friend* (qq.v.) actively sought authors and published them. New independent periodicals, especially *Dialogue: A Journal of Mormon Thought* and *Sunstone* (qq.v.), provided additional outlets for poetry, essays, and stories as well as reviews making judgments of quality. Deseret Book Company (q.v.) enlarged its publication scope to include fiction, and other publishers proved receptive to Mormon subjects. The Association of Mormon Letters (q.v.) gave conscious attention to the subject, provided a forum for discussion and the presentation of new work, and made annual awards. Not least important, Brigham Young University (q.v.) became an academic home for several literary historians as well as poets and novelists.

So fertile has been Mormon literature in the present generation—in novels and short stories, drama, poetry, essays, and even religious and devotional pieces—that a listing quickly becomes a bibliography. A few examples must suffice. The poet of greatest output and influence from mid-20th century to the present has been Clinton F. Larson, but many others, including Carol Lynn Pearson, Emma Lou Thayne, and Dennis Clark, have produced poetry on Mormon themes. Edward Geary, Mary Bradford, and Eugene G. England Jr. (q.v.) are notable essayists. Among the many now writing Mormon fiction must be mentioned Levi Peterson (q.v.) (*Canyons of Grace, The Backslider*), Neal Chandler (*Benediction*), Donald R. Marshall (*The Rummage Sale, Frost in the Orchard*), Douglas H. Thayer (*Under the Cottonwoods*), and Orson Scott Card (q.v.). Linda Sillitoe, Judith Freeman, and Phyllis Barber are three among many women fiction writers who have made a mark.

Persistent tensions in Mormon literature include realism vs. idealism, faithfulness vs. outsider perspective, moralism vs. open-ended description, seriousness vs. humor (q.v.). In publication there is also tension between sponsored and unsponsored work. Pieces published by Deseret Book or appearing in Church magazines understandably must meet certain standards of the faith. Independent journals and publishers have greater latitude. Significant literature has emanated from both directions.

Almost entirely unrealized to the present is the literary potential of the international Church. Considering the different traditions, one might anticipate Mormon poetry and novels, hymns and essays, biographies and autobiographies, from Peru, the Philippines, France, Tonga, Russia, and other countries. *See also* MEMBERSHIP; PLAN OF SALVATION; UTAH PERIOD.

LUDLOW, DANIEL HANSEN (1924–). Educator, administrator, writer, and tour director. Born in Benjamin, Utah, on 17 March 1924, Ludlow was raised and attended school in Spanish Fork. He graduated from Utah State University in 1946, served on the faculty there for a period of time, and then moved to the Midwest, receiving an M.A. from Indiana University in 1953. He received a Ph.D. from Columbia University in 1955 and returned to a faculty appointment in religious instruction at Brigham Young University (q.v.).

In addition to teaching classes, Ludlow served as dean of his college. In 1972 he was called to be the Church's director of correlation (q.v.), continuing until 1988 except for a two-year mission presidency in Perth, Australia, from 1981 to 1983.

A gifted teacher, Ludlow became known far beyond his college classrooms. He participated regularly as a lecturer in the extension series "Know Your Religion." He directed three different semester-abroad programs in Israel and as a tour director has taken more than 40 groups there.

More recently he has conducted tours to Mexico and Central America (q.v.).

A prolific author of at least 10 books in addition to many articles and manuals, Ludlow was editor in chief of the five-volume *Encyclopedia of Mormonism* published in 1992.

LYON, JOHN (1803–1889). Poet, missionary, drama critic. Born on 4 March 1803 in Glasgow, Scotland, John Lyon was raised by his mother after his father's death in 1811. He left home to become a weaver's apprentice and then a spinner's apprentice, but lost both positions when economic conditions became tight. Anxious for self-improvement, he took classes in the local charity schools.

At 21, John moved to Kilmarnock and found work as a weaver. He married Janet Thomson, and twelve children came one after the other, eight surviving to adulthood. He joined a local literary society and worked hard to master basic writing skills. To supplement his primary income he worked as a canvasser and correspondent for several newspapers of the region. During the 1830s and early 1840s he published sketches, news items, and poems.

In 1843 he heard a Mormon preacher. After reading the Book of Mormon (q.v.) and various tracts, he was baptized in March 1844. Soon after, his wife and older children also joined the new religion. During the next five years he became presiding elder (q.v.) of the Mormon congregation in Kilmarnock. He wrote poetry on Mormon themes and published in the *Millennial Star* (q.v.).

From 1849 he served as a missionary (q.v.) in Worcester, England, baptizing at least 360 persons. He continued to write and publish poetry. At the end of 1851 he moved to Glasgow as president (q.v.) of the missionary district. Preaching, baptizing, and traveling, he also found time to write poetry and collect poems previously written. In early 1853 his collected poems were published as *Harp of Zion*, all proceeds being earmarked for the assistance of Mormon immigrants.

Emigrating with his family to Utah in 1853, 50-year-old Lyon plunged into Church activity. Deciding in favor of polygamy (q.v.), he took a second wife in 1856. He was appointed president of the Endowment House, where ordinances (q.v.) of the temples (q.v.) were provided while awaiting the completion of the Salt Lake Temple, and for 30 years he supervised and officiated there regularly. He also became official territorial librarian. In addition to publishing many poems in the newspapers, he wrote others that remained unpublished. As drama critic for the

Deseret News (q.v.) he attended opening nights at the Salt Lake Theatre and gave his evaluations of the plays.

An excellent biography by great-grandson T. Edgar Lyon Jr. acknowledges that much of the creative work of the self-taught John Lyon was undistinguished. Yet he often successfully communicated the values and aspirations of his fellow believers, and he was among those who sought to raise the standards of Mormon literary expression. Recognizing his own limitations, he was optimistic for the future.

LYON, THOMAS EDGAR (1903–1978). Educator, missionary, (q.v.) and historian. Born in Salt Lake City in 1903, T. Edgar Lyon was the son of David and Mary Cairns Lyon and a grandson of poet John Lyon (q.v.). After the usual early schooling he attended the University of Utah for two years and then was called as a missionary to the Netherlands. After his return he married Hermana Forsberg; they would go on to have six sons.

After graduating he taught high school in Rigby, Idaho, and then became a seminary (q.v.) teacher. When summer seminars at Brigham Young University from Sidney B. Sperry (qq.v.) piqued his interest, Lyon arranged a leave of absence and attended the University of Chicago, studying with Edgar Goodspeed and William W. Sweet and earning a master's degree.

Upon his return Lyon was called at age 30 to be president of the Netherlands Mission, serving from 1933 to 1937. Under the direction of European Mission president John A. Widtsoe (q.v.) he concentrated on training local leadership, which turned out to be timely when World War II forced the evacuation of U.S. missionaries.

Returning to Utah, Lyon was assigned to the new institute of religion (q.v.) at the University of Utah. For more than 30 years this was his station, as he taught classes in the Bible, Book of Mormon, Doctrine and Covenants (qq.v.), and Mormon history. His close associate and fellow teacher was Lowell L. Bennion (q.v.). Persisting in his desire to earn a doctorate, Lyon entered the graduate program in history at the University of Utah and in 1962 was awarded the Ph.D. A prolific writer, he authored many articles and manuals.

In the 1960s, at an age when many would be preparing for retirement, Lyon moved vigorously into two new activities. He was named official historian for Nauvoo Restoration, Inc. (q.v.), exerting his influence to encourage authenticity in the project and compiling impressive files on the Illinois Period (q.v.). He became one of the early members and in

1967 president of the Mormon History Association (q.v.) and attended many of its meetings. He launched a major new history of Nauvoo and made impressive, methodical progress through its early stages. Historian Glen M. Leonard inherited this project when T. Edgar Lyon died in 1978.

-M-

MCCONKIE, BRUCE REDD (1915–1985). Attorney, missionary (q.v.), and prolific writer on doctrinal subjects, Apostle. Born on 29 July 1915 in Ann Arbor, Michigan, McConkie was raised in Utah. After serving a mission in the Eastern States Mission from 1934 to 1936, he attended the University of Utah Law School, receiving his law degree in 1939. In 1937, while still a student, he married Amelia Smith, daughter of Joseph Fielding Smith (q.v.). McConkie was assistant Salt Lake City attorney and city prosecutor until entering the U.S. Army as an intelligence officer in 1941. By the end of World War II he was a lieutenant colonel.

At the relatively young age of 31 he was called as one of the First Council of the Seventy (q.v.). From 1946 he traveled to stake (q.v.) conferences, addressed general conferences (q.v.), and for three years served as president of the Southern Australia Mission. In 1972 he became a member of the Quorum of the Twelve Apostles (q.v.).

McConkie was a diligent student of the scriptures (q.v.) and came to be acknowledged as a doctrinal authority. As a young man he started the systematic scriptural study that provided the basis for his later exposition. His marriage to the daughter of Joseph Fielding Smith increased his appreciation of an approach that was rather literal but thoroughly grounded in the sacred writings. The publication of *Mormon Doctrine* (1958) made his name a household word throughout the Church. Also important was his three-volume commentary on the New Testament.

His personal commitment to Jesus Christ (q.v.), the subject of many of his sermons, led to a six-volume work on the life and mission of the Savior, a hymn entitled "I Believe in Christ," and a moving testimony (q.v.) in his final conference address in April 1985. Less than two weeks later he died of cancer.

MCKAY, DAVID OMAN (1873–1970). Educator, Apostle, counselor in the First Presidency, and 9th president of the Church (qq.v.). McKay was born on 8 September 1873 in Huntsville, Utah, and lived his early life in a rural environment. A popular and handsome young man, McKay played football and was president of his student body in college. After graduating from the University of Utah in 1897, he was a missionary (q.v.) in Scotland. Upon his return he married Emma Ray Riggs and took a teaching job at Weber Academy in Ogden, Utah. He became its principal from 1902 to 1908. In the stake Sunday School (qq.v.) superintendency, he attempted to upgrade the quality of teaching.

He was called to be a General Authority of the Church and a member of the Quorum of the Twelve Apostles (qq.v.), in 1906. In addition to the usual responsibility of visiting stakes, he became a leader in the general Church Sunday School organization and Church commissioner of education. In 1922–24 he was president of the European Mission.

Tall and handsome (six feet, one inch), with a head of wavy white hair, McKay was striking. Exuding confidence and goodwill, he was popular among his people. His sermons were often illustrated with quotations from Shakespeare or his favorite poet, Robert Burns. The McKay family (q.v.) seemed a model with seven children and an obvious affection and respect between the parents. When he could find time, McKay would return to his rural Huntsville, where he could ride horses and breathe fresh air.

In 1934 he was called as a counselor to Church president Heber J. Grant (qq.v.) and for the rest of his life was at or near the top of the Church hierarchy. His close associate for many years was Joshua Reuben Clark (q.v.). During the 1930s and the 1940s he and his colleagues shepherded the Church through the Great Depression and World War II.

In 1951 David O. McKay became ninth president of the Church. Membership (q.v.) had passed the million mark. In addition to continuing emphasis on the family, he highlighted missionary work. "Every member a missionary" was an oft-repeated saying of his. The number of missionaries rose from 2,000 to 13,000 between 1951 and 1971, the number of stakes from 184 to 500.

Ever since his missionary experience as a young man and more especially after a trip around the world in 1924, McKay had an international outlook. During his administration, temples (q.v.) were constructed at Los Angeles and Oakland but also in Switzerland, New Zealand, and England.

Among his published books, mostly collected from his sermons, are *Ancient Apostles* and *Gospel Ideals*.

MCMURRAY, W. GRANT (1947–). President, RLDS Church. Born on 12 June 1947 in Toronto, Canada, McMurray was raised in the Reorganized Church of Jesus Christ of Latter Day Saints (q.v.). He received a B.A. in religious instruction from Graceland College in 1969 and in 1975 the Master of Divinity degree from St. Paul School of Theology in Kansas City, Missouri. Since 1971 McMurray has been employed by the RLDS Church, serving as assistant to the director of the Division of Program Planning (1971–72), historical research assistant (1972–73), church archivist (1973–76), assistant commissioner of history (1976–82), World Church secretary and executive assistant to the first Presidency (q.v.) (1982–92), and member of the Quorum (q.v.) of the First Presidency (1992–96). Ordained as president of the RLDS Church on 15 April 1996, McMurray is the first president who is not a direct descendant of Joseph Smith (q.v.).

McMurray is also a scholar. He has served on the executive council of the Mormon History Association (q.v.) and is a past president of the John Whitmer Historical Association (q.v.). He is an avid reader, an astute observer of politics and culture, and has published numerous articles in religious and historical publications. McMurray and his wife, Joyce Lynette McMurray, are the parents of two sons—a journalist and a communications major.

MAESER, KARL GOTTFRIED (1828–1901). Educator and moralist. Born in Vorbrucke, Meissen, Germany, Maeser enjoyed a good education. Private tutoring instructed him in French, Italian, and Latin. He learned the piano and organ and conducted choirs. He studied at the Krenz Schule and the Friederich Stadt normal school, from which he graduated. He became a teacher (q.v.) for a while in Dresden and then took employment as a private tutor in Bohemia. In 1854 he married Anna Meith.

In 1855 he came in contact with Mormonism. An agnostic, he was impressed by the sincere testimonies of the Mormon missionaries (qq.v.). After being baptized he was named president (q.v.) of the Dresden branch, leading this small group to the United States the next year. Out of money, he stopped in the East and worked teaching music until he could go on to Utah.

From 1860 on, except for a three-year mission back to Germany, he was an educator. He taught a variety of subjects for a fee. He headed the Union Academy and tutored Brigham Young's (q.v.) children.

In 1876 he was named principal of the new Brigham Young Academy in Provo. Young's instructions to Maeser included, "I want you to remember that you ought not to teach even the alphabet or the multiplication tables without the Spirit of God." (Ernest L. Wilkinson and W. Cleon Skousen, *Brigham Young University: School of Destiny*, 67.) Maeser's students long remembered him for his aphorisms and moral lessons.

Appointed general superintendent of Church schools, he was released from the Brigham Young Academy so that he could travel and supervise scattered academies. In 1894 he became a member of the superintendency of the Sunday School (q.v.).

Crusty but tender of heart, Maeser spoke with a slight accent. Students like Reed Smoot and James E. Talmage (qq.v.) long remembered him. He expressed his philosophy of education in *School and Fireside* (1898). He died on 14 February 1901. *See also* BRIGHAM YOUNG UNIVERSITY.

MANIFESTO. Document issued by Church president Wilford Woodruff (qq.v.) in 1890 that is often regarded as a great dividing point in Mormon history in that it marked the end of polygamy (q.v.). Actually, the facts are a little more complex. The Manifesto itself (Doctrine and Covenants, Official Declaration 1) falls short of an absolute prohibition: "my advice to the Latter-day Saints is to refrain from contracting any marriage forbidden by the law of the land." Moreover, there was a distinction between the contracting of a new marriage and the continuation of an existing relationship. Even those willing to discontinue the former would find it difficult to end the latter.

Following the 1890 manifesto, Mormon polygamy went into a sharp decline. A relatively few new plural marriages were performed, mostly outside of the United States. Then in 1904 a second manifesto was issued and much more rigidly enforced.

The importance of the 1890 manifesto remains. It was an official statement of intent. Signaling the beginning of the end of polygamy, it prepared the way for Utah's admission to the union as a state.

MARRIOTT, JOHN WILLARD (1900–1985). Businessman and Church leader. Born in Ogden, Utah, on 17 September 1900, J. Willard (or Bill) Marriott had the experience of working on farms, herding sheep and cattle. For two years, from 1919 to 1921, he was a missionary (q.v.) in New England. Paying his way with summer jobs, he graduated from Weber College and then in 1927 from the University of Utah.

He opened a root beer stand in Washington, D.C., and returned to Utah to marry Alice Sheets. Another root beer stand was followed by a restaurant, the Hot Shoppe. Other restaurants followed: Hot Shoppe Number One, Number Two, and so on. Marriott weathered the Great Depression and expanded his chain of restaurants as well as moving into airline catering and hotels. After World War II he became president of the National Restaurant Association.

Always active in the Church, Marriott became a counselor in the stake presidency (q.v.) in 1946 and two years later stake president in Washington, D.C. His accomplishments include seeing the completion of the first Mormon chapel there, supervising the development of leaders and expansion of membership (q.v.) from one little branch to several stakes, and finally acquiring property and watching the completion of the Washington, D.C., Temple in 1976.

Active Republicans, both Marriott and his wife participated in party politics and supported the arts. He chaired the inauguration committees in 1969 and 1973. For several years he chaired the American Historical and Cultural Society, which sponsored Honor America concerts at the Kennedy Center.

He was awarded an honorary degree by the University of Utah. In return for a substantial gift to the University of Utah, the J. Willard Marriott Library was named after him. To Brigham Young University (q.v.) he made another generous donation; the Marriott Activities Center there houses major athletic events.

MASON, JAMES O. (1930–). Physician, public health administrator, Church leader. Born in Salt Lake City, Utah, Mason served a full-time mission in Denmark. He received a bachelor's degree and then a medical degree from the University of Utah. From Harvard University he received a master's degree and doctorate of public health. He interned at the Johns Hopkins University Hospital in Baltimore, Maryland. He served in the military branch of the U.S. Public Health Service and became an epidemiologist.

Mason was director of the infectious diseases division at a Salt Lake City hospital before being named Church commissioner of health services. In 1978 he returned to the University of Utah School of Medicine as chairman of the Division of Community Medicine. Then he served for four years as executive director of the Utah Department of Health.

In 1983 Mason was named director of the National Center for Disease Control and in 1989 became assistant secretary for health and head of the U.S. Public Health Service. Mason has served in the Church as bishop, stake president, and regional representative (qq.v.). In 1994 he was called to the Second Quorum of the Seventy (q.v.). Mason and his wife, Marie, are the parents of seven children.

MAXWELL, NEAL A. (1926–). Educator, political scientist, Apostle. Born on 6 July 1926 in Salt Lake City, Neal Maxwell was raised and received his education there, including a degree in political science from the University of Utah. For two years he was a missionary (q.v.) in eastern Canada.

After serving as a legislative assistant to U.S. Senator Wallace F. Bennett, Maxwell accepted teaching and administrative positions at the University of Utah. In 1970 he became executive vice president of the University. At the same time he was called to be commissioner of education for the Church Educational System, serving from 1970 to 1976.

Already, his Church experience had been extensive. Bishop (q.v.), general board member for the Young Men's (q.v.) organization, member of the Adult Correlation (q.v.) Committee, regional representative (q.v.): he had grown in these different assignments and had performed conscientiously.

In 1974, his record as commissioner of Education already impressive, he was named an assistant to the Twelve (q.v.). Two years later he was one of the presidency of the First Quorum of the Seventy (q.v.). In 1981, at the age of 55, Maxwell became a member of the Quorum of the Twelve Apostles (q.v.).

Known for his eloquent preaching, Maxwell is the author of about 30 books. An effective counselor and skilled manager, he serves on several committees. He is on the executive committee of Brigham Young University's (q.v.) board of trustees. In 1998, the Neal A. Maxwell Presidential Endowed Chair in political theory, public policy, and public service was established by private donors at the University of Utah. Maxwell and his wife, Colleen, are the parents of four children.

MELCHIZEDEK PRIESTHOOD. The higher priesthood, to which every worthy adult male in the Church is eligible. It is conferred by the laying on of hands of those who are in authority.

Offices within the Melchizedek Priesthood include elder, high priest, patriarch, seventy, or apostle (qq.v.). As an indispensable part of the restoration (q.v.) of the gospel (q.v.), Joseph Smith and Oliver Cowdery (qq.v.) received the Melchizedek Priesthood when Peter, James, and John appeared to them in 1829 or early 1830 and conferred it upon them. At the same time they were ordained Apostles and received the keys of the dispensation (q.v.) of the fullness of times.

This priesthood, or authority to act in God's name, is eternal, going back to the pre-mortal stage. It has been held by various individuals during the history of the world. The patriarch (q.v.) Abraham received it from Melchizedek, a priest (q.v.) and king of Salem, after whom it is named in order to avoid the frequent use of God's name.

Although it is a lay organization with no professional clergy (q.v.), the Church regards priesthood as anything but unimportant; to the contrary, it is an absolute prerequisite to the authorized preaching of the gospel and administration in the ordinances (q.v.). *See also* AARONIC PRIEST-HOOD; ARTICLES OF FAITH, 5; PRIESTHOOD.

MEMBERSHIP. Technically one becomes a member of the Church upon baptism and confirmation (qq.v.). Since age eight, the "age of account-ability," is the minimum age for baptism, younger children of Mormon families are considered "children of record." The membership figures here will include these.

Starting with the original six members on 6 April 1830, the Church membership reached 10 million by 1998. But a straight line between those two dates would not give the picture of growth, for it did not oc-cur at the same pace throughout those 168 years.

Although the figures might be subject to some question in early years, official membership totals were as follows. In 1844, the year of Joseph Smith's (q.v.) death, there were 26,000 members. The year of Brigham Young's (q.v.) death, 1877, saw the total reach 115,000. At the turn of the 20th century there were more than 283,000 Mormons. Of course the United States and world populations were also much smaller than they are now.

In 1919 membership passed 500,000. To appreciate the growth in the 20th century it will be of interest to note how long it took to achieve a doubling. Here is the pattern:

1919	500,000	22 years from 250,000
1947	1,000,000	28 years
1963	2,000,000	16 years
1979	4,000,000	16 years
1991	8,000,000	12 years

At the end of 1998, the official report of membership was 10,354,241. If the rate of growth continues, during the first decade of the 21st cen-tury there will be 16 million Latter-day Saints, and during the next de-cade—certainly in the lifetime of many now living—the number could surpass 30 million. Sociologist Rodney Stark has used these figures as the basis for his prediction that Mormonism is on the way to becoming a major world religion.

The growth has not been uniform geographically. By February 1996 more than half the membership lived outside the United States. At the end of 1998, Mexico and Central America (q.v.) accounted for more than 1.3 million members, South America (q.v.) more than 2.3 million, Asia (q.v.) and the South Pacific more than a million. True, the United States and Canada still had over 5.1 million, but the time when Mormonism was exclusively a U.S. or Utah church (never completely the case, of course, except at the very beginning) was obviously over. Differing rates of growth in the different continents will produce a different, less Anglo-Saxon mix in the future.

To cope with the demands of a skyrocketing membership, Church leaders have sought simplification and coordination through the correlation (q.v.) program, divided administrative responsibilities into different world areas (q.v.), and increased the number of General Authorities (q.v.).

MENLOVE, COLEEN K. (1943–). President (q.v.), Young Women (q.v.), 1999– . Born on 1 July 1943, Coleen married Dean W. Menlove in 1964. They have seven children. She earned a B.S. degree in elementary education from the University of Utah and a master's degree in elementary curriculum from Brigham Young University (q.v.). Her church service includes serving on the Young Women general board and in ward and stake Relief Society, Young Women, and Primary callings (qq.v.).

MEXICO. *See* CENTRAL AMERICA AND MEXICO.

MILLENNIAL STAR. Official publication of the British Mission from its founding in 1840 to its termination in 1970. The complete title was *The Latter-day Saints Millennial Star.* Especially for the 19th century, it is a valuable primary source. Its contents include editorials, poetry, sermons, baptisms (q.v.), names of missionaries (q.v.) and their activities, immigration organization and departures, and letters from various locations in Great Britain as well as the distant Zion (q.v.) of Utah. Starting publication when Joseph Smith (q.v.) was still alive, it included some of the earliest documents and historical writings of the Church.

MILLENNIUM. Like some other Christians, Mormons believe in a future era of a thousand years when the earth will be renewed (Articles of Faith, 10). In a strict and narrow sense of the word, they are *premillennialists,* believing that the millennial reign will be ushered in by the Second Coming of Jesus Christ (q.v.). However, the obligation to work for improvement in the present is an integral part of the belief. Moreover, during the Millennium life will not be one of simply basking in the sun. Among other activities will be a great missionary (q.v.) work and much service in the temples (q.v.).

Some early Mormons thought the Second Coming and the Millennium were very near. As time has gone on, the expectation has faded but not disappeared. The term *latter-day* in the title of the Church designates the present age as the final dispensation (q.v.). The official belief in the prophesied winding-up scene and Millennium is still intact. The standard works, or scriptures (q.v.), which are regularly studied, all have passages pointing forward to such a final act in the drama of human existence. But Mormon leaders do not harp on this as a matter of immediate concern; they are not among the millennialists who are counting the days or selling off property in order to await the great event. They insist that they do not know the exact timetable. It is simply *near*—a relative term. The important message for members is that they should be ready—that is, have their "house in order" by following the commandments (q.v.).

MISSION OF THE CHURCH. Building upon scriptural passages and earlier statements by previous Church leaders, Presidents Spencer W. Kimball and Ezra Taft Benson (qq.v.) brought the mission of the Church into sharp focus. It is to "invite all to come unto Christ and be perfected in him" (Doctrine and Covenants 20:50; Moroni 10:32). This mission has three dimensions: (1) proclaim the gospel (q.v.) to every nation, kindred, tongue, and people; (2) perfect the Saints (q.v.) by preparing them to receive the ordinances (q.v.) of the gospel and by caring for the poor and needy; and (3) redeem the dead by performing vicarious ordinances of the gospel for them.

In other words, through the missionary (q.v.) program nonmembers were to be addressed; through the various programs of the Church members were to receive the saving ordinances and experience development and opportunities for service; and through genealogy and temples (qq.v.) those who are dead would receive the blessings of the gospel.

MISSIONARIES. It is sometimes said that "all" Mormon young people go on missions. This is not true. Although it is strongly urged that young men (q.v.) prepare themselves for mission calls, only 32 percent of males between ages 19 and 21 actually serve missions. These figures come from a survey done in 1991 by the Correlation (q.v.) Department's Evaluation Division for the Priesthood (q.v.) Executive Committee. (*Deseret News*, 26 September 1992, p. A8.)

Nevertheless, from the beginning (Doctrine and Covenants, Section 4) the Church has been a missionary organization. Members were anxious to invite their friends and relatives to share the joy they had found in the restored gospel (q.v.). On their own sometimes, or as called by their leaders, Mormon men would depart on missionary preaching tours. Some degree of organization, with leaders of certain mission areas and missionaries organized into conferences or districts, began to take shape. By the last generation of the 19th century, especially in the British Mission and the Southern States Mission, the basic outline was established: mission president, mission office, missionaries going two by two and being assigned by their president, periodic relocations, and a formal release at the end of the mission.

In the 20th century the following developments took place. Young women (q.v.) were called as missionaries. Training programs for the departing missionaries were developed. Systematic programs for presenting Mormonism to investigators (q.v.) were developed to ensure consistency and to ensure adequate instruction. The number of missions was increased as opportunity allowed. Married couples were called as missionaries.

Those willing to serve as missionaries so indicate in an interview with their bishop (q.v.). Worthiness (q.v.) is ascertained and financial arrangements are discussed. People are not paid to go on missions. The great majority support themselves from savings, donations from family (q.v.), a ward (q.v.) mission fund, a general mission fund, or some combination of these. When the official letter comes from Church headquarters calling (q.v.) one to be a missionary, the specific mission is indicated. The place of service is determined by need and inspiration of the General Authorities (q.v.) and not the desire of the prospective missionary.

At the end of 1998 57,953 full-time missionaries were serving in 331 missions. During that year they had brought into the Church 299,134 converts. *See also* MISSIONARY TRAINING CENTERS.

MISSIONARY TRAINING CENTERS (MTC). Very early, missionaries (q.v.) were advised to study the scriptures (q.v.) and prepare themselves to be effective representatives of the Church (Doctrine and Covenants, sections 14–19, 88). To assist them a school operated briefly at Kirtland, Ohio. During the Utah Period (q.v.) several academies, including the one that became Brigham Young University (q.v.), offered brief missionary training classes by the end of the 19th century. For several decades in the early 20th century a "mission home" in Salt Lake City provided lodging for missionaries as they followed a series of classes that lasted about one week.

A more comprehensive program of instruction and a change of location came with the Missionary Language Institute at Provo in 1961, renamed the Language Training Mission in 1963. In 1978, after buildings had been constructed in Provo, it was called the Missionary Training Center and all missionaries, even those not learning a foreign language, were required to attend.

Following a rigorous program, outgoing missionaries receive instruction in the scriptures, missionary techniques, and, where applicable, language. The language instruction is intensive, following the "total immersion" approach earlier pioneered by the U.S. military. Some introduction to culture and customs is also included. The typical MTC term for those learning a foreign language is eight weeks.

To accommodate the expanding missionary force, missionary training centers have also been established in South America, Europe, Asia, and the Pacific (qq.v.).

MISSOURI PERIOD. For about nine years Missouri was the location of passionate activity on the part of the Mormons. Sometimes the taxing experience there is summed up by the phrase "the Missouri persecutions."

The first Mormons in Missouri were the missionaries (q.v.)—Oliver Cowdery, Parley P. Pratt (qq.v.), Peter Whitmer Jr., and Ziba Peterson—sent in mid-1830 by Joseph Smith (q.v.) on an assignment to preach to the Indians. After unusual success in Ohio these missionaries proceeded westward, arriving in January 1831, completing a 1,500-mile journey from western New York. Preaching to the Indians was thwarted by the Indian agents, but a foothold had been established. Western Missouri was declared the site of the New Jerusalem (Doctrine and Covenants, Section 28). Joseph Smith traveled there and declared Independence to be "the center place" and the site for a temple (q.v.) (Doctrine and Covenants, Section 57). The Mormons from Colesville, New York, moved there. The gathering to Missouri had begun. During the same years Ohio was also serving as a magnet to converts.

By 1832 several hundred Mormons had come to Missouri. A printing press was established, two newspapers began publication, and schools were started. The next year saw the publication—interrupted by violence but partially successful—of the *Book of Commandments* (q.v.), a compilation of Joseph Smith's revelations (q.v.). Mormons were settling not only in Independence but also in nearby Kaw Township and three other small settlements.

The problems in Missouri included internal bickering and jealousies. Some of the new arrivals came, contrary to instructions, with no visible means of support. Some Mormons made themselves obnoxious by boasting of how they were going to take over Jackson County. But the problem of internal discipline might well have been solved had it not been for the fuming opposition that finally burst forth into mob violence in 1833. The printing press was destroyed and one of the Mormon leaders tarred and feathered. Several were killed. By November the Mormons were fleeing across the Missouri River northward to Clay County. In an effort to restore his people to their lawful property Joseph Smith came from Ohio at the head of a military force of untrained volunteers, but, recognizing the reality of the situation, disbanded them before any actual battle.

Still looking for a place in Missouri where they might live peaceably, the Mormons moved northward into Caldwell County, newly created in 1836. A center was established at Far West, to which Smith moved his headquarters in 1838. Another center was begun in Daviess County. With the collapse of Kirtland, hundreds came from there to the new Missouri settlements. Some optimism was in the air, as a temple (q.v.) was announced for construction in Far West. There was still hope that through legal processes some return to the lands back in Jackson County might be possible.

But friction seemed unavoidable. The Mormons were not faultless. Sidney Rigdon (q.v.) spoke out against dissenters, threatening them with violence, and declared that if mobs attacked again there would be a war of extermination. One Mormon formed an unauthorized paramilitary group, the Danites (q.v.), and encouraged vengeance against Church enemies. Moreover, the Mormons did not limit their settlements to Caldwell County, as many in the Missouri legislature had thought they would, but insisted on their right to settle anywhere.

There was an abundance of guilt on the other side as well. Rabid anti-Mormons were eager to drive their enemies out and seize their property. A riot occurred when Mormons tried to exercise their right to vote. Seventeen were killed in a massacre at Haun's Mill. Militias armed on both sides. It was in this setting that Missouri's Governor Lilburn W. Boggs issued his "extermination order": Mormons must leave the state or suffer extermination. When Far West was besieged and tensions were high, Joseph Smith and a few of his colleagues attempted to meet with the other side and negotiate. Instead, they were seized and thrown into prison.

The stage was set for the exodus of the Mormons from Missouri. This was accomplished in late 1838 and early 1839 under the direction of Brigham Young (q.v.) and his close associate and fellow Apostle Heber C. Kimball. In the cold season of the year, carrying such few belongings as they could salvage, some 12,000 Mormons straggled—in companies, as families, even individually—eastward to seek refuge in Illinois.

The Reorganized Church of Jesus Christ of Latter Day Saints (q.v.) later made its headquarters in Independence.

On 25 June 1976 Governor Christopher S. Bond rescinded the infamous 1838 extermination order. At the end of 1997, 48,000 Mormons lived in Missouri, divided into 13 stakes and 92 wards (qq.v.). That same year a temple was completed and dedicated in St. Louis. *See also* ANTI-MORMONISM; ILLINOIS PERIOD; OHIO PERIOD; ZION'S CAMP.

MONSON, THOMAS SPENCER (1927–). Businessman, Apostle, counselor in the First Presidency (qq.v.). Born on 21 August 1927 in Salt Lake City, Monson grew up and received his primary and secondary education there. He served in the U.S. Navy during World War II and subsequently graduated from the University of Utah with a degree in business management.

Having married Frances Beverly Johnson, Monson became a bishop (q.v.) at the age of 22. He was employed by the Newspaper Agency Corporation as executive in the advertising division. For *Deseret News* (q.v.) Press he took the position of sales manager, later becoming general manager. He was president of Printing Industry of Utah and a member of the board of directors of Printing Industry of America.

The Church experience of this young bishop continued to expand. He became a counselor in the stake presidency (q.v.). In 1959 he was called to be president of the Canadian Mission and lived at its headquarters in Toronto for three years. The missionaries (q.v.) who served under him and many Church members from Canada remember his positive spirit and his assurances that the future of the Church in Canada was bright.

Soon after his return, at age 36, he was called to be a member of the Quorum of the Twelve Apostles (q.v.). Chairman of the board of the Deseret News Publishing Company and a member of the board of Newspaper Agency Corporation, he also serves on the National Executive

Board of Boy Scouts (q.v.) of America. He has received both the Silver Beaver and Silver Buffalo awards. An active participant in community affairs, he has belonged to the Utah Association of Sales Executives, the Salt Lake Advertising Club, and the Salt Lake Exchange Club. For many years he was a member of the State Board of Regents.

In 1985, Monson became second counselor in the First Presidency, and in 1995 he became first counselor to President Gordon B. Hinckley (q.v.). Appreciated for his vigor and positive attitude, President Monson gave many addresses before Church and other groups. He has traveled extensively to area (q.v.) conferences and temple (q.v.) dedications, and in general supervises the operations of the Church worldwide.

MORMON. 1. The proper name of a great Book of Mormon (q.v.) prophet (q.v.) who lived at the end of the fourth century. In addition to leading his people militarily, Mormon abridged previous records into the plates later used by Joseph Smith (q.v.) in translating the Book of Mormon. The book is thus named after a person.

2. Nickname for members of the Church of Jesus Christ of Latter-day Saints (q.v.). Because it falsely suggests a primary loyalty to this individual prophet and, among the uninformed, leaves an impression of being non-Christian, the term has long been discouraged or carefully placed within quotation marks. But because of the length of the official title of the Church the shorter term has proved irresistible. Even Church writers and journalists use it. Properly used, the term applies strictly to the Church of Jesus Christ of Latter-day Saints, not fundamentalism (q.v.) and not the Reorganized Church of Jesus Christ of Latter Day Saints (q.v.). *See also* CHURCH OF JESUS CHRIST OF LATTER-DAY SAINTS.

MORMON BATTALION. A battalion of the U.S. Army during the Mexican War (1846–47) recruited from the Mormon refugees encamped in Iowa after their forced departure from Nauvoo, Illinois. Approximately 500 men signed up. Accompanying them were about 80 women, some working as laundresses, and a few children. Recruiter Captain James Allen (promoted to colonel) first led the battalion. When he died en route, after an interim arrangement, Colonel Philip St. George Cooke became commander.

The battalion proceeded overland to Santa Fe. One group of sick, including nearly all the women and children, after wintering at Pueblo, Colorado, went on to the Salt Lake Valley, where they arrived on 28 July

1847, just four days after Brigham Young (q.v.). The rest of the battalion left Santa Fe, marched in a southwestward direction through New Mexico, across southern Arizona and southern California, and arrived at San Diego in January 1847. Most of them were discharged at Los Angeles in July 1847.

During a pivotal year in the colonization (q.v.) of the West, the Mormon Battalion found itself involved in important events: in the settling of San Diego, in the gold discovery at Sutter's Mill that precipitated the great California gold rush, and finally most of them rejoining the main Mormon group in colonizing the Salt Lake Valley.

This is one of those historic events whose motivation is not simple. The point of view of the U.S. government is revealed in a passage from the diary of President James K. Polk: "Col. Kearny was also authorized to receive into service as volunteers a few hundred of the Mormons who are now on their way to California, with a view to conciliate them, attach them to our country, & prevent them from taking part against us." (2 July 1846; Polk, *The Diary of a President*, ed. Allan Nevins [London, 1929]). The Mormons, on the other hand, saw this as a chance to gain government help in their westward migration. Not only were the battalion members fed and clothed during their westward march, but also the pay they earned as soldiers was made available to help their families (q.v.). *See also* ILLINOIS PERIOD.

MORMON HISTORY ASSOCIATION (MHA). An organization formed in December 1965 to further the research and publication of Mormon history. Since its first sponsored meeting in 1966, the MHA has held annual meetings, organized adjunct sessions in connection with other professional associations, given awards, and published a newsletter and the *Journal of Mormon History*.

MORMON TABERNACLE CHOIR. A celebrated singing group started in the 1860s. For many years its leader was Evan Stephens (q.v.), who increased its size to more than 300 voices.

The choir became more widely known with the beginning of weekly live radio broadcasts in 1929, later extended to television, which included also a brief "sermonette," the "spoken word," by Richard L. Evans (q.v.). Its members, amateur in the sense that they are unpaid, are trained musicians, selected by audition, who rehearse every Thursday evening. From 1975 to 1999 its director was Jerold D. Ottley (q.v.). He was succeeded by Craig D. Jessop (q.v.).

In addition to its weekly Sunday morning broadcast, the Tabernacle Choir has made recordings for CBS Masterworks Records, London-Decca, Argo, and Bonneville Records. It has performed major choral works with the Philadelphia Symphony, Utah Symphony, and Jerusalem Symphony Orchestras. Tours within Utah and the United States started under director Evan Stephens (q.v.) These have been extended in recent years as the choir has performed concerts in Japan, Korea, Brazil, northern Europe, Russia, and Israel.

MORMON YOUTH SYMPHONY AND CHORUS (MYSC). Dual group of musicians between ages 18 and 33 established in 1969. Like the Mormon Tabernacle Choir (q.v.), the MYSC was sponsored by the Church. Trained musicians with experience in other orchestras and choruses were selected by audition. Performances included appearances at general conferences, firesides (qq.v.), and tours. Commercial recordings are available. Conductor since 1974 was Robert C. Bowden, who also composed and arranged some of the group's music. He retired after 25 years of service.

In 1999 this organization was superseded by the Temple Square (q.v.) Chorale, a training choir for the Mormon Tabernacle Choir, and the Orchestra at Temple Square, with no age requirement for membership.

MORONI. (Pronounced with the accent on the second syllable and a long final vowel: more-own-eye.) 1. A prominent leader at the close of the Book of Mormon (q.v.). 2. As a resurrected being, Moroni appeared to Joseph Smith (q.v.) several times. 3. The statue on the top spire of many temples (q.v.), mistakenly thought by many to be the angel Gabriel. Moroni is sometimes identified as fulfilling Revelation 14:6.

MOUNTAIN MEADOWS MASSACRE. Incident that took place on 7–11 September 1857 in which virtually an entire wagon company, at least 87 people, was killed by Mormons and Indians as they were passing through southern Utah on their way to California.

Unless one sees Mormons as congenitally bloodthirsty, anxious for the first opportunity to slaughter infidel nonbelievers, the incident must be explained by specific factors that happened to converge at Mountain Meadows in 1857. These included war conditions, poor communications, and perhaps provocation.

The summer of 1857 had brought the announcement that U.S. troops were on their way to install a new governor in Utah Territory. On the grounds that he had not been notified of his replacement, Brigham Young (q.v.) announced that the army would be treated as a hostile force. During the latter part of 1857 and early 1858 the militia was mobilized, preparations were made to evacuate Salt Lake City, and the supply trains of the advancing army were harassed. The Mormons hoped for assistance from Indian allies, who had no love for Americans in general. This was the Utah War.

The Fancher company was from Arkansas. As they moved southward through Utah, they required supplies. Rumors spread among the Mormons that they included in their number some of the persecutors from the 1830s, that they were taunting the Mormons, that they had poisoned a watering hole, and that they were spies for the advancing army. It was an atmosphere of hysteria.

While the company was camped at Mountain Meadows in southern Utah, local leaders in the Cedar City area determined to take action in cooperation with their Indian allies. A messenger was sent on horseback to Salt Lake City to obtain instructions from Brigham Young. Traveling more than 100 miles a day, the messenger reached his destination and rushed back with Young's instructions: "You must not meddle with them."

But it was too late. The Fancher party had been surrounded and, starting 7 September, almost all were killed by Indians and White Mormons working together. Their property was divided among local residents. Some children were spared, 17 of whom were returned to Arkansas in 1859.

It was not a pretty picture. With the conclusion of hostilities in 1858, violence elsewhere having been averted by the negotiating skills of Colonel Thomas L. Kane, a friend of the Mormons from Philadelphia, investigation into the massacre began. In 1876 John D. Lee, Mormon Indian farmer and one of the participants in the massacre, was tried, convicted, and executed by firing squad. Juanita Brooks (q.v.), who wrote the most thorough study of the subject, saw the massacre as a result of a collective hysteria. She did not hold Brigham Young responsible, although she did see the execution of Lee as an act of scapegoating in the sense that others on the local level had also been involved in the unfortunate decision.

Mormon leaders have denounced the act ever since it occurred. They do not consider it justified by the fact of their own persecution (q.v.). In 1990 a monument in honor of the victims was dedicated at Mountain Meadows. On 11 September 1999, the dedication of a monument at the site was attended by descendants of those in the wagon train and descendants of the Mormons who participated. Seeking emotional closure to a painful chapter of history, President Gordon B. Hinckley (q.v.) said: "I come as a peacemaker. This is not a time of recrimination or the assignment of blame. . . . It is time to leave the entire matter in the hands of God who deals justly in all things. His is a wisdom far beyond our own." Speaking for the descendants of the victims, the Reverend Stanton Cram of Springdale, Arkansas, said: "We are finding out that we are good people on both sides, decent people—people who want to do the right thing. . . . No one in this world today has any blame for that, and we don't have any right to hold this evil against the Mormon Church or the people here." *See also* MISSOURI PERIOD.

MOYLE, HENRY D. (1889–1963). Attorney, Apostle, counselor in First Presidency (qq.v.). Born on 22 April 1889 in Salt Lake City, Utah, Henry Dinwoody Moyle was the son of James H. and Alice Moyle. Intelligent and highly motivated, Henry enrolled at the University of Utah in 1905, receiving his B.S. degree in mining engineering. From 1909 to 1911, he served a full-time mission in the Swiss-German Mission and remained in Europe (q.v.) for one year to study at Freiberg University. Returning to the United States, he pursued a law degree at the University of Chicago and earned the J.D. degree in 1915.

Enlisting in the U.S. Army, Moyle became an officer but remained in the United States during World War I. After the war, he began his own law practice and in October 1919 married Clara Alberta Wright. Moyle invested in several businesses, including the Deseret Livestock Company, the Wasatch Oil Company, and a silver mining company. A lifelong Democrat, he served as Utah's Democratic Party chairman and unsuccessfully ran for governor in 1940

After serving in ward and stake (qq.v.) positions, Moyle was called to be an Apostle in 1947. Active in organizing and promoting the welfare program (q.v.), he assisted the Church in legal and business affairs. In June 1959, Moyle became second counselor in the First Presidency under President David O. McKay (q.v.). He died in Florida on 18 September 1963.

MUSEUM OF CHURCH HISTORY AND ART. Continuing a series of earlier museums housing artifacts, the present building was dedicated and opened in 1984. Staffed by curators, historians, and art historians, the museum is administratively part of the Historical Department of the Church (q.v.). Its basic purpose is to preserve and exhibit the significant material remains, crafts, and art from the Mormon past as well as work being produced at the present.

A voluntary staff of docents assists in greeting, providing tours and explanations, and visiting schools.

An especially interesting part of the permanent exhibit consists of works by Mormon artists of the 19th century who studied in France and brought back the style of the French impressionists. A handsome volume entitled *Harvesting the Light* prepared by art historian Linda Gibbs was published by the museum. Portraits of Church leaders from the beginning are numerous. For each of the Church presidents a collection of artifacts has been assembled.

Temporary exhibits are changed every few months. For the sesquicentennial of the Relief Society (q.v.) in 1992, an exhibit displayed works by and about women throughout the world. For the centennial of the Salt Lake Temple in 1993, an exhibit of old photographs and relics traced the construction through its duration of 40 years. Competitions from time to time on subjects like the Book of Mormon (q.v.) result in submissions from many countries and using different artistic media. *See also* ART.

MUSIC. From the beginning of the Church, music has been included as part of Mormon worship. Although Mormon musicians have sometimes achieved success as composers or performers in the larger arena, here we shall consider music as it has developed in the Church setting.

As early as 1830 Emma Hale Smith (q.v.) received instructions (Doctrine and Covenants, section 25) to compile a hymnal, which she did, publishing her collection in 1835. Hymns from the Protestant tradition were included, adapted where necessary, as well as new works by Mormons. As opportunity allowed, this hymnal was revised and expanded in a series of later editions, with music being added to the text by the 1870s. The present official edition was published by the Church in 1985. Editions in Spanish, French, German, and other languages have versions of 100 or more of the English hymns but also add others from their respective traditions.

Congregational singing was supplemented by choirs on occasion, as for the dedication of the Kirtland Temple in 1836. During the Illinois Period (q.v.) singing instructors and the arrival of trained musicians among converts from England led to some resplendent public performances. Bands also performed, starting in Nauvoo and continuing through the exodus (q.v.) across the plains.

During the Utah Period (q.v.) bands and orchestras were popular. Concerts featured local performers and touring instrumental and vocal virtuosi. An examination of the concert offerings in Salt Lake City during the last quarter of the 19th century shows a provincial capital with about as much urbanity and refinement as other cities of the same size. The great Adelina Patti and Jenny Lind thrilled Utah audiences. Gilbert and Sullivan operettas were heard and enjoyed.

Helping to raise the standards of music among Mormons were several immigrant converts, including C. J. Thomas, John Tullidge, and George Careless, who gave lessons, wrote criticism, and directed groups.

Many wards (q.v.) had choirs, their quality depending on the available voices and the talent of the directors. The choir with the greatest prestige was the one that came to be known as the Mormon Tabernacle Choir (q.v.). When Evan Stephens (q.v.) took over its direction, its fame expanded through many tours in Utah and eventually outside as well. In 1893 it performed at the great Chicago Columbian Exposition and won second prize.

In the 20th century the Mormon Tabernacle Choir has continued to be the most public exemplar of Mormon musicianship, especially as it began its network radio broadcasts in 1929 (later extended to television). Director J. Spencer Cornwall and later Jerold Ottley (q.v.) chose the voices carefully on the basis of audition and in weekly rehearsals achieved a quality surprisingly high for a volunteer choral group. Recordings by the Tabernacle Choir sold well in the national market. In the present generation the group has extended its touring schedule to Asia, Europe (qq.v.), and Israel.

Also in the Tabernacle (q.v.) was a great pipe organ. Constructed originally by Australian convert Joseph Ridges, the organ has been improved periodically. The most recent upgrading, completed in 1988, was described by organ historian Barbara Owen in *The Mormon Tabernacle Organ: An American Classic* (1990). Frank W. Asper and Alexander Schreiner (q.v.) were the two famed organists for many years. Tabernacle organists Robert Cundick, John Longhurst, and Clay Christiansen, along with assistant organists Richard Elliot, Bonnie Goodliffe, and Linda Margetts, have occupied the great console recently both as accompanists for the choir and in solo performances.

The universities have contributed significantly in teaching composition and in training instrumental and vocal performers. Brigham Young University (q.v.) sponsors impressive choir performances on a regular basis. Ricks College (q.v.) does the same. Brigham Young University–

Hawaii Campus (q.v.) does much to preserve Polynesian (q.v.) music and its choral tradition.

Mormon musical composition goes back to the 19th century. Evan Stephens was one of the most prolific music writers. In the 20th century B. Cecil Gates wrote many single numbers, cantatas, and oratorios. Leroy J. Robertson (q.v.) completed *Oratorio from the Book of Mormon*. Crawford Gates, Robert Cundick, and Merrill Bradshaw are among those who have composed serious works.

On the more popular level some music has carried Mormon ideas. The 1947 musical drama *Promised Valley*, composed by Crawford Gates, was produced for many years because its catchy, Broadway-style tunes appealed to tourists. Lex d'Azevedo's *Saturday's Warrior*, a dramatic presentation of the Plan of Salvation (q.v.), incorporated rhythms that could appeal to the post-Lawrence Welk generation. Similar songs, sometimes called "Mormon pop," continue to appear. Not considered appropriate for sacrament meetings (q.v.), these songs and the groups that sing them nevertheless demonstrate one aspect of what is happening in Mormon music.

With the expansion into parts of the world outside the United States and western Europe, two principles are in tension. Creativity and a rich diversity are consistent with the scriptural injunction to "prove all things and hold fast to that which is good" (1 Thess. 5:21). Mormonism does not insist on transforming everyone into a single mold. On the other hand, the Church desires to have unity, to have some practices, including worship services, that will be the same for its members throughout the world. Allowing centrifugal forces to operate without restriction could create chaos.

Up to the present it is the unifying principle that has predominated, as when African Mormons were told that drums were not appropriate to sacrament meetings. Yet they have been allowed as part of weekday Church activities, and cultural evenings featuring national and indigenous music and dance have been a popular activity in different parts of the world.

In whatever form their music takes, retaining favorite hymns from the past century, adding and adapting, Mormons are still fond of the revealed declaration to Emma Smith in 1830: "The song of the righteous is a prayer unto me" (Doctrine and Covenants, section 25). *See also* MEMBERSHIP.

MYSTICISM. Belief in and practice of direct contact, or union, with God, found in both Christian and non-Christian traditions. In its classic formulation, as represented by Plotinus and St. John of the Cross, Mormons are not mystics. A close analysis demonstrates that their concepts of God and man are simply not conducive to the kind of absorption described by Plotinus as "the flight of the alone to the alone." According to a looser definition, emphasizing direct communication from God to humans, Mormons might qualify, although they do not use the term *mysticism,* preferring *revelation, inspiration, Holy Ghost* and other terms (qq.v.).

-N-

NADAULD, MARGARET D. (1944–). Educator, young women (q.v.) leader. Born in Manti, Utah, Margaret Dyreng studied at Snow College there before going on to complete a bachelor's degree in speech and English at Brigham Young University (q.v.). She married Stephen D. Nadauld, and they became the parents of seven sons. She taught high school English and speech in Boston, Massachusetts, and Salt Lake City, Utah. Besides teaching piano to supplement the family income, she served as a chapter president of Freedoms Foundation at Valley Forge, vice president of American Mothers, Inc., president of Management Women of Marriott School of Management at Brigham Young University, and founder of a personal development course taught through a national department store chain. She was ward Relief Society president, ward Young Women president, and member of the Relief Society general board (qq.v.). In 1997 she became general president of the Young Women.

NATIVE AMERICANS. American Indians, or Amerindians. The relationship between White Mormons and Indians has been one of unusual interest. On the one hand, the early Mormons, practically all of whom were of White American or European ethnicity, experienced most of the same difficulties with the native population as other westward-moving Americans. On the other hand, Indians were regarded as descendants of the Lamanites (q.v.) described in the Book of Mormon (qq.v.). A glorious future was promised for them.

Repeated efforts to missionize the western American Indians had minimal success in the 19th century. In the 20th century, starting especially in the 1940s, Mormon converts have been made among Utes, Shoshone, Navajo, Hopi, and other Native American tribes. An Indian Student Placement Service was established to provide foster families for children from the reservation who voluntarily wished to take advantage of schools in the urban area for nine months of the year. With the improvement of reservation schools the program has been sharply reduced, but a total of 70,000 children have participated. Brigham Young University (q.v.) provided special scholarships and had probably the largest contingent of Indian college students in the nation.

Because of the large number of Indians and mestizos in Central and South America, the growth of the Church in those regions is also seen as fulfillment of the scriptural promise. *See also* LAMANITE.

NAUVOO. *See* ILLINOIS PERIOD.

NAUVOO RESTORATION, INC. (NRI). A Church-founded nonprofit corporation that supervises the partial restoration of historic Nauvoo, Illinois, which was occupied by the Mormons from 1839 to 1846.

For the previous eight years Dr. James LeRoy Kimball, a Salt Lake City internist and cardiologist, purchased old Mormon homes as they became available. With the founding of Nauvoo Restoration, Inc. in 1962, he became its president. As stated in the articles of incorporation, the mission of NRI is "to acquire, restore, protect, and preserve, for the education and benefit of its members and the public, all or a part of the old city of Nauvoo."

A board of trustees was established, including among its members David M. Kennedy and John Willard Marriott (qq.v.). Historical consultant was Thomas Edgar Lyon (q.v.).

Over the next several years about 1,000 acres were purchased, including more than 40 homes or buildings from the period of the 1840s. A major project of historical restoration was begun; seven structures were totally reconstructed while others were finished on the exterior. A visitor center (q.v.) was built, near which a sculptural Monument to Women was placed by the Relief Society (q.v.) in 1978.

Called to assist at NRI were young missionaries (q.v.) and older couples, who could play the roles of such period figures as blacksmiths and act as guides for visitors. Restored Nauvoo has become a major attraction not only for tourists but also for school children on field trips. *See also* ILLINOIS PERIOD.

NELSON, RUSSELL M. (1924–). Physician, Apostle. Born on 9 September 1924, Nelson grew up in Salt Lake City and graduated from the

University of Utah in 1945. His medical studies, also at the University of Utah, led to the M.D. degree in 1947. After a residency at Massachusetts General Hospital in Boston he moved to the University of Minnesota, earning a Ph.D. in 1954.

A skilled surgeon, Nelson has been director of the Thoracic Surgery Residency at the University of Utah and chairman of the Thoracic Surgery division at LDS Hospital. Among other professional positions he has been president of the Society for Vascular Surgery, a director of the American Board of Thoracic Surgery, chairman of the Council on Cardiovascular Surgery for the American Heart Association, and president of the Utah State Medical Association.

In addition to his busy professional life and family (q.v.) responsibilities (he and his wife, Dantzel, have 10 children), Nelson has served extensively in the Church. After serving as a stake president (qq.v.) for seven years, he became general president of the Sunday School (q.v.) in 1971. Later he was a Regional Representative (q.v.). In 1984 he became a member of the Quorum of the Twelve Apostles (q.v.).

Among his many other responsibilities as a General Authority (q.v.), Nelson has been especially energetic and effective in gaining recognition in Europe and Asia (qq.v.), thus promoting the international growth of the Church.

NEW ERA, THE. Monthly magazine for youth (q.v.), which began publication in January 1971. It contains photographic essays, features on youth activities in different parts of the world, and inspirational articles and stories.

NEW YORK PERIOD. Organized on 6 April 1830, the Church had its first home in upper New York State. The family of Joseph Smith (q.v.) lived in Palmyra. It was there that the First Vision (q.v.) occurred in 1820, there that Smith gained his first followers during the translation of the Book of Mormon (q.v.), which was published there in the spring of 1830.

While the manuscript of the Book of Mormon was being prepared, with Oliver Cowdery (q.v.) writing as Joseph Smith dictated the translation, a passage about baptism (q.v.) prompted prayer (q.v.) to God for direction. A heavenly messenger, who identified himself as John the Baptist, appeared and bestowed on Smith and Cowdery the Aaronic Priesthood (q.v.), which included the authority to baptize. During the next few months others were baptized.

The Church was officially organized in early 1830. Some of the early sources identify the place of this organizational meeting as Manchester, while others say Fayette. After comparing their memories, Mormon leaders determined that Fayette, where the Whitmer farm was located, was where it happened, although it is not improbable that an important meeting, even with some organizing functions, took place in Manchester at about the same time. To satisfy legal requirements, six men—Joseph Smith, Oliver Cowdery, and four others—were listed as charter members. A group of perhaps 50 people, filling and overflowing the house, were in attendance. Immediately, of course, the Church grew larger with the addition of those already baptized and other converts.

The New York phase of the Church as an organization lasted only nine months, from April through December 1830. Three centers were the foci of the fledgling organization: Fayette (the Whitmers), Manchester (the Smiths), and Colesville (the Knights). Conferences were held at Fayette in June and September.

Not all of the activity was confined to New York State. Missionaries embarked on preaching journeys, including the important mission of Oliver Cowdery, Parley P. Pratt (qq.v.), Peter Whitmer Jr., and Ziba Peterson to Missouri via Ohio. As he had done the previous year, Joseph Smith sometimes stayed at the home of his wife's parents in Harmony, Pennsylvania, more than a hundred miles from Palmyra and just across the state boundary.

To judge how much of Mormonism was introduced during this initial phase, one must look at the Book of Mormon, which became the chief missionary (q.v.) tool and gave the new religion its nickname. Joseph Smith began work on his "inspired revision" of the Bible (q.v.). Approximately the first 40 revelations (q.v.), published as sections of the Doctrine and Covenants (q.v.), emanate from the New York period. Among the topics introduced were: Priesthood (q.v.) authority, the obligation of missionary work, the sacramental prayers, the assignment of preparing a hymnal, description of the duties of different offices, and the gathering (q.v.). Although the Twelve Apostles (q.v.) were not yet called, this future development was predicted. The proclamation of the Mormon gospel (q.v.) to the Indians was begun, and the place where Zion (q.v.) was to be built (Missouri) was specified. Apocalyptic and millennial, Mormonism was already showing some of the characteristics it would retain throughout its history.

It also began to experience persecution (q.v.). Ridicule had been the lot of Joseph Smith from the time of his First Vision. He was taken to the local court and charged with being a disorderly person. The early Mormons were harassed, as on the occasion when a mob broke up the temporary dam placed in a stream in order to allow baptisms.

In December 1830 the beleaguered New York Mormons were instructed to move to Ohio (Doctrine and Covenants, Section 37), which most of them did in the first two or three months of 1831. For the next phase of Church history, read the Ohio Period and Missouri Period (qq.v.) entries.

In the 20th century the Church developed monuments and historic sites in the vicinity of Palmyra, New York. Conversions produced a buildup of the Church in the state. At the end of 1997 New York State had 57,000 Mormons, including 10 stakes (q.v.). *See also* CHURCH OF JESUS CHRIST OF LATTER-DAY SAINTS; NATIVE AMERICANS.

NEW ZEALAND. *See* COWLEY, MATTHEW; PACIFIC.

NIBLEY, HUGH (1910–). Professor of ancient history, linguist, scholarly defender of Mormonism. Born on 27 March 1910 in Portland, Oregon, Nibley early showed signs of precociousness in his avid reading. He served as a Swiss-German missionary. Upon his return he attended UCLA, graduating summa cum laude in 1934. His Berkeley doctorate of 1938 was awarded after completing a dissertation in ancient history on "The Roman Games as the Survival of an Archaic Year-Cult."

During World War II Nibley was a noncommissioned intelligence officer, first in England and then in the battle of Normandy and on the Continent. After the war he took a post at Brigham Young University (q.v.), where for some 40 years he offered courses on ancient history, Greek literature, patristics, and the Mormon scriptures (q.v.).

A gifted linguist, Nibley read voraciously in Greek, Latin, Hebrew, Arabic, Egyptian, and numerous modern languages. He studied Egyptian at the Oriental Institute in Chicago and Coptic at Berkeley. He has poured out a stream of writings, some of them published in the learned journals, many of them in Church magazines. In 1990 a two-volume Festschrift, *By Study and Also by Faith*, was published in his honor, containing contributions by former students and colleagues, both in and out of the Church.

Because his works often respond to anti-Mormon critics Nibley is sometimes called an apologist, which in the best sense of a defender he undoubtedly is. His witty responses to critical historians expose their inconsistencies and speculation based on their secular assumptions. His massive work on the Book of Mormon (q.v.) treats it with deep respect and offers example after example of its congruity with the ancient world. His erudition enables him to show striking parallels between Joseph

Smith's (q.v.) Book of Abraham and ancient Egypt, between Mormonism and early Christianity (q.v.). To critics who say that such parallels fall short of proof he responds with the challenge to explain how, short of revelation (q.v.), a relatively uneducated Joseph Smith could come up with such details. He is also a penetrating observer of the foibles of modern society and a captivating speaker on eternal patterns.

His voluminous writings—including such titles as *Lehi in the Desert*, *The World and the Prophets*, *The Ancient State*, *Temple and Cosmos*, and *Approaching Zion*—have been published in *Collected Works of Hugh Nibley*. See also PEARL OF GREAT PRICE.

NORTH AMERICA. Organized in New York State in 1830, the Church has always had its main center in the United States. But its message was preached to "all the world" as opportunity allowed. It has always been a misunderstanding, at least partially, to describe it as "an American church," just as it would not be accurate to describe the Catholic Church as "an Italian church."

Nevertheless, throughout the 19th century 90 percent or more of its members lived in the United States. As converts joined, they responded to the doctrine of gathering (q.v.) and moved to headquarters. Only gradually was that practice reversed, starting with recommendations to remain where they were around the turn of the 20th century, becoming much more emphatic after World War II.

Membership (q.v.) remains strong in Utah (1,551,000 members at the end of 1997) and in other western states: Idaho (333,000), Arizona (289,000), Nevada (133,000), Colorado (105,000), Oregon (130,000), Washington (219,000), and California (733,000).

Yet the 20th century, especially since World War II, has witnessed a dispersion of membership into other parts of the United States. Every state now has Mormon stakes and wards (qq.v.). To meet the needs of members in parts of the country away from the intermountain West, temples (q.v.) have been constructed in California, Washington, Oregon, Idaho, Nevada, Colorado, Georgia, Texas, Illinois, Missouri, and several other states.

Early preaching expeditions into eastern Canada in the 1830s led to some conversions, but gathering and the successive persecutions (q.v.) and moves of the Church left no permanent membership there. At the end of the 19th century, as part of a continuing program of colonization (q.v.), Mormons moved into Alberta, Canada, and established settlements at Cardston and elsewhere. A stake was organized there in 1895.

At the end of 1997 there were 61,000 members in Alberta, divided into 19 stakes and 135 wards. Just as there had been an outward, centrifugal tendency in the United States, so membership in Canada spread. As a result of proselytizing, movement of people from other areas, and births, Mormons could be found in all parts of the country: British Columbia (27,000), Manitoba (3,700), New Brunswick (2,000), Newfoundland (600), Nova Scotia (4,200), Ontario (39,000), Prince Edward Island (400), Quebec (8,300), Saskatchewan (4,500), Northwest Territories (200), and Yukon Territory (200). In addition to the Cardston, Alberta, Temple, constructed in 1923, temples were completed at Brampton, Ontario, in 1990, and in 1999 at Halifax, Nova Scotia, and Regina, Saskatchewan. For information on church membership in Mexico and countries south of Mexico, read the entry entitled Central America and Mexico (q.v.).

-O-

OAKS, DALLIN H. (1932–). Lawyer, jurist, educator, Apostle. Born in Provo, Utah, on 12 August 1932, Dallin Oaks was raised in Provo by Stella Harris Oaks, his accomplished, widowed mother. He attended Brigham Young University (q.v.), from which he received a B.A. degree in accounting in 1954. After three years at the University of Chicago Law School, serving as editor of the law review his senior year, Oaks graduated with a J.D. degree in 1957.

After serving as a law clerk to Chief Justice Earl Warren of the U.S. Supreme Court, he moved back to Chicago, where he specialized in corporate litigation for a law firm before accepting a faculty position at the University of Chicago. In addition to serving as associate dean of the law school, he became executive director of the American Bar Foundation. He authored many articles on legal and historical subjects.

In 1971 Oaks became president of Brigham Young University. For nine years he presided over BYU during a period of continued growth. He became president of the American Association of Presidents of Independent Colleges and Universities, 1975–78.

In 1980 he left his university presidency and became a Utah Supreme Court justice for three and a half years. Also in 1980 he became chairman of the board of directors of the Public Broadcasting Corporation (PBS), continuing until 1985.

Through the years Dallin Oaks has served in a variety of Church positions: stake mission president in Chicago, member of the presidency of the Chicago South Stake, and regional representative (qq.v.). In 1984 he was called to be a member of the Quorum of the Twelve Apostles (q.v.). Like the other Apostles, he travels extensively, concerned with everything that affects the Church and its programs. He is chairman of the board of the Polynesian Cultural Center (q.v.) in Laie, Hawaii. Dallin Oaks and his wife, June (who died of cancer in 1998), are the parents of six children.

OHIO PERIOD. A main center of Mormonism from early 1831 to 1838. During the same years western Missouri was the second center of Mormon activity.

A mission to the Indians of western Missouri by Parley P. Pratt (q.v.) and others stopped in the vicinity of Kirtland, Ohio, a suburb of modern Cleveland. Finding seekers or restorationists there, the missionaries (q.v.) succeeded in converting more than a hundred of them, which immediately gave Ohio about as many members as lived in New York. Among these early Ohio converts was Sidney Rigdon (q.v.), a preacher known for his eloquence and leadership ability.

Not long after Joseph Smith (q.v.) heard of these developments— Rigdon having traveled to New York—instructions were given that the New York Mormons should move to Ohio. (Doctrine and Covenants, sections 37, 38). Smith moved to Kirtland in February with his family (q.v.). Not long after, in the summer of 1831, he traveled to Missouri and designated Independence as a gathering (q.v.) place. For the next few years, then, many Mormon converts flowed either into Ohio or Missouri, with Smith living for most of the time in or near Kirtland, Ohio.

An examination of the Doctrine and Covenants (q.v.) shows Ohio to be the scene of many important developments during the 1830s. It was there that the Church organization made important advances from its simple beginnings. The office of bishop (q.v.) was created. A high council (q.v.) was established. In 1835 the Quorum of the Twelve Apostles was formed along with the Quorum of the Seventy (qq.v.). A School of the Prophets (q.v.) provided instruction for missionaries and Church officers. Periodicals were published, providing an outlet for revelations (q.v.) received by Smith as well as other instructions. In 1835 many of these revelations, which had earlier circulated in handwritten form or appeared in the periodicals, were published as the Doctrine and Covenants (q.v.).

Kirtland became a nerve center of missionary activity, with proselytizers traveling outward through Ohio and wider regions and then returning. As new converts arrived in the Kirtland vicinity, a boomtown atmosphere was created. Many houses were constructed. In 1836 the Kirtland Temple was finished and dedicated. An impressive structure for a religion that had been in existence just six years and whose members were mostly poor, the temple (q.v.) was the scene of visions to Joseph Smith and pentecostal experiences for many others.

Although even in the brief New York Period (q.v.) several basic characteristics of Mormonism took form, the few years in Ohio saw important developments not only in organization but in doctrine. The health code, known as the Word of Wisdom (q.v.), was issued. The gradations of eternal salvation were described (Doctrine and Covenants, section 76). An economic program of consecration and stewardship was introduced (Doctrine and Covenants, section 42). Joseph Smith continued work on his inspired revision of the Bible (q.v.) and produced the Book of Abraham after acquiring Egyptian papyri.

The creativity of the Ohio Period both organizationally and doctrinally took place against a backdrop of obstacles and opposition. Simply providing for the incoming Mormons was an enormous economic challenge. Not surprisingly, the influx, which meant Mormon domination, led to opposition and persecution (q.v.) by others in the region. To provide capital for construction, a Mormon bank was established. In an era of largely unregulated banking, the failure of wildcat banks was not unusual, but when the Kirtland Anti-banking Society (renamed to circumvent a statute) collapsed, all who suffered losses were bitter, including not only outside investors but, more importantly, some of the Mormon leaders. Historian Milton Backman has estimated that as many as 10 to 15 percent of the membership (q.v.) withdrew from the Church. It was the tumult over these matters, with opposition from within and without, that led to the flight of Joseph Smith and the great majority of Mormons in 1838.

Kirtland rapidly waned as a Mormon center. A few members lingered there for the next several years, but for practical purposes it was abandoned. The Kirtland Temple, later acquired by the Reorganized Church of Jesus Christ of Latter Day Saints (q.v.), still stands.

In the second half of the 20th century Mormonism enjoyed a resurgence in Ohio as some Church members from the West moved there and as convert baptisms (q.v.) increased their number. At the end of 1998 there were 43,000 members in the state, with 11 stakes and 71 wards (qq.v.). *See also* MISSOURI PERIOD; PEARL OF GREAT PRICE; STAKE.

ORDINANCE. A ceremony or procedure by which special blessings of God are mediated to the recipient. Roughly equivalent to the term *sacrament* (q.v.) as used in the general Christian tradition. While the form and words are important, an ordinance, to be valid, must be performed by authority of the priesthood (q.v.).

Essential to salvation are baptism and confirmation (qq.v.), although these may be performed vicariously for the deceased in the temples (q.v.). Priesthood ordination and certain temple rites are considered prerequisites for salvation in the highest degree. Other ordinances include the sacrament, the naming of children, and administering to the sick. *See also* SACRAMENT MEETING.

OSMOND, DONNY (1957–). Singer, actor. Born on 9 December 1957 in Ogden, Utah, Donny Osmond is the son of George and Olive Osmond. At age five, Donny launched his career in music when he sang with his siblings on the *Andy Williams Show.* By his early 20s, he had released 23 top-40 songs. In 1976, Donny and his sister Marie began their own television show on the ABC network, which lasted four seasons. In the 1980s Donny's status as a teen idol faded, but in 1992 his career was revived when he began acting in Andrew Lloyd Weber's *Joseph and the Amazing Technicolor Dreamcoat*, which he starred in for five years. Osmond now cohosts a syndicated television talk show with his sister Marie Osmond (q.v.). Donny Osmond married Debra Gleen in 1978, and they are the parents of five sons.

OSMOND, MARIE (1959–). Singer, actress. Born 13 October 1959 in Ogden, Utah, Marie performed as a child with her siblings, the children of George and Olive Osmond. By the time she was a teenager, Marie had appeared on the *Andy Williams Show,* recorded the hit record "Paper Roses," and performed with her brothers before a sold-out crowd at New York's Madison Square Garden. Besides her career in the entertainment industry, Marie has written several books, developed the Marie Osmond Doll Collection, and helped raise money for charitable foundations. She cohosted a syndicated television talk show with her brother Donny Osmond (q.v.) and with him hosted the Miss America Pageant at Atlantic City in 1999. She has seven children.

OTTLEY, JEROLD (1934–). Musician, director of Mormon Tabernacle Choir (q.v.). Born in Salt Lake City on 7 April 1934, Jerold Ottley received his basic primary and secondary education there. In 1951 he moved to New Zealand, where he served as a missionary (q.v.) from 1953 to 1955. Returning from his mission, he married JoAnn South in 1956. They have two children.

Ottley graduated from the University of Utah in 1961. His master's degree in music was awarded by Brigham Young University (q.v.) in 1967, the doctorate, the D.M.A., by the University of Oregon in 1972. He also studied at the Academy of Music in Cologne, Germany.

Director of the Mormon Tabernacle Choir from 1975 to his retirement in 1999, Ottley raised the level of its performance to new heights by a scrupulous selection of voices through auditions and intensive rehearsal. His wife, JoAnn Ottley, a respected, highly accomplished soprano, assisted the choir as vocal coach. Jerold Ottley is an adjunct professor of music at the University of Utah. *See also* MUSIC.

-P-

PACIFIC. In addition to the Philippines, other Pacific islands have experienced steady expansion of Church membership (q.v.) from the 19th century. The following membership figures are for the end of 1997:

	members	stakes	temples
American Samoa	12,000	4	
Cook Islands	900		
Fiji	11,000	4	
Guam	1,400		
Marshall Islands	3,400		
Micronesia	3,100		
Niue	300		
North Mariana Islands	600		
Papua New Guinea	5,600		
Tahiti	15,000	6	1
Tonga	43,000	16	1
Western Samoa	56,000	16	1

The state of Hawaii has 54,000 members in 14 stakes (q.v.). Its temple (q.v.) at Laie was the first constructed outside the continental United States. Another temple, at Kona, was completed in 2000.

Somewhat different because of size are Australia and New Zealand, which administratively are in the Pacific Area. The first preaching of Mormonism in Australia started as early as 1840, but it was in 1851 that a mission was established. In the 19th century progress was slow. Anti-Mormon speeches and newspaper articles discouraged converts, and the gathering (q.v.) policy led many of the strong members to emigrate. Finally, in 1904, the first meetinghouse in Australia was constructed at Wooloongabba. As elsewhere, the latter half of the 20th century saw greater progress. At the end of 1997, 96,000 Australian Mormons were divided into 28 stakes and 178 wards (q.v.). Temples were dedicated at Sydney in 1984 and at Adelaide and Melbourne in 2000.

In New Zealand the trajectory was similar. Missionaries (q.v.) arriving in the 1850s were able to convert only a few. By 1880 there were only 133 members. Then the missionaries began preaching to the Maoris and, because of a similarity of beliefs, enjoyed much greater success. One of the great missionaries to the Maoris was Matthew Cowley (q.v.). From the 1930s on expansion also occurred among New Zealanders of European ancestry. In 1958 two institutions were completed and dedicated: the Church College of New Zealand and the New Zealand Temple, both at Hamilton, south of Auckland. By the end of 1997, 86,000 New Zealand Mormons were divided into 25 stakes and 142 wards. *See also* BRIGHAM YOUNG UNIVERSITY–HAWAII CAMPUS; POLYNESIAN CULTURAL CENTER; POLYNESIANS.

PACKER, BOYD KENNETH (1924–). Educator, Apostle. Born on 10 September 1924 in Brigham City, Utah, Boyd Packer grew up there. He enlisted and became a bomber pilot during World War II, serving in the Pacific Theater. Upon his return he studied at Weber College and Utah State University, from which he received B.S. and M.S. degrees. Subsequently he earned a doctor of education degree at Brigham Young University (q.v.).

After accepting a position with the Church Educational System, Packer proved to be a successful classroom teacher and became supervisor of seminaries and institutes of religion (qq.v.). Active in community affairs, he served as a city councilman. He was then called to serve as president (q.v.) of the Church's New England Mission.

In 1961 he became one of the Assistants to the Twelve (q.v.), and in 1970, at the age of 45, a member of the Quorum of the Twelve Apostles (q.v.). During about 40 years as General Authority (q.v.), Packer has traveled throughout the world, given countless sermons, officiated in the formation of stakes (q.v.), and published several books. With the other

Apostles he has deliberated on all matters concerning the Church. Special areas of responsibility have included correlation (q.v.) and education. He has served on the Church Board of Education and the Board of Trustees of BYU. He married Donna Edith Smith in 1947. They have 10 children.

PAGEANTS. Dramatic presentations of historic or scriptural events in an outdoor setting, pageants have become a popular means of commemoration. Usually produced locally, they vary in quality. Their large casts ensure a theatrical experience for many who would not have it otherwise. Scheduled in the summer, they attract not only the local population but also tourists as audiences. The largest of the pageants is the Cumorah Pageant at Palmyra, New York. Another, in Cache Valley, Utah, portrays the life of Martin Harris (q.v.).

PATRIARCH. Priesthood (q.v.) holders, at least one per stake (q.v.), who are called and ordained to give patriarchal blessings (q.v.) to stake members. Until 1979 a general Church patriarch, a descendant of the Joseph Smith Sr. family (qq.v.), was counted among the General Authorities (q.v.), but on the grounds that stake patriarchs performed the function adequately, the general patriarch was retired.

PATRIARCHAL BLESSINGS. After receiving a recommend (q.v.) from one's bishop (q.v.), one is given an individual blessing.

Placing his hands on the head of the recipient, the patriarch (q.v.) solemnly pronounces the person's lineage, whether by blood or adoption, leading back to Abraham. Seeking inspiration, the patriarch gives additional promises and counsel to guide one in life.

Blessings are recorded and transcribed. One copy is preserved in the Church archives. Another copy is retained by the individual receiving the blessing. Mormons look upon their patriarchal blessing as a source of comfort and guidance.

PATRIOTISM. Mormons have expressed their loyalty to governments in general from the beginning. Although frustrated at the failure of state and federal governments to protect them in Missouri and Illinois, Mormons insisted on their devotion to the country. The Constitution of the United States (q.v.) was divinely inspired (Doctrine and Covenants, Section 101); corrupt individuals were responsible for the problems. Despite being forced to flee to the West, Mormons enlisted in the Mormon Battalion (q.v.) during the Mexican War, and some fought in the Civil War. During the antipolygamy prosecutions of the 1870s and 1880s enthusiasm for the country may have cooled, but this did not prevent a vigorous effort to obtain statehood for Utah, which was accomplished in 1896. During the Spanish-American War and World Wars I and II, Mormons participated with more than normal enthusiasm. Patriotic, even flag-waving, talks were sometimes heard in General Conference (q.v.).

With the expansion of the Church into other countries, especially since the 1960s, expressions of U.S. patriotism have been less frequent. Wherever they live, Mormons are expected to be loyal to their country. *See also* ARTICLES OF FAITH, 12; POLITICS.

PEARL OF GREAT PRICE. One of the four standard works along with the Bible, Book of Mormon, and Doctrine and Covenants (qq.v.).

First published as a pamphlet in 1851 by Apostle Franklin D. Richards, the book is a compilation of five writings previously published in Church periodicals: portions of the first eight chapters of the Genesis text that restored by revelation (q.v.) the writings of Moses; the Book of Abraham, a translation from Egyptian papyri brought to Joseph Smith (q.v.) in 1835; Matthew 24—a selection from Smith's inspired revision of the Bible; an autobiographical account of Joseph Smith's early life and visions, including the First Vision (q.v.), as written in 1838; and the Articles of Faith (q.v.)

In 1967 11 fragments of the papyri once in the possession of Joseph Smith were discovered. They turned out to be from an Egyptian religious work called *The Book of Breathings*. Mormon defenders, especially Hugh Nibley (q.v.), raised questions as to whether those particular fragments were the ones underlying the Book of Abraham, stated that we are in the dark as to what Smith meant by "translation," and pointed out many parallels between the Book of Abraham and ancient writings.

Some other items once included in the Pearl of Great Price are no longer there, the most important of these now placed in the Doctrine and Covenants. The Pearl of Great Price was accepted as a standard work by a vote of approval in the General Conference (q.v.) on 10 October 1880.

PERRY, L. TOM (1922–). Business administrator, Apostle. Born in Logan, Utah, on 5 August 1922, Lowell Tom Perry became a missionary (q.v.) to the northern states at age 20. Upon his return, he entered the U.S. Marines and served for two years in the Pacific.

After the war he married Virginia Lee (they had three children) and attended Utah State University, receiving a B.S. degree in finance in 1949 and doing some graduate work.

He took employment with retail business companies as treasurer and vice president. His professional career took him to Idaho, California, New York, and Massachusetts. During this itinerary he served in two bishoprics, on a high council, and in two stake presidencies (qq.v.). He was president (q.v.) of the Boston Stake.

Called to be an Assistant to the Twelve in 1972, Perry became a member of the Quorum of the Twelve Apostles (qq.v.) in 1974. In addition to traveling to different parts of the Church to supervise conferences and select leaders, Perry has served as a member of the Church Board of Education and the General Welfare Services Committee. A special assignment was to head the Church's part in the bicentennial of the United States. His wife Virginia died in 1974. Two years later he married Barbara Dayton.

PERSECUTION. Opposition or harassment, especially when motivated by religious or ethnic prejudice. Mormons were opposed from the beginning. The activities against them have included verbal denunciation and misrepresentation, ridicule, deliberately throwing nuisances and irritants in their path, vexatious lawsuits, imprisonment, mob demonstrations and violence, tarring and feathering, burning homes and barns, driving off cattle, raping, and killing. There has also been opposition on the level of the antipolygamy statutes and the attempts to enforce them, which led to fines, terms in prison, denial of the right to vote, and finally confiscation of Church property. All such harassment was regarded by Mormons as persecution.

Joseph Smith (q.v.) described the reaction to his account of the First Vision (q.v.) as persecution. Among other things, the label served to identify Mormons with the New Testament saints, who were told by the Lord: "Blessed are ye when men shall revile you, and persecute you, and shall say all manner of evil against you falsely, for my sake" (Matt. 5:11).

From the point of view of their opponents, of course, the activity was perfectly justified. When mobs or individuals struck out against the Mormons, this was justifiable self-defense, consistent with the history of vigilantism in the 19th century. When it was the government who promoted the activity, as in the campaign against polygamy (q.v.), they were not persecuting people for religious belief but prosecuting stubborn lawbreakers. Point of view was all important.

Motivation for the opposition to Mormonism was not merely disgust with polygamy. That stick was used to beat them with, especially from the end of the Civil War to the 1890 Manifesto (q.v.). But denunciation and harassment started much earlier and continued to flare up after the abandonment of polygamy. Religious differences provoked antagonism, but this was exacerbated by fears of the Mormons as a political or economic power. For details of some of the persecution, *see also* ANTI-MORMONISM; EXODUS; ILLINOIS PERIOD; MISSOURI PERIOD; NEW YORK PERIOD; OHIO PERIOD; UTAH PERIOD.

PETERSON, LEVI S. (1933–). Fiction writer and biographer. Born in Snowflake, Arizona, Peterson received a bachelor's and master's degree at Brigham Young University (q.v.) and a Ph.D. at the University of Utah in 1965. Since then he has taught English at Weber State University in Ogden, Utah, where he was director of the honors program. Peterson's short stories and novels almost always have Mormon characters, and a strong comic streak is present, most notably in *The Backslider*. The incongruities of the religious life in a secular world also produce scenes of tragedy. Two collections of short stories and a second novel, *Aspen Marooney*, have been well received. In 1988 Peterson published a biography of Juanita Brooks (q.v.), which won the Evans Biography Award.

PINEGAR, PATRICIA P. (1937–). Children, youth (q.v.), and women leader. Born in Cedar City, Utah, Patricia Peterson attended Brigham Young University (q.v.). She married Ed J. Pinegar, a dentist, and had eight children. She served as PTA president. In the Church she was ward Young Women president, ward Relief Society president, ward and stake Primary president, and member of the Primary general board (qq.v.). She served with her husband when he was president of the Missionary Training Center (q.v.) in Provo, Utah, and president of the England London South Mission. After serving as second counselor in the Young Women general presidency, she was called as general president in 1994.

PIONEER(S). 1. Anyone who clears the way or the original settlers of an area. 2. The specific company, then known as "the pioneer company," led by Brigham Young (q.v.) to go ahead of the others and establish the place of settlement in 1847. 3. All early settlers in the West. Needing to have a cut-off date for membership qualification, the Daughters of Utah Pioneers and Sons of Utah Pioneers specified 1869, when the railroad reached Utah, as the year before which the settlers were "pioneers."

4. Those who went out in a process of continuing colonization (q.v.) to establish settlements in adjacent states, in Mexico, in Canada, in the last two or three decades of the 19th century. 5. By extension, the original persons converted to Mormonism in any state or country, those who establish the foundation for Church growth there, are sometimes described as pioneers. In this sense there are 20th-century pioneers in different U.S. states, and in the Philippines, Korea, Thailand, France, Russia, and Nigeria. *See also* EXODUS.

PIONEER DAY. July 24. It was on this date in 1847 that Brigham Young (q.v.) emerged from the mountains, beheld the Salt Lake Valley and verified that it was indeed "the right place" for settlement. As early as 1849 Church members began celebrating the date as Pioneer Day.

Like other commemorations celebrating past events, Pioneer Day has always included a parade as well as speeches, picnics, and various kinds of recreation. Since it is a state holiday in Utah, the long parade has been expanded to include many high school bands, civic groups, politicians, U.S. military units, and different denominations. A strong Mormon tone remains in that many floats are sponsored by wards (q.v.) and the historical themes they commemorate have to do with Mormon history.

PLAN OF SALVATION. A view of the purpose of human life drawn from the standard works, especially the modern scriptures (q.v.). All humans naturally confront the questions "Where do I come from? Why am I here? Where am I going?" Mormons find their answers in the plan of salvation.

Essentially it consists of three acts or three phases of existence, each of which can be subdivided. First, the preexistence, or pre-mortal stage, during which all humans existed as spirit children of God. In a great council in heaven the Heavenly Father put forth a plan by which the spirits would come to earth. His firstborn son, Jesus Christ (q.v.), offered to come to earth to atone for the sins of the world and to be the first fruit of the resurrection (q.v.). All human beings born on earth accepted this plan in their pre-mortal state.

Born on earth, a veil of forgetfulness preventing any recollection of the prior existence, human beings enter a state in which two purposes are achieved. First, one gains a physical body. This is considered important in that it is this physical body that will be recovered at the time of resurrection (q.v.); without it the spirit could never obtain a "fullness of joy." Earth life is also a time of probation, a time in which to demonstrate one's real character, one's ability to withstand temptation or willingness to repent. On our own, so to speak, we show the kind of person we really are.

At death one enters the post-mortal phase of existence. Death is in essence the separation of the spirit from the body. The physical body, a mere shell, is placed in the grave and deteriorates. The spirit never ceases to exist. During a period it enters the spirit world, still conscious, still having awareness of one's self-identity. This is a time during which instruction, even missionary (q.v.) proselytizing, is provided for those who, through no fault of their own, never had the opportunity to hear the gospel (q.v.) during earth life.

Then come the resurrection and final judgment. Resurrection is the reuniting of the physical body (or the reassembled component elements of that body) and the spirit. By Christ's atonement it comes to all, regardless of goodness or badness of one's actions.

The judgment determines where one then goes, the ultimate reward or punishment. In revelations now compiled in the Doctrine and Covenants (Sections 76, 88) Joseph Smith (q.v.) described not a simple division into heaven or hell but a graded salvation. There were three kingdoms or glories. The lowest was the telestial kingdom, followed by the terrestrial and celestial kingdoms. Each kingdom was in turn subdivided into different levels. It is in the highest level of the celestial kingdom that the righteous regain the presence of God.

One other point should be mentioned. Eternal salvation is not basking in heavenly bliss or playing a harp. It includes continued activity and progression. Ultimately those who qualify at the highest level, in the eons to come, become coheirs with Christ and, joining God the Father in a heavenly aristocracy of character, even have the capacity to create worlds.

Understanding "the merciful plan of the great Creator" (Book of Mormon [q.v.]), Mormons do not see life as "a tale told by an idiot, full of sound and fury, signifying nothing" (Shakespeare, *Macbeth* 5.5).

PLURAL MARRIAGE. *See* POLYGAMY.

POLITICS. In general, Mormons proclaim loyalty to nation and acknowledge the inappropriateness of Church involvement in political matters. This basic stance is emphasized when the Church seeks permission for its missionaries (q.v.) to proselytize in a country. It is a good-faith statement and not a subterfuge. Still, historically, there have been countertendencies.

During the Illinois Period (q.v.) and later in territorial Utah where Mormons were the great majority of the population they might effectively control the government as well as the Church. This led to charges of "theocracy." A standard answer at the time was that people who chose to be represented by leaders of their own faith were only exercising their rights. The introduction of the national political parties prior to statehood, with Mormons in both parties, reduced fear of ecclesiastical domination.

Some few Mormons have been conscientious objectors in times of war, a position they are allowed to take individually but not while claiming Church support. A particularly awkward challenge (not unique to Mormonism) arose in Germany under Hitler. Practically all German Mormons fell in line with the führer's government and obeyed "the law of the land," but a few, notably three young men, joined to resist Nazism.

In the U.S. setting, while not endorsing candidates and scrupulously keeping meetinghouses out of bounds for political campaigning, the Church has felt free to make pronouncements in the area of morals. Election returns clearly show that all Mormons do not fall into line behind a Church position. For example, despite the recommendation of President Heber J. Grant (q.v.) a number of Church members voted with non-Mormons to repeal the prohibition amendment.

POLYGAMY. The practice by which an individual husband may take more than one wife, known technically as polygyny and more popularly as polygamy. Publicly announced in 1852, Mormon plural marriage was officially terminated when a Manifesto (q.v.) was issued by Church President Wilford Woodruff (q.v.) in 1890. Since only a minority of members practiced it even then, and remembering the spectacular growth in the late 20th century, it is obvious that only a very small percentage of all the Mormons who have ever lived practiced polygamy. Yet polygamy continues to be associated with Mormonism, and the work of scholars allows us to consider the subject in somewhat greater detail with respect to its origins, its extent, its success or failure, and its termination.

Origins. As the Church was organized in 1830, polygamy was not part of its practice. The revelation (q.v.) authorizing it is dated 12 July 1843, the year prior to Joseph Smith's (q.v.) death (Doctrine and Covenants, Section 132). There is some evidence that Smith considered the possibility as early as 1830–31, and it is probable that he married Fanny Alger as a second wife before leaving Kirtland in 1838. Nevertheless, it was in Nauvoo, Illinois, after 1842 that polygamy was privately introduced to some persons along with the new temple ordinances (qq.v.).

The original reaction was usually shock and rejection. But after personal struggle and prayer (q.v.)—on the part of Joseph Smith, his wife Emma, Hyrum Smith, other Apostles (qq.v.), their wives, and the women who became plural wives—a small number of Church leaders became polygamists. Since the practice was not publicly acknowledged, exact numbers are difficult to come by. As an educated guess, fewer than 100 began practicing polygamy before the departure of the Mormons from Nauvoo in early 1846.

Motives are difficult to determine with any confidence. Not surprisingly, critics of the practice have always assumed that lust was behind it. Clearly, however, Mormons saw it in a religious context. It was defended as a biblical practice that by specific divine authorization could again be allowed. It was part of "the restoration of all things."

Extent. How many Mormons were polygamous in the 19th century? As already indicated, practically none until 1843, after which a relatively small group of leaders were inducted into it. The practice was officially admitted and defended from 1852. Its formal termination, with the Manifesto (q.v.) of 1890, came 38 years later. Yet the evidence is not clear. At the end of the 19th century a figure sometimes heard was 2 percent of the population, but this estimate was disingenuous, for it included only polygamist males in the numerator, while the entire Church membership was the denominator.

Estimates for the late 19th century have varied between 10 and 30 percent. The higher figure refers to certain settlements or wards (q.v.) and includes in the numerator all children whose mothers were married, or had been married, to a polygamist male. Certainly a more accurate estimate for the entire Church population would be 15 or 20 percent, with variations from place to place and from decade to decade.

Even if 20 to 30 percent of Mormons were involved in polygamy in some way, that is still a minority of the population. Yet virtually all of the leadership—General Authorities, stake presidents, bishops (qq.v.)—were polygamists, and the practice loomed very large in the public perception of Mormons.

Success or Failure. Contemporary charges of miserable failure, portraying plural wives as chattels and the children as neglected waifs, are inaccurate. Likewise, glowing descriptions by some Mormon defenders of polygamy are too good to be true. The several hundred divorces (q.v.) granted to plural wives and approved by Brigham Young (q.v.) are sufficient evidence of some marital malfunction. The fact seems to be that the success of these marriages depended on the persons involved. Anecdotal evidence and diary accounts indicate that there could be cooperation and mutual support between the wives. Allegations to the contrary notwithstanding, children of plural marriages tended to be healthy and intelligent. On the other hand, there is no evading the inherent limitations of time and financial resources; a polygamist father could not give the same time and attention to wives and children as could a monogamist.

For purposes of discussion it might be suggested that polygamy was about as successful or unsuccessful as monogamy. A simple examination of divorce ratios is sufficient to prove that monogamy too varies greatly across a spectrum, ranging from beautiful harmony to disastrous breakdown, with most probably coming somewhere in between. Without knowing exact percentages, it could be suggested that something of the same sort was true of polygamy.

Termination. Succumbing to a determined antipolygamy campaign, Church President Wilford Woodruff issued a Manifesto in the fall of 1890. Often cited as the end of Mormon polygamy, the document itself did not claim so much. Its concluding words are: "And I now publicly declare that my advice to the Latter-day Saints is to refrain from contracting any marriage forbidden by the law of the land." It was not possible to make a clean break that would suddenly cause the system to vanish. The following points seem worthy of consideration:

1. Many husbands continued to support, live with, and have children by plural wives married before the Manifesto. While agreeing not to enter any new plural marriages they could not abandon those they already had even if a strict reading of the law seemed to require it. By a gentleman's agreement these were not prosecuted. Continuing to support wives and families (q.v.) seemed fair, and in time, if there were no new plural marriages, the system would die out.

2. Some new plural marriages, perhaps 100 to 300, were secretly performed between 1890 and 1904. Some of these were performed outside the boundaries of the United States, even on the high seas, where it was reasoned no law of the land made them illegal. Others used different forms of casuistry to justify their action: the Manifesto had only "recommended"; promises made under coercion need not be observed; the Manifesto was addressed "to whom it may concern" and it does not concern me. When the clandestine plural marriages following 1890 were uncovered during the hearings for the seating of Senator Reed Smoot (q.v.), a second manifesto was issued by Church President Joseph F. Smith (q.v.) in 1904 with a greater determination to enforce it.

3. Those who engaged in plural marriages performed after 1904 are the "Fundamentalists" (q.v.), who see themselves as adhering to the principle as taught by Joseph Smith and his successors. They are excommunicated (q.v.) when discovered.

See also UTAH PERIOD.

POLYNESIAN CULTURAL CENTER. A theme park located in Laie, Hawaii, on the island of Oahu. While providing employment to hundreds of Polynesian students at the campus of Brigham Young University–Hawaii (q.v.), the center also seeks to preserve and display different Polynesian cultural traditions through song, dance, and crafts. A major tourist attraction, the center is a nonprofit corporation. *See also* POLYNESIANS.

POLYNESIANS. Missionary (q.v.) proselytizing began as early as 1843 among some of the Polynesians and was resumed later in the 19th century. Each of the groups has its own history of pioneer (q.v.) conversions, persecutions (q.v.), and continuity. Although not clearly stated in the scriptures (q.v.), the idea is often expressed that Polynesians are heirs of the Abrahamic covenant by their descent from Book of Mormon (q.v.) peoples.

In addition to substantial numbers of Mormon Polynesians in New Zealand, Hawaii, Samoa, Tonga, and Tahiti, many have imigrated to other locations, such as Australia or the United States. *See also* PACIFIC.

PORTER, L. ALDIN (1931–). Businessman, Church leader. Born in Salt Lake City, Utah, Porter was raised in southeastern Idaho. After serving as a missionary (q.v.) in the west central States, he married Shirley Palmer and graduated from Brigham Young University (q.v.). An insurance agent in Boise, Idaho, he rose to become head of the agency. Church leadership experience included serving as bishop, stake president, regional representative, and counselor in the Boise temple presidency (qq.v.), and president of the Louisiana Baton Rouge Mission. In 1987 Porter became a member of the First Quorum of the Seventy (q.v.) and in 1992 a member of its presidency. The Porters have six children.

PRATT, ORSON (1811–1881). Mathematician, intellectual, Apostle. Born in Hartford, New York, on 19 September 1811, Pratt had little formal schooling but avidly pursued different subjects on his own.

In 1830 his older brother Parley P. Pratt (q.v.) taught him the new religion of Mormonism and baptized him. As was common at the time, Orson immediately went on a preaching mission. He participated in many of the experiences at Kirtland, Ohio, was a member of Zion's Camp (q.v.), and in 1835 at the age of 24 became one of the original members of the Quorum of the Twelve Apostles (q.v.). In 1836 he married Sarah Marinda Bates.

Pratt was one of the great missionaries (q.v.), traveling through the eastern states, Canada, Scotland, and England. Returning from England in 1841, he found a crisis. His wife had been introduced to polygamy (q.v.) in his absence. During much of 1842 Pratt was in turmoil, refusing to support Joseph Smith (q.v.) and the other Apostles on some matters. He and his wife were excommunicated in August. Before the year had ended they were rebaptized and Orson Pratt was again one of the Twelve.

After the Mormons were forced out of Nauvoo, Illinois, during the great move to the West, Pratt was in the pioneer (q.v.) party that led the way. One of a group of advance scouts, he entered the Salt Lake Valley on 21 July 1847, three days before Brigham Young (q.v.). He invented an odometer to measure the mileage during the trip and supervised the surveying of the new location after their arrival.

Somewhat of a philosopher and mathematician, Pratt was not working within the context of the major universities of the Victorian era. But on the Mormon frontier audiences found him interesting and stimulating as he gave lectures on subjects such as light and causation. Sometimes he went too far, or was too abstruse, for Brigham Young, who occasionally reprimanded him. In 1875 President Young declared that Pratt's position of seniority in the Twelve was determined not by his original ordination but by his readmission in 1842—which had the practical effect of putting Orson behind John Taylor (q.v.). Yet Young recognized Pratt's deep commitment to Mormonism and did not want to lose his services.

In addition to Sarah, Pratt had married four other wives before the move to the West. Two others were added later. Eventually he was the father of 45 children. Such personal involvement in plural marriage made Pratt the ideal choice as its defender. When the practice of polygamy was publicly announced in 1852, Pratt preached the main sermon and immediately began publishing *The Seer*, a periodical in Washington, D.C., dedicated to defending the practice. In 1870, when the prominent minister John P. Newman attacked polygamy, Pratt was designated to face him in a debate, the text of which was published in newspapers and as a pamphlet. *See also* OHIO PERIOD.

PRATT, PARLEY PARKER (1807–1857). Poet, missionary (q.v.), Apostle. Born in Otsego County, New York, Parley Pratt married Thankful Halsey in 1827 and moved to Ohio. Having been a Baptist, he became a follower of Sidney Rigdon's (q.v.) brand of the Campbellites. In 1830 he sold out and with his wife traveled to New York. Leaving her on a canal boat to continue their intended journey, he suddenly left her to go on his own for a while, explaining that he felt strongly that there was some special work for him in that part of the country. There he first saw the Book of Mormon (q.v.). After reading it with enthusiasm, he traveled to the Palmyra area, met Hyrum Smith (q.v.), and was soon baptized.

With Oliver Cowdery (q.v.) he was called on a mission to the Indians in Missouri (Doctrine and Covenants, section 32). During the journey, they stopped at Kirtland, Ohio, and introduced Mormonism to Sidney Rigdon, who earlier had been Pratt's minister, and his congregation. The conversion of Rigdon and most of his congregation paved the way for the establishment of a new center for the Church. Continuing on to Missouri, Pratt and his travel companions made contact with the Indians and, more important historically, provided the information leading to the declaration of Missouri as the new Zion (q.v.).

During the remainder of the 1830s Parley Pratt and his family (q.v.) were in the middle of most of the most exciting and trying events of early Mormon history. They were driven from Jackson County, Missouri, in 1833. In 1834 he served in Zion's Camp (q.v.). In 1835 he was named one of the original members of the Quorum of the Twelve Apostles (q.v.).

He served on many missions, including one to Canada and in 1840 to England. There he edited the *Millennial Star* (q.v.). His literary skills were also employed in the writing of pamphlets like *Voice of Warning* (1837). His hymns were among the most popular in Mormon worship, including "An Angel from on High," "Jesus, Once of Humble Birth," and "The Morning Breaks, The Shadows Flee."

After the Mormons moved west to Utah, Pratt assisted in drafting a constitution. He served in the territorial legislature. Much of his time was taken in settling and providing for his families. His wife Thankful had died in 1837, after which he married Mary Ann Frost. Then starting in 1843 he took plural wives and eventually became the father of 30 children.

The last of these plural wives, Eleanor McComb McLean, had not been legally divorced from her husband, an alcoholic in San Francisco. McLean, the father, kept the children and took them to Arkansas. A nasty custody suit followed. Pratt was attempting to recover Eleanor's children when he was charged with alienation of affection, acquitted, and murdered. He had been trying to return to Utah by joining an immigration company when McLean overtook him, stabbed him twice, and shot him in the neck. Pratt was unarmed.

Although just 50 years old at the time of his death in 1857, Parley P. Pratt had made important contributions during Mormonism's first generation. His autobiography, prepared from unpublished manuscripts, was later published and is considered a classic. *See also* OHIO PERIOD.

PRAYER. A basic part of Mormon religious practice on the individual and group level. Individually a devout Mormon approaches God in prayer evening and morning as well as any other time there is a special need or desire. Family (q.v.) prayers are pronounced, often twice daily. A prayer of blessing and thanks is uttered at mealtime. All Church meetings are started and ended with prayers, known respectively as invocations and benedictions.

Except for the sacrament and baptism (qq.v.), fixed or written prayers are not used. Although standard usage includes addressing God at the beginning of the prayer and saying "in the name of Jesus Christ (q.v.)" at the end, the prayer should otherwise come from the heart and be appropriate for the occasion.

PRESIDENT. A common title in the Church organization, referring to the person who stands at the head. Thus there is a president of a stake (q.v.), of priesthood quorums (q.v.), and of such auxiliary organizations as Primary, Sunday School, Young Men, and Young Women on the ward, stake, and general level (qq.v.). Although the head of the ward is a bishop (q.v.), a congregation not yet large enough to achieve ward status is led by a branch president. Each of the 276 missions is presided over by a mission president.

The president of the Church stands at the head of the whole Church on earth, although the real head is regarded as Jesus Christ (q.v.). In addition to his title of president, the Church president is sustained as "prophet (q.v.), seer, and revelator" and is often referred to as "the prophet." He is the presiding high priest (q.v.) of the Church and holds all the keys, or authority, for its functioning on earth.

One characteristic of Mormon organization is that each of these presidents is assisted by two counselors (q.v.), the three of them constituting a presidency. Clerks or secretaries as needed also assist.

The term is regularly used as the accepted form of address for the president of the Church and presidents of stakes and missions. Although not improper for the others holding the title, they are more commonly addressed as brother or sister (q.v.).

PRESIDING BISHOP. One of the General Authorities (q.v.) of the Church. The Presiding Bishop and his two counselors (q.v.) form the Presiding Bishopric. Unlike other bishoprics, with responsibility for a single ward (q.v.), the Presiding Bishopric oversees the entire Church.

Under the direction of the president (q.v.) of the Church, the Presiding Bishop and his counselors exercise specific responsibility over receiving tithing (q.v.) and other income, helping the poor, planning and erecting buildings, and maintaining membership (q.v.) records. In addition the Presiding Bishopric has had responsibility for the Aaronic Priesthood (q.v.), the young men from 12 to 18 years of age, and even for young women of the same age. In 1977 these were officially assigned to the presidency of the Young Men and Young Women (qq.v.).

The rapid growth of Church membership led to an expansion of duties in 1977. To assist the Presiding Bishop in the different areas local directors for temporal affairs were established. After 1986 Area (q.v.) Presidencies supervised the local Area directors, with the Presiding Bishopric providing training, planning, and technical support.

PRIEST. An office in the Aaronic Priesthood (q.v.). Eligible for ordination as priests at age 16, young men (q.v.) thereby acquire authority to perform not only the functions of deacons and teachers (qq.v.) but, in addition, to baptize, administer the sacrament (q.v.), ordain other priests, teachers, and deacons under the direction of their bishop (q.v.). This is the highest office of the Aaronic Priesthood.

The priests in a ward are organized in a quorum (qq.v.) of 48 or fewer. Their president is the ward bishop, with two priests serving as counselors (q.v.). They meet regularly on Sundays with an adult adviser for study and training. In principle they are preparing for the Melchizedek Priesthood and missionary service (qq.v.).

PRIESTHOOD. The power or authority of God granted to mankind to act in his holy name. Different from a blessing or a diffuse approbation by

God, Priesthood must be specifically received by ordination from someone who holds it. It is not, therefore, a right that one arrogates to himself and not the prerogative of every baptized believer.

For the restoration (q.v.) of the Church to be efficacious, the authority to act in God's name had to be restored, which Joseph Smith (q.v.) described as having occurred by means of heavenly messengers. A church without such authority, or where the founder simply decides to work on his own, is an empty shell. Baptisms or any of the other ordinances (qq.v.) performed without priesthood authority lack the essential ingredient that makes them efficacious.

While insisting on the indispensability of Priesthood, Mormons do not connect it with professional preparation in divinity school. It is widely distributed by the ordination of every worthy male 12 years of age and older.

The two major divisions are the Aaronic Priesthood and Melchizedek Priesthood (qq.v.). In the Aaronic Priesthood are three offices: deacon, for which one is eligible at age 12; teacher, at age 14; and priest, at age 16 (qq.v.). Each of these has specific rights and prerogatives; for example, one may pass the sacrament (q.v.) to the congregation as a deacon, but not until becoming a priest may one perform baptisms.

At age 18 one is eligible to be ordained an elder (q.v.) in the Melchizedek Priesthood. All male missionaries (q.v.) are elders. Later, depending on responsibilities, one may be ordained a high priest (q.v.).

In each ward (q.v.) during Priesthood meeting there are separate classes for the different offices: deacon, teacher, priest, elder, high priest.

Two important qualifications limit Priesthood claims by any individual. First, God will recognize those things done in his name only to the extent that they are done in righteousness. Priesthood must not be used as an excuse for intimidation or unkindness. Second, in practice one exercises the Priesthood authority under the direction of ecclesiastical superiors, who possess the keys, or authority, of administration. Thus before performing a baptism, one must have approval from one's file leader. *See also* ARTICLES OF FAITH, 5.

PRIMARY. Organization for children under the age of 12. Founded in 1878 when Aurelia Spencer Rogers received approval from Church leaders, Primary soon spread to other wards (q.v.) and settlements.

A general presidency of three women began to supervise the different Primaries in the 1890s. In 1902 they began publication of *The Children's Friend*, a magazine containing lessons as well as stories and pictures to interest children. A program of sequential classes—with manuals, goals, and badges for achievement—was organized for both boys and girls.

In 1980 Primary meetings were moved from weekdays to Sunday. Through classes and discussion, by participation in prayer (q.v.) and singing, children learn principles that prepare them for baptism and, in the case of the boys, Priesthood (qq.v.) ordination at age 12.

PROPHECY. Statements inspired by God. Although often thought to refer specifically to the future, prophecy as found in the Bible (q.v.) often referred to the present. Prophecy, expressing God's will and warning, is found in the Bible, in other scriptures, in statements from Joseph Smith (qq.v.) and other prophets (q.v.) down to the present.

PROPHET. One who legitimately transmits the will of God to the human race. Somehow a prophet must have been designated by God and be the recipient of divine communications. The Biblical prophets are the prototypes. Part of the restoration (q.v.) that was Mormonism was the reappearance of prophets.

In a general sense all have access to this heavenly gift, for "the testimony of Jesus is the spirit of prophecy" (Rev. 19:10). More specifically, however, the title is reserved to those who are God's designated spokespersons on earth. In Mormon usage, all of the Apostles are "prophets, seers, and revelators" but it is the president (q.v.) of the Church who specifically holds the keys of authority during his administration. It is he who is sometimes called simply "the prophet." The word designates not his administrative role, that of president, but his closeness to God, his capability and responsibility to convey God's message to Church members and all mankind. Not only is he endowed with this authority by being specially set apart by the other Apostles, but also he is sustained by the uplifted hand of members throughout the Church, who thus testify that they accept him in the prophetic role.

From the time of prophet Joseph Smith to the present, Mormon leaders have worn the prophetic mantle. The title does not imply divinity or sainthood in the traditional sense of the word; as human beings prophets are not worshiped, but faithful Latter-day Saints listen to their counsel with great respect. A common injunction, expressed in a song for children, is "Follow the prophet."

PROTESTANTISM. Some consider Protestants to be all Christian churches that are not Roman Catholic or Greek Orthodox. During the

Protestant Reformation of the 16th century mainstream, or magisterial, Protestants included Lutherans, Calvinists, and Anglicans, each with different subgroups. Common principles were said to include salvation by faith, the unique authority of the Bible (q.v.), the priesthood (q.v.) of all believers, and the two sacraments of baptism (qq.v.) and the Eucharist. But even these main groups could not agree on everything, as witness Zwingli and Luther denouncing each other's view of the Eucharist.

More radical 16th-century Protestants, including the Anabaptists, were rejected and persecuted by Catholics and mainstream Protestants alike. As everyone knows, new groups came into existence later, notably Baptists and Methodists, and with new organizations and repeated division and subdivision, by the 20th century there were hundreds of churches.

Mormons are not Protestants. They do not trace their origin to the Protestant Reformation. Sometimes they emphasize their belief in a *restoration* (q.v.) as opposed to a *reformation*, but this ignores the existence of Protestant restorationism. Each of the so-called Protestant principles—salvation by faith alone, the inerrancy and sufficiency of the Bible—would be found unacceptable by Mormons, but of course many Protestants now also find these slogans to be inadequate.

The major premise that all Christianity (q.v.) is divided between Catholics and Protestants, followed by the minor premise that Mormons are neither Catholic nor Protestant, leads inevitably to the conclusion that they are not part of Christianity. Mormons see themselves as neither Catholic nor Protestant but decidedly Christian, even uniquely faithful to the purity of original Christianity.

Theological distinctions notwithstanding, Mormons have much in common with many Protestants in worship, lifestyle, and social agenda. Mormon and Protestant congregations have occasionally been able to cooperate, help one another, and achieve mutual respect.

PUBLIC AFFAIRS. The department responsible for disseminating information about the Church to media. News releases are prepared about programs and events. Radio and television programs are also produced.

In addition to the central office at Church headquarters, area (q.v.) offices with full-time directors have been established in such major cities as Washington, D.C., Toronto, and London. More than 3,500 local public affairs directors on the level of stakes (q.v.) and missions are coordinated from the central and regional offices.

-Q-

QUORUM. Designation for different governing or priesthood (q.v.) units in the Church organization. Thus the quorum of the First Presidency, the Quorum of the Twelve Apostles, the First Quorum of the Seventy, the Second Quorum of the Seventy (qq.v.).

On the level of ordinary Church members living in wards and stakes (qq.v.), when a male receives the priesthood, he enters a quorum for the particular office to which he is ordained: deacon, teacher, priest, elder, or high priest (qq.v.). Quorum meetings are held regularly.

QUORUM OF THE TWELVE APOSTLES. *See* TWELVE APOSTLES; GENERAL AUTHORITIES.

-R-

RECOMMEND. A certificate of worthiness (q.v.) necessary for entrance into the temples (q.v.). A searching interview by one's bishop (q.v.) determines one's faithfulness to commitments and attitude toward the Church and its leaders. A follow-up interview is conducted by a member of the stake (q.v.) presidency.

A similar determination of worthiness, although not resulting in a signed certificate, is made prior to being called as a missionary (q.v.) or to fill different positions of responsibility.

REFERRAL. The name of a person who has shown an interest in the Church that is turned over to the missionaries (q.v.), who then attempt to schedule meetings for teaching the gospel (q.v.) prior to conversion and baptism (q.v.). Church members are encouraged to explore such a possibility with friends and family (q.v.). Otherwise missionaries have to rely on random door knocking or other inefficient and tedious methods of finding people willing to investigate Mormonism. Growth of the Church has been most spectacular in areas where members have been diligent in making referrals.

REGION. A grouping of several stakes (q.v.). Smaller than an area (q.v.), the region is an intermediate level. *See also* REGIONAL REPRESENTATIVES.

REGIONAL REPRESENTATIVES. Leaders holding the Priesthood (q.v.) and called to provide supervision over regions (q.v.). They trained local leaders and visited conferences in the region, but were not considered General Authorities (q.v.). In 1995, this position was discontinued and replaced with that of Area (q.v.) Authority.

RELIEF SOCIETY. Women's organization of the Church. One of the auxiliary (q.v.) organizations.

Organized in Nauvoo, Illinois, in 1842, with Emma Smith, wife of Joseph Smith (qq.v.), as first president (q.v.), the Female Relief Society, as it was first called, performed charitable service and solicited contributions. Joseph Smith explained that it was essential to the completeness of the Church. By 1844 it had reached a membership of 1,341.

With the death of Joseph Smith in June 1844 and the subsequent turmoil and exodus (q.v.), the Relief Society suspended official operations. Women worked and met together on occasion, but not until 1854 did Brigham Young (q.v.) initiate a society to make clothing for Indian women and children. In 1866 the Relief Society was reorganized with Eliza R. Snow (q.v.) as president.

During the last generation of the 19th century the society responded to a call from Church leaders by raising silk worms in the effort to establish sericulture. A grain storage program was organized. Nurses, midwives, and even doctors were selected, and money was raised to assist in their training. The organization founded and operated a hospital. Relief Society women were outspoken in defending Mormonism and in agitating for female suffrage. A semimonthly publication, *Woman's Exponent*, provided instruction and inspiration. Two of the organization's prominent leaders were Eliza R. Snow and Emmeline B. Wells (q.v.).

In the 20th century the Relief Society expanded its educational role. Through the *Relief Society Magazine* (q.v.) lesson materials were provided in theological, cultural, and homemaking areas. Some Relief Society leaders having been professionally trained as teachers, psychologists, and social workers, it was natural for the organization to enlarge its role in child placement, in cooperation with other agencies, and to sponsor health clinics. As the Welfare Program (q.v.) got under way during the 1930s, Relief Society presidents throughout the Church worked in close cooperation with ward bishops (qq.v.).

For many years Relief Society women studied courses in literature (q.v.) and comparative cultures, but this has been superseded by greater emphasis on spiritual training. Homemaking, considered broadly, continues to be a central part of the society's program. The voluntary membership and dues requirement was replaced in 1971 by automatic membership for all Mormon women. One of the central features of the organization, whose origins go back to Nauvoo, continues to be the visiting teaching (q.v.) program, with each adult female member of the Church—all of whom are members of the Relief Society—receiving regular visits, support, and needed compassionate service.

Although conservative in opposing the Equal Rights Amendment and promoting the home as a primary area of woman's responsibility, the organization has tried to meet the many needs of its members. The increasingly diverse life patterns of women in the United States combined with the growth of the Church abroad have combined to present major challenges. In 1992, the sesquicentennial year of its organization, the Society announced that each ward unit would undertake a community service or literacy project.

Remembering the number of stakes (q.v.) and wards in the Church, one notes that thousands of women are receiving administrative, teaching, and service experience. Passivity or timidity have not been the characteristics of this dynamic organization. Its motto from the beginning has been "Charity never faileth." *See also* MEMBERSHIP; VISITING TEACHING.

RELIEF SOCIETY **MAGAZINE.** Monthly magazine published by the Relief Society (q.v.) from 1915 to 1970. Intended to reflect and serve the women of the Church, it included reports on Relief Society activities, recipes, articles, and addresses given at the annual Relief Society conference. Creativity was encouraged by the publication of poetry and short stories as well as annual contests. Lessons supporting the wide-ranging courses of study were published on religion, art, social science, and literature (q.v.). The magazine had 301,000 subscribers in 1970, when it was terminated.

REORGANIZED CHURCH OF JESUS CHRIST OF LATTER DAY SAINTS (RLDS). A church that came into existence after the middle of the 19th century as an alternative to The Church of Jesus Christ of Latter-day Saints then led by Brigham Young (qq.v.). In the aftermath of the death of Joseph Smith (q.v.) some fragmentation occurred as different groups put forth claims. Most remained small and later disappeared. The RLDS Church continues and, though small by comparison—

approximately 250,000 versus 10 million plus—expresses an alternative vision of the Restoration (q.v.).

The departure of the main body of the Church for the West after their expulsion from Nauvoo, Illinois, left a minority of scattered Mormons who needed more time to prepare, followed one or another rival claimant, apostatized, or had not made up their minds what to do. By 1851–52 Jason W. Briggs and Zenos H. Gurley Sr. were rallying followers in Wisconsin. In addition to rejecting the leadership of the Quorum of the Twelve Apostles and Brigham Young (qq.v.), who had been ordained president (q.v.) of the Church in late 1847, Briggs and Gurley looked forward to the time when "young Joseph," the prophet's (q.v.) son, could take the leadership.

It was on 6 April 1860 that Joseph Smith III traveled to Amboy, Illinois, and accepted the position of prophet and president of the Reorganized Church of Jesus Christ of Latter Day Saints. (In addition to the adjective at the front, this designation omits the hyphen used by the main group of Latter-day Saints.)

From its beginning the RLDS Church disassociated itself from its larger rival. Not only was the practice of polygamy (q.v.) forbidden but the fact, now well established, that Joseph Smith had introduced it was denied. Other practices characteristic of early Mormonism, such as the gathering (q.v.), were abandoned. The ceremonies of the temples (q.v.) were rejected. (Actually for many generations the RLDS people looked forward to the construction of a temple in Independence, Missouri, as the founding prophet (q.v.) had foretold, but when it was completed in 1993 it became a place of worship and education "dedicated to the pursuit of peace" with no special temple rituals being practiced.)

In 1881 headquarters was established at Lamoni, Iowa, where in 1895 Graceland College was created. (A liberal arts college, Graceland had an enrollment of 1,163 on the main campus in the fall of 1998, with 2,500 in satellite programs elsewhere.) When Joseph Smith III died in 1914, three of his sons in a row succeeded to the presidency, followed by a grandson. Then the commitment to lineal succession was forsaken. Currently the RLDS Church is led by W. Grant McMurray (q.v.).

Through most of its existence the RLDS Church tried to draw sharp distinctions between themselves and the LDS Church, on the one hand, and Protestantism (q.v.) on the other. However, beginning in the 1960s the RLDS Church began to identify itself more with mainstream Christianity (q.v.) in its liberal or progressive forms. This tendency has required soul-searching and redefinition. A 1970 report entitled *Exploring the*

Faith discusses many topics that would be readily subscribed to by other Christians while at the same time trying to maintain some of the original Mormon distinctiveness.

"Inspired declarations" from the RLDS Church president have been issued from time to time. On this basis Blacks were ordained to the priesthood (1865), polygamists in Asia and Africa (qq.v.) were allowed to join the Church if they would not take on more wives (1972), women were ordained to the priesthood (1984), and the temple was announced (1984) and subsequently completed. These last two issues have turned out to be quite divisive, as some congregations have disaffiliated from the RLDS Church. The majority, however, have accepted the changes as part of a positive redefinition. *See also* EXODUS.

REPENTANCE. One of the first principles of the gospel (q.v.). When Peter was asked by his listeners what they should do, thus demonstrating their faith, he replied, "Repent, and be baptized every one of you in the name of Jesus Christ (q.v.) for the remission of sins, and ye shall receive the gift of the Holy Ghost" (Acts 2:38). Since faith and repentance precede baptism (q.v.), Mormons do not baptize infants. There is no prescribed ritual such as penance, but Mormon writers, echoing a centuries-old Christian description, have said that proper repentance includes recognition, remorse, confession to proper Church authorities, and restitution where possible. With most humans the need for repentance continues throughout life. *See also* ARTICLES OF FAITH, 5.

RESTORATION. The basic idea of bringing back something that was there before. In Christian religious thought, the bringing back of the beliefs and practices of original Christianity (q.v.).

Mormons are restorationists. Joseph Smith (q.v.) sought to bring back the organization of the primitive Christian church and the true doctrines that had been lost during a Great Apostasy (q.v.). Unlike some other restorationists, he also brought back such Old Testament concepts and usages as Zion, polygamy, and temples (qq.v.). Of central importance to the restoration as Smith conceived it was the appearance of heavenly beings and the actual transmission of the keys of authority from previous dispensations to the present. It was not to be a scholarly enterprise but one infused with divine power.

All of Mormonism is not summed up by the idea of restoration. The reestablishment of prophets (q.v.), who would be the recipients of continuing revelation (q.v.), meant that a direct channel of communication existed between God and the human race.

RESURRECTION. The reuniting of the spirit with the physical body. The spirit of individual humans is indestructible. It could live forever, a disembodied presence, but never could it thus obtain a fullness of joy. It was Jesus Christ (q.v.) who broke the bonds of death by his own resurrection and then made possible the resurrection of the entire human race.

Resurrection comes to all, good and evil, thanks to the atoning sacrifice of Jesus Christ. Without pretending to know the exact mechanism by which it is accomplished, Mormons believe in a physical and literal resurrection, first of Jesus, then of others, ultimately of the entire human race.

REVELATION. Communication from God. While accepting the Bible (q.v.) as scripture (q.v.) and thus God's word to the human race, Mormons usually use the term *revelation* to describe not the written scriptures but additional heavenly manifestations.

The First Vision of Joseph Smith (qq.v.) was an example of such revelation. Angelic messengers from God appeared to Smith on many occasions. Communications have sometimes come in dreams, as in the Bible. Probably the most common form of divine revelation is by means of "the still small voice," the whisperings of the Holy Spirit.

Rejecting the idea that such miraculous intervention was limited to biblical times, Mormons are strongly convinced of the importance of "continuing revelation."

Who is eligible to receive revelation from God? Here two principles must be kept in salutary tension. On the one hand, all may petition God for guidance. Especially after baptism and confirmation (qq.v.), Church members, if worthy, may enjoy the constant companionship of the Holy Ghost, which includes promptings to assist in decisions. On occasion individuals may receive more dramatic manifestations. Such revelation is available for one's personal needs or responsibility, as parent in a family (q.v.), as bishop (q.v.) over a congregation, and the like.

On the other hand, guidance for the entire Church comes through the president and other General Authorities (qq.v.). The First Presidency and the Quorum of the Twelve Apostles (qq.v.) are sustained by approving vote of the membership as "prophets (q.v.), seers, and revelators." The instruction that comes from these leaders, especially the current president (q.v.), is considered to have the same status as the canonical scriptures. Church members are urged to read the conference addresses as they are published in the *Ensign* (q.v.) twice a year and apply them to their lives. Members are also to seek personal manifestation to confirm that these messages come from God and to show how they may be applied.

What might appear to be anarchic decentralization, with everyone having access to the divine source, is in fact qualified by a subsidiarity principle. Divine guidance for the whole Church comes to the president. Guidance for a congregation may come to its bishop, guidance for a family to its mother or father. *See also* ARTICLES OF FAITH, 9.

REYNOLDS, SYDNEY S. (1943–). First counselor in general presidency of the Primary (qq.v.), 1999– . After growing up in Burbank, California, she attended Brigham Young University (q.v.), where she earned a bachelor's degree in history with a minor in political science and a teaching certificate in secondary education. She married educator and scholar Noel B. Reynolds in 1965. They have 11 children. In addition to community service as president of PTA and member of the steering committee for women's conference, she has filled many church callings (q.v.): seminary teacher, ward Relief Society (qq.v.) president, ward and stake Young Women (qq.v.) president, Primary (q.v.) general board member, teacher.

RICHARDS, LEGRAND (1886–1983). Businessman, Presiding Bishop (q.v.), Apostle. Born in Farmington, Utah, LeGrand Richards spent much of his early life in Tooele, Utah, where his father, George F. Richards, was stake (q.v.) president (q.v.). George F. went on to become one of the Twelve Apostles (q.v.) in 1906.

Much of LeGrand's early years were spent in farming. He graduated from the eighth grade in 1901. Then he attended business college in Salt Lake City. In 1905 he departed on a mission to the Netherlands. Upon his return in 1908 he met Ina Ashton, whom he married the following year.

After about a year of employment in Portland, Oregon, the young family (q.v.) returned to Salt Lake City, where he worked for a lumber company. Then he was called to be president of the Netherlands Mission, serving from 1913 to 1916.

Back in Salt Lake City, Richards founded a realty company. He became bishop of his Sugar House ward (qq.v.) during several years of the 1920s. Then, after a short-term mission in the East, he moved his family to Glendale, California. After serving as bishop of the Glendale Ward he became president of the Hollywood Stake (q.v.). In 1934 he was called to be president of the Southern States Mission.

After returning to Utah in 1937, Richards again established a real estate business, briefly became bishop of the University Ward, and in 1938 was called to be the Church's Presiding Bishop.

For the remainder of his life LeGrand Richards was one of the General Authorities (q.v.) of the Church. As Presiding Bishop he was responsible generally for "temporal affairs" but also for the young men of the Aaronic Priesthood (qq.v.). Procedures were modernized, record keeping improved, a major building program launched.

In 1954 he became a member of the Quorum of the Twelve Apostles (q.v.). In the many conferences he visited and twice a year in general conferences (q.v.) he addressed the people, urging them to live their religion, bearing testimony to his faith. A personable man with an enthusiastic preaching style, he was much appreciated by Church members.

Perhaps the accomplishment that touched more people than any other was his book. As a mission president in the southern states he had prepared a topical plan to assist his missionaries (q.v.) in teaching Mormonism. Responding to requests he expanded on his earlier plan and in 1950 published *A Marvelous Work and a Wonder*, a presentation of Mormonism on the introductory level, buttressed by scriptural passages that he had used from the time he was a young missionary in Holland. The book went through many editions, and its proceeds were consecrated to the missionary program.

In declining health, LeGrand Richards lost his wife, Ina, in late 1977. Continually alert, retaining his enthusiasm and sense of humor, he lived on until 1983.

RICKS COLLEGE. Two-year accredited college at Rexburg, Idaho, owned by the Church. Originally the Bannock Academy, one of several stake (q.v.) academies at the time, the institution was renamed after stake president (q.v.) Thomas E. Ricks in 1903. It was once a relatively small school of fewer than 200 students, but attendance at Ricks College had expanded to 5,150 by 1971.

With 7,500 students (its ceiling) and 300 faculty, Ricks offers liberal arts training and programs in nursing, agriculture, and other technical areas. Many of its students go on to complete bachelor's degrees at four-year institutions.

The students come from all 50 states and 30 different foreign countries. They take one religion class each semester along with the usual academic subjects. For their religious and social needs they are divided into about 40 student wards (q.v.). In June 2000, it was announced that Ricks would become a four-year college and would be renamed Brigham Young University–Idaho.

RIGDON, SIDNEY (1793–1876). Prominent early Mormon leader and associate of Joseph Smith (q.v.). Born on 19 February 1793 near Pittsburgh, Pennsylvania, Sidney experienced a Christian conversion as a young man and became a Baptist preacher. He married Phebe Brooks. His popular preaching style made his First Baptist Church one of the largest in Pittsburgh.

Rigdon was one of those in his generation who longed for the purity of early Christianity (q.v.). He became connected with the Mahoning Baptist Association, which included among its leaders Alexander Campbell and Walter Scott, who would soon found the Disciples of Christ. Rigdon did not follow them, however, but instead pastored a congregation in Mentor, Ohio, and among his parishioners formed a communal society called "the Family."

In October 1830 four Mormon missionaries (q.v.) came to Ohio, including Parley P. Pratt (q.v.), whom Rigdon had converted to the Reformed Baptist faith. After hearing their message and reading the Book of Mormon (q.v.), Rigdon accepted baptism (q.v.). Perhaps a hundred of his congregation followed him into Mormonism. He traveled to Fayette, New York, met Joseph Smith (q.v.), and soon was assisting the prophet (q.v.) as a scribe.

During the Ohio Period, Missouri Period, and Illinois Period (qq.v.) of Mormon history Rigdon was a prominent figure. He participated with Joseph Smith in the great revelation (q.v.) on the graded salvation of souls after death (Doctrine and Covenants, section 76). He became a counselor in the First Presidency (qq.v.). He taught classes in Kirtland and assisted in preparing a series of "Lectures on Faith." In Illinois he served on the Nauvoo City Council and as postmaster. When Joseph Smith declared his candidacy for president of the United States, Rigdon became the vice-presidential candidate.

Despite this prominence, Rigdon was not always stable. In 1832 when he and Smith were seized by a mob and tarred and feathered, he suffered head injuries and perhaps never fully recovered. Whatever the reason, he could be an unsettling influence. In Missouri he gave two inflammatory sermons that exacerbated the ill will already present. Upon the death of Joseph Smith in June 1844, he rushed from Pittsburgh and offered himself as "guardian" of the Church. By this time, however, the steadier hand of Brigham Young (q.v.) had demonstrated itself, and the Church members voted in favor of Young and the Twelve Apostles (q.v.) over Rigdon.

Rigdon lived for 32 more years, but they were anticlimactic. He established a Church of Christ in Pennsylvania, but it soon fizzled. In 1863, living in Freedom, New York, he founded the Church of Jesus Christ of the Children of Zion, but it too proved short-lived.

A common charge from anti-Mormons was that Rigdon was the real brains behind Mormonism, that he provided the theology, that he had written or at least transmitted to Joseph Smith the transcript that became the Book of Mormon. None of this holds up. He made important contributions during the first 14 years of Mormonism and then, somewhat pathetically, went his separate way.

ROBERTS, BRIGHAM HENRY (1857–1933). Missionary (q.v.), newspaper editor, politician, General Authority (q.v.). Born in England, Roberts immigrated to Utah as a boy and worked on farms, in mines, and in a blacksmith shop. Possessed of a powerful drive for self-improvement, he read voraciously and graduated from the territorial University of Deseret.

At age 21 he married Sarah Louisa Smith; six years later he took a second wife and six years after that, a third. Employment included school and working as a journalist. Church assignments included missions in the United States and Great Britain. From 1888 he was a General Authority, a member of the First Council of the Seventy (q.v.).

Politically Roberts became a Democrat during the 1890s when national parties came to Utah. He served in the convention that drafted a constitution for the new state. After losing a close race for the House of Representatives in 1895, he was elected in 1898, only to become the center of a storm of controversy as a national campaign was organized to oppose seating him. After hearings he was denied his seat on the grounds of his being a polygamist. For the remainder of his life he continued to be an outspoken Democrat.

Although lacking the advanced degrees that have come to be considered essential in the 20th century, Roberts had a brilliant mind and a forceful prose style. His works of apologetics included defenses of the Book of Mormon and of Brigham Young as Joseph Smith's (qq.v.) lawful successor. As a historian he compiled a massive, multivolume source collection (Joseph Smith, *History of the Church of Jesus Christ of Latter-day Saints*) and wrote a magisterial narrative history in six volumes (*Comprehensive History of the Church*) that, even with its flaws, retains its value.

A surviving set of notes on some problems that had been raised about the claims of the Book of Mormon, with reflections and reactions by Roberts, were published as B. H. Roberts, *Studies of the Book of Mormon.* Some have seen these as proof that he had privately lost his faith in the Mormon scripture (q.v.), about which he had earlier written eloquent and voluminous defenses. But his continued willingness to accept Church callings (q.v.), including the presidency of the Eastern States Mission, and later fervent testimony (q.v.) of the Book of Mormon, make it more likely that the unpublished notes were tentative, exploratory, or intended to provoke answers rather than his own definitive faith statement.

ROBERTSON, LEROY JASPER (1896–1971). Musician, composer. Born on 21 December 1896 in Fountain Green, Utah, Robertson grew up on a farm and received his primary schooling locally. He showed musical aptitude but had little opportunity for formal training. He was sent to Provo to attend Brigham Young High School, after which he attended the Boston Music Center, graduating in 1923.

Robertson became a professor of music (q.v.) at Brigham Young University (q.v.) in 1925. While there he continued his own formal training, receiving his A.B. and M.A. in music. In 1948 he accepted the chairmanship of the music department at the University of Utah. By determination he persisted in the pursuit of a doctorate, receiving the Ph.D. from the University of Southern California in 1954. He retired in 1964.

Robertson was a serious composer. Among his compositions an overture won first prize in a 1923 competition, a quintet for piano and string won first place in 1936, and *Trilogy* won the coveted Reichhold award in 1947. His compositions were performed by many symphony orchestras and chamber groups in both Europe (q.v.) and the United States. In 1952 he completed an oratorio based on the Book of Mormon (q.v.); its recording was pronounced by critic Lowell Durham to be perhaps the high point in serious music among the Mormons. Robertson also contributed several works to the Church hymnal.

ROCKWELL, ORRIN PORTER (1813–1878). Joseph Smith's (q.v.) bodyguard, hotelier, deputy sheriff. A neighbor of the Joseph Smith family (q.v.) near Palmyra, New York, Rockwell joined the Church at age 17 or 18. He followed the course of the Mormons to Ohio and Missouri and finally to Nauvoo, where in 1840 he became one of Smith's bodyguards. The Mormon leader felt threatened by enemies within the Church as well as by non-Mormon opponents in Illinois and especially in Missouri. In 1842 Rockwell was caught in Missouri and arrested for the attempted murder of Governor Lilburn Boggs, who had issued an extermination order against the Mormons. Unable to convict him, the Missouri court released him after eight months.

After the murder of Joseph and Hyrum Smith (q.v.), Rockwell participated in the defense of Nauvoo. He shot and killed an anti-Mormon leader named Franklin Worrell. During the migration to the West, he was a guide and hunter.

In Utah he was a deputy sheriff. He established a Pony Express station and hotel and raised horses. For several years he refused to cut his hair (claiming a promise from Joseph Smith that no harm would befall him if he let his hair grow). Just how many men were victims of his weapons is difficult to determine, for he became a popular folk hero; rumors and unconfirmed stories circulated. Sometimes he was called "the Destroying Angel" of Mormonism. In 1877 he was arrested and charged with a murder that had taken place in 1858, but he died before the trial.

ROMNEY, GEORGE (1907–1995). Businessman, civic leader, politician, Church leader. Born on 8 July 1907 in the Mormon colonies in Mexico, Romney was five when his parents moved to Los Angeles in 1912 during the Mexican Revolution. The next year they moved to Oakley, Idaho, where his father began farming. Low prices forced abandonment of the farm and moves to Salt Lake City and Rexburg, Idaho. In 1921 the family moved back to Salt Lake City. In addition to construction work on his father's house building projects, George attended high school and played football, baseball, and basketball. He also courted Lenore LaFount.

In 1926 he began two years of foreign missionary (q.v.) proselytizing in Scotland. Inspired by mission president John A. Widtsoe (qq.v.), George was transferred to London and gained administrative experience as a secretary in the mission office. Returning home in 1928, he entered the University of Utah and also took speedwriting classes at a business college. Anxious to be in Washington, D.C., where Lenore had moved and had graduated from George Washington University, George landed a job on the staff of Senator David I. Walsh, Democrat of Massachusetts. In 1930 he accepted a job with Aluminum Company of America (Alcoa), moving to California, where Lenore was pursuing a movie career. Finally, they married in 1931.

Moving back to Washington, D.C., the Romneys participated in different community activities. Then he took a job with the Automobile

Manufacturers Association in Detroit. In 1941 he became managing director of the Automotive Council for War Production. After the war he went to work for Nash-Kelvinator. In 1954 he became CEO of American Motors, which enjoyed a rise in production and profits under his direction.

He headed the Citizens Advisory Committee on School Needs, became chairman of Citizens for Michigan, and in 1962 was elected governor of Michigan, serving three terms. A front-runner for the Republican presidential nomination in 1968, Romney lost out partly because he claimed, with perfect justification, that he had been "brainwashed" during a tour of Vietnam.

In the Church, Romney served in many capacities, including several years as stake president (q.v.) in Detroit. After his retirement he continued to promote volunteerism throughout the country.

-S-

SABBATH DAY. From the beginning Mormons have sought to remember the Sabbath day and keep it holy. Like other Christians, they have designated Sunday for this purpose, although in countries where this proves difficult, like Israel, they have readily shifted to the seventh day.

The central activity of the Sabbath is worship. At sacrament meeting (q.v.) Mormons pray, sing, listen to sermons, and most importantly partake of the emblems of the sacrament (q.v.) in remembrance of the sacrifice of Jesus Christ (q.v.). Other meetings include Priesthood, Relief Society, and Sunday School (qq.v.). In 1980 these meetings were consolidated into a single time block, including Young Women and Primary (qq.v.) meetings. For bishops (q.v.) and other leaders there is usually an additional preparation meeting.

During the remaining hours of the Sabbath, members are on their own but they are urged to avoid regular work where possible as well as secular recreation. The hours of this day are to be dedicated to prayer (q.v.), letter writing, visiting the sick and lonely, appropriate family (q.v.) activities, music (q.v.), and study. Somehow this day should be set apart from the rest of the week and provide nourishment for the spiritual side of human nature that is so easily neglected.

In a revelation (q.v.) in 1831 (Doctrine and Covenants, section 59) Joseph Smith (q.v.) announced: "And that thou mayest more fully keep thyself unspotted from the world, thou shalt go to the house of prayer and offer up thy sacraments upon my holy day; for verily this is a day appointed unto you to rest from your labors, and to pay thy devotions unto the Most High."

SACRAMENT. In Mormon usage the sacrament of the Lord's Supper repeated each week in sacrament meeting (q.v.). Bread and wine (gradually replaced by water after a revelation [q.v.] had authorized it) are blessed in prayers (q.v.) specified in the Book of Mormon and Doctrine and Covenants (qq.v.). Regarded as a solemn remembrance and acknowledgment of Jesus Christ's (q.v.) sacrifice, the sacrament includes no claim of transubstantiation or real presence. The regular partaking of the emblems by Church members is also considered an act of recommitment and renewal of covenants. Sacraments in the broad sense are usually described by Mormons as ordinances (q.v.).

SACRAMENT MEETING. The main meeting for worship held in wards (q.v.) throughout the Church each Sabbath (q.v.). Although appearing somewhat informal when compared with the highly structured worship of liturgical traditions, sacrament meetings follow a standard format:

Hymn by congregation
Announcements
Opening prayer (q.v.) or invocation
Sacramental hymn
Blessing and distribution of the sacrament (q.v.)
Speakers
Musical selection
Closing hymn
Closing prayer or benediction

Those unfamiliar with Mormon practices sometimes find the sacrament meeting lacking because of the inclusion of small children in the congregation with some inevitable noise and the unprofessional quality of music (q.v.) and sermons. On the other hand, if one recalls that a lay organization, entirely volunteer, is putting on the meeting, it can be recognized that it performs its basic purpose entirely adequately. Certainly the personal growth that goes with participation is abundantly evident.

One sacrament meeting each month, normally the first, is designated as a Fast and Testimony (q.v.) meeting. Instead of the usual sermons, members of the congregation who feel the desire to do so stand and "bear testimony," telling what their religious faith means to them.

SACRED GROVE. In the spring of 1820 Joseph Smith (q.v.), desiring to know which church he should join, retired to a grove of trees near his home in Palmyra, New York. The First Vision (q.v.) set in motion the events that led to the organization of the Church in 1830. The grove of trees that Smith prayed in, or one that seems to fit the requirements, has been designated the Sacred Grove and is a popular tourist site.

SAINTS. Synonymous with "members of the Church." Following the New Testament usage according to which Paul wrote to "the saints" at Ephesus or Corinth or other cities where there were Christians, Mormons do not assign any special sanctity to the term, although obviously members are expected to live a life dedicated to God. There is no canonization process. The venerable dead, the heroic figures of the past, are not the subject of any special cult or veneration. Prayers (q.v.) are not addressed to them.

SALVATION. *See* PLAN OF SALVATION.

SATAN. A real spirit personage who leads the forces of evil and tries to defeat God's purposes. In the pre-mortal existence this spirit, also a child of God, rebelled and took with him a portion of the host of Heaven, that is other spirits. Since then Satan has tried to frustrate the Plan of Salvation (q.v.). Clever, knowing human weaknesses, he often tempts individuals to the path of destruction. But those who keep the commandments (q.v.), who have faith and follow the path of the Church, will be safe, for God is more powerful and will ultimately prevail.

SATANISM. Rituals and cultic practices that have included the worship of Satan (q.v.). Found in different time periods and geographical locations, Satanism has appeared even in modern, relatively educated communities. Mormons are warned by their leaders to have nothing to do with such practices.

SCHREINER, ALEXANDER (1901–1987). Musician, Tabernacle (q.v.) organist. Born in Nuernberg, Germany, on 31 July 1901, Schreiner attended the Melanchthon School. His parents were musical and gave him the opportunity to learn piano. At a very young age he began accompanying at the Mormon branch. In 1912 his family (q.v.) moved to Salt Lake City.

Young Schreiner was placed in school and learned English by the "assimilation" method (he decried bilingual education). He was quickly enlisted as an accompanist and resumed piano study. Then he added organ study and earned money by playing as a theater organist. In 1922–24 he served as a missionary (q.v.) in California.

Returning to Salt Lake City, he became one of the Tabernacle organists. On leave, he studied organ and theory in Paris with Henri Libert, Charles-Marie Widor, and Louis Vierne. He also received an appointment as university organist at the University of California at Los Angeles, where he performed recitals and taught classes for nine years.

Anxious to pursue his education, Schreiner took classes and in 1942 obtained a B.A. from the University of Utah. Continuing on the graduate level in musical composition under Leroy J. Robertson (q.v.), he earned a Ph.D. in 1954. For more than 30 years he was on concert tour yearly. He composed many organ voluntaries as well as *Concerto for Full Orchestra and Organ*. Schreiner set several Church hymns to music, including "God Loved Us, So He Sent His Son." He was the recipient of several honorary degrees, and he retired in 1977. Schreiner was married to Margaret Lyman, and they had four children.

SCIENCE. The basic attitude of Mormonism toward science has always been positive. Truth will not contradict truth. Especially in the 20th century many Mormons have become scientists. Studies demonstrated that Utah had more scientists per capita than any other state. Examples of Mormon scientists are Henry B. Eyring (q.v.), prominent chemist; Harvey Fletcher, physicist and inventor; and Philo Farnsworth (q.v.), inventor of television.

Controversy over scientific issues has flared up from time to time, as Mormons with a literal interpretation of scripture (q.v.) and doctrine have condemned those with a more flexible interpretation. These controversies have been of short duration and have been contained. The emphasis remains one of insisting on God's ultimate power while acknowledging that His will may be worked through a variety of means. *See also* CREATION.

SCOTT, RICHARD GORDON (1928–). Nuclear engineer, Apostle. Born on 7 November 1928 in Pocatello, Idaho, Scott grew up in the Washington, D.C., area, where his father was employed by the Department of Agriculture. He graduated from George Washington University in mechanical engineering and, after serving a mission for the Church in Uruguay, returned to do postgraduate work in nuclear engineering at Oak Ridge, Tennessee.

From 1953 to 1965 Scott served on the immediate staff of Admiral Hyman Rickover. He directed research and application of the use of nuclear energy for military purposes and land-based power plants. Later he was a consultant for nuclear power companies.

In 1965 he was called to be president (q.v.) of the Argentina North Mission in Cordoba. After his return in 1969 he was a regional representative (q.v.) in Uruguay, Paraguay, and the eastern United States. In 1977 he became one of the First Quorum of the Seventy and in 1988 a member of the Quorum of the Twelve Apostles (qq.v.). He and his wife, Jeanene (who died in 1995), are the parents of seven children, five of them living.

SCRIPTURE. 1. The four "standard works": the Bible, the Book of Mormon, the Doctrine and Covenants, and the Pearl of Great Price (qq.v.). The proclaiming of the Book of Mormon as scripture at the Church's beginning in 1830 signaled a belief in an open, not a closed, canon. The acceptance of both the Doctrine and Covenants and the Pearl of Great Price as standard works was made official by a sustaining (q.v.) vote of the members of the Church in General Conference (q.v.).

Whatever is spoken by God's representatives when they are divinely inspired (Doctrine and Covenants, Section 68.). Although in common parlance "scripture" or "scriptures" as used among Mormons refers to the four standard works, this broader meaning is a reminder that revelation (q.v.) continues, that the living prophets (q.v.) express God's will to the current generation, and that God, the ultimate source of truth, is not to be constrained. *See also* PROPHET; REVELATION.

SEALING. Ordinance (q.v.) performed in the temples (q.v.) by which one is permanently connected to another person, as in wife-husband, or parents-children. This relationship is to continue after death as well as during mortality. When a temple marriage establishes such a sealing between husband and wife, children born to that union are considered "born in the covenant" and do not have to be sealed in a separate ceremony, for the eternal family (q.v.) unit was created by the temple marriage. Persons who earlier had been married outside of the temple only until their death may, upon their conversion or a later decision to do so, go to the temple to have their marriage sealed. Any children they have may go with them and participate in the sealing ordinance. Participation in temple

ordinances is always dependent upon worthiness (q.v.), which is determined by a bishop (q.v.), who issues a recommend (q.v.). Ultimate en-
joyment of the eternal blessings is always contingent upon faithfulness.

SECT. *See* CULT.

SEMINARIES. Religious instruction for youth (q.v.) of high-school age,
roughly 14 to 18, provided on a released-time basis for one class period
each day in buildings adjacent to or nearby the regular school. The first
seminary of this type began in 1912 in Salt Lake City; the program then
expanded through those western states with a sufficient population of
Church members.

Classes are taught by teachers (q.v.) with the same training and cre-
dentials as those in the public schools. The four-year curriculum includes
Old Testament, New Testament, Doctrine and Covenants (q.v.) and
Church History, and Book of Mormon (q.v.).

Where the released-time arrangement has not been allowed because
of an insufficient population of Church members, seminaries are conducted in the early morning prior to the beginning of the school day.
Alternatively, especially for scattered students where the other arrangements are not feasible, correspondence or home-study courses are available. *See also* INSTITUTES OF RELIGION.

SENIOR CITIZENS. In the late 19th century organized outings and celebrations for "old folks" at least gave some recognition to the most advanced age group. In the 20th and present centuries, their health enhanced
by their adherence to the Word of Wisdom (q.v.), more and more Mormons, like everyone else, are living many years beyond retirement.

The inherent problems of old age—dependency, loneliness, pain, dis-
orientation—are faced by Mormons like everyone else. The increased
incidence of Alzheimer's disease has been a challenge, sometimes tragi-
cally painful, for many individual families (q.v.).

On the other hand, the "golden years" for many Mormon senior citizens are alleviated by the following: a program of home teaching (q.v.)
and visiting teaching (q.v.) that, when it works, sees to it that each person has others assigned to provide friendship, assist, and report special
needs; activity (q.v.) in the temples (q.v.), which occupies many, giving
them something to do, people to associate with, and a sense of usefulness; missions, with retired couples especially in demand, some of them
serving one mission after another; and the strength of Mormon families

(not perfect by any means but superior to many other groups) and their continued acceptance of responsibility for providing love and care to aging parents and grandparents.

SEVENTY. An office in the Priesthood (q.v.). First established during the Ohio Period (q.v.) in 1835, the Seventies had primarily a missionary (q.v.) responsibility. They were to work under the direction of the Quorum of the Twelve Apostles (q.v.).

For most of its history the Seventy were simply those holders of the Melchizedek Priesthood (q.v.) who were ordained to this office with special orientation toward proselytizing. The seven presidents were called the First Council of the Seventy and were regarded as General Authorities (q.v.) of the Church.

In 1975 to meet the needs of the expanding membership (q.v.), the First Quorum of the Seventy (q.v.) was organized. It included those who previously had been called Assistants to the Twelve (q.v.). Its leadership was a presidency of seven. In 1986 stake seventy quorums (qq.v.) were discontinued. In 1989 a Second Quorum of the Seventy was organized, also under the direction of the same seven presidents, the Presidency of the Seventy. Membership in the Second Quorum was to last about five years.

Under the direction of the First Presidency (q.v.) and the Quorum of the Twelve Apostles, members of the First and Second Quorums of the Seventy supervise training of leaders, attend stake conferences (q.v.), and especially serve as presidencies over the areas (q.v.) of the Church throughout the world. In 1997 three additional quorums were created— the Third, Fourth, and Fifth Quorums—made up of men called to serve for five or six years on a Church-service basis. That is, they were to continue their present employment and reside in their homes. Of the 134 men first called to this position, 128 had already been serving as Area Authorities and henceforth would be identified as Area Authority Seventies. *See also* GENERAL AUTHORITIES.

SHUMWAY, ERIC B. (1939–). President, Brigham Young University–Hawaii (qq.v.). Raised in St. Johns, Arizona, Shumway served as a missionary (q.v.) in Tonga before going on to graduate from Brigham Young University (q.v.) with bachelor's and master's degrees in English. After receiving his doctorate at the University of Virginia, he accepted a position as instructor of English at Brigham Young University–Hawaii, starting in 1966. In 1975 he became chair of the Communications and Language Arts Division and in 1980 was named vice president for academics.

President of the Tongan Mission from 1986 to 1989, Shumway returned to Hawaii where, in addition to his other duties, he became acting president of the Polynesian Cultural Center (q.v.). In 1994 he was named university president.

SINGLES. Unmarried adults who are Mormons face the same economic and social challenges as other singles. In addition, they must find their way in a Church that clearly includes marriage among the prerequisites for the highest salvation. Sometimes they feel unappreciated in meetings where it is assumed that everyone is in a traditional family (q.v.).

A variety of factors have increased the number of single adults: later marriage age, increased divorce (q.v.), and acceptance of the single lifestyle in the larger society. One study showed that LDS single adults were divided into three groups: divorced or separated, 23 percent; widowed, 13 percent; never married, 63 percent. Among these singles there is consistently a gender disproportion, with more single women than men.

The Church has attempted to respond by providing recreational activities, appointing committees for single adults on the ward and stake (qq.v.) level, establishing wards or branches for singles where the demand is sufficient, and including material on singles in manuals and Church periodicals.

SISTER. *See* BROTHER AND SISTER.

SMITH, BARBARA BRADSHAW (1922–). Women's leader, Relief Society president (qq.v.). Born in Salt Lake City on 26 January 1922, Barbara Bradshaw attended the local schools. She married Douglas H. Smith, an insurance executive, who later became a General Authority as a member of the Second Quorum of the Seventy (qq.v.). They have seven children.

In the Relief Society she had experience as a teacher and as ward president (qq.v.). (Her mother and sister were presidents of their ward Relief Societies at exactly the same time.) She served on the Relief Society stake (q.v.) board and then on the general board.

From 1974 to 1984 she was general president of the Relief Society. It was a decade during which the movement for women's liberation became more assertive and women's issues assumed an unprecedented prominence. Employment, birth control (q.v.), abortion, divorce (q.v.), one-parent families—such issues could not be ignored. In the meantime, economic conditions created welfare needs, and the women leaders of the Relief Society participated on every level of Welfare Services.

An outspoken opponent of the Equal Rights Amendment, Barbara Smith found herself under attack from those on the other side. In many addresses, in the women's meetings of the International Women's Year, she patiently explained her position: "I stand as a representative of an organization that is in favor of rights for women. However, we may differ with some people on the best way or ways to achieve these rights. In my opinion, the Equal Rights Amendment is not the way." (Barbara Smith, *A Fruitful Season* [Salt Lake City, 1988], 227.) Responding to a difficult situation, she appeared on Phil Donahue's television show to explain this position.

To celebrate the achievements and contribution of women, a Monument to Women was created in Nauvoo, Illinois, and dedicated in June 1978 in a stunning three-day ceremony. Attempting to meet the needs of a variety of Mormon women—old and young, different races, ethnic groups, and nationalities, married and single—the Relief Society under President Smith's leadership adapted its teaching materials and introduced new resources.

Upon her release as general president of the Relief Society in 1984, Barbara Smith accompanied her husband to Hong Kong, where he served in the presidency of the area (q.v.). For three years she taught Asian women, many of them converts, about the Relief Society, as well as the Primary and Young Women (qq.v.) programs.

SMITH, EMMA HALE (1804–1879). Wife of Joseph Smith (q.v.). Born in Harmony, Pennsylvania, where she grew up and received basic schooling, she met Joseph Smith when he was working as a laborer in her area. When permission to marry him was not given, she did so anyway (she was 22) on 18 January 1827, after which the newlyweds moved to Manchester, New York.

Joining the new Church in 1830, Emma experienced persecution (q.v.) and frequent moves along with her husband. Her first three children, including a set of twins, died soon after their birth, as did two other infants and an adopted baby boy. Surviving sons were Joseph III, Frederick, Alexander Hale, and David Hyrum. Caring for these children was physically and emotionally taxing for Emma.

She was appointed to select hymns for the new Church; her compilation was published in 1835. In Nauvoo, Illinois, she became president in 1842 of the organization for women, the Relief Society (q.v.). She was among the first women to experience the new ordinance (q.v.) of endowment even prior to the completion of the Nauvoo Temple in 1846.

A major challenge came with the introduction of polygamy (q.v.) about 1840. She consented to her husband's marriage to plural wives but soon had second thoughts. Torn between aversion to this practice and loyalty to her husband, she suffered great emotional stress. After Joseph's death in June 1844, she refused to accept the leadership of Brigham Young (q.v.), quarreling with him over property claims.

During the remainder of her life Emma remained in Nauvoo, denying that her late husband had introduced polygamy, a denial psychologically understandable but untrue to historical reality. She married Lewis Bidamon, who assisted in raising her remaining five children. In 1860 her oldest son, Joseph III, became president of the Reorganized Church of Jesus Christ of Latter Day Saints (q.v.), which she joined.

Although tension continued to exist between her and the leaders of the Church of Jesus Christ of Latter-day Saints in the West, she treated Mormon visitors kindly. In time they preferred to overlook the closing phase of her life by emphasizing instead the courage, faith, and loyalty of her life down to the death of her husband in 1844. *See also* TEMPLES.

SMITH, GEORGE ALBERT (1870–1951). Apostle and president (q.v.) of the Church. Tall and thin, with a white goatee, he was a striking figure known for his kindliness.

Born in Salt Lake City of a prominent family (q.v.), George was the son of John Henry Smith and grandson of George A. Smith, both of whom were Apostles and counselors in the First Presidency (qq.v.). His advanced education was at Brigham Young Academy and the University of Utah. He married Lucy Emily Woodruff, a granddaughter of Wilford Woodruff (q.v.).

He was a missionary (q.v.) in the Southern States Mission from 1892 to 1894. Work for the Republican Party led to his being appointed as receiver for the Land Office in 1896 and again in 1902. In 1903, at the age of 33, Smith was called to the Quorum of the Twelve Apostles (q.v.).

In addition to the routine of visiting stakes (q.v.) throughout the Church, he had a special interest in the Young Men's (q.v.) Mutual Improvement Association. He served on its general board and, from 1921 to 1935, as its general superintendent. He was especially interested in the Boy Scout (q.v.) organization and promoted its inclusion in the Church youth (q.v.) program. For years of service in scouting he was awarded the Silver Beaver and the Silver Buffalo.

Although afflicted with poor eyesight and chronic debilitation (from lupus erythematosus), Smith kept busily involved. President of the European Mission from 1919 to 1921, he made a special effort to make friends with government leaders. In 1938 he visited the Church missions in Australia, New Zealand, and several Pacific (q.v.) islands.

Perhaps because of his family heritage, he took a keen interest in Church history sites and trails. He attended the dedication of a monument to Joseph Smith (q.v.) at Sharon, Vermont, in 1905. He helped to found the Utah Pioneer Trails and Landmarks Association, which erected many monuments, including the "This Is the Place" Monument (q.v.).

By seniority he became president of the Quorum of Twelve Apostles in 1943. Then, upon the death of President Heber J. Grant (q.v.) in 1945, Smith became president of the Church. He was 75 years old.

For six years, from 1945 to 1951, he led the Church. Among the achievements of these postwar years were the dedication of the new Idaho Falls Temple in 1945, the construction of many meetinghouses, the expansion of a program for microfilming genealogical records, and the rapid growth of missionary (q.v.) activity. Under his direction the Church sent substantial relief supplies to Europe (q.v.).

His personal creed, which he allowed to be published in 1932, was an inspiration to many. Among its 10 goals or ideals were: "I would be a friend to the friendless and find joy in ministering to the needs of the poor" and "I would not be an enemy to any living soul." (Merlo Pusey, *Builders of the Kingdom* [1981], 255.) He died on 4 April 1951.

SMITH, HYRUM (1800–1844). Older brother and close associate of Joseph Smith (q.v.), he was Associate President of the Church at the time of his death.

Born in Vermont, where he received some primary schooling, Hyrum moved with family (q.v.) to Manchester, New York, about 1816. For the next several years he worked hard on the family farm and occasionally hired out. He married Jerusha Barden in 1826.

When his brother Joseph was working on the manuscript of the Book of Mormon (q.v.), Hyrum, a believer from the first, assisted. He was one of the eight witnesses (q.v.) allowed to see and handle the metal plates. When the Church was organized on 6 April 1830, Hyrum was among the six original members. Immediately he began preaching, going on several missions in New York and later in Ohio and Missouri.

Hyrum experienced the persecutions (q.v.) along with the rest of the Church, moved to Missouri, served several months in jail, and spent the closing years of his life in Illinois. After bearing six children, his wife

Jerusha died. His second wife, Mary Fielding, bore two more children, including Joseph F. Smith (q.v.).

In addition to being the companion and confidant of his brother, Hyrum held important positions in the Church: Assistant President from 1834, counselor in the First Presidency (qq.v.) from 1837, Presiding Patriarch (q.v.), and Associate President.

In June 1844 he refused the opportunity to take his family to Cincinnati, instead staying by his brother Joseph during their imprisonment in Carthage Jail. There both of them were killed by a mob on 27 June 1844. Latter-day Saints regard both of them as martyrs.

SMITH, JOSEPH (1805–1844). Founding prophet (q.v.) of the Church of Jesus Christ of Latter-day Saints (q.v.). Sometimes known as Joseph Smith Jr., to distinguish him from his father.

The external life of Smith—his places of residence, his travels, his public statements—is easily enough recounted, although even on this level his life was not easily lived, for he had more than his share of pain and trial. The internal life, the religious experiences, the dimension of revelation or prophecy (qq.v.)—these are of course understood differently by believers and nonbelievers. He recognized the ultimate ineffability of such matters in a famous statement at the end of his life: "No man knows my history; I cannot tell it. I shall never undertake it. If I had not experienced what I have, I should not have believed it myself." (*Teachings of the Prophet Joseph Smith* [1977], 361.) In the present brief sketch the emphasis will be on the external matters, with the religious experiences and contributions presented in the way Smith told them to others and the way they have been accepted by his followers.

Born in Sharon, Vermont, on 23 December 1805, Joseph was the third living son of Joseph Smith Sr. and Lucy Mack Smith. Poor but hardworking, the Smith family (q.v.)—nine children, not counting stillbirths or infant deaths—moved from farm to farm. In 1816, like other New Englanders, they moved into New York State, settling on a farm near Palmyra.

Broadly Christian, reading and believing the Bible (q.v.), the Smiths became unsettled over the question of religion during revivals. In this context, young Joseph, still a teenager, prayed to God, asking what he should do. The result was the First Vision (q.v.), during which the Lord instructed him to join none of the existing churches, for they had all gone astray.

During the 1820s, between the ages of 15 and 25, Joseph Smith grew to adulthood, worked on the family farm, and hired out as a laborer.

Reputed to be able to find treasure through a seer stone, he was briefly employed to dig for buried Spanish gold, but the enterprise failed. The most important events of these years, as he later saw them, were the appearances of an angel, who told him where to find buried metal plates. He was not allowed to take them at first, for he coveted them for their monetary value, but after four years of discipline and purifying his heart, he was allowed in 1827 to take possession of them for purposes of translation. The same year he married Emma Hale Smith (q.v.).

During the next two and a half years, Joseph moved to Harmony, Pennsylvania, and, with the assistance of scribes, worked on translating the hieroglyphics from the plates into English. Although ridiculed by ministers and others, he had the confidence of his parents, his siblings, his wife, and a few friends who provided financial support. Some of these were selected as witnesses of the Book of Mormon (qq.v.).

When the resurrected John the Baptist appeared to Smith and Cowdery and gave them Priesthood (q.v.) authority, they baptized each other and began baptizing others. In the spring of 1830 the Book of Mormon was published and on 6 April the Church was organized with six men to satisfy the legal requirement.

During the next 14 years, from age 24 to 38, Joseph Smith's life was anything but dull. The head of a church, a movement, he had to answer many specific questions. Revelations (q.v.) on matters ranging from instruction to individuals on their duty to administrative details to lofty theological principles were issued by the prophet (q.v.) one by one. Eventually these were compiled into a volume entitled Doctrine and Covenants (q.v.).

Smith led the fledgling church, with a hundred or so members, to a new location at Kirtland, Ohio. At the same time he announced that the new Zion (q.v.) was in western Missouri. During most of the 1830s, therefore, Mormon converts converged on these two locations. Smith himself lived at Kirtland but led an expedition to assist his persecuted followers in Missouri and in 1837 moved there with his family.

Opposition to the new religion had started early. Harassment in New York, verbal denunciation in both Ohio and Missouri, finally tarring and feathering, beatings, and lynchings of outright terrorism—all of this the early Mormons saw as persecution (q.v.), the expected fate of the Lord's disciples. Smith himself was tarred and feathered in Ohio. In Missouri, where the opposition became most ferocious, the Mormons were driven from Jackson County. An election-day incident led to open confrontation between Mormon militia and a mobilized state militia, called out by Governor Lilburn W. Boggs after he issued an infamous extermination order. While his family and several thousand Mormon refugees fled the state, Joseph Smith and several of his associates were imprisoned for several months in a jail at Liberty, Missouri. In the depths of despair, he still managed to maintain the rightness of his position, to provide inspiration to his followers, and to produce some of his most sublime religious revelations (Doctrine and Covenants, sections 121–3).

After escaping his captors, Joseph joined the bedraggled Mormons in western Illinois and there on the banks of the Mississippi River established a new center at Commerce, renamed Nauvoo. From 1839 on Nauvoo was the Mormon center. Converts flocked in, including several hundred from as far away as England, and the city's population grew to more than 10,000 by the mid-1840s, even 15,000 if one includes the surrounding area. Illinois was the stage of the final period of Smith's life.

Two themes played themselves out in a relentless counterpoint. On the one hand, the Church prospered in many ways. Conversions continued unabated. The city grew and commanded a steadily increasing political and economic position in the area. A special charter from the Illinois legislature granted extraordinary powers to Nauvoo, for example a militia known as the Nauvoo Legion. In addition to his position as president of the Church, Smith became mayor of the city.

Significant developments in doctrine and practice occurred at Nauvoo. These included giving to the Quorum of the Twelve Apostles (q.v.) jurisdiction over the entire Church, the introduction of temple ordinances (q.v.) and the construction of a temple (q.v.), establishment of the Relief Society (q.v.) organization for women, and the cautious, secretive introduction of polygamy (q.v.) to a few Apostles and other leaders. Fears of a theocratic state, which earlier had provoked Missourians, intensified as Mormons became sufficiently numerous to dominate county elections and especially in early 1844 with the establishment of the Council of Fifty (q.v.).

Missouri officials had continued to demand Smith's extradition. Efforts to obtain protection or relief from the federal government came to naught. In addition to the rising tide of anti-Mormonism (q.v.) in surrounding towns, a small number of apostates (q.v.) raised their heads within the Church, and to some extent the two groups cooperated. Running counter to all of the apparent growth and prosperity, therefore, was increasing opposition.

Matters came to a head with the publication of an opposition newspaper, *The Nauvoo Expositor*, and a decision by the city council, including Smith, to destroy the press. Outraged opponents decried the act as inimical to freedom of the press. Some of these enemies in speeches and editorials called for solving the Mormon problem by the violence of "powder and ball." Smith was charged with riot for destroying the press and, assured by the state's governor that he would be safe, was arrested and placed in Carthage Jail. Accompanying him were his brother Hyrum Smith, Apostle John Taylor (qq.v.), and others.

Whipped up by anti-Mormons, the militia assigned to guard the jail transformed itself into a lynch mob. With blackened faces, they fired into the jail from the outside and, charging up the stairs, attacked from the inside with guns blazing. In a few moments Hyrum Smith and Joseph Smith were killed. John Taylor was wounded. It was 27 June 1844.

It is hard to be neutral about Joseph Smith. His enemies and detractors viewed him as an imposter, a con man who took advantage of the gullibility of people. Mormons remembered him with great fondness, recalling incidents of kindness and humor and charismatic leadership. At no time has this respect required Mormons to believe that he was perfect. They do not worship him. For them he was a human being but one chosen by God to be the prophet of the last dispensation. He brought back to earth Priesthood authority, restored the Church, brought forth the Book of Mormon, the Doctrine and Covenants, and the Pearl of Great Price (q.v.), led his people through times of perilous persecution and displacement, founded a city, and revealed many important religious truths. When he died, he was 38 years old. See also APOSTASY; CHURCH OF JESUS CHRIST OF LATTER-DAY SAINTS; COWDERY, OLIVER; TEMPLES; ZION'S CAMP.

SMITH, JOSEPH F. (1838–1918). Apostle and Church president (q.v.). Although Fielding is his middle name, he is traditionally known as Joseph F. to distinguish him from his son.

Born to Hyrum Smith (q.v.) and Mary Fielding Smith in Far West, Missouri, on 13 November 1838, he was carried by his mother through a "trail of tears" to refuge in Illinois. His father and his uncle, the prophet (q.v.) Joseph Smith (q.v.), were incarcerated. He was only five years old when his father and uncle were killed. As his mother took charge of seven children during the flight from Nauvoo and the trek to the Salt Lake Valley, young Joseph F. drove his mother's wagon. He was nine when they arrived in Salt Lake City.

As was common among those pioneering the new location, Joseph F. worked hard in the fields and tending cattle. He was only 13 when his mother died. Two years later, having had only minimal schooling, he was called as a missionary (q.v.) to Hawaii, where for the next four years he mastered the language and gained leadership experience.

Soon after his return he married Levira Smith. With her permission he married as a plural wife Julina Lambson, who was later followed by four others. He eventually fathered 43 children.

His leadership experience continued to increase. From 1860 to 1863 he was a missionary in Great Britain. He was elected to the Utah Territorial legislature and the Salt Lake City council. In the Church he served on his stake high council (qq.v.), worked in the Historian's Office, and officiated in ceremonies in the Endowment House. In 1867 he was ordained a member of the Quorum of Twelve Apostles (q.v.). In 1874–75 and again in 1877 he was president of the European and British Missions. For a while he was president of the Davis County stake. In 1880, at the age of 41, he became second counselor (q.v.) in the First Presidency of the Church; he and George Q. Cannon would be counselors to three successive presidents (qq.v.).

For much of the next decade Joseph F. lived in hiding. When John Taylor (q.v.) died in 1887, Smith continued as one of the Twelve and became a counselor to Wilford Woodruff (q.v.) upon his becoming Church president. As one of the First Presidency Joseph F. was closely involved in the decision to issue the Manifesto (q.v.) in 1890, which announced the formal end of polygamy (q.v.) and prepared the way for Utah's admission to the Union as a state.

With the coming of national political parties to Utah, Joseph F. became a Republican. He participated in the Church policy decisions of the 1890s, continuing as a counselor to Lorenzo Snow (q.v.) in 1898. When Snow died in 1901, Joseph F. Smith became president of the Church.

He worked to bring Mormonism into the 20th century by emphasizing its loyalty to the United States, first in the Spanish-American War and later during World War I. Although anti-Mormonism (q.v.) continued during the hearings for Senator-elect Reed Smoot (q.v.) and afterward, President Smith emphasized education, missionary expansion, the construction of needed Church buildings, and the acquisition of historic sites. Known for his sensible discussions of doctrinal matters, he gave many sermons and wrote articles, from which the book *Gospel Doctrine* was compiled in 1918. His 1918 "Vision of the Redemption of the Dead" was added to the Doctrine and Covenants (q.v.) in 1981.

Respected for his faithfulness, intelligence, and spirituality and venerated for his blood relationship to the martyred prophets, Joseph F. Smith died on 19 November 1918.

SMITH, JOSEPH FIELDING (1876–1972). Historian, doctrinal authority, Apostle, Church president (q.v.). Born in Salt Lake City on 19 July 1876, Joseph Fielding Smith was the son of Joseph F. Smith (q.v.) and Julina Lambson. Since his father was out of the country during much of the 1880s, the boy was supervised by his mother, a midwife. He milked cows and did other farmwork. In 1898 at the age of 22 he married Louie Shurtliff and the next year was called as a missionary (q.v.) to England.

Returning in 1901, Joseph took employment in the Church Historian's Office. When his father became president of the Church that same year, he became a confidant and assistant. In 1905 and again in 1907 he wrote pamphlets defending the Church's practices against critics.

Smith and his wife had two daughters, but during her third pregnancy Louie had complications and died. After several months of loneliness, Joseph married Ethel Reynolds, who went on to become the mother of five sons and four daughters.

It was at April general conference (q.v.) in 1910 that Joseph was called to the Quorum of the Twelve Apostles (q.v.). During the next 60 years he would meet regularly with the other Apostles (q.v.), visit the different stakes (q.v.) on assignment, and give counsel. He had special interests. Temple (q.v.) and genealogical work were themes he often stressed, and he edited the *Utah Genealogical and Historical Magazine*. For 20 years he was in the presidency of the Salt Lake Temple either as a counselor (q.v.) or as president. Church history was also one of his passions. From his initial appointment as Assistant Church Historian in 1906 he went on to become Church Historian from 1921 to 1970.

In 1937 his wife Ethel died. The next year, at age 62, he married Jessie Evans, a well-known contralto. A loving companion for the remaining 34 years of his life, she had a keen sense of humor that made her a well-known character in her own right.

From 1950 he was president (or acting president) of the Twelve Apostles. In 1965 he was called to be also a counselor to the First Presidency (q.v.). Then in 1970, at age 94, he became president of the Church. Leading effectively, he supervised the reorganization of some departments, the expansion of missionary work, and the dedication of two temples. Some feared that he would be harsh and judgmental, but instead he was patient and loving, which was no surprise to his family (q.v.) and those close to him. He died on 2 July 1972.

SMOOT, MARY ELLEN WOOD (1933–). Youth (q.v.) and women's leader. Born in Ogden, Utah, Mary Ellen Wood studied elementary education at Utah State University. She and her husband, Stanley, are the parents of seven children. A full-time homemaker, she also did community service (q.v.), writing a local history and organizing a local historical society. Smoot served on the board of United Way and on the board of a community hospital. She wrote a newspaper column for youth. When her husband was called as mission president (q.v.) in Ohio, she enlarged her experience, becoming very involved in public affairs. With her husband she worked with church hosting, the two of them finally becoming directors. In 1997, Smoot was called to be general president of the Relief Society (q.v.).

SMOOT, REED (1862–1941). U.S. senator from Utah, Apostle. Although born in Salt Lake City in 1862, Smoot was raised in Provo, Utah, where his father was mayor. Reed studied at the new Brigham Young Academy from 1876. As a young man of 22 he became superintendent of the Provo Woolen Mills and also married Alpha Eldredge. Except for about a year's absence as a missionary (q.v.) in England (1890–91) his base of operations was Provo, where he enjoyed considerable success in business. Manager of Provo Commercial and Savings Bank, he was also vice president of Grant Central Mining and a director of Los Angeles and Salt Lake Railroad. From 1884 he was appointed a director of the Utah Territorial Insane Asylum in Provo. In 1900 he became a member of the Quorum of the Twelve Apostles (q.v.).

Elected U.S. Senator from Utah in 1902, after clearing his candidacy with the Church Presidency, Smoot was immediately challenged. For two and a half years the Senate Committee on Privileges held hearings. Accusers testified. Church leaders were summoned and cross-examined. Issues included the continuation of polygamy (q.v.) among the Mormons and Smoot's status as a Church General Authority (q.v.). Although the committee voted against Smoot, the Senate itself allowed him to keep his seat.

For about 30 years Reed Smoot was an Apostle in the Church, a leader of Utah Republicans, and a highly regarded and powerful member of the U.S. Senate.

SNOW, ELIZA ROXCY (1804–1887). Poet, author of hymns, leader of Mormon women. Born in Massachusetts but raised in Ohio, Eliza learned of Mormonism and in 1835, with other family (q.v.) members, joined the new faith. With other Latter-day Saints the Snows were forced to leave Ohio, then to leave Missouri, and then to seek refuge in Illinois. Eliza published poems defending and encouraging her people and became a schoolteacher.

In 1842 she participated in the founding of the Relief Society (q.v.), serving as secretary. She also became a plural wife of Joseph Smith (q.v.), following whose death in 1844 she became a plural wife of Brigham Young (q.v.).

With the other Mormons who were driven from Nauvoo, she made her way westward, arriving in the Salt Lake Valley in the fall of 1847. There she continued to write and publish poetry, participated in a study group known as the Polysophical Society, and after 1866 led the reorganized and revitalized Relief Society. Eliza R. Snow also helped found organizations for children and young women (q.v.). She traveled throughout Mormon country, visiting the different communities, carried on extensive correspondence, and in general until her death in 1887 was looked upon as leader of the Church's women.

Her hymn "O My Father"—which includes the idea of a pre-mortal existence and of a Heavenly Mother—continues to be a favorite.

SNOW, LORENZO (1814–1901). Missionary, Apostle, president (qq.v.) of the Church at the turn of the 20th century. Raised on a farm in Ohio, Snow received not only a common school education but, unusual for the time, completed high school and one term at Oberlin College. Becoming acquainted with Mormonism when Joseph Smith (q.v.) briefly resided at nearby Hiram, Ohio, the Snow family, including Lorenzo's sister Eliza R. Snow (q.v.), became converts—Lorenzo in 1836. During his 20s he gained experience through a series of missions, presiding over several congregations in London, and leading a party of emigrants from England to Illinois.

Participating in the Mormon migration to the West, Snow arrived in Salt Lake City in 1848 and one year later was named to the Quorum of Twelve Apostles (q.v.). Another mission took him to Italy, Switzerland, and Malta. In the 1860s he went to the Hawaiian Islands for a brief time and helped impose proper discipline on a rebellious leader.

When not away on such missions, Snow was a community leader in Utah. For 29 years he served in the territorial legislature. He led the settlement of Brigham City, which became a model of economic cooperation and later impressed the visitor Edward Bellamy.

Like all General Authorities (q.v.) of the period, Snow was involved in polygamy (q.v.), having married four wives before leaving Illinois. In 1886 he served a prison term for violating the Edmunds Act but was released in early 1887 when his conviction was overturned by the U.S. Supreme Court.

By seniority he became president (q.v.) of the Twelve Apostles in 1889 and in 1893 president of the newly dedicated Salt Lake Temple. In 1898, although old and weak, at the death of Wilford Woodruff (q.v.) Lorenzo Snow became president of the Church. During his three-year administration he extricated the Church from serious financial indebtedness by strongly urging members to pay tithing (q.v.), extended missionary (q.v.) proselytizing to Japan, and issued with his counselors an address to the world. He died of pneumonia on 10 October 1901. *See also* EXODUS.

SORENSEN, DAVID E. (1933–). Businessman, entrepreneur, Church leader. Born in Aurora, Utah, Sorensen attended Brigham Young University (q.v.), Utah State University, and the University of Utah. He was a missionary (q.v.) in the Central Atlantic States Mission. After military service in the U.S. Army he had a successful career as president of United Homes, Inc., chief executive officer of North American Health Care, chairman of Cal-Utah Feeders, and board vice chairman of Nevada Community Bank. In the church he was a bishop, high councilor, stake president, and president of the Canada Halifax Mission (qq.v.) Called to the Second Quorum of the Seventy (q.v.) in 1992, Sorensen became a member of the First Quorum of the Seventy in 1995. He and his wife, Verla, are the parents of seven children.

SORENSON, JOHN L. (1924–). Mormon anthropologist and expert on the Book of Mormon (q.v.). Born on 8 April 1924 in Smithfield, Utah, John Sorenson received his early education there. After service as a first lieutenant in the U.S. military during World War II, being trained as a meteorologist, he served as a missionary (q.v.) in New Zealand and the Cook Islands. From Brigham Young University (q.v.) he received a B.S. and M.A. degree in archaeology, after which he pursued a doctorate in anthropology at UCLA, receiving the Ph.D. in 1961.

After teaching anthropology at Brigham Young University for a few years, Sorenson became director of Social Sciences for General Research Corporation, Santa Barbara, California, from 1964 to 1969. He headed his own research corporation before returning to BYU in 1971. For 15 years he taught courses in anthropology there and served as consultant in applied social sciences, chairman of University Studies, and Department of Anthropology chairman.

Sorenson's interests have been varied. From a Rarotongan grammar he prepared as a missionary, he went on to publish articles and reviews on different Mesoamerican topics. His dissertation explored the effects of Geneva Steel on two Utah communities. Unconventional warfare and insurgency, along with transportation policy, were the focus of his research in the 1960s. A cultural anthropologist in the broad sense, Sorenson has been interested in language, cultural networks, and group personality.

Throughout his adult life Sorenson has also been especially persevering as a student of the Book of Mormon, attempting to see its text through the eyes of an anthropologist and exploring its possible Mesoamerican milieu. One of the participants in the University Archaeology Society and the New World Archaeological Foundation, he gave reports and published papers on many specific topics. His early *The World of the Book of Mormon* (1955), a prescient series of lectures, was followed by studies of such topics as the Book of Mormon as a Mesoamerican codex, writing systems, "brass plates" and Biblical scholarship, and wheeled figurines.

In 1985 appeared his *An Ancient American Setting for the Book of Mormon*, an unrivaled work in showing respect for the text and equally showing due regard for geographical reality and the present state of knowledge about ancient Mesoamerica. In 1990, after earlier preliminary versions, he published with Martin H. Raish a two-volume bibliography of pre-Columbian transoceanic contacts with America. In 1998, he published *Images of Ancient America: Visualizing Book of Mormon Life*, a massive photographic compilation of suggested parallels, and the same year he began editing *Journal of Book of Mormon Studies*.

Among the founders of the Foundation for Ancient Research and Mormon Studies (q.v.), Sorenson has been highly effective in organizing team research, facilitating publication of information as it becomes available, and encouraging other younger scholars.

In addition to his service as a missionary, Sorenson has at different times been a bishop and high councilor (qq.v.) in the Church. His wife, Kathryn, died in 1991. He retired from his university duties as an emeritus professor in 1986 but has continued his scholarly interests.

SORENSON, VIRGINIA EGGERTSON (1912–1991). Novelist. Born on 17 February 1912 in Provo, Utah, Virginia Eggertson also lived in Manti and American Fork during her childhood. In the early 1930s she was a student at Brigham Young University (q.v.). After marrying Frederick Sorenson, an English professor, she moved to California. She had two children. Later after a divorce (q.v.), she married the novelist Alec Waugh, with whom she lived in Tangier. In 1981 they returned to the United States. She died in North Carolina in 1991.

Sorenson's writings included such children's books as *Miracles on Maple Hill* (1957), for which she won the Newbery Award. But her Mormon people and culture provided the subject matter for most of her fiction, including *A Little Lower than the Angels* (1942), *On This Star* (1946), *The Neighbors* (1947), *The Evening and the* Morning (1949), *Many Heavens* (1954), and *Kingdom Come* (1960). She wrote a series of semifictional pieces that first appeared in *The New Yorker* and were later published as *Where Nothing Is Long Ago* (1963).

SOUTH AMERICA. Parley P. Pratt (q.v.) attempted to proselytize in Chile in 1851–52, but had practically no success. In 1925 the South American continent was dedicated for the preaching of Mormonism. Except for a few German immigrants, however, practically no conversions were made.

After World War II missionaries (q.v.) were sent to most countries of South America. Chapels were constructed. Scriptures (q.v.), lesson materials, and other publications were translated into Spanish and Portuguese. By the 1960s the Church was experiencing spectacular growth.

In Brazil the first stake (q.v.) was created in 1966; by the end of 1997 there were 173 stakes, 1,144 wards (q.v.), and about 640,000 members. A temple (q.v.) was constructed at São Paulo in 1978. Two General Authorities (q.v.) have been Brazilians—Helio da Rocha Camargo and Helvecio Martins, the first Black General Authority.

Other South American countries have seen the Church grow from small beginnings, in some cases from zero, to impressive heights. At the end of 1997, Mormon presence in South America stood as follows:

Country	Members	Stakes	Wards	Temples
Argentina	268,000	62	376	1
Bolivia	100,000	20	152	
Brazil	640,000	173	1,144	1
Chile	462,000	111	723	1
Colombia	122,000	24	159	
Ecuador	139,000	31	225	
Paraguay	37,000	6	34	
Peru	312,000	81	633	1
Uruguay	69,000	15	86	
Venezuela	80,000	16	117	

Missionary work had also begun in Guyana, Surinam, and French Guiana. South America was divided into six areas (q.v.): South America

North, South America South, South America West, Chile, Brazil North, and Brazil South. Much of the success of the Church in South America can be attributed to the buildup of local leadership. As much as one-third or even one-half of the missionary force in these countries is made up of indigenous young men and women. After completion of their missions, they form a pool of talent and leadership experience.

SPAFFORD, BELLE SMITH (1895–1982). President of the Relief Society (q.v.). Born on 8 October 1895 in Salt Lake City, Belle was educated through the secondary school level and then spent two years at the University of Utah. Thirsty for education, she later took many additional courses. In 1921 she married Earl Spafford.

Spafford taught religion classes and gained administrative experience in her Young Women's (q.v.) Mutual Improvement Association. In the 1930s she worked energetically in the Relief Society, serving in leadership positions in her ward and stake (qq.v.). In 1935 she became a member of the Relief Society general board. By 1942 she was a counselor in the general presidency (qq.v.).

Named general president of the Relief Society in 1945, Spafford occupied a prominent leadership role for nearly 30 years. Her accomplishments included raising funds for the construction of a beautiful Relief Society building, encouraging women to do voluntary work in the community, and establishing a health missionary (q.v.) program. She also participated in national and international organizations, including the National Council of Women, which she served as president in 1968–70. *See also* YOUNG WOMEN.

SPERRY, SIDNEY BRANTON (1895–). Educator, linguist. Born in Salt Lake City in 1895, Sperry received his elementary and secondary education there and in 1917 graduated from the University of Utah, majoring in chemistry and minoring in geology. After working for the U.S. Bureau of Metallurgical Research, he preached Mormonism as a missionary (q.v.) in the Southern States Mission from 1919 to 1921. He then married Eva Lila Braithwaite.

Sperry became a teacher in the Church's seminary and institute system (qq.v.). Pursuing advanced training, he obtained an M.A. from the University of Chicago in Old Testament studies and Hebrew in 1926. In 1931 he received the doctorate in Old Testament languages and literature. He did postdoctoral study in archaeology at the American School of Oriental Research in Jerusalem.

In 1932 Sperry accepted a faculty appointment at Brigham Young University (q.v.). For 39 years he taught courses and supervised students in Old Testament, New Testament, languages, and the Book of Mormon (q.v.). For part of this time he was director of the Division of Religion. Not limited to the home base of his campus, Sperry gave lectures in many other places, particularly during Education Week (q.v.), which he helped to establish.

In his lectures, articles, and manuals written for the auxiliary (q.v.) organizations he explicated and defended the scriptures (q.v.). He aligned himself with conservative scholars regarding some of the issues of biblical scholarship. Among his titles are *Our Book of Mormon*, *The Voice of Israel's Prophets*, *Paul's Life and Letters*, and *Doctrine and Covenants Compendium*.

SPORTS. From almost the beginning of the Church sports activities have been participated in to some degree. We know, for example, that Joseph Smith (q.v.) enjoyed wrestling, pitching quoits, and even playing an early form of baseball, or one-o-cat. It was really after the Mormons moved west that sports blossomed. In the latter half of the 19th century, especially after the Civil War, Utah Territory witnessed cricket, baseball, bowling, boxing, wrestling, horse racing, and later football and basketball. Some of these activities took place at the Church academies and Brigham Young University (q.v.).

It was in conjunction with the Young Men and Young Women (qq.v.) programs, first called Mutual Improvement Associations, that sports were most directly sponsored by the Church. By the early years of the 20th century, manuals for leaders and Church magazines were giving guidelines for activity on the ward (q.v.) level in which young people might participate not only in softball and basketball but also volleyball, swimming, gymnastics, and track-and-field events. Those involved in Boy Scouting (q.v.) often enjoyed camping as well.

Tournaments with competition on the stake (q.v.), then regional, and finally the all-Church level were organized after World War II. In 1962 more than 50,000 players participated on 3,500 basketball teams. Softball and other sports had similar tournaments.

In 1971, with a rapidly expanding membership (q.v.), Church leaders ended the all-Church competitions but encouraged a continuation of sports activity on the local level. Anxious to provide wholesome activities for young people, local leaders of Young Men and Young Women have included sports in their weekday programs. During winter months these often take place in ward (q.v.) cultural halls. And of course full programs of intercollegiate and intramural athletics are sponsored by Brigham Young University, Brigham Young University–Hawaii, and Ricks College (qq.v.). *See also* DANCE.

STAKE. Comparable in some ways to a diocese, a stake is an administrative subdivision of the Church comprising several wards (q.v.) and usually 2,000 or more members. The term is derived from Isaiah 54:2: "Enlarge the place of thy tent and let them stretch forth the curtains of thine habitations: spare not, lengthen thy cords, and strengthen thy stakes."

A stake is presided over by a stake president and two counselors (qq.v.), constituting the presidency, and a high council (q.v.). They are responsible for calling bishops (q.v.) of wards, supervising training of ward officers, and holding leadership meetings. Stake presidencies and high councils also serve as judicial bodies for disciplinary cases. Conferences for all of the members living within the stake boundaries are held semiannually.

Since the full program of the Church is available in a stake, it has been called by Ezra Taft Benson (q.v.) "a miniature Church to the Saints (q.v.) in a specific geographic area" (*Ensign* (q.v.), January 1991, 4). The organization of a stake in an area is an indication of maturity in the organizational development there. For this to take place there must be sufficient members. Also essential is a certain mass of qualified and worthy leadership to serve as members of the stake presidency, the high council, bishoprics in the five to 10 wards, leaders of the stake and ward auxiliary (q.v.) organizations, and teachers (q.v.) for the many classes.

In addition to total membership (q.v.), therefore, an important indication of development is the number of stakes. By decade, here are the figures:

1950	180
1960	319
1970	537
1980	1,218
1990	1,784

By the end of 1998 there were 2,505 stakes.

STANDARD WORKS. *See* SCRIPTURE.

STEPHENS, EVAN (1854–1930). Director, Mormon Tabernacle Choir (q.v.), 1890–1916. Converts to Mormonism in Wales, the Stephens family emigrated in 1866. From a childhood of relative poverty in Willard, Utah, Evan showed an interest in music (q.v.) and obtained lessons. He performed in the local choir, gave voice lessons, and began composing songs. After living in Logan for a time, he moved to Salt Lake City and during the 1880s became well known for his training choirs, including teaching hundreds of children how to read music.

Named director of the Mormon Tabernacle Choir in 1890, Stephens reorganized the group and enlarged it. In the World Columbian Exposition at Chicago in 1893 this choir won second place. Several other tours followed during the next two decades, giving Stephens and his choir a high reputation. He served as director until 1916.

Largely self-trained, Stephens attended the New England Conservatory in 1886. He composed cantatas, two oratorios, and many choruses and anthems. Many of his compositions were popular among Mormons. Some of them are still in the Church hymnal: "Let Us All Press On," "True to the Faith," "For the Strength of the Hills," "We Ever Pray for Thee," and others. For some of these he wrote the words as well as the music.

In addition to directing the Mormon Tabernacle Choir, Evan Stephens had private students and conducted special choruses of children and youth (q.v.). For a period he headed the Stephens Opera Company.

STRANG, JAMES J. (1813–1856). Leader of a schismatic group. Born on 21 March 1813 in Scipio, New York, Strang was baptized in 1844 shortly before the death of Joseph Smith (q.v.). Claiming to have received a letter from Smith appointing him successor, Strang was rejected by the main body of the Church and excommunicated. He formed a small religious community on Beaver Island in Lake Michigan that grew to nearly 3,000 members. At first opposed to polygamy (q.v.), Strang soon embraced the practice and married his first plural wife in 1849. Strang's theocratic community encountered internal dissension and outside opposition and on 16 June 1856 Strang was assassinated. The group fell apart, but several small "Strangite" groups survived in the United States.

SUCCESSION. When Joseph Smith (q.v.) was murdered in 1844, the Church faced a crisis of succession. Who was the lawful successor as prophet and president (qq.v.)? Had this been provided for in the revelations? Or must there be a struggle between competing claimants?

Various principles were advanced. Membership in the Council of Fifty (q.v.) and a personal call from Joseph Smith led to the departure of Lyman Wight (q.v.) for Texas; James J. Strang (q.v.) claimed a letter from the prophet had appointed him; Sidney Rigdon (q.v.), surviving member of the First Presidency (q.v.), put forth a proposal that he act as "guardian"; some asserted that leadership now devolved upon the Church patriarch (q.v.); and some insisted that "young Joseph," age eight, was the leader designate and would become prophet as soon as he grew up.

Despite such confusion and potential anarchy, the leadership of the Quorum of the Twelve Apostles (q.v.) was quickly agreed upon by the great majority at a conference on 8 August 1844. The vote in favor of the Twelve was virtually unanimous. In practical terms the Twelve were experienced leaders. In legal terms they remembered not only their equal authority with the First Presidency (Doctrine and Covenants, section 107) but also a "last charge" in which Joseph Smith had told them they would lead if he should die. It was the Twelve, then, with Brigham Young (q.v.) as president, who effectively rallied the members, directed their preparations and flight from Nauvoo, organized them into companies, and led them to the Salt Lake Valley. In late 1847 Brigham Young became president of the Church, not just president of the Twelve.

At the death of every Church president since, it has been the president of the Twelve who succeeded. On two occasions, 1877–80 and 1887–89, some time lapsed before the reestablishment of the First Presidency. Since then, the transition has taken place immediately. A sustaining (q.v.) by the membership of the Church in conference expresses support and approval for the new leader, but this is not an election. *See also* EXODUS.

SUNDAY SCHOOL. Church auxiliary (q.v.) organization founded in 1867, building on a local Sunday School started in 1849 by Richard Ballantyne (q.v.). The first general superintendent was George Q. Cannon (q.v.). A general board was appointed, lesson materials were produced, a periodical (*The Juvenile Instructor*) was started, and supervision instituted.

At present Sunday School meets for about an hour each week. Classes are offered for all those over 12, ranging from the adult Gospel Doctrine course on the scriptures (q.v.) through different moral, historical, and scriptural subjects for youth (q.v.). For new members and those interested in investigating Mormonism, a course on gospel essentials is offered. Classes are taught by lay members of the congregation. Children under 12 attend Primary (q.v.).

SUNSTONE. Independent magazine published by the Sunstone Foundation, a nonprofit corporation. Subtitled "Mormon Experience, Scholarship, Issues, and Art," *Sunstone* states on its title page that it is interested in "feature- and column-length articles relevant to Mormonism from a variety of perspectives; news stories about Mormons and the LDS (q.v.) church, and poetry, psalms, and limericks." Short stories are published and an annual award given for the best fiction.

Annually in Salt Lake City and at irregular intervals in other cities, *Sunstone* sponsors a symposium, including papers and panel discussions on a variety of Mormon-related issues.

SUSTAINING. A vote and an attitude.

1. When individuals are named to positions in the Church ("called" to the responsibility by those over them), those in the same jurisdiction have the opportunity to express their "common consent" by vote. The person conducting the meeting says, "All those willing to sustain *X* as bishop of the ward (qq.v.) please express it by raising the hand," or words to this effect. With rare exceptions the resulting votes are unanimous. The action is not construed as an election with competing candidates but as an opportunity to express one's support and willingness to follow leadership. If there is a reason that might impair the leader's ability to function, if there is some moral unworthiness for example, the member who knows of this votes in the negative and has an opportunity after the meeting to explain the reasons to the presiding authorities. Mere personal dislike or preference for someone else is not considered grounds for exclusion.

2. The attitude expressed by the vote and the term *sustain* is that of willingness to follow the leadership and do what is in one's power to support and assist.

-T-

TABERNACLE. 1. Building in Salt Lake City used for general church conferences and other large assemblies or concerts. Completed in 1867, the Tabernacle is 250 feet long and 150 feet wide. Its dome-shaped roof has the appearance of half an eggshell or, as some have suggested, the back of a turtle. Constructed before the railroad arrived, the structure was made with many wooden dowels and even rawhide was used to reinforce and strengthen the lattice trusses in the attic. A great pipe organ, which has been modernized and replaced from time to time, resounds in daily recitals and on weekly broadcasts. The Tabernacle is considered an architectural and historic landmark.

2. The word *tabernacle*, of Old Testament origin, was also used to describe buildings put up in some of the stakes (q.v.), but that usage is now rare.

TALMAGE, JAMES EDWARD (1862–1933). Educator, university president, Apostle. Leading Mormon theologian for many years.

Born in England on 22 September 1862, Talmage was a Diocesan Scholar at Oxford. But his education was interrupted by the conversion of his family (q.v.) and their immigration to Utah in 1876. He entered Brigham Young Academy and studied with Karl G. Maeser (q.v.). After teaching science and English at the Brigham Young Academy he pursued advanced training at Lehigh University and the Johns Hopkins University.

Returning to Utah in 1884, Talmage was professor of geology and chemistry at Brigham Young Academy. In 1888 he was president of Latter-day Saints College (now defunct) in Salt Lake City and six years later became president of the University of Utah. For health reasons Talmage resigned as university president in 1897 but remained as professor of geology. He affiliated with many scientific societies.

In addition to works on science such as *First Book of Nature* (1888) and *Domestic Science* (1891), Talmage wrote important books on the Mormon religion: *The Articles of Faith* (1899); and *The Great Apostasy* (1909). In 1911 he was named to the Quorum of the Twelve Apostles (q.v.). He continued writing, producing *The House of the Lord* (1912) and *Jesus the Christ* (1915).

During the 1920s and early 1930s Talmage was a central figure in attempting to explain the consistency of the Mormon religion with some of the findings of modern science. His view was that the means of creation were not known, or at least were not part of the Mormon religious understanding, but that the human race was created by God. *See also* CREATION.

TANNER, NATHAN ELDON (1898–1982). Canadian businessman and politician, Apostle, counselor in the First Presidency (q.v.). Born in Salt Lake City, Tanner was quickly taken by his mother back to the family (q.v.) homestead several miles outside Cardston, Alberta, Canada. Growing up, he learned the rigors of farmwork. His education consisted of classes in one-room schools and, after the family moved into Cardston, completion of secondary school. He then went to normal school in Calgary, became certified as a teacher, and took a position as principal of a school in Hill Spring. In 1919 he married Sarah Merrill, also a schoolteacher. As children came (eventually five daughters), Eldon acquired a general store to bring in additional income. Accepting an assignment as scoutmaster, he started a long career in the Boy Scouts (q.v.), in which he would influence hundreds of boys.

In 1927 Tanner became high school principal in Cardston. In the Church he was called as a counselor to the ward bishop (qq.v.). In 1933 he became bishop and was elected to the city council. During these depression years he was attracted to the Social Credit Party and in 1935 was elected to the provincial legislature at Edmonton on its ticket. There he became speaker of the Assembly and the next year minister of lands and mines. In this position he acquired a reputation for honesty and steady leadership in developing Alberta's natural resources, especially the oil industry.

Living in Edmonton, the Tanners were active in the little branch of the Church, of which Eldon became president and his wife, Sarah, the Relief Society (q.v.) president. He oversaw the growth of the branch and the construction of a chapel. During these Edmonton years the five daughters married.

After his retirement from the government in 1952 Tanner moved to Calgary and became president of Merrill Petroleums. Then he was named president of Trans-Canada Pipelines Company, the world's largest natural gas pipeline project—2,300 miles long—which would challenge his administrative skills for the next several years. Continuing to live in Calgary, he became president of the Church's Calgary Stake (q.v.) and supervised its expansion.

In 1960 Tanner was called to be an Assistant to the Twelve (q.v.). The next year he became president of the Western European Mission, with headquarters in London, where for the next two years he supervised the beginnings of a remarkable building program and laid the groundwork for the growth that would continue. In 1962 he became a member of the Quorum of the Twelve Apostles (q.v.). One of his specific assignments was to be president of the Genealogical Society of the Church, which was embarking on an ambitious worldwide program of microfilming records. The next year he was named to be a counselor in the First Presidency (q.v.) of the Church. The president at the time was David O.

McKay (q.v.), while the other counselor was Tanner's uncle Hugh B. Brown, also a Canadian.

During the next two decades Tanner served in the highest council of the Church, steadily acquiring experience and becoming the indispensable right-hand man of four presidents, who because of advanced age were at times weak or partially incapacitated. Tanner was a counselor to Presidents David O. McKay, Joseph Fielding Smith, Harold B. Lee, and Spencer W. Kimball (qq.v.). His loyalty to each of these presidents was unquestionable, and they relied on him as an experienced administrator and a force for continuity. His previous experience equipped him especially for guiding Church businesses, building communications through the media, forming policy for colleges and schools, and directing building programs. He took an active role in many different community programs.

Reflecting admiration for his many accomplishments and contributions, the Salt Lake Area Chamber of Commerce named Tanner "Giant in our City" in 1978. In 1980 Brigham Young University (q.v.) named him Executive of the Year and named the new Management School building after him. "President N. Eldon Tanner will go down in history as one of the greatest counselors ever to serve in the First Presidency of the Church," said Apostle Marvin J. Ashton (q.v.). "He is a man of few words and much performance."

TAYLOR, JOHN (1808–1887). Missionary (q.v.), Apostle, Church president (q.v.). Born in England, where he received several years of primary education, John Taylor immigrated to Canada with his parents in 1832. At first a Methodist preacher and then a seeker, he and his wife were converted to Mormonism in 1836. Two years later, in Missouri, he became a member of the Quorum of the Twelve Apostles (q.v.).

Participating in the forced exodus (q.v.) from Missouri and the establishment of a settlement at Nauvoo, Illinois, Taylor joined several of his fellow Apostles on a mission to England in 1839 and there enjoyed phenomenal success. Later, in the early 1850s, he led the first Mormon proselytizing in France and Germany.

Always a strong defender of Joseph Smith (q.v.), Taylor accompanied him to Carthage Jail in June 1844, where Smith and his brother Hyrum (q.v.) were killed. Taylor incurred several wounds but survived. He was among the organizers of the great exodus to the West, leading, with fellow Apostle Parley P. Pratt (q.v.), a large company of 1,500 people to the Salt Lake Valley in 1847.

Except for his missionary tour in Europe, Taylor had his hands full providing for his families (q.v.). (Among the first to be introduced by Joseph Smith to plural marriage, he eventually had seven wives and 35 children.) A major expenditure of time and money was his project, at Brigham Young's (q.v.) request, of introducing sugar beets and sugar processing to Utah, which failed for lack of proper equipment. Civic responsibilities included the territorial legislature, where he was speaker of the house and territorial superintendent of schools.

Articulate and pugnacious, Taylor participated in several debates with Protestant ministers and others. He edited Mormon newspapers in Nauvoo and New York as well as founding *Etoile du Deseret* in France. His tribute to Joseph Smith was included as section 135 of the Doctrine and Covenants (q.v.).

In addition to many sermons, he wrote *The Government of God* (1852) and *The Mediation and Atonement of Our Lord and Savior Jesus Christ* (1882). Following Brigham Young's death in 1877, Taylor at first led the Church simply as president of the Quorum of the Twelve Apostles but in 1880 was ordained president (q.v.) of the Church.

His was a holding action. The Edmunds Act (1882) and Edmunds-Tucker Act (1877) brought intense pressure on the Mormons, which by 1890 would bring about the Manifesto formally ending polygamy (qq.v.). But during his lifetime Taylor refused to yield. His motto was "The Kingdom of God or nothing." With other Mormon leaders he went into hiding, leading the Church from "the underground." There he died of heart failure in 1887.

TEACHER. In addition to its general meaning, an office in the Aaronic Priesthood (q.v.). Having already served as a deacon (q.v.), a young man is advanced to teacher at 14. Then at age 16, assuming worthiness (q.v.), he is advanced to the office of priest (q.v.).

Teachers in the Aaronic Priesthood retain the right to perform all the duties of a deacon. In addition, they prepare the sacrament (q.v.), do home teaching (q.v.), and in general respond to the request of the bishop (q.v.) in ushering and assisting people.

They are organized into a quorum (q.v.) of 24 or less and, like other holders of the Priesthood (q.v.), meet on Sundays for instruction. During weekdays they often have service projects and social activities.

TEMPLE SQUARE. A square block at the center of Salt Lake City, surrounded by a wall, within which stand some of the Church's most historic and sacred buildings and monuments: the Salt Lake Temple (q.v.), the Tabernacle (q.v.), the Assembly Hall, two visitor centers (q.v.), and several sculptural works, including a replica of Thorvaldsen's renowned *Christus*.

"Here we will build a temple to our God," Brigham Young (q.v.) said, touching his cane to the ground soon after the arrival of the pioneer (q.v.) company in July 1847. But not until 1853 was the spot dedicated and construction begun, and because of interruptions and financial difficulties the temple was not completed until 1893. An Endowment House was razed upon the completion of the Temple.

A bowery, a simple shelter providing protection against the sun, was replaced by an early tabernacle, which gave way to the present Tabernacle (q.v.) in 1867. The frame visitor centers of the early 20th century were replaced by the present commodious centers during the second half of the 20th century.

Even in pioneer times Temple Square attracted visitors. You could not very easily visit the city without noticing it. Guides were showing people around as early as 1875. For much of the 20th century guided tours were conducted by volunteers. In the 1990s, under the direction of a mission president, most tours were conducted by full-time missionaries (q.v.), young women from different countries. Tours were available in French, German, Spanish, Japanese, Chinese, and other languages. During the holiday season each year the trees are illuminated with 750,000 lights. More than 5,000,000 visitors came annually to Temple Square, making it one of the major tourist attractions in the nation. *See also* TEMPLES.

TEMPLE SQUARE CONCERT SERIES. Concerts performed almost every Friday and Saturday evening of the year in the Assembly Hall on Temple Square (q.v.). Admission is free and open to everyone over eight years of age. Orchestras, choirs, ensembles, instrumental and vocal soloists are included. Performers are selected by a volunteer committee on the basis of tapes submitted. Sponsored by the Church Missionary Department, the concerts are sometimes held more often, as the piano performances given in connection with the Gina Bachauer International Piano Competition.

TEMPLES. Structures or buildings that differ from the usual meetinghouse. Temples are not for regular worship services but are places in which "worthy" Church members participate in sacred ceremonies or ordinances (q.v.). In this general sense Mormon temples are analogous not to a synagogue but to the ancient temples described in the Bible (q.v.).

The first modern temple was constructed at Kirtland, Ohio, in 1836. Its dedicatory prayer (q.v.) is found in the Doctrine and Covenants (q.v.), section 109. When it was dedicated, according to participants, a pentecostal outpouring of heavenly manifestations occurred. Ceremonies included anointings and the washing of feet. Plans to construct a temple in Missouri were frustrated. During the Illinois Period Joseph Smith introduced baptism for the dead (qq.v.), the endowment, and eternal marriage, ordinances participated in by more than 5,000 people in the Nauvoo Temple before their forced departure in early 1846.

In Utah these ceremonies were performed in an Endowment House until it was superseded by the Salt Lake Temple in 1893. Earlier temples had been completed at St. George (1877), Logan (1884), and Manti (1888). To make the temple ordinances more readily available to Mormons elsewhere the early 20th century saw the completion of temples in Hawaii, Alberta, Arizona, and Idaho. After mid-century Switzerland, New Zealand, and England were the sites of temple construction.

Especially since the 1970s temple construction has accelerated as the sacred edifices have gone up in many states and foreign countries, wherever the population of Mormons was deemed sufficient. By 1995, there were temples in Brazil, Japan, Samoa, Tonga, Chile, Tahiti, Mexico, Australia, the Philippines, Taiwan, Guatemala, Germany, Sweden, South Africa, Korea, Peru, Argentina, and Hong Kong.

Although the proceedings within Mormon temples are considered sacred and are not discussed or described by faithful members, authorized publications give all of the basic factual information. In fonts containing water to the level of three or four feet, persons of age 12 or over are baptized by immersion as proxies for deceased individuals. In another section washings and anointings are received. In the endowment ceremony participants observe a series of dramatic reenactments of the purpose of the creation and the mortal probation, and special vows or covenants are entered into having to do with faithfulness and moral purity and service to the Lord. In small rooms containing an altar, persons are married and "sealed" together not just for this life but for eternity. The endowments and the sealings (q.v.) can also be performed by proxy for the dead.

Faithful Mormons describe the temple experience as a noble, Christ-centered service, a spiritual high point in their lives. To participate in the temples one must be not only a member of the Church but the holder of a signed recommend (q.v.), or certificate of worthiness (q.v.), from one's bishop and stake president (qq.v.). That curious nonmembers are not allowed into the temples has to do not so much with secretiveness as with the sacredness of the temples. Observation by tourists would be clearly disruptive to the purpose of the buildings. They are scheduled for virtually constant use from early in the morning until late at night. Prior to its dedication a new temple is normally open to public viewing for a specified period of time.

On 4 October 1997 President Gordon B. Hinckley announced that "smaller" temples would be constructed throughout the world in certain locations where the number of Church members did not justify the larger structures. Even the smaller buildings were considerably larger than the average meetinghouse and contained all essentials for administering temple ordinances. As construction accelerated, the number of functioning Mormon temples was expected to reach 100 during the year 2000. *See also* BAPTISM FOR THE DEAD; MISSOURI PERIOD.

TESTIMONY. The conviction or assurance of the truth and goodness of the gospel, or more specifically of Jesus Christ and the modern prophets (qq.v.). When this conviction is expressed in words one "bears testimony." Although study and experience are at its basis, such testimony is ultimately dependent on the Holy Ghost. Such certitude is promised to and claimed by readers of the Book of Mormon (q.v.): "And when ye shall receive these things, I would exhort you that ye would ask God, the Eternal Father, in the name of Christ, if these things are not true; and if ye shall ask with a sincere heart, with real intent, having faith in Christ, he will manifest the truth of it unto you, by the power of the Holy Ghost." (Moroni 10:4–5.)

Those seeking such testimony are advised of four prerequisites: (1) desire, (2) study, (3) practice, and (4) prayer (q.v.). Anyone who fails to receive the personal conviction known as testimony is probably lacking in one or more of these.

One Sunday each month Mormon congregations have a "fast and testimony meeting," in which individuals who wish can stand and express their feelings, that is, bear their testimony, about the gospel. Testimonies are expressed by Mormons in other meetings as well, often in conjunction with a sermon and with missionary (q.v.) proselytizing.

THEOLOGY. Both in the technical sense of a doctrine of God and in the larger sense of religious beliefs about life and its purpose, Mormons have a theology. Indeed, students of Mormonism describe their belief system as rather complex, requiring more than a little study in the standard works (q.v.) and various Church publications to master. But in two related respects Mormonism fits uneasily into usual theological discourse. First, it proceeds from revealed truth with virtually no effort made to employ standard philosophical terminology. Second, there is no class of professionally trained Mormon theologians. Although some individual Mormons have had advanced study in philosophy, theology, or religious studies, such training is not considered necessary.

"THIS IS THE PLACE" MONUMENT. Monument on the east bench overlooking the Salt Lake Valley, commemorating the arrival of the original pioneers (q.v.) in July 1847. According to later recollections, when Brigham Young (q.v.), whose party came out of the mountains on 24 July, first beheld the valley below, he said, "This is the right place. Drive on." Abbreviated to "This is the place," the saying was often repeated as an indication of divine protection and selection. A smaller memorial was replaced in 1947, the centennial year, by the present imposing monument designed and sculpted by Mahonri M. Young. *See also* EXODUS.

THOMAS, CAROL B. (1942–). Born in Salt Lake City, Utah, Carol Burdett married Ray Thomas, who became a medical doctor. They lived in California, Washington, and Kansas before returning to Utah. She is mother of seven children. She served in the ward and stake Relief Society (qq.v.) presidencies and as stake Young Women (q.v.) president (q.v.). In 1997 she became second counselor (q.v.) in the general Young Women presidency.

THREE WITNESSES. *See* WITNESSES OF THE BOOK OF MORMON.

TIMES AND SEASONS. 1. Mormon newspaper published in Nauvoo, Illinois, 1839–46. Motto: "Truth Will Prevail." Editors included Ebeneezer Robinson, Don Carlos Smith, and Robert B. Thompson as well as Joseph Smith, Wilford Woodruff, and John Taylor (qq.v.). 2. Public service television broadcast, starting in 1991.

TINGEY, EARL C. (1934–). Corporate lawyer, church leader. Born in Bountiful, Utah, Tingey served as a missionary (q.v.) in Australia and then graduated from the University of Utah Law School with a juris doctorate. At New York University he received a master of corporate law degree. For three years he was a captain in the U.S. Army with the Judge

Advocate General Corps. Tingey was an attorney on Wall Street. After representing other corporations he became attorney for Kennecott Corporation. He was bishop of the Manhattan Ward, counselor in the Eastern States Mission presidency, president of the Australia Sydney Mission, and regional representative (qq.v.). Tingey was called to the First Quorum of the Seventy (q.v.) in 1990 and in 1996 became a member of its presidency. He and his wife, Joanne, have four children.

TITHING. One-tenth of income, paid to the Church on a voluntary and confidential basis. At an individual interview with their bishop (q.v.) at the end of the year, members verify the amount of their contribution and state whether or not they consider it a full tithing.

Not mandatory in the sense of coercion being imposed or excommunication (q.v.) resulting from failure to pay, tithing is nevertheless considered a commandment (q.v.) and is paid faithfully by fully committed members. Tithing funds are sent by the bishop to Church headquarters, where they are accounted for and dispensed for such purposes as building and maintaining meetinghouses and temples (q.v.) and support of missions and church educational activity. *See also* AUDITORS.

TRIPLE COMBINATION. Three of the standard works of scripture (q.v.)—the Book of Mormon, Doctrine and Covenants, and Pearl of Great Price—when published together as a single volume. These works are of course also published separately.

TWELVE APOSTLES, QUORUM OF THE. Group of General Authorities (q.v.) who have been ordained to this office in the Melchizedek Priesthood (q.v.). When selected as an Apostle, one's name is presented in general conference (q.v.) for the sustaining (q.v.) vote of the Church membership (q.v.). He then receives an ordination by the laying on of the hands of the First Presidency and the other members of the Quorum of the Twelve Apostles (qq.v.).

The authority of the apostolic calling (q.v.) was given to Joseph Smith and Oliver Cowdery (qq.v.) by the ancient Apostles Peter, James, and John in late 1829. The first Quorum of the Twelve Apostles was named in 1835 after having been selected by the Three Witnesses of the Book of Mormon (q.v.). The body has maintained uninterrupted continuity ever since; as vacancies occur, they are filled.

Historically the role of the Twelve grew steadily as they supervised missionary (q.v.) work, organized the forced departure of thousands of Mormons from Missouri, implemented a highly successful proselytizing venture in England, and were given increased responsibilities by Joseph Smith (q.v.) during the Illinois Period (q.v.). Having authority next to that of the First Presidency (q.v.), according to Doctrine and Covenants, section 107, the Twelve were also the recipients of a special charge from Joseph Smith in early 1844 by which he placed on their shoulders the responsibility for carrying on the work. In August 1844, after Smith's murder, it was the Twelve with Brigham Young (q.v.) as president (q.v.) who were approved as leaders of the Church by a nearly unanimous vote of the members assembled in a conference.

Apostles hold their office for life. Special witnesses of Jesus Christ (q.v.), possessing the keys or rights of presidency, Apostles have automatically assumed leadership of the Church at the death of every Church president. After being sustained by a vote in general conference (q.v.), the president of the Apostles has then been ordained the new president of the Church. *See also* SUCCESSION.

-U-

UCHTDORF, DIETER F. (1940–). Airline pilot, Church leader. Born in Ostrava, Czechoslovakia, Uchtdorf grew up in Frankfurt, Germany, as a member of the Church. After service in the German Air Force he graduated from airline pilot school in Bremen, Germany, attended Business Administration School in Cologne, Germany, and the International Management Institute in Lausanne, Switzerland. An airline captain, he headed pilot school for Lufthansa and became senior vice president for flight operations. He served as Young Men president in his ward, stake high councilor, and stake president (qq.v.). In 1994 Uchdorf was called as a member of the Second Quorum of the Seventy (q.v.). He and his wife, Harriet, have two children.

UNITED ORDER. A system of cooperation not now in operation in which Church members would give all their property to the Church, receive back a portion of it as a stewardship, continue to donate surplus production, and generally live in a context of mutual support and equality.

The ideal, ultimately going back to primitive Christianity (q.v.) (Acts 2:44–45; 4:32) and even to the ancient day of Enoch, was proclaimed by Joseph Smith (q.v.) in 1831 (Doctrine and Covenants, section 42) in what was then called the Law of Consecration. When early efforts to practice the system collapsed, it was replaced by the law of tithing and later fast offerings (qq.v.). In the last quarter of the 19th century efforts were made once again to implement communal living in several Utah settlements. Part of the effort to create social and economic unity, self-sufficiency, and survival in the desert, these experiments were analogous to the kibbutz of modern Israel. These were called United Orders, but they varied in types. They were essentially disbanded after Brigham Young's (q.v.) death.

Some scholars have seen this aspect of the Mormon experience as a parallel to the communal or utopian societies found elsewhere in the 19th century, with utopian idealism floundering because of the recalcitrance of human nature. Undoubtedly internal differences contributed to the Mormon failures, but lack of capital and outside pressure were additional obstacles. Some of the spirit of consecration and the United Order remains in the tradition of dedicating one's life to God's work on earth, commitments made in the temples (q.v.), financial donations such as tithing and fast offering, and the ideal of equality, which allows lay leaders of different wealth and background to work together as brothers and sisters (q.v.). In the Welfare Program (q.v.) also they have banded together in the spirit of fellowship to provide for those in need.

UTAH PERIOD. Roughly the second half of the 19th century. Following its origins in New York and unsuccessful efforts to establish itself in Ohio, Missouri, and Illinois, the great majority of Church members moved westward in a great exodus (q.v.) and established themselves in the Great Basin of the Rocky Mountains, with the headquarters in the Salt Lake Valley.

The original pioneer (q.v.) company of July 1847 was followed by other companies. By the end of the year, some 3,000 Mormons were living in wagon boxes, tents, and simple cabins, hoping to survive the winter and then enjoy crops they had planted soon after their arrival. Survive they did, although under conditions of privation. During the next two or three years groups continued to arrive, both those who had been temporarily encamped in Iowa or Nebraska, and converts from England and elsewhere. When the 1850 census was taken, 11,380 people were counted. Ten years later, reinforced by continued immigration and new births, the population had reached 40,273.

Unsuccessful in achieving early statehood, the newly settled area was recognized as a U.S. territory. At first Brigham Young (q.v.) was both president (q.v.) of the Church and presidentially appointed governor, but in 1857 he was replaced as governor. Church and state would not be combined, although Church members looked to their president for leadership in all kinds of things, and because of their numerical preponderance in the territory they dominated much of economic, political, and social life.

Until his death in 1877 Brigham Young (q.v.), sometimes called "the Lion of the Lord," was the Mormon leader. Under his direction missionary proselytizing continued and an ambitious gathering (qq.v.) was organized. Year after year companies of converts from the United States or Europe arrived. A revolving fund was established to assist the immigrants and allow them to repay later. For a few years some companies crossed the plains using handcarts (q.v.). The transcontinental railroad was completed in 1869, after which almost all immigrants arrived by rail.

To sustain their expanding population in a hostile, arid environment the Mormons developed irrigation agriculture. An extraordinary program of colonization (q.v.) extended over several decades and resulted in the settlement of most of the parts of Utah that seemed to provide the necessary soil and water. In fact, the colonization extended more broadly through the western states—and before the century's end northern Mexico, and southern Canada—but Utah remained the center. Young and his successors did what they could to achieve economic self-sufficiency in the region but were never wholly successful.

In terms of religious history the Utah period was one of continuing hostility from outside. The formal announcement of polygamy (q.v.) proved to be a lightning rod, providing a focus for the resentment of the Mormons' enemies. Some of the Latter-day Saints saw it as an excuse, and they may have been right, at least in part, for the persecution (q.v.) had started long before the vexing marriage system, and throughout complaints about political and economic domination were also heard. In any case, the negative press, including a flow of sometimes funny but cruel, barbed cartoons, caricatured the Mormons as superstitious, authoritarian, and lascivious.

Conflict between the Mormons and the federal government almost developed into a bloody military confrontation in 1857, when the new governor headed west accompanied by U.S. troops. Brigham Young, who had not been officially notified of his release, rallied his people, called out the militia, and prepared to resist. This was the so-called Utah War. Miraculously, despite the lamentable Mountain Meadows Massacre (q.v.), the conflict ended after skirmishes and no other loss of life.

After the Civil War a series of antipolygamy statutes signaled the determination of the Congress to bring the Mormons into conformity with the rest of the nation. Church leaders, both Brigham Young and his successor John Taylor (q.v.), insisted that these efforts were in violation of their constitutional rights. In 1879 a landmark Supreme Court decision *(Reynolds v. United States)* drew a crucial distinction, finding that antisocial practices such as polygamy could be prohibited even though they might have a religious basis. The Edmunds Act of 1882 and the Edmunds-Tucker Act of 1887 were increasingly punitive. Many Mormon polygamists, including such Church leaders as George Q. Cannon (q.v.), served time in prison ("for conscience sake," they said). The Church was dissolved as a legal corporation; property in excess of $50,000 was confiscated; female suffrage was abolished; and a test oath was used to bar polygamists from voting. After the first such test oath was declared unconstitutional, another one, even more stringent, was devised and, starting with an Idaho case, was enlarged to bar all who supported a polygamous system—in other words, all Church members.

This was the situation when Taylor's successor, Wilford Woodruff (q.v.), issued the 1890 Manifesto (q.v.) formally ending polygamy. Although that document has often been misunderstood and given too much credit for effecting an immediate transformation, the fact is that a watershed had been reached. Making concessions not only on polygamy but also in their political and economic goals, the Mormons retained their theology and temples (q.v.). By this process, sometimes called accommodation, they gave up on peripheral matters in order to retain and emphasize the central thrust of the restoration (q.v.).

The Utah Period was not only a time of troubles. It was also a time of growth and consolidation. The 40,000 Utah population of 1860 reached 276,749 in 1900, including several thousand non-Mormons. Including Mormons outside the state, Church membership (q.v.) in 1900 has been calculated at 236,628. From the Church's beginning in 1830 or even from the arrival in Utah in 1847, the ascent had been steadily upward.

Institutional developments included the standardization of wards and stakes (qq.v.); the creation of the auxiliary organizations known then or later as Relief Society, Sunday School, Primary, Young Men, and Young Women (qq.v.); and an emphasis on temples, with such sacred edifices constructed not only in Salt Lake City but also in St. George, Manti, and Logan. Priesthood quorums were divided with the Aaronic Priesthood for teenage youths and the Melchizedek Priesthood (qq.v.) for adult males. The missionary (q.v.) program was reorganized and standardized. In many ways, therefore, the Utah Period, building on the foundations of the earlier experiences in Ohio, Missouri, and Illinois, formed the detailed structure of the Church as it exists today.

Statehood for Utah was achieved in 1896. During the closing quarter of the century the Church was already showing signs of being much more than a one-state Church. Outposts had been established in Colorado, Arizona, Nevada, New Mexico, Idaho, Wyoming, and even Canada and Mexico. Missionaries were having success in Samoa, Tonga, New Zealand, the southern United States, and Europe (q.v.), and many of the convert families (q.v.) were staying put rather than migrating. But for half a century at least Utah had been a place of refuge and consolidation as well as continued adaptation. *See also* ANTI-MORMONISM; ILLINOIS PERIOD; MISSOURI PERIOD; OHIO PERIOD.

-V-

VINAS, FRANCISCO J. (1946–). Educator, church leader. Born in Spain, Vinas was raised as a member of the church in Uruguay. After graduating with a bachelor's degree, he was employed as a product cost supervisor for Bayer Q.U., Ltd. Later he became coordinator for the Church Educational System in Spain. In Uruguay, he served as bishop, stake president, regional representative, mission president, and area authority (qq.v.). In 1996 Vinas was called to be a member of the Second Quorum of the Seventy (q.v.). He and his wife, Cristina, have three children.

VISITING TEACHING. Program of the Relief Society (q.v.) by which each member of the organization—now automatically including all adult female members of the Church—is visited regularly, at least quarterly with additional telephone contacts. Those assigned as visiting teachers normally go as a team of two. They bring as a teaching message, an item of instruction or inspiration. Most importantly, they show a personal interest in the person being visited. Where personal or family (q.v.) problems exist they render whatever help they can. If these are extreme or if financial problems loom large, the visiting teachers report back to the Relief Society president, who is able to enlist the help of the ward bishop (q.v.) in providing an appropriate response. *See also* HOME TEACHING.

VISITORS' CENTERS. Departments or bureaus at historic sites where visitors can ask questions and obtain literature. Visitors' centers are staffed by Church members, some of them serving as full-time missionaries (q.v.), others as part-time volunteers.

The first such center was established in 1902 at Temple Square (q.v.) in Salt Lake City following complaints about the misrepresentation being purveyed to tourists by anti-Mormons or uninformed cab drivers. Other visitor's centers are located near Palmyra, New York, in Nauvoo, Illinois, in Independence, Missouri, and at several of the temples (q.v.). *See also* HISTORIC SITES.

-W-

WARD. The Church's basic ecclesiastical unit, similar to a parish. Membership (q.v.) is somewhere between 300 and 700. A lay bishop with his two counselors (qq.v.) presides over the ward. Ward clerks assist with membership and financial records. An executive secretary coordinates. The bishop selects and calls ward members to serve in the many teaching positions, music director, accompanists, auxiliary (q.v.) leaders, and so on.

Mormon wards provide a weekly worship service, the sacrament meeting (q.v.). In addition there are bishopric meetings, Priesthood meetings for the males over age 12, Relief Society for the adult women, programs for Young Women and Young Men (including Scouting), Primary for children, and Sunday School (qq.v.). Wards sometimes sponsor social and sports (q.v.) activities. Much of the life of active Mormons centers on their ward.

When Church members are few in number, they worship in families (q.v.) or in branches. When they are sufficiently numerous, they are organized into wards. When membership in an existing ward passes a certain point, the ward is divided, thus providing opportunities of service to many more people. Like the membership generally and like stakes (qq.v.), wards have sharply increased in number.

1951	1,666
1961	3,143
1971	5,135
1981	11,063
1991	15,511

At the end of 1998, the official report claimed 25,551 wards and branches in the Church. *See also* CALLING.

WARNER, SUSAN L. (1940–). Educator and church leader. Born in Salt Lake City, Utah, Susan Lillywhite was raised in California. She received a bachelor's degree in elementary education and psychology from Brigham Young University (q.v.). She married Terry Warner, who earned a doctorate at Yale University and became a professor of philosophy. They have 10 children. After teaching elementary school, Susan Warner worked as a volunteer substitute teacher, in the unwed mother placement program, on the child abuse council, and on a committee for gifted and talented children. Her church callings (q.v.) included teacher and counselor in ward Primary, ward Relief Society president, ward Young Women president, and member of the Primary general board (qq.v.). In 1994 Warner became second counselor in the general Primary presidency.

WELCH, JOHN W. (1946–). Lawyer, writer, editor, and student of scriptures (q.v.). Born in Boston, Massachusetts, on 15 October 1946, John Welch was raised in the Los Angeles, California, area. He was a missionary (q.v.) in southern Germany, 1966–68, and in 1970 graduated as social sciences valedictorian with highest honors from Brigham Young University (q.v.). After receiving an M.A. degree in Latin and Greek from BYU, Welch studied Greek philosophy, ancient Greek history, and modern British analytic philosophy at Oxford for two years. At Duke Law School he was articles editor on the law journal, graduating with a J.D. in 1975.

For five years Welch worked at a Los Angeles law firm. He later accepted a position as professor of law at BYU's J. Reuben Clark Law School in 1980. He has published several law journal articles on such topics as deferred compensation, shareholder derivative actions, and qualified pension plans. A member of the Jewish Law Association, he follows the research in biblical law, coediting *Religion and Law: Biblical, Jewish and Islamic Perspectives.* In 1990 he published a bibliography of biblical law.

While still an undergraduate Welch detected the presence of chiasmus, an intricate parallel literary form known especially from Jewish scripture, in the Book of Mormon (q.v.). In 1974 he published an article on chiasmus in Ugaritic and in 1981 edited an ambitious book on chiasmus in antiquity. It was a natural step, too, for him to pay close attention to legal matters in the Book of Mormon, leading to articles on "Judicial Process in the Trial of Abinadi" and "Lehi's Last Will and Testament." Combining interests, he published "Chiasmus in Biblical Law" in 1990.

In 1979 Welch founded and became president and director of the new Foundation for Ancient Research and Mormon Studies (q.v.) In addition to encouraging the scholarship of others and producing books and articles on different aspects of the Book of Mormon, he published *The Sermon at the Temple and the Sermon on the Mount* (1990). One of the editors of the five-volume *Encyclopedia of Mormonism* published by Macmillan (1992), he was named editor of *Brigham Young University Studies* (q.v.) in 1991.

Welch and his wife, Norma Jean, have four children. In the Church he has taught Sunday School classes, served as a bishop, and, on the stake level he has been a high councilor and a counselor in the stake presidency (qq.v.).

WELFARE PROGRAM. A continuing program instituted by the Church during the 1930s when the Great Depression had produced high unemployment and hardship.

With a view to provide food for those in need while avoiding "the evils of the dole," the program started by allowing Church members from the city to harvest crops that were so unprofitable that the farmers would have allowed them to remain in the fields. Leading the way in these early efforts was a Salt Lake City stake (q.v.) whose president was Harold B. Lee (q.v.). Storehouses were established for the storage and distribution of food and clothing. A network of outlets of contributed clothing, furniture, and other items provided essentials at a nominal cost while also offering employment.

As the program developed, members were instructed in basic principles of self-reliance. Having an emergency supply of food and other basics was repeatedly urged. Farms of different sizes and specialties were acquired to produce for the welfare storehouses through the voluntary labor of Church members. By 1985 there were 199 agricultural production projects and 51 canneries. Goods were processed and sent to regional and branch storehouses. Families in need would consult with leaders of the Relief Society and bishop of the ward (qq.v.), who had the responsibility of evaluation and attempting to match assistance with donated voluntary labor. Much of the labor was donated by Church members simply as charitable service.

Responding to different needs, career counseling, financial management, and assistance from social workers are also available. With the expansion into different parts of the world, welfare missionaries (q.v.), often young women, are sent to offer instruction in nutrition, health care, hygiene, and agriculture.

Persons in need are expected to look first to the resources of their family (q.v.). Any assistance from the Church is regarded as temporary. Moreover, there is an expectation of work; one should not expect a handout. The underlying objective is not a dependency class but self-reliant members.

WELLS, EMMELINE B. (1828–1921). Leader of Mormon women, editor, Relief Society president (qq.v.). Born in Petersham, Massachusetts, on 29 February 1828, Emmeline Blanche Woodward became a schoolteacher and married James H. Harris. Converts to Mormonism, they moved to Nauvoo, Illinois, in early 1844. In the fall her husband left in search of work. He never returned, leaving her confused and destitute. Only many years later did she discover that he had died in an accident on a ship in the Indian Ocean.

Mormon polygamy (q.v.) proved an answer for her situation. She became the plural wife of Newel K. Whitney, who provided for her during the trip across the plains to Utah. When he died, she became a plural wife of Daniel H. Wells, a prominent Church leader. The disadvantages of the system became apparent in her lack of companionship.

Emmeline B. Wells became a staunch advocate of women's rights. She published articles in *Woman's Exponent,* an outspoken organ for Mormon women, and in 1877 became its editor. It was in this capacity that she became a recognized spokesperson for women. Attending national meetings for female suffrage, she became acquainted with Susan B. Anthony and Elizabeth Cady Stanton. Wells held office in several organizations, including the National Council of Women and the International Council of Women.

In 1910 Wells became general president of the Relief Society and thus official leader of Mormon women. In the Utah State Capitol stands a marble bust from the women of Utah in honor of "A Fine Soul Who Served Us." *See also* ILLINOIS PERIOD.

WHITMER, DAVID (1805–1888). Early follower of Joseph Smith (q.v.) and one of the special three witnesses, along with Oliver Cowdery and Martin Harris (qq.v.), who testified that an angel showed them the metal plates from which the Book of Mormon (q.v.) was translated.

Born on 7 January 1805 in Pennsylvania, Whitmer moved with his family (q.v.) to Fayette, New York, in 1809. When he was a young man, he learned of Joseph Smith's project of translation, traveled to Harmony, Pennsylvania, and there was elated when Smith received a special revelation (q.v.) for him (Doctrine and Covenants, section 14). Soon Joseph and Emma Hale Smith (q.v.) were on their way to the Whitmer farm in Fayette, where the project was completed. The importance of the Whitmers at this stage is suggested by the fact that of the Eight Witnesses who saw the metal plates four were Whitmers and a fifth, Hiram Page, was a brother-in-law. Of the Three Witnesses, David was a Whitmer and Oliver Cowdery would be a brother-in-law. Martin Harris, the third witness, was unrelated. It was this special status as one of the Three Witnesses that remained David Whitmer's claim to fame for the remainder of his life.

Whitmer moved to Kirtland, Ohio, in 1831 and shortly thereafter moved on to Jackson County, Missouri. He and other members of his family established themselves along the Big Blue River (present Kansas City), but were among those forced to leave in 1833. Relocated in Clay County, David Whitmer became president of a stake (qq.v.) organized there. This prestigious assignment was short lived, for in late 1834 he moved back to Kirtland. With Oliver Cowdery and Martin Harris he selected the first Quorum of the Twelve Apostles (q.v.) in 1835. The following year he attended the dedication of the Kirtland Temple and witnessed a spiritual outpouring.

The next two years were emotionally taxing. Failure of a banking enterprise led many in Kirtland to question Joseph Smith's leadership in temporal affairs. The persecution intensified both in Ohio and Missouri. Jealousies led to bitter disputes over leadership. It was in this context that David Whitmer was excommunicated on 13 April 1838. His own grievances, to judge from a pamphlet he wrote later, stemmed in part from his refusal to accept evolution in the organization and doctrines.

Whitmer moved to Richmond, Missouri, where for 50 years he ran a livery stable and became a respected citizen. Many thought that his complaints about Joseph Smith would lead him to disavow his testimony (q.v.). But he held consistently to his sworn statement to the end of his life. *See also* EXCOMMUNICATION; WITNESSES OF THE BOOK OF MORMON.

WIDTSOE, JOHN ANDREAS (1872–1952). Scientist, educator, Apostle. Born in Norway, Widtsoe at age six moved with his mother to Trondheim after the death of his father. Reading some Mormon tracts, his mother investigated and converted to the new religion. With two young boys she immigrated to the United States in 1883, ending up in Logan, Utah. After elementary classes Widtsoe attended Brigham Young College, graduating in 1891.

Widtsoe left for Harvard University, where he graduated with highest honors in chemistry in 1894. His first position was at Utah State Agricultural College. In addition to teaching chemistry he was a chemist at the experiment station. In 1898 he married Leah Eudora Dunford and three months later left with his bride for study in Europe (q.v.), having received a Harvard fellowship. At Göttingen, Germany, he earned the M.A. and Ph.D.

From 1900 he was director of the Utah State Agricultural Experiment Station. Extensive research and travel assisting the farmers of the state led to early publications on dry farming. In 1905 he moved to Brigham Young University (q.v.), where he organized a department of agriculture. Then in 1907 Widtsoe was appointed president of Utah State Agricultural College. He published *Dry Farming: A System of Agriculture for Countries Under a Low Rainfall* in 1910 and in 1912, a book on irrigation. For nine years he administered a university as it went through significant development. In 1916 Widtsoe was selected as president of the University of Utah in Salt Lake City.

While pursuing his professional life, Widtsoe had continued to be a practicing Mormon. He had taught classes and served in different assignments. A series of lessons had been published as *Joseph Smith as Scientist* in 1908 and another in 1915 as *A Rational Theology*. In 1921, he was called as a member of the Quorum of the Twelve Apostles (q.v.). In 1927 he became president (q.v.) of the European and British Mission, living in London until 1933. As one of the Twelve, he participated in the many changes and institutional developments of his generation, stretching from the 1920s to the 1950s. He had direct responsibility for *The Improvement Era* (q.v.) the official Church magazine, and published a monthly column, "Evidences and Reconciliations," in which he answered many historical and doctrinal questions. His total record of published titles, scientific and religious, was prodigious.

WIDTSOE, LEAH DUNFORD (1874–1955). Home economist, granddaughter of Brigham Young (q.v.), daughter of Susa Young Gates.

After graduating from the University of Utah in 1896, Leah Dunford studied at the Pratt Institute, then taught home economics at Brigham Young Academy, from which she received a bachelor's degree in 1899. She had met John A. Widtsoe (q.v.) in 1893 when she visited Boston in company with other prospective summer school students. The acquaintance blossomed into a romance and, after a correspondence, eventually resulted in their marriage in 1898.

Leah D. Widtsoe was an accomplished instructor, specializing in nutrition. She studied, lectured, and wrote. She was an advocate and model of the educated Mormon woman, serving as president of the Salt Lake Federation of Women's Clubs and on the board of the Salt Lake Council of Women. With her mother she wrote on Brigham Young. Collaborating with her husband, she wrote *The Word of Wisdom: A Modern Interpretation*. She had seven children, three of whom reached maturity.

WIGHT, LYMAN (1796–1858). Early Mormon leader, Apostle, and schismatic. Born in Fairfield, New York, on 9 May 1796, Lyman Wight served in the U.S. Army during the War of 1812. After the war he married Harriet Benton and by 1830 was living near Kirtland, Ohio. A "seeker" for the primitive Christian gospel (q.v.), he and others had joined in a cooperative living arrangement called "The Family." When the first Mormon missionaries (q.v.) arrived that year, he accepted the new faith along with Sidney Rigdon (q.v.). Soon he was ordained an elder and then a high priest (qq.v.)

Moving to Missouri, he was among the Mormon leaders forced to sign an agreement that they would leave Jackson County. When a rescue group called Zions Camp (q.v.) was organized, Wight was among its leaders. When a stake (q.v.) was organized in Missouri in 1838, he was selected as a counselor (q.v.) in the presidency. A colonel in the militia, he helped organize the military defense of his people. When taken captive and ordered to stand before a firing squad, he defiantly said, "Shoot and be damned." He was not shot but was placed in prison at Liberty Jail along with Joseph Smith (q.v.).

After his escape he moved to Nauvoo, Illinois, and then became a counselor in the stake presidency across the river in Iowa Territory. In 1841 two new assignments came his way: member of the committee responsible for raising funds for the Nauvoo House, and, more importantly, a member of the Quorum of the Twelve Apostles (q.v.). In the winter of 1843–44 he led a group conducting a logging operation on the Black River in Wisconsin. He corresponded with Joseph Smith about the possibility of leading a colony in Texas (at that time an independent country) and then, in the spring, departed on a preaching mission in New England on behalf of Smith's candidacy for the U.S. presidency. Hearing of the Prophet's (q.v.) assassination, he and the other Apostles returned to Nauvoo.

Insisting that he had orders from Joseph Smith to lead his group to Texas, Wight did so, although Brigham Young (q.v.) and the other

Apostles counseled him not to persist. The two strong-willed men did not see eye to eye. Wight saw his authority as deriving from his apostleship, his membership in the Council of Fifty (q.v.), and a special ordination from Joseph Smith.

In Texas the Wight colony of 200 people established themselves briefly near Austin. In 1847 they established a communitarian settlement called Zodiak on the Pedernales River. A pamphlet he wrote that year reached Salt Lake City at the end of 1848, when Wight was cut off from the Church and replaced as an Apostle. Meanwhile, a flood washed out the dam at Zodiak. Wight and his dwindling followers moved to Hamilton's Creek, then to the Medina River, and finally in 1854 to Mountain Valley.

He was among those who looked to "young Joseph," Joseph Smith III, to become leader of the Church, but since Wight was faithful to such practices as polygamy and temple (qq.v.) ceremonies, he would have been a stormy petrel had he lived to participate in the Reorganized Church of Jesus Christ of Latter Day Saints (q.v.). He died in central Texas in 1858 while attempting to move his followers north to Missouri. The movement, sometimes called the Wightites, quickly dissolved. *See also* COWDERY, OLIVER; MISSOURI PERIOD; OHIO PERIOD; PRATT, PARLEY P.

WILKINSON, ERNEST LEROY (1899–1978). Attorney, educator, university president. Born on 4 May 1899 in Ogden, Utah, Wilkinson received his early education in Ogden. At Weber College, he was a debater, editor of the school newspaper, and student body president. Going on to attend Brigham Young University (q.v.), he graduated with an A.B. degree in 1921. He then returned to teach English and public speaking at Weber until 1923, when he married Alice Ludlow.

For the next three years the Wilkinsons lived in Washington, D.C. He received his law degree summa cum laude from George Washington University in 1926 and the following year attended Harvard Law School on a scholarship, earning the S.J.D. Admitted to the bar, he went on to head his own law firm and in Washington, D.C., to represent many large corporations. Representing the Ute Indians, he won the largest judgment ever obtained against the United States.

In 1951 Wilkinson responded to a call from his Church and became president of Brigham Young University for 20 years, finally resigning in 1971. During his presidency BYU grew from about 5,000 to over 20,000 students, the faculty was enlarged and improved, and the library became one worthy of a first-class institution. Most noticeably, an ambitious building program was undertaken. He was also chancellor of the Church's Unified School System, which placed him over Ricks College, 130 institutes of religion, and more than a thousand seminaries (qq.v.). Wilkinson became Republican candidate for the U.S. Senate in 1964 but lost. He served on the board of directors of many corporations and received many awards, including the George Washington Medal from the Freedom Foundation and the Distinguished Service Award from his alma mater.

WILSON, WILLIAM A. "BERT" (1933–). Folklorist, educator. Born on 23 September 1933 at Tremonton, Utah, Wilson received his BA and MA degrees from Brigham Young University (q.v.). At Indiana University he earned a Ph.D. in folklore (q.v.). At Utah State University Wilson served as director of the Folklore Program from 1978–84. In 1985 Wilson moved to Brigham Young University, taking the position of chair of the English department and also serving as director of the Charles Redd Center for Western Studies and director of the BYU Folklore Archives. Wilson has published more than 35 articles and one book on Mormon folklore. He was named the Karl G. Maeser (q.v.) Distinguished Faculty Lecturer at BYU and received the Grace Arrington Award for Historical Excellence and the Utah's Governor's Award in the Arts. Among other Church positions, Wilson has served as bishop and high councilor (qq.v.). He married Birgit H. Blomqvist in 1957. They are the parents of four children

WINDER, BARBARA WOODHEAD (1931–). Relief Society general president (q.v.). Born on 9 May 1931 in Midvale, Utah, Barbara Woodhead attended local schools and the University of Utah. In 1951 she married Richard K. Winder. They have four children.

President of the sorority for Mormon students, she also accumulated a great variety of Church experience as ward president of Primary and Young Women (qq.v.). For five years she was on the Relief Society (q.v.) general board. In 1982 she accompanied her husband when he was named president of the California San Diego Mission.

The mission was cut short when she was sustained as general Relief Society president in April 1984. She selected as her counselors Joy F. Evans and Joanne B. Doxey. With women's issues still very prominent in society generally, Winder stressed partnership with the priesthood (q.v.) and the importance of home and family (q.v.). At the same time she and her colleagues recognized the diversity of their women members in national and ethnic background and in family situations. The increased number of single women, including single mothers, led to workshops and conferences to counsel and assist them.

A new statement of mission was prepared, stating that the purpose of the Relief Society was to help women have faith in God and build individual testimonies (q.v.) of Jesus Christ (q.v.), strengthen the families of the Church, render compassionate service, and sustain the priesthood (q.v.).

Several developments during Barbara Winder's presidency deserve mention. The Relief Society Building was renovated into an office building for all three "women's" organizations: Relief Society, Young Women, and Primary (qq.v.). Stake boards were eliminated, freeing up those qualified women for specific service in their wards (qq.v.). The teaching assignments in the wards were made more flexible. Special efforts were made to reach out and assist Latter-day Saint women among Native Americans (q.v.) and in areas where new missions were established.

In April 1990, having served for six years, Barbara Winder was released in order to accompany her husband to Czechoslovakia, where he became president (q.v.) of the revived Czechoslovakia Mission.

WIRTHLIN, ANNE G. (1939–). Educator, young women (q.v.) and children leader. Born in Salt Lake City, Anne Goalen received a bachelor's degree in elementary education from the University of Utah. She married David B. Wirthlin, who became a hospital administrator. They have six children. In addition to serving on PTA boards Anne Wirthlin taught at an inner-city school in Minneapolis, Minnesota. She has been ward Primary president, counselor in Young Women presidency, ward Relief Society president, and member of the Young Women general board (qq.v.). From 1989 to 1992 she served with her husband when he was president of the Germany Frankfurt Mission. In 1994 she was called as a counselor in the Primary general presidency.

WIRTHLIN, JOSEPH BITNER (1917–). Businessman and Apostle. Born on 11 June 1917 in Salt Lake City, Wirthlin grew up in an active Latter-day Saint family. His father, Joseph L. Wirthlin, served as a counselor in the Presiding Bishopric and then as Presiding Bishop (q.v.) of the Church. Young Joseph became an Eagle Scout, participated in high school athletics, and went on to play football at the University of Utah, where he received a degree in business administration. He also served as a missionary (q.v.) in Germany, Austria, and Switzerland prior to World War II.

In 1941 he married Elisa Young Rogers. They became the parents of eight children. A successful businessman, Wirthlin was president of a trade association in Utah.

In the Church he was a counselor in a bishopric and for 10 years, bishop. After a period as stake high councilor, he served as a counselor in his stake presidency (qq.v.). In 1971 he became a counselor in the Sunday School (q.v.) general presidency. In 1975 he became an Assistant to the Twelve, in 1976 a member of the presidency of the First Quorum of the Seventy, and in 1986, an Apostle (qq.v.).

Drawing upon his wealth of business and church experience, Wirthlin made significant contributions in many areas of activity (q.v.). As supervisor or executive administrator he had responsibility for the southeast United States and Caribbean Islands (1978–82) and Brazil (1982–84). He was president of the Europe area (qq.v.) of the Church from 1984 to 1986.

WIRTHLIN, RICHARD B. (1931–). Economist, pollster, Church leader. Born in Salt Lake City, Utah, Wirthlin served as a missionary (q.v.) in Switzerland and Austria. After graduating with a bachelor's degree in economics and a master's degree in economics and statistics from the University of Utah, he earned a doctorate in economics at the University of California at Berkeley. In 1969 Wirthlin founded a survey research firm in Los Angeles. Moving to Washington, D.C., in 1981, he became influential in national politics. Church callings included service as bishop, high councilor, counselor in stake presidencies, and regional representative (qq.v.). He was called to the Second Quorum of the Seventy (qq.v.) in 1996. Wirthlin and his wife, Jeralie, are the parents of eight children.

WITNESSES OF THE BOOK OF MORMON. In each copy of the Book of Mormon (q.v.) is found a page containing "The Testimony of the Three Witnesses" and "The Testimony of the Eight Witnesses."

The Three Witnesses—Oliver Cowdery, David Whitmer, and Martin Harris (qq.v.)—testify to having seen the metal plates from which the Book of Mormon was translated as well as an angel who "brought and laid before our eyes" and to having heard the voice of the Lord command them to bear record. In 1835 these three witnesses, after receiving authority from the First Presidency (q.v.), selected the members of the original Quorum of the Twelve Apostles (q.v.).

The Eight Witnesses did not tell of seeing an angel or hearing a voice, but they touched the plates and examined the engraved hieroglyphics.

"And this we bear record with words of soberness," they write, "that the said Smith has shown unto us, for we have seen and hefted, and know of a surety that the said Smith has got the plates of which we have spoken."

Although many of these witnesses became disaffected from the Church, they did not repudiate their testimony (q.v.). Their lives have been studied in depth by historian Richard L. Anderson (q.v.).

WOMEN, ROLES OF. In a large sense Mormon women have experienced the same understanding of gender roles as the rest of U.S. or Western society. The assumption was that most women would be wives and mothers. The idealized notion of "true womanhood"—woman as the refined, cultured, and religious influence in the home—was readily accepted by 19th-century Mormons. In the late 20th century, Mormon women enjoyed increased education, a higher percentage remained unmarried, divorce (q.v.) became more common, and paid work outside the home attracted (through desire or necessity) more and more women.

Many Mormon women worked even in the 19th century, in the fields or as domestics for example, but this is not inconsistent with what we know about other women of the same period. Obviously, to see Mormon women as strikingly divergent, or somehow immune, from the general cultural trends would be misleading.

On the other hand, there are differences and influences unique to the Mormon situation. In the 19th century, for example, the needs of pioneering and settlement put an unusually onerous burden on women, who through necessity assisted with every conceivable task. Absences of husbands on Church missions forced them either into poverty and discouragement or, often, increased independence. Women managed ranches, edited newspapers, taught in schools, and worked in retail stores. They were not recluses. Participating in the Relief Society and the Young Women (qq.v.) organizations, they had opportunities to learn, to teach, and to lead. They raised their hand along with the men in sustaining (q.v.) their Church leaders. They early received the vote in secular government, only to be deprived of it temporarily by the antipolygamy statutes of the 1880s. Mormon women spoke out on a variety of issues and participated enthusiastically in the national movement for women suffrage.

In the latter 20th century, with the rise of women's liberation, Mormon women have reacted differently. A small number of women have criticized what they see as the narrow conception of their role. When Relief Society president Barbara B. Smith (q.v.) counseled against voting for the Equal Rights Amendment, on grounds familiar to its other opponents, some Mormon feminists were outraged. Some single (q.v.) or divorced women resented the emphasis placed on the family (q.v.) and the necessity of marriage for salvation in the highest degree.

By far the majority of Mormon women saw such protest as unnecessary. Rejecting a gender-based paranoia, they loyally supported their prophet (q.v.) and the women leaders of the Relief Society. They were encouraged to seek all the education possible, to equip themselves for good employment, to enter the workforce and make contributions if necessary or at appropriate periods of their lives. But the priority of home and their duty to provide personal care for their children if at all possible continued to be emphasized.

By comparison with some of the activists of the women's movement, certainly with those who disparage the role of wife and mother, Mormon women appear highly conservative. Those who are familiar with many of them will acknowledge, however, that they are articulate and talented. In the Church they occupy positions of leadership in the Relief Society, Young Women, and Primary (q.v.) organizations, serve as teachers in those organizations and in Sunday School (q.v.) and Church schools, and in many cases serve as full-time missionaries (q.v.). *See also* FEMINISM; POLYGAMY; RELIEF SOCIETY.

WOODRUFF, WILFORD (1807–1898). Missionary, Apostle, president of the Church (qq.v.). Born in Farmington, Connecticut, in 1807, Woodruff grew up in hard surroundings, his mother having died in his infancy. He worked, suffered many accidents and injuries, and as a young adult became a seeker, looking for a true church, one that corresponded to the New Testament description. Baptized by Mormon missionaries (qq.v.) in 1833, he traveled directly to Kirtland, Ohio, where he met Joseph Smith (q.v.). He joined the Zion's Camp (q.v.) expedition to Missouri and preached as a missionary in several southern states and the Fox Islands. In 1838 he was named to the Quorum of the Twelve Apostles (q.v.).

Woodruff became one of Mormonism's legendary missionaries. On two different missions to England, starting in 1839, he baptized hundreds of people.

In addition to his ecclesiastical position he was a member of the Nauvoo City Council and, after the long move to Utah in 1847, a delegate in the Utah territorial legislature, president of the Cooperative Stock Company Association, president of the Universal Scientific Society, president of the Agricultural and Manufacturing Society, and chairman of the Medical Board of Examiners.

Like other General Authorities (q.v.), Woodruff accepted polygamy (q.v.) when it was introduced in Nauvoo by Joseph Smith. Eventually he had nine wives (four of whom divorced him) and 33 children.

When John Taylor (q.v.) died in 1887, Woodruff, at age 80, assumed leadership of the Church, first in his capacity as president of the Quorum of the Twelve Apostles and, after 1889, as president of the Church. Because of the continued practice of polygamy, pressure had become relentless, including the dissolution of the Church as a legal entity and the confiscation of much of its property. In 1890, Woodruff issued the Manifesto (q.v.) announcing a discontinuation of the practice, which, although complete enforcement took several years to accomplish, has been regarded as a major watershed in Mormon history.

Financial pressure continued to hound the Church for several years, and bickering over political differences soured the 1890s as national parties entered Utah politics. Nevertheless, Woodruff's administration had its high points, including the completion and dedication of the Salt Lake Temple (1893), attendance of Woodruff along with the Tabernacle Choir (q.v.) at the World Columbian Exposition in Chicago (1893), the achievement of Utah statehood (1896), and the jubilee celebration (1897).

One of the monumental achievements of Woodruff's life was his diary. Begun at the time of his conversion in 1834, this detailed record preserves many of Joseph Smith's and other early leaders' sermons, describes spiritual manifestations experienced by its author, and graphically conveys an abundance of concrete detail. *See also* EXODUS; POLYGAMY.

WORD OF WISDOM. Code of health announced by Joseph Smith (q.v.) in 1833 (Doctrine and Covenants, Section 89). Not good for human consumption were alcohol, tobacco, and "hot drinks" (soon defined by Hyrum Smith [q.v.] as tea and coffee). Meat was to be used sparingly. Wholesome grains and fruits were recommended.

Health reformers of the Jacksonian era were advocating similar ideas, but Joseph Smith presented the Word of Wisdom differently: it was a revelation (q.v.) from God. Originally presented as a recommendation, the Word of Wisdom was observed rather laxly throughout the 19th century. In the 20th century, especially during the administration of Heber J. Grant (q.v.), it received greater emphasis. Church members who held official positions or who participated in the temples (q.v.) were expected to adhere to the basic proscriptions: no tea, coffee, alcohol, or tobacco.

The Word of Wisdom and its requirements became a factor in the degree of Church activity (q.v.): many who had acquired the habits stopped attending Church services, while those who managed to come back into full activity did so in part by overcoming the forbidden practices. Converts to the Church, in addition to becoming convinced of the correctness of Mormonism doctrinally, often had to abandon habits of long standing. Children raised in the Church were instructed in the standards of the Word of Wisdom. One result, confirmed by several studies, was that Mormons on the whole had better health.

The Word of Wisdom is "a principle with a promise." Consistent with the principle of caring for one's physical health, the lifestyle of Mormons includes cleanliness, physical exercise, recreation, abstinence from mind-altering drugs, regular medical examinations, and avoidance of excesses.

WORLD CONFERENCE ON RECORDS. Sponsored by the Utah Genealogical Society, the first World Conference on Records was held in Salt Lake City on 8 August 1969 and attracted nearly 3,000 participants from different countries. Its theme, addressed by many speakers in concurrent sessions, was "Records Protection in an Uncertain World." A second such conference was held in Salt Lake City in 1980. Emphasizing the compilation of pedigree charts and family (q.v.) histories, it attracted 11,500 registrants from many different countries.

WORLD RELIGIONS. In 1930, when the Church celebrated its 100th year, Brigham H. Roberts (q.v.) insisted that it was not a narrow sect but a world movement. In her interpretation that Mormonism has the same relationship to Christianity (q.v.) that Christianity has to Judaism, historian Jan Shipps also comes close to granting Mormonism the status of an incipient world religion. Sociologist Rodney Stark has advanced the possibility, based on his analysis of growth statistics, that in Mormonism we are seeing the emergence of another major world religion right before our eyes. Critics who emphasize its lack of correspondence to Christian orthodoxy at certain points tend to label it a cult (q.v.), sect, or new religious movement. Even the Mormon self-definition is ambivalent. On the one hand, Mormons see themselves as a subset of Christianity; on the other hand, their claim to exclusivity, to being the only true church, sets them apart.

The traditional world religions include Christianity, Judaism, Islam, Buddhism, Jainism, and others. A First Presidency (q.v.) statement of 1978 reads: "The great religious leaders of the world such as Mohammed, Confucius, and the Reformers, as well as philosophers including

Socrates, Plato, and others, received a portion of God's light. Moral truths were given to them by God to enlighten whole nations and to bring a higher level of understanding to individuals." (Spencer J. Palmer, ed., *Mormons and Muslims* [1983], 208.) Appropriate in a period when Mormon missionaries (q.v.) are in all the continents, this general attitude was stated by Joseph Smith (q.v.) and other early Church leaders. *See also* CATHOLICISM; CHRISTIANITY; MEMBERSHIP; PROTESTANTISM.

WORTHINESS. A condition or status of moral uprightness considered essential for those performing certain Church functions or responsibilities. A general sincerity, while important, is not sufficient. Performance is expected. Regular attendance at meetings, payment of tithing and fast offering, observance of the Word of Wisdom (qq.v.), moral strictness, honesty in dealing with others, sustaining (q.v.) the Church leadership—these are among the determinants of worthiness.

While Church members are urged to adhere to these standards at all times, certain occasions require an examination of individual worthiness: qualifying for a recommend (q.v.) to enter the temples (q.v.), service as a missionary (q.v.), or a call to any position of responsibility. If for some specific reason one does not measure up, the standards are not to be relaxed; instead, one should repent and bring about the necessary changes. A period of probation is sometimes required, depending on the gravity of the infraction.

Without claiming perfection, Mormons who are missionaries, bishops, seminary teachers (qq.v.), and the like, have passed a worthiness check. Preaching or teaching principles they do not themselves practice would be rank hypocrisy.

Mormons are under no illusion that ultimate salvation is determined only by a simple checklist. The heart must be right. But for determining minimal requirements for service in the Church on the earthly level, the concept of worthiness serves a useful purpose.

-Y-

YOUNG, BRIGHAM (1801–1877). Missionary, Apostle, colonizer of the American West, and president of the Church (qq.v.). Born in Whitingham, Vermont, on 1 June 1801, Young was the ninth of 11 children. His parents moved to New York State when he was three. Growing up, he did every kind of farmwork. At the age of 15 he left home and worked as an apprentice carpenter, eventually becoming highly skilled. At age 23, he married Miriam Works. After living in Port Byron they moved to Oswego and in 1828 to Mendon.

Converted to Mormonism in 1832 by reading the Book of Mormon (q.v.), Brigham was baptized along with several siblings, his wife, and other members of his family (q.v.). Miriam, already an invalid, died the same year. He traveled to Kirtland, Ohio and met Joseph Smith (q.v.). In 1834 he volunteered as a member of Zion's Camp (q.v.). In 1835 he became one of the original members of the Quorum of the Twelve Apostles (q.v.). Alternately preaching the gospel as a missionary (qq.v.) and working in Kirtland, he used his skills to assist in the construction of the Kirtland Temple. An ardent defender of Joseph Smith, he acquired a reputation for loyalty and steadfastness.

After moving to northern Missouri in 1838, Young found himself in the midst of terrible persecutions (q.v.). With Joseph Smith and other leaders in prison, Young supervised the evacuation of the Mormon refugees from the state and their original establishment in Illinois.

At a time when the Mormons were struggling to survive, Young and other Apostles were called to preach the gospel in England. In the depths of poverty they started out and arrived at Liverpool in April 1840. Young, president of the Twelve, directed an incredible program of proselytizing several thousand converts, printing books and tracts, establishing a periodical, and shepherding emigrants. This beginning of the history of Mormonism in Great Britain resulted in the infusion of new blood through conversions and migration. Young's leadership experience was also growing.

Returning to Nauvoo, Illinois, Young was among the first to begin the practice of polygamy (q.v.). After the death in 1832 of Miriam he had married Mary Ann Angel two years later. Now, with Mary Ann's permission he took Lucy Ann Decker as a plural wife in 1842. As president of the Quorum of the Twelve Apostles he participated in many of the defining events of the Illinois Period (q.v.). He received the new ordinances such as endowments. He was a member of the Council of Fifty (q.v.). When Joseph Smith proposed western exploration preparatory to a possible move, Brigham participated in the discussions. When Smith ran for the U.S. presidency in 1844, Young and most of the Apostles went out on preaching missions to promote his candidacy.

News of Joseph Smith's assassination was slow in reaching the Apostles. When Young heard about it, he returned immediately to Nauvoo and, in a dramatic showdown with Sidney Rigdon (q.v.), won endorsement by almost all of the Mormons as leader of the Church.

The next year and a half were times to try men's souls. Young and his colleagues continued construction of the Nauvoo Temple, tried to maintain the viability of the city, received new immigrants, and tried to withstand the increasing persecution and demands for their departure. Gathering the best information available to them, especially the report of John C. Frémont's voyage, they studied possible sites for settlement in the West and in February 1846 began their departure from Illinois.

Young's leadership abilities would now be tested as never before. As thousands of refugees moved westward out of the city, they lived in covered wagons, tents, and brush shelters, huddling around campfires against the winter cold. Young organized them into companies, arranged for some to seek temporary employment, approved the enlistment of 500 men in the Mormon Battalion (q.v.), and kept most of his people together as they tried to maintain their westward momentum. After a stop on the Missouri River during the winter of 1846–47, he led the pioneer (q.v.) company that, in July 1847, reached the Salt Lake Valley.

The remaining 30 years of Brigham Young's life were spent in Utah (except for one trip to the Salmon River in Idaho). He led the Mormons in his capacity as president of the Quorum of the Twelve Apostles until December 1847, when in a conference he was sustained as president (q.v.) of the Church. When Utah became a territory in 1850, he was its first governor and also served as superintendent of Indian affairs. Even after his replacement as governor, in 1857, he continued to lead in establishing economic projects and in colonization (q.v.).

At the same time his family continued to grow. Plural wives were added. By 16 of his wives, according to the most thorough biography (Leonard J. Arrington [q.v.]), he had a total of 57 children. Using his skills as a carpenter, painter, and glazier, he constructed (or supervised the construction of) several homes, including the Lion House and the Beehive House in Salt Lake City. He was a kind father who took a personal interest in his children, as his letters to them demonstrate.

Young gave hundreds of sermons, many of which are preserved in the *Journal of Discourses* (q.v.), advising his people what crops to plant, where to settle, how to discipline their children, and the meaning of their Mormon faith. He also traveled up and down the region, visiting the smaller settlements in order to advise the people and inspire them by his charisma. Although non-Mormons criticized him as a tyrant, there is every indication that he was much loved by almost all of the Mormons.

He was a practical man. He took a personal interest in the company that brought supplies from the East. He encouraged the construction of the railroad, which reached Utah in 1869, and negotiated contracts to build part of the line. He organized the smaller rail lines that spread out to connect the Utah economy to the national network. Motivated by ideals found in the teachings of Joseph Smith and the Mormon scriptures (q.v.), he promoted different forms of economic cooperation.

Near the end of his life he founded Brigham Young Academy, later Brigham Young University (q.v.), in Provo (1875) and Brigham Young College in Logan. His practical bent did not mean a lack of spirituality. Especially devoted to the importance of temples (q.v.), he organized the continuation of the temple ceremonies at an Endowment House in Salt Lake City and in 1877 dedicated the St. George Temple.

A man of impressive versatility and strength of character, Young was able to hold the Church together and lead it to a new stability during crucial years. He died on 29 August 1877. *See also* EXODUS; ILLINOIS PERIOD; OHIO PERIOD; SUCCESSION; TEMPLES.

YOUNG, STEVE (1961–). Professional football player. Born in Salt Lake City, Young was raised in Greenwich, Connecticut. A great-great-great-great grandson of Brigham Young (q.v.), he also has another famous ancestor: Massasoit, the well-known, kindly Native American (q.v.) of colonial times. Young played football in high school and at Brigham Young University (q.v.) under coach LaVell Edwards. Following quarterback Jim McMahon, Young won his own plaudits. In 1984 he completed 71.3 percent of his 429 passes for 3,902 yards and 33 touchdowns—a National Collegiate Athletic Association record. During his senior year he passed for more than 300 yards in each of the season's 12 games and was runner-up for the Heisman Trophy.

After graduating from BYU with a double major in international relations and business finance, Young began his professional football career playing for the Los Angeles Express of the United States Football League. Then he played for the National Football League's Tampa Bay Buccaneers for two seasons. Finally he joined the San Francisco Forty-Niners. At first he was backup to the famous Joe Montana but went on to become the starting quarterback. Young's records are numerous. He was on the all-NFL team in 1992 and 1993 and was Player of the Year in 1992 and 1994. In 1995 his team won the Super Bowl and he was named Most Valuable Player.

Young participates in a variety of charitable causes. During the off-season he returned to Brigham Young University and earned a law degree.

YOUNG MEN. Auxiliary (q.v.) organization of the Church with programs to assist young male members develop socially, physically, and especially spiritually.

Early improvement societies were consolidated into the Young Men's Mutual Improvement Association (YMMIA) in 1875. By the early 20th century, classes had been formalized and various athletic and social activities added. Boy Scouts (q.v.) was added in 1913. Working in close conjunction with the parallel organization known as the Young Women's Mutual Improvement Association, the YMMIA developed ambitious programs in sports, dance (qq.v.), drama, music (q.v.), and public speaking.

A series of changes from the 1960s brought the organization under direction of the Priesthood (q.v.), with activities centered around the quorums (q.v.). In 1977 the name was changed to Young Men. By age groups the young men meet on Sundays for religious instruction and on one evening during the week for scouting, service projects, sports, or career education. Joint activities, including social dances (q.v.) and the production of theatrical plays and skits, are also held with the Young Women (q.v.).

YOUNG WOMEN. Starting in 1869 with a small organization founded by Brigham Young (q.v.) for his daughters, a Retrenchment Association expanded to include young women in the different wards of Salt Lake City. Avoiding the expense and pretense of worldly fashions was one goal, but spiritual development, the study of literature (q.v.), instruction in public speaking, and social projects were quickly added.

In the 1870s the organization was called the Young Ladies (later Women's) Mutual Improvement Association (YWMIA) as a sister organization to the Young Men's Mutual Improvement Association (YMMIA). Officers met in annual planning conferences from at least 1888. A magazine called *Young Woman's Journal* was published by the organization until 1929.

Instruction in music and dance (qq.v.), in public speaking and drama, originated at headquarters and then was transmitted to local leaders and the young women. At annual June conferences a great dance festival with more than 2,000 participants would take place, culminating months of preparation on the local level. Manuals were prepared for the different classes.

From the 1960s on, the Young Women began to meet on Sundays at the same time as Priesthood (q.v.) meetings were held for the Young Men (q.v.). A meeting during the week allowed opportunities for recreation and social development. Sensitive to the inroads of secularism and temptation, leaders emphasized spiritual values.

YOUTH. In all human societies some kind of "coming of age" occurs. In the late 20th-century United States, the stresses often included more than a little experimentation with alcohol and drugs, sexual activity, teenage pregnancy, confusion over gender identity, and of course violence.

During these years, that ambiguous zone stretching from youth into adulthood, one is also expected to complete a satisfactory education, choose a career, become economically self-sufficient, and, for many, embark on a commitment to marriage and family (q.v.). Societies outside of the United States face many if not all of these same challenges.

In navigating this minefield, the Mormon youth population is assisted by consistent teachings of a traditional moral code, including the Word of Wisdom (q.v.) and chastity (q.v.); activities, adult guidance, and peer support in Young Men, Young Women, seminaries, and institutes (qq.v.); and the missionary (q.v.) program, which, while pursuing its primary objective of preaching the gospel (q.v.), shepherds tens of thousands of young people through a process of expanding cultural awareness, acquiring habits of discipline, and deepening religious commitment.

For those who succumb to worldly standards and become inactive (q.v.), the path back of repentance (q.v.) is always open. Through home teaching and visiting teaching (qq.v.) the Church seeks constantly to bring the wayward of all ages back to keeping the commandments (q.v.).

-Z-

ZION. 1. The pure in heart (Doctrine and Covenants, 97:21). 2. The center established in Independence, Missouri, where a temple (q.v.) is to be built. The hopes to accomplish this in the 1830s were frustrated by persecution (q.v.) and expulsion, but Mormons look forward to a future establishment there. 3. All of North and South America. 4. The Great Salt

Lake Valley and the surrounding area where Mormons colonized after 1847. 5. Any place in any country where the Saints (q.v.) of God live and worship, especially stakes (q.v.).

The expectations of an imminent Millennium (q.v.) explain the emphasis placed on definition 2 at the Church's beginning, while the doctrine of gathering (q.v.) explains the usage embodied in definition 4. The cessation of efforts to gather converts from foreign lands and the growth of the Church membership (q.v.) in all of the states and many foreign countries, beginning early in the 20th century but especially emphatic in the latter half of the century, help to explain the current emphasis on definitions 1 and 5. *See also* ARTICLES OF FAITH, 10.

ZION'S CAMP. An expedition of 1834 intending to come to the aid of persecuted Mormons in Missouri. Living in Ohio at the time, Joseph Smith (q.v.) responded to appeals from his Missouri followers by issuing a revelation (Doctrine and Covenants, Section 103) commanding the organization of volunteers. Eventually about 200 men banded together, organized themselves into units, and trained as they made their way westward in May and June. After a journey of 600 or 700 miles the army reached the trouble spot in western Missouri. Internal dissension, sickness, and the collapse of negotiations with the Missourians led to the disbanding of the expedition.

Although it had not achieved its objective of restoring the Missouri Mormons to their property, Zion's Camp provided valuable experience in organization. Most of the Apostles named in 1835 had served in the expedition. Brigham Young (q.v.) and others later looked back upon it as a time of trial and seasoning. *See also* MISSOURI PERIOD.

Appendix 1
Church Presidents

Joseph Smith, 1830–44
Brigham Young, 1847–77
John Taylor, 1880–87
Wilford Woodruff, 1889–98
Lorenzo Snow 1898–1901
Joseph F. Smith, 1901–18
Heber J. Grant, 1918–45
George Albert Smith, 1945–51
David O. McKay, 1951–70
Joseph Fielding Smith, 1970–72
Harold B. Lee, 1972–73
Spencer W. Kimball, 1973–85
Ezra Taft Benson, 1985–94
Howard W. Hunter, 1994–95
Gordon B. Hinckley, 1995–

Appendix 2
Temples

Location	Dedicated
Kirtland, Ohio	27 March 1836
Nauvoo, Illinois	30 April 1846
St. George, Utah	6 April 1877
Logan, Utah	17 May 1884
Manti, Utah	17 May 1888
Salt Lake City, Utah	6 April 1893
Laie, Oahu, Hawaii	27 November 1919
Cardston, Alberta, Canada	26 August 1923
Mesa, Arizona	23 October 1927
Idaho Falls, Idaho	23 September 1945
Zollikofen, Switzerland	11 September 1955
Los Angeles, California	11 March 1956
Hamilton, New Zealand	20 April 1958
Newchapel, Surrey, England	7 September 1958
Oakland, California	17 November 1964
Ogden, Utah	18 January 1972
Provo, Utah	9 February 1972
Kensington, Maryland	19 November 1974
São Paulo, Brazil	30 October 1978
Tokyo, Japan	27 October 1980
Bellevue, Washington	17 November 1980
South Jordan, Utah	16 November 1981
Sandy Springs, Georgia	1 June 1983
Apia, Western Samoa	5 August 1983
Nuku'alofa, Tonga	9 August 1983
Santiago, Chile	15 September 1983
Pirae, Tahiti	17 October 1983
Mexico City, Mexico	2 December 1983
Boise, Idaho	25 May 1984
Carlingford, Australia	20 September 1984

Quezon City, Philippines	25 September 1984
Dallas, Texas	19 October 1984
Taipei, Taiwan	17 November 1984
Guatemala City, Guatemala	14 December 1984
Freiberg, Germany	29 June 1985
Vasterhaninge, Sweden	1 July 1985
Glenview, Illinois	9 August 1985
Johannesburg, South Africa	24 August 1985
Seoul, Korea	14 December 1985
Lima, Peru	10 January 1986
Buenos Aires, Argentina	17 January 1986
Littleton, Colorado	24 October 1986
Friedrichsdorf, Germany	28 August 1987
Oswego, Oregon	19 August 1989
Las Vegas, Nevada	16 December 1989
Brampton, Ontario, Canada	25 August 1990
San Diego, California	25 April 1993
Orlando, Florida	9 October 1994
Bountiful, Utah	8 January 1995
Hong Kong	26 May 1996
American Fork, Utah	13 October 1996
St. Louis, Missouri	1 June 1997
Vernal, Utah	2 November 1997
Preston, England	7 June 1998
Monticello, Utah	26 July 1998
Anchorage, Alaska	9 January 1999
Colonia, Juarez, Chihuahua, Mexico	7 March 1999
Madrid, Spain	19 March 1999
Bogotá, Colombia	26 April 1999
Guayaquil, Ecuador	1 August 1999
Spokane, Washington	21 August 1999
Columbus, Ohio	4 September 1999
Bismarck, North Dakota	19 September 1999
Columbia, South Carolina	16 October 1999
Detroit, Michigan	23 October 1999
Halifax, Nova Scotia	14 November 1999
Regina, Saskatchewan	14 November 1999
Billings, Montana	20 November 1999
Edmonton, Alberta	11 December 1999
Raleigh, North Carolina	18 December 1999

St. Paul, Minnesota	9 January 2000
Kona, Hawaii	23 January 2000
Ciudad Juárez, Mexico	26 February 2000
Hermosilla, Mexico	27 February 2000
Albuquerque, New Mexico	6 March 2000
Oaxaca, Mexico	11 March 2000
Tuxtla Gutiérrez, Mexico	12 March 2000
Louisville, Kentucky	19 March 2000
Palmyra, New York	6 April 2000
Fresno, California	9 April 2000
Medford, Oregon	16 April 2000
Memphis, Tennessee	23 April 2000
Reno, Nevada	23 April 2000
Cochabamba, Bolivia	30 April 2000
Tampico, Mexico	20 May 2000
Villahermosa, Mexico	21 May 2000
Nahsville, Tennessee	21 May 2000
Montreal, Canada	4 June 2000
San José, Costa Rica	4 June 2000
Fukuoka, Japan	11 June 2000
Adelaide, Australia	15 June 2000
Melbourne, Australia	16 June 2000
Suva, Fiji	18 June 2000
Merida, Mexico	25 June 2000
Vera Cruz, Mexico	9 July 2000

Appendix 3

The Family:
A Proclamation to the World

We, the First Presidency and the Council of the Twelve Apostles of The Church of Jesus Christ of Latter-day Saints, solemnly proclaim that marriage between a man and a woman is ordained of God and that the family is central to the Creator's plan for the eternal destiny of his children.

All human beings—male and female—are created in the image of God. Each is a beloved spirit son or daughter of heavenly parents, and, as such, each has a divine nature and destiny. Gender is an essential characteristic of individual pre-mortal, mortal, and eternal identity and purpose.

In the pre-mortal realm, spirit sons and daughters knew and worshiped God as their Eternal Father and accepted His plan by which His children could obtain a physical body and gain earthly experience to progress toward perfection and ultimately realize his or her divine destiny as an heir of eternal life. The divine plan of happiness enables family relationships to be perpetuated beyond the grave. Sacred ordinances and covenants available in holy temples make it possible for individuals to return to the presence of God and for families to be united eternally.

The first commandment that God gave to Adam and Eve pertained to their potential for parenthood as husband and wife. We declare that God's commandment for His children to multiply and replenish the Earth remains in force. We further declare that God has commanded that the sacred powers of procreation are to be employed only between man and woman, lawfully wedded as husband and wife.

We declare the means by which mortal life is created to be divinely appointed. We affirm the sanctity of life and of its importance in God's eternal plan.

Husband and wife have a solemn responsibility to love and care for each other and for their children. "Children are an heritage of the Lord" (Psalms 127:3). Parents have a sacred duty to rear their children in love and righteousness, to provide for their physical and spiritual needs, to teach them to love and serve one another, to observe the commandments of God and to be law-abiding citizens wherever they live. Husbands and wives—

mothers and fathers—will be held accountable before God for the discharge of these obligations.

The family is ordained of God. Marriage between man and woman is essential to His eternal plan. Children are entitled to birth within the bonds of matrimony, and to be reared by a father and a mother who honor marital vows with complete fidelity. Happiness in family life is most likely to be achieved when founded upon the teachings of the Lord Jesus Christ. Successful marriages and families are established and maintained on principles of faith, prayer, repentance, forgiveness, respect, love, compassion, work, and wholesome recreational activities. By divine design, fathers are to preside over their families in love and righteousness and are responsible to provide the necessities of life and protection for their families. Mothers are primarily responsible for the nurture of their children. In these sacred responsibilities, fathers and mothers are obligated to help one another as equal partners. Disability, death, or other circumstances may necessitate individual adaptation. Extended families should lend support when needed.

We warn that individuals who violate covenants of chastity, who abuse spouse or offspring, or who fail to fulfill family responsibilities will one day stand accountable before God. Further, we warn that the disintegration of the family will bring upon individuals, communities, and nations the calamities foretold by ancient and modern prophets.

We call upon responsible citizens and officers of the government everywhere to promote those measures designed to maintain and strengthen the family as the fundamental unit of society.

—presented by President Gordon B. Hinckley
at the General Relief Society meeting, 23 September 1995

Appendix 4
Relief Society Declaration (1999)

We are beloved spirit daughters of God, and our lives have meaning, purpose, and direction. As a worldwide sisterhood, we are united in our devotion to Jesus Christ, our Savior and Exemplar. We are women of faith, virtue, vision, and charity, who:

Increase our testimonies of Jesus Christ through prayer and scripture study.
Seek spiritual strength by following the promptings of the Holy Ghost.
Dedicate ourselves to strengthening marriages, families, and homes.
Find nobility in motherhood and joy in womanhood.
Delight in service and good works.
Love life and learning.
Stand for truth and righteousness.
Sustain the priesthood as the authority of God on earth.
Rejoice in the blessings of the temple, understand our divine destiny, and strive for exaltation.

—presented by Relief Society general president Mary Ellen Smoot
at general Relief Society meeting on 25 September 1999

Appendix 4
Quotations

"Adam fell that men might be; and men are, that they might have joy."

—Book of Mormon[1]

"Wickedness never was happiness."

—Book of Mormon[2]

"The glory of God is intelligence, or, in other words, light and truth."

—Doctrine and Covenants[3]

"There is a law, irrevocably decreed in heaven before the foundations of this world, upon which all blessings are predicated—and when we obtain any blessing from God, it is by obedience to that law upon which it is predicated."

—Doctrine and Covenants[4]

"Behold, this is my work and my glory—to bring to pass the immortality and eternal life of man."

—Pearl of Great Price[5]

"Happiness is the object and design of our existence; and will be the end thereof, if we pursue the path that leads to it; and this path is virtue, uprightness, faithfulness, holiness, and keeping all the commandments of God."

—Joseph Smith[6]

"We teach them correct principles and they govern themselves."

—Joseph Smith[7]

"The standard of truth has been erected: no unhallowed hand can stop the
work from progressing, persecutions may rage, mobs may combine, armies
may assemble, calumny may defame, but the truth of God will go forth
boldly, nobly, and independent till it has penetrated every continent, visited every clime, swept every country, and sounded in every ear, till the
purposes of God shall be accomplished and the great Jehovah shall say the
work is done."

—Joseph Smith[8]

"There has been a great difficulty in getting anything into the heads of this
generation. It has been like splitting hemlock knots with a corn-dodger for
a wedge, and a pumpkin for a beetle. Even the Saints are slow to understand."

—Joseph Smith[9]

"Gentlemen, your cause is just, but I can do nothing for you. If I take up
for you I shall lose the vote of Missouri."

—Martin Van Buren[10]

"To Martin Van Buren and all mobocrats: May they be winked at by blind
men, kicked across lots by cripples, nibbled to death by ducks, and carried
to hell through the keyhole by bumblebees."

—Jedediah M. Grant[11]

"Stenhouse, when I was a boy on the farm in Illinois there was a great deal
of timber on the farm which we had to clear away. Occasionally we would
come to a log which had fallen down. It was too hard to split, too wet to
burn, and too heavy to move, so we plowed around it. You go back and tell
Brigham Young that if he will let me alone I will let him alone."

—Abraham Lincoln[12]

"My religion embraced all the truth they all had and a great deal more. I
could put on paper all the knowledge of salvation that all the religious sects
possess, and put that paper into a snuff-box, and never miss the room it
occupied. I would say, I know how much truth you have embraced; you
have bounds to your religion, but I have no bounds to mine: the faith I have
embraced is broad as eternity."

—Brigham Young[13]

"I do not argue with the men who say the earth is only six thousand years old, or those who say it is six hundred thousand years old, or those who say it is six million. I know we are here on earth, and I know the Lord has told us why we are here. The time will come when we will know all the rest."

—Anthony W. Ivins[14]

"There have been some who have belittled him [Joseph Smith], but I would like to say that those who have done so will be forgotten and their remains will go back to mother earth, if they have not already gone, and the odor of their infamy will never die, while the glory and honor and majesty and courage and fidelity manifested by the Prophet Joseph Smith will attach to his name forever."

—George Albert Smith

"I would be a friend to the friendless and find joy in ministering to the needs of the poor.
I would visit the sick and afflicted and inspire in them a desire for faith to be healed.
I would teach truth to the understanding and blessing of all mankind.
I would seek out the erring one and try to win him back to a righteous and a happy life.
I would not seek to force people to live up to my ideals but rather love them into doing the thing that is right.
I would live with the masses and help to solve their problems that their earth life may be happy.
I would avoid the publicity of high positions and discourage the flattery of thoughtless friends.
I would not knowingly wound the feelings of any, not even one who may have wronged me, but would seek to do him good and make him my friend.
I would overcome the tendency to selfishness and jealousy and rejoice in the success of all the children of my Heavenly Father
I would not be an enemy to any living soul.
Knowing that the Redeemer of mankind has offered to the world the only plan that will fully develop us and make us really happy here and hereafter, I feel it not only a duty but a blessed privilege to disseminate this truth."

—George Albert Smith[15]

"The choice is given, whether we live in the physical world as animals, or whether we use what earth offers us as a means of living in the spiritual world that will lead us back into the presence of God. This means specifically—

1. Whether we choose selfishness or whether we will deny ourselves for the good of others;
2. Whether we will cherish indulgence of appetite, passion, or whether we will develop restraint and self-control;
3. Whether we choose licentiousness or chastity;
4. Whether we will encourage hate or develop love;
5. Whether we practice cruelty or kindness;
6. Whether we be cynical or sanguine—hopeful;
7. Whether we be traitorous—disloyal to those who love us, to our country, to the Church, or to God—or whether we will be loyal;
8. Whether we be deceitful or honest, our word our bond;
9. Whether we have a slanderous or a controlled tongue."

—David O. McKay[16]

"No other success can compensate for failure in the home."

—David O. McKay[17]

"I am grateful that the mysteries of the kingdom have never troubled me much. I think that the simple truths of the gospel are so plain and so beautiful that I don't worry much about the things that no man can explain; and I am sure in my own heart that if we will just live as well as we know how to live, we will be all right here and hereafter. It won't be the things that we don't know that will give us trouble. It will be the things that we do know and fail to abide by."

—Richard L. Evans[18]

"For years I have been waiting for someone to do justice in recording in song and story and painting and sculpture the story of the struggles and frustrations; the apostasies and inner revolutions and counter-revolutions of those first decades; of the exodus; of the miracle man, Joseph Smith; and of the giant colonizer and builder, Brigham Young."

—Spencer W. Kimball[19]

"I asked him about himself. He was in college, still single, and fairly miserable. I asked him about his service in the Church and the light in his eyes went out and a dull, disappointed face fashioned itself as he said, 'I am not very active in the Church now. . . .'

"Not one single time had he opened the sacred books. He had been reading negative and critical and faith-destroying things and wondered why he could never smile. He never prayed anymore yet wondered why he felt so abandoned and so alone in a tough world. For a long time he had not partaken of the sacrament of the Lord's Supper and wondered why his spirit was dead.

"Not a penny of tithing had he paid and wondered why the windows of heaven seemed closed and locked and barred."

—Spencer W. Kimball[20]

"Our missionaries are not salesmen with wares to peddle; rather, they are servants of the Most High God, with testimonies to bear, truths to teach, and souls to save."

—Thomas S. Monson[21]

"If you can control your thoughts, you can overcome habits—even degrading, personal habits. If you can master them, you will have a happy life."

—Boyd K. Packer[22]

"As I understand it, our mission to the world in this day is to testify of Jesus Christ. Our mission is to bear record that he is the Son of the Living God and that he was crucified for the sins of the world; that salvation was, and is, and is to come, in and through his atoning blood; that by virtue of his atonement all men will be raised in immortality, and those who believe and obey the gospel law both in immortality and eternal life.

And the position which Joseph Smith holds in the scheme of things is that he is the chiefest witness of Christ that there has been in this world since the Son of God personally walked among men and bore record of himself saying, 'I am the Son of God.'"

—Bruce R. McConkie[23]

"As Latter-day Saints, we believe God to be the living Father of all men. Never has he turned his back on them. He is not estranged from men. The opposite is true. Men frequently estrange themselves from God. Men leave God, the fountain and source of their lives, and, like the Prodigal Son, go into a far country to spend their lives in riotous living. God, like the father in the parable, is waiting for his children to return and is ready to run to meet them."

—Lowell L. Bennion[24]

"No man can learn enough in a lifetime to count for very much, and no one knows that better than the man who diligently seeks knowledge—that is the lesson of *Faust*. How then can any honest man believe that his modicum of knowledge can supersede revelation and supplant the authority of the priesthood?"

—Hugh Nibley[25]

"We must reach out beyond the walls of our own church. In humanitarian work, as in other areas of the gospel, we cannot become the salt of the earth if we stay in one lump in the cultural halls of our beautiful meetinghouses. We need not wait for a call or assignment from a Church leader before we become involved in activities that are best carried out on a community or individual basis."

—Glenn L. Pace[26]

"There are those who are exceedingly anxious to proclaim, 'I did it my way!' Such selfish assertions are seen by some as a validation of individuality, while obedience to God is seen as a lessening of self. Yet obedience to God is really what makes the flowering of the full self possible."

—Neal A. Maxwell[27]

"Brilliance, by itself, is not wholeness nor happiness. Knowledge, if possessed for its own sake and unapplied, leaves one's life unadorned. A Church member, for instance, might describe the Lord's doctrines but not qualify to enter the Lord's house. One could produce much commentary without being exemplary. One might be intellectually brilliant but Bohemian in behavior. One might use his knowledge to seek preeminence or dominion. Such are not Jesus' ways, for He asks that perception and implementation be part of the same spiritual process."

—Neal A. Maxwell[28]

"Meekness of mind is essential, salvationally. It is likewise vital if we are to experience true intellectual growth and to heighten our understanding of the great realities of the universe. Such meekness is a friend to, not a foe of, true education."

—Neal A. Maxwell[29]

"It was never intended that home become a prison for a Latter-day Saint woman, or for any woman. It was never anyone's intent in the Church to circumscribe the ways in which a woman might contribute to society or to the world in which she lives. On the contrary, women have been encouraged to utilize and expand their abilities—but not at a time when we would threaten the potential of those nearest and dearest to us. Women must understand the purpose of the home as a great learning center where the nurturing and training of children take place. There have always been mitigating circumstances that make it necessary for some women to leave their children and work outside the home; but for the majority of homes, the responsibility for the care of the children must be carried out by mothers who give their children their time, their full concern, and their loving attention."

—Barbara Smith[30]

"A loving Heavenly Father knew we would need help to learn again the basic things we had once been taught in the heavenly councils. So He gave us the gift of the Holy Ghost to bring all things to our remembrance, and living prophets to direct us. He also provided scriptures to teach us, commandments to help us become like the Savior, and covenants to remind us of our solemn responsibility to remember Him."

—Joanne B. Doxey[31]

"When the pioneers ended a day's journey, each night they checked their wagons for any needed repairs. They united in prayer for continued guidance and protection and took a reading of both distance and direction to see how far they had traveled and make sure they were on the right trail. We would do well to follow the same pattern today. A good measurement to ask concerning every important decision is whether or not this decision will move you toward or away from making and keeping sacred covenants and preparing for the ordinances of the temple."

—Ardeth G. Kapp[32]

"It is the diversity of colors in a spectrum that makes a rainbow. It is the diversity of our circumstances that gives us compassionate hearts. It is the diversity of our spiritual gifts that benefits the Church."

—Chieko N. Okazaki

"If you're doing the best you can, that's good enough. I don't know many women who aren't doing their absolute level best in every way, but plenty of those women keep track only of the things they *don't* do perfectly. The women I know accomplish a phenomenal amount, but often they don't pay attention to what they've done. Rather they concentrate on what has been left undone or what remains still to do."

—Chieko N. Okazaki[33]

"The Lord works from the inside out. The world works from the outside in. The world would take people out of the slums. Christ takes the slums out of the people, and then they take themselves out of the slums. The world would mold men by changing their environment. Christ changes men, who then change their environment. The world would shape human behavior, but Christ can change human nature."

—Ezra Taft Benson[34]

"Let the Church be your dear friend. Let it be your great companion. Serve wherever you are called to serve. Do what you are asked to do. Every position you hold will add to your capacity. I have served in many responsibilities in this great organization. Every bit of service brought its own reward.

"This, too will require your unselfish devotion, your unyielding loyalty and faith. You will serve in many capacities before your lives are complete. Some of them may seem small, but there is no small or unimportant calling in this Church. Every calling is important. Every calling is necessary to the advancement of the work. Never demean a responsibility in the Church. . . .

"Make room for the Church in your life. Let your knowledge of its doctrine grow. Let your understanding of its organization increase. Let your love for its eternal truths become ever and ever stronger.

"The Church may call upon you to make sacrifice. It may call upon you to give of the very best that you have to offer. There will be no cost in this, because you will discover that it will become an investment that will pay you dividends for as long as you live. The Church is the great reservoir of eternal truth. Embrace it and hold fast to it."

—Gordon B. Hinckley[35]

"Are we Christians? Of course we are! No one can honestly deny that. We may be somewhat different from the traditional pattern of Christianity. But no one believes more literally in the redemption wrought by the Lord Jesus Christ. No one believes more fundamentally that He was the Son of God, that he died for the sins of mankind, that He rose from the grave, and that He is the living resurrected Son of the living Father.

"All of our doctrine, all of our religious practice stems from that one basic doctrinal position. 'We believe in God, the Eternal Father, and in His Son, Jesus Christ, and in the Holy Ghost.' This is the first article of our faith, and all else flows therefrom."

—Gordon B. Hinckley[36]

"Let me say that we appreciate the truth in all churches and the good which they do. We say to the people, in effect, you bring with you all the good that you have, and then let us see if we can add to it. That is the spirit of this work. That is the essence of our missionary service."

—Gordon B. Hinckley[37]

SOURCES FOR QUOTATIONS

1. Book of Mormon, 2 Nephi 2:25.
2. Book of Mormon, Alma 41:10.
3. Doctrine and Covenants 93:36.
4. Doctrine and Covenants 130:20–21.
5. Pearl of Great Price, Moses 1:39.
6. Joseph Fielding Smith, ed., *Teachings of the Prophet Joseph Smith* (Salt Lake City: Deseret Book, 1976), 255–56.
7. *Journal of Discourses* 10 (1865): 57–8; *Millennial Star*, 15 November 1851, 339.
8. Dean C. Jessee, ed., *The Papers of Joseph Smith* vol. 1 (Salt Lake City: Deseret Book, 1989), 436.
9. *Teachings of the Prophet Joseph Smith*, 331.
10. *Teachings of the Prophet Joseph Smith*, 302, 327.

11. Jay A. Parry and Larry E. Morris, *The Mormon Book of Lists* (Salt Lake City: Bookcraft), 29.

12. *The Mormon Book of Lists*, 13.

13. *Journal of Discourses* 5 (1857): 342.

14. Eugene E. Campbell and Richard D. Poll, *Hugh B. Brown: His Life and Thought* (Salt Lake City: Bookcraft, 1975), 285.

15. *Improvement Era*, March 1932, 295.

16. David O. McKay, *Gospel Ideals* (Salt Lake City: Improvement Era, 1953), 346.

17. Leonard J. Arrington, ed., *The Presidents of the Church* (Salt Lake City: Deseret Book, 1986), 292.

18. *Conference Reports*, October 1948, 67.

19. *Ensign*, July 1977, 5.

20. Edward L. Kimball, ed., *The Teachings of Spencer W. Kimball* (Salt Lake City: Bookcraft, 1982) 128–9.

21. *Ensign*, November 1987, 42.

22. Boyd K. Packer, *Teach Ye Diligently* (Salt Lake City: Deseret Book, 1975), 46–7.

23. Mark L. McConkie, ed., *Doctrines of the Restoration* (Salt Lake City: Bookcraft, 1989), 87.

24. Eugene England, ed., *The Best of Lowell L. Bennion* (Salt Lake City: Deseret Book, 1988), 99.

25. Gary P. Gillum, comp., *Of All Things: A Nibley Quote Book* (Salt Lake City: Signature Books, 1981), 134.

26. *Ensign*, January 1992, 66.

27. Neal A. Maxwell, *Not My Will, but Thine* (Salt Lake City: Bookcraft, 1988), 7.

28. *Ensign*, April 1993, 69.

29. Neal A. Maxwell, *Meek and Lowly* (Salt Lake City: Deseret Book, 1987), 34.

30. Barbara Smith, *A Fruitful Season* (Salt Lake City: Bookcraft, 1988), 181–2.

31. *Ensign*, November 1989, 89.

32. *Ensign*, November 1990, 95.

33. Chieko Okazaki, *Lighten Up* (Salt Lake City: Deseret Book, 1993), 5.

34. *Ensign*, November 1985, 6.

35. *Ensign*, February 1998, 73.

36. *Ensign*, February 1998, 73.

37. *Church News*, 4 July 1998, 2.

Bibliography

The explosion in scholarship on Mormonism has made it impossible to include anything like a complete bibliography. I have been especially desirous here of including works that have been helpful in providing information for the present dictionary. In addition, I have listed the standard bibliographies and a generous sampling of the monographs that should enable one to go further.

Titles in the Bibliography are grouped according to the following categories:

Periodicals and Yearbooks
Reference Works
Bibliographies
Published Primary Sources
Diaries and Autobiographies
Biographies
Histories
    General
    New York Period
    Ohio Period
    Missouri Period
    Illinois Period
    The Exodus
    Utah Period
    Twentieth Century
    Local and Regional United States
    Countries outside the United States and Immigration
Social Science
Philosophy
Folklore
Personal Essays
Doctrinal and Apologetic
Literature and Art

PERIODICALS AND YEARBOOKS

Brigham Young University Studies, 1 (1959–).
Church News, 1943– . Weekly.
Church Section, Deseret News, 1931–43.
Conference Reports, 1880, 1897, 1899– .
Deseret News Church Almanac. Salt Lake City: Deseret News, 1973– .
Dialogue: A Journal of Mormon Thought, 1 (1966–).
Ensign, 1971– . Monthly.
Exponent II, 1974– . Quarterly.
FARMS Review of Books 1 (1989–). Originally titled *Review of Books on the Book of Mormon*.
Improvement Era, 1897–1970. Monthly.
The John Whitmer Historical Association Journal, 1 (1981–).
Journal of Book of Mormon Studies, 1 (1992–).
Journal of Discourses, 1–25 (1854–84).
Relief Society Magazine, 1–56 (1915–70).
The Saints Herald, 1 (1860–). Official monthly magazine of the Reorganized Church of Jesus Christ of Latter Day Saints.
Sunstone, 1 (1975–).

REFERENCE WORKS

Brown, S. Kent, Donald Q. Cannon, and Richard H. Jackson, eds. *Historical Atlas of Mormonism*. New York: Simon and Schuster, 1994.
Jenson, Andrew. *Church Chronology: A Record of Important Events*. 2nd ed. Salt Lake City: Deseret News, 1914.
————. *Encyclopedic History of the Church of Jesus Christ of Latter-day Saints*. Salt Lake City: Deseret News, 1941.
Ludlow, Daniel H., ed. *Encyclopedia of Mormonism*. 5 vols. New York: Macmillan, 1992.
Olpin, Robert S. *Dictionary of Utah Art*. Salt Lake City: Salt Lake Art Center, 1980.
Whittaker, David J. *Mormon Americana: A Guide to Sources and Collections in the United States*. Provo, Utah: BYU Studies, 1995.

BIBLIOGRAPHIES

Alder, Douglas D. "Writing Southern Utah History: An Appraisal and a Bibliography." *Journal of Mormon History* 20 (Fall 1994): 156–78.

Alexander, Thomas G. "Historiography and the New Mormon History: A Historian's Perspective." *Dialogue: A Journal of Mormon Thought* 19 (Fall 1986): 25–49.

———. "Toward the New Mormon History: An Examination of the Literature on the Latter-day Saints in the Far West." In Michael P. Malone, ed., *Historians and the American West.* Lincoln: University of Nebraska Press, 1983.

Alexander, Thomas G., and James B. Allen, eds. "The Mormons in the Mountain West: A Selected Bibliography." *Arizona and the West* 9 (Winter 1967): 365–84.

Allen, James B., David J. Whittaker, and Ronald W. Walker. *Studies in Mormon History, 1830–1997: An Indexed Bibliography.* Urbana: University of Illinois Press, 2000.

Arrington, Leonard J. "Scholarly Studies of Mormonism in the Twentieth Century." *Dialogue: A Journal of Mormon Thought* 1 (Spring 1966): 15–32.

Bitton, Davis. *Guide to Mormon Diaries and Autobiographies.* Provo, Utah: Brigham Young University Press, 1977.

———. "Mormon Polygamy: A Review Article." *Journal of Mormon History* 4 (1977): 101–8.

A Catalogue of Theses and Dissertations concerning the Church. Provo, Utah: College of Religious Instruction, Brigham Young University, 1971.

Clement, Russell T. *Mormons in the Pacific: A Bibliography.* Laie, Hawaii: Institute for Polynesian Studies, 1981.

Cowan, Richard O., and Frank A. Bruno. *Bibliography on Temples and Temple Work.* Provo, Utah: Brigham Young University, 1982.

Crawley, Peter. "A Bibliography of the Church of Jesus Christ of Latter-day Saints in New York, Ohio, and Missouri." *Brigham Young University Studies* 12 (Summer 1972): 465–537.

———. *A Descriptive Bibliography of the Mormon Church. Vol. One 1830–1847.* Provo, Utah: Religious Studies Center, Brigham Young University, 1997.

Crawley, Peter, and David J. Whittaker. *Mormon Imprints in Great Britain and the Empire.* Provo, Utah: Friends of the Brigham Young University Library, 1987.

Dennis, Ronald D. *Welsh Mormon Publications from 1844 to 1862: A Historical Bibliography.* Provo, Utah: Brigham Young University Religious Studies Center, 1988.

England, Eugene. "The Dawning of a Brighter Day: Mormon Literature after 150 Years." *Brigham Young University Studies* 22 (Spring 1982): 131–60.

Fales, Susan L. *An Addendum to Mormons and Mormonism in U.S. Government Documents: A Bibliography*. Provo, Utah: N.p., 1989.

Fales, Susan L., and Chad J. Flake, comps. *Mormons and Mormonism in U.S. Government Documents: A Bibliography*. Salt Lake City: University of Utah Press, 1989.

Fales Susan L., and Lanell M. Reeder. "Mormonism: Bibliography of Bibliographies." *Mormon History Association Newsletter* 72 (April 1989): 5–8.

Flake, Chad J., ed. *A Mormon Bibliography, 1830–1930*. Salt Lake City: University of Utah Press, 1978.

Flake, Chad J., and Larry Draper. *Supplement to a Mormon Bibliography*. Salt Lake City: University of Utah Press, 1989.

Flake, Chad J., and Susan L. Fales, eds. *Mormons and Mormonism in U.S. Government Documents: A Bibliography*. Salt Lake City: University of Utah Press, 1989.

Frazier, Karen Purser. *Bibliography of Social Scientific, Historical, and Popular Writings about Mormon Women*. Provo, Utah: Women's Research Institute, Brigham Young University, 1990.

Grover, Mark L. *The Mormon Church in Latin America: A Periodical Index, 1830–1976*. Provo, Utah: Brigham Young University Press, 1977.

Hawkins, Chester Lee. "Selective Bibliography on African-Americans and Mormons, 1830–1890." *Dialogue: A Journal of Mormon Thought* 25 (Winter 1992): 113–31.

Hill, Marvin S. "The Historiography of Mormonism." *Church History* 28 (December 1959): 418–26.

Homer, Michael W. "The Church's Image in Italy from the 1840s to 1946: A Bibliographic Essay." *Brigham Young University Studies* 31 (Spring 1991): 83–114.

Laughlin, David L. "A Selective, Evaluative, and Annotated Bibliography on Mormonism." *Bulletin of Bibliography* 48 (June 1991): 75–101.

———. "It Began with a Book: A Didactically Annotated Bibliography on Mormonism." *Journal of Religious and Theological Information* 2 (1994): 45–94.

Launius, Roger D. "A Bibliographical Review of the Reorganized Church in the Nineteenth Century." *Mormon History Association Newsletter* 64 (January 1987): 5–8.

———. "A New Historiographical Frontier: The Reorganized Church in the Twentieth Century." *John Whitmer Historical Association Journal* 6 (1986): 53–63.

————. "The Reorganized Church in the Nineteenth Century: A Bibliographical Review." In Marjorie B. Troeh and Eileen M. Terril, eds., *Restoration* Studies *IV* (Independence, Mo.: Herald, 1988): 171–87.

Leonard, Glen M. "Recent Writing on Mormon Nauvoo." *Western Illinois Regional Studies* 11 (Fall 1988): 69–93.

————. "Selected Nauvoo Bibliography: Work Since 1978." *Mormon History Association Newsletter* 71 (January 1989): 4–8.

Madsen, Carol Cornwall, and David J. Whittaker. "History's Sequel: A Source Essay on Women in Mormon History." *Journal of Mormon History* 6 (1979): 123–45.

Mauss, Armand L., and Jeffrey R. Franks. "Comprehensive Bibliography of Social Science Literature on the Mormons." *Review of Religious Research* 26 (September 1984): 73–115.

Paul, Rodman W. "The Mormons as a Theme in Western Historical Writing." *Journal of American History* 54 (December 1967): 511–23.

Poll, Richard D. "Nauvoo and the New Mormon History: A Bibliographical Survey." *Journal of Mormon History* 5 (1978): 105–23.

Scott, Patricia Lyn. "Mormon Polygamy: A Bibliography, 1977–91." *Journal of Mormon History* 19 (Spring 1993): 133–55.

Shields, Steven L. *The Latter Day Saint Churches: An Annotated Bibliography*. New York/London: Garland, 1987.

Taylor, P. A. M. "Recent Writing on Utah and the Mormons." *Arizona and the West* 4 (Fall 1962): 249–60.

Wahlquist, Wayne L. "A Review of Mormon Settlement Literature." *Utah Historical Quarterly* 45 (Winter 1977): 3–21.

Whittaker, David J. "Bibliography: LDS Missionary Work." *Mormon History Association Newsletter* 69 (July 1988): 5–8.

————. "History—Educational System of the LDS Church." *Mormon History Association Newsletter* 68 (April 1988): 2–5.

————. *Mormon Americana: A Guide to Sources and Collections in the United States*. Provo, Utah: BYU Studies, 1995.

————. "Mormon Social History: A Selected Bibliography." *Mormon History Association Newsletter* 6 (April 1986): 2–5.

————. "Mormonism in Great Britain, 1837–1987." *Mormon History Association Newsletter* 66 (July 1987): 1–4.

————. "Mormons and Native Americans: A Historical and Bibliographical Introduction." *Dialogue: A Journal of Mormon Thought* 18 (Winter 1985): 33–64.

————. "Sources on Mormon Origins in New York and Pennsylvania." *Mormon History Association Newsletter* 43 (March 1980): 8–12.

Whittaker, David J., and Chris McClellan. *Mormon Missions and Missionaries: A Bibliographic Guide to Published and Manuscript Sources.* Provo, Utah: Harold B. Lee Library, Brigham Young University, 1993.

Wilson, William A. "A Bibliography of Studies in Mormon Folklore." *Utah Historical Quarterly* 44 (Fall 1976): 389–94.

PUBLISHED PRIMARY SOURCES

Bagley, Will, ed. *Scoundrel's Tale: The Samuel Brannan Papers.* Vol. 3 of *Kingdom in the West: The Mormons and the American Frontier.* Spokane, Wash.: Arthur H. Clark, 1999.

Barney, Ronald O., ed. "Letters of a Missionary Apostle to His Wife: Brigham Young to Mary Ann Angell Young, 1839–1841." *Brigham Young University Studies* 38 (1999): 156–201.

Baugh, Alexander L. "Joseph Young's Affidavit of the Massacre at Haun's Mill." *Brigham Young University Studies* 38 (1999): 188–202.

Berrett, William E., and Alma P. Burton. *Readings in L.D.S. Church History from Original Manuscripts.* 3 vols. Salt Lake City: Deseret Book, 1953–58.

The Book of Mormon. Salt Lake City: The Church of Jesus Christ of Latter-day Saints, 1981.

Buchanan, Frederick Stewart, ed. *A Good Time Coming: Mormon Letters to Scotland.* Salt Lake City: University of Utah Press, 1988.

Campbell, Eugene E., ed. *The Essential Brigham Young.* Salt Lake City: Signature, 1992.

Cannon, Donald Q., and Lyndon W. Cook, eds. *Far West Record: Minutes of the Church of Jesus Christ of Latter-day Saints, 1830–1844.* Salt Lake City: Deseret Book, 1983.

Clark, James R., ed. *Messages of the First Presidency of the Church of Jesus Christ of Latter-day Saints.* 6 vols. Salt Lake City: Bookcraft, 1971–75.

Collier, Fred C., and William S. Hartwell, eds. *Kirtland Council Minute Book.* Salt Lake City: Collier's, 1996.

Cook, Lyndon W. "'Brother Joseph Is Truly a Wonderful Man, He Is All We Could Wish a Prophet to Be': Pre-1844 Letters of William Law." *Brigham Young University Studies* 20 (Winter 1980): 207–18.

Cook, Lyndon W. *The Revelations of the Prophet Joseph Smith.* Provo, Utah: Seventy's Mission Bookstore, 1981.

Cook, Lyndon W., and Milton V. Backman Jr. *Kirtland Elders' Quorum Record, 1836–1841.* Provo, Utah: Grandin, 1985.

Cook, Lyndon W., and Matthew K. Cook, eds. *David Whitmer Interviews: A Restoration Witness*. Orem, Utah: Grandin, 1991.

Cracroft, Richard H., and Neal E. Lambert. *A Believing People: Literature of the Latter-day Saints*. Provo, Utah: Brigham Young University Press, 1974.

Crawley, Peter L. *The Essential Parley P. Pratt*. Salt Lake City: Signature, 1990.

Dahl, Larry E., and Charles D. Tate Jr., eds. *The Lectures on Faith in Historical Perspective*. Provo, Utah: Religious Studies Center, Brigham Young University, 1990.

Daughters of Utah Pioneers. *Chronicles of Courage 1–* . Daughters of Utah Pioneers, 1990– .

———. *An Enduring Legacy*. 12 vols. Daughters of Utah Pioneers, 1978–89.

———. *Heart Throbs of the West*. 12 vols. Daughters of Utah Pioneers, 1939–51.

———. *Our Pioneer* Heritage. 20 vols. Daughters of Utah Pioneers, 1958–77.

———. *Treasures of Pioneer History*. 6 vols. Daughters of Utah Pioneers, 1952–57.

The Doctrine and Covenants. Salt Lake City: The Church of Jesus Christ of Latter-day Saints, 1981.

Durham, G. Homer, comp. *The Discourses of Wilford Woodruff*. Salt Lake City: Bookcraft, 1946.

Ehat, Andrew F., and Lyndon W. Cook, eds. *The Words of Joseph Smith*. Provo, Utah: Religious Studies Center, Brigham Young University, 1980.

Ellsworth, Maria S., ed. *Mormon Odyssey: The Story of Ida Hunt Udall, Plural Wife*. Urbana: University of Illinois Press, 1992.

Ellsworth, S. George. *Dear Ellen: Two Mormon Women and Their Letters*. Salt Lake City: Tanner Trust Fund, University of Utah Library, 1974.

Godfrey, Kenneth W., Audrey M. Godfrey, and Jill Mulvay Derr, eds. *Women's Voices: An Untold History of the Latter-day Saints*. Salt Lake City: Deseret Book, 1982.

Gospel Ideals: Selections from the Discourses of David O. McKay. Salt Lake City: Improvement Era, 1953.

Grant, Heber J. *Gospel Standards: Selections from the Sermons and Writings of Heber J. Grant*. Salt Lake City: Improvement Era, 1941.

Hansen, Jennifer Moulton, ed. *Letters of Catharine Cottam Romney, Plural Wife*. Urbana: University of Illinois Press, 1992.

Harris, James, ed. *The Essential James E. Talmage*. Salt Lake City: Signature, 1997.

Harwell, William S., ed. *Manuscript History of Brigham Young, 1847–1850.* Salt Lake City: Collier's, 1997.

Higbee, Marilyn. "'A Weary Traveler': The 1848–50 Diary of Zina D. H. Young." *Journal of Mormon History* 19 (Fall 1993): 86–125.

Hill, Marvin S., ed. *The Essential Joseph Smith.* Salt Lake City: Signature, 1995.

Holzapfel, Jeni Brobert, and Richard Neitzel Holzapfel, eds. *A Woman's View: Helen Mar Whitney's Reminiscences of Early Church History.* Provo, Utah: Brigham Young University Religious Studies Center, 1997.

Huntress, Keith C., ed. *Murder of an American Prophet.* San Francisco: Chandler, 1960.

Jessee, Dean C., ed. *Letters of Brigham Young to His Sons.* Salt Lake City: Deseret Book, 1974.

———. *The Papers of Joseph Smith.* Vols. 1– . Salt Lake City: Deseret Book, 1989– .

Johnson, Clark V., comp. *Mormon Redress Petitions: Documents of the 1833–1838 Missouri Conflict.* Religious Studies Center, Brigham Young University. Salt Lake City: Bookcraft, 1992.

Kimball, Edward L., ed. *The Teachings of Spencer W. Kimball.* Salt Lake City: Bookcraft, 1982.

Kirkham, Francis W. *A New Witness for Christ in America.* 2 vols. Independence, Mo.: Zion's, 1942, 1951.

Knight, Greg R., ed. *Thomas Bullock Nauvoo Journal.* Orem, Utah: Grandin, 1994.

Larson, Stan. "A 'Meeting of the Brethren': The Discovery of Official Minutes of a 1902 Meeting of the First Presidency and Twelve Apostles." *Dialogue: A Journal of Mormon Thought* 31 (Summer 1998): 77–95.

Larson, Stan, ed. *Prisoner for Polygamy: The Memoirs and Letters of Rudger Clawson at the Utah Territorial Penitentiary, 1884–87.* Urbana: University of Illinois Press, 1993.

Lieber, Constance L. "'The Goose Hangs High': Excerpts from the Letters of Martha Hughes Cannon." *Utah Historical Quarterly* 48 (Winter 1980): 37–48.

Lieber, Constance L., and John Sillito, eds. *Letters from Exile: The Correspondence of Martha Hughes Cannon and Angus M. Cannon, 1886–1888.* Salt Lake City: Signature, 1989.

McKiernan, F. Mark, and Roger D. Launius, eds. *An Early Latter Day Saint History: The Book of John Whitmer.* Independence, Mo.: Herald, 1980.

Madsen, Carol Cornwall. *In Their Own Words: Women and the Story of Nauvoo.* Salt Lake City: Deseret Book, 1994.

Millett, Robert L., ed. *Joseph Smith: Selected Sermons and Writings*. New York: Paulist, 1989.

Mulder, William, and A. Russell Mortensen, eds. *Among the Mormons: Historic Accounts by Contemporary Observers*. New York: Knopf, 1967.

The Pearl of Great Price. Salt Lake City: The Church of Jesus Christ of Latter-day Saints, 1981.

Smith, Hyrum M., ed. *From Prophet to Son: Advice of Joseph F. Smith to His Missionary Sons*. Salt Lake City: Deseret Book, 1981.

Smith, Joseph. *History of the Church of Jesus Christ of Latter-day Saints*. 7 vols. Ed. B. H. Roberts. Salt Lake City: Deseret Book, 1902–12.

Smith, Joseph F. *Gospel Doctrine*. 2nd ed. Salt Lake City: Deseret News, 1919.

Smith, Joseph Fielding, comp. *Teachings of the Prophet Joseph Smith*. Salt Lake City: Deseret Book, 1938.

Taylor, John. *Gospel Kingdom: Selections from the Writings and Discourses of John Taylor*. Comp. G. Homer Durham. Salt Lake City: Bookcraft, 1943.

Van Orden, Bruce, ed. "Writing to Zion: The William W. Phelps Kirtland Letters (1835–1836)." *Brigham Young University Studies* 33 (1993): 542–93.

Vogel, Dan, ed. *Early Mormon Documents: Vol. 1*. Salt Lake City: Signature, 1995.

———. *Early Mormon Documents: Vol. 2*. Salt Lake City: Signature, 1998.

Watson, Elden J., ed. *Manuscript History of Brigham Young, 1846–1847*. Salt Lake City: Elden J. Watson, 1971.

Westergren, Bruce N., and Julie J. Westergren, eds. *From Historian to Dissident: The Book of John Whitmer*. Salt Lake City: Signature, 1994.

Whittaker, David J., ed. *The Essential Orson Pratt*. Salt Lake City: Signature, 1991.

Widtsoe, John A., comp. *Discourses of Brigham* Young. Salt Lake City: Deseret Book, 1925.

Williams, Clyde J., comp. *The Teachings of Lorenzo Snow*. Salt Lake City: Bookcraft, 1984.

DIARIES AND AUTOBIOGRAPHIES

Allen, James B., and Thomas G. Alexander, eds. *Manchester Mormons: The Journal of William Clayton, 1840 to 1842*. Santa Barbara: Peregrine Smith, 1974.

Arrington, Leonard J. *Adventures of a Church Historian*. Urbana: University of Illinois Press, 1998.

Arrington, Leonard J., ed. "Crusade against Theocracy: The Reminiscences of Judge Jacob Smith Boreman of Utah, 1872–1877." *Huntington Library Quarterly* 24 (November 1960): 1–45.

———. "James Gordon Bennett's 1831 Report on 'The Mormonites,'" *Brigham Young University Studies* 10 (Spring 1970): 353–64.

———. "Oliver Cowdery's Kirtland, Ohio, 'Sketch Book.'" *Brigham Young University Studies* 12 (Summer 1972): 410–26.

Bagley, Will, ed. *Frontiersman: Abner Blackburn's Narrative*. Salt Lake City: University of Utah Press, 1992.

———. *The Pioneer Camp of the Saints: The 1846 and 1847 Mormon Trail Journals of Thomas Bullock*. Vol. 1 of *Kingdom in the West: The Mormons and the American Frontier*. Spokane, Wash.: Arthur H. Clark, 1997.

Beecher, Maureen Ursenbach, ed. "'All Things Move in Order in the City': The Nauvoo Diary of Zina Diantha Huntington Jacobs," *Brigham Young University Studies* 19 (Spring 1979): 285–320.

———. "Eliza R. Snow's Nauvoo Journal." *Brigham Young University Studies* 15 (Summer 1975): 391–416.

———. "The Iowa Journal of Lorenzo Snow." *Brigham Young University Studies* 24 (Summer 1984): 261–73.

———. *The Personal Writings of Eliza Roxcy Snow*. Salt Lake City: University of Utah Press, 1995.

Bergera, Gary James, ed. *The Autobiography of B. H. Roberts*. Salt Lake City: Signature, 1990.

Bigler, David L., ed. *The Gold Discovery Journal of Azariah Smith*. Salt Lake City: University of Utah Press, 1990.

Brimhall, Sandra Dawn Allen, ed. *Journal of Isaiah Moses Coombs (1855–1856)*. Vol. 1. Salt Lake City: privately published, 1993.

Brooks, Juanita, ed. *On the Mormon Frontier: The Diary of Hosea Stout, 1844–1861*. Salt Lake City: University of Utah Press, 1964.

———. *Quicksand and Cactus: A Memoir of the Southern Mormon Frontier*. Salt Lake City: Howe Brothers, 1982.

Buice, David. "'All Alone and None to Cheer Me': The Southern States Mission Diaries of J. Golden Kimball." *Dialogue: A Journal of Mormon Thought* 24 (Spring 1991): 35–54.

———. "Excerpts from the Diary of Teancum William Heward, Early Mormon Missionary to Georgia." *Georgia Historical Quarterly* 64 (Fall 1981): 317–25.

Bullock, Thomas. "Journal of Thomas Bullock, 31 August 1845 to 5 July 1846." *Brigham Young University Studies* 31 (Winter 1991): 15–75.

Cannon, M. Hamlin, ed. "The Prison Diary of a Mormon Apostle." *Pacific Historical Review* 16 (November 1947): 393–409.

Clayton, William. *William Clayton's Journal: A Daily Record of the Journey of the Original Company.* Salt Lake City: Clayton Family Association, 1921.

Cleland, Robert Glass, and Juanita Brooks, eds. *A Mormon Chronicle: The Diaries of John D. Lee.* 2 vols. San Marino, Calif.: Huntington Library, 1955.

Creer, Leland H., ed. "Journey to Zion: From the Journal of Erastus Snow." *Utah Humanities Review* 2 (April and July 1948): 107–28, 264–84.

Crookson, Douglas L., ed. *Henry Ballard: The Story of a Courageous Pioneer.* Layton, Utah: privately published, 1994.

Egan, Howard R. *Pioneering the West, 1846–1878: Major Howard Egan's Diary.* Richmond, Utah: Howard R. Egan Estate, 1917.

Ellsworth, Maria S., ed. *Mormon Odyssey: The Story of Ida Hunt Udall, Plural Wife.* Urbana: University of Illinois Press, 1992.

Ellsworth, S. George, ed. *The History of Louisa Barnes Pratt: Being the Autobiography of a Mormon Missionary Widow and Pioneer.* Logan: Utah State University, 1998.

———. *The Journals of Addison Pratt.* Salt Lake City: University of Utah Press, 1990.

England, Eugene, ed. "George Laub's Nauvoo Journal." *Brigham Young University Studies* 18 (1978): 151–78.

Evans, Cleo H., comp. *Curtis Edwin Bolton: Pioneer Missionary.* Fairfax, Va.: privately published, 1968.

Firmage, Edwin Brown, ed. *An Abundant Life: The Memoirs of Hugh B. Brown.* Salt Lake City: Signature, 1988.

Garner, Hugh, ed. *A Mormon Rebel: The Life and Travels of Frederick Gardiner.* Salt Lake City: Signature, 1993.

Godfrey, Donald G., and Brigham Y. Card, eds. *The Diaries of Charles Ora Card: The Canadian Years, 1886–1903.* Salt Lake City: University of Utah Press, 1993.

Groberg, John H. *The Fire of Faith.* Salt Lake City: Bookcraft, 1996.

———. *In the Eye of the Storm.* Salt Lake City: Bookcraft, 1993.

Hart, Edward L. *Mormon in Motion: The Life and Journals of James H. Hart, 1825–1906.* Provo, Utah: Windsor, 1978.

Hartley, William G. *My Best for the Kingdom: History and Autobiography of John Lowe Butler, a Mormon Frontiersman.* Salt Lake City: Aspen, 1993.

Heath, Harvard S., ed. *In the World: The Diaries of Reed Smoot.* Salt Lake City: Signature, 1994.

Jenson, Andrew. *Autobiography of Andrew Jenson, Assistant Historian of the Church.* Salt Lake City: Deseret News, 1938.

Jessee, Dean C., ed. "The John Taylor Nauvoo Journal." *Brigham Young University Studies* 23 (Summer 1983): 1–124.

————. "The Kirtland Diary of Wilford Woodruff." *Brigham Young University Studies* 12 (Summer 1972): 365–99.

Jessee, Dean C., and David J. Whittaker, eds. "The Last Months of Mormonism in Missouri: The Albert Perry Rockwood Journal." *Brigham Young University Studies* 28 (1988): 5–41.

Johnson, Benjamin F. *My Life's Review: The Autobiography of Benjamin F. Johnson.* Provo, Utah: Grandin, 1997.

Jones, Daniel W. *Forty Years among the Indians.* Salt Lake City: Juvenile Instructor Office, 1890.

Kenney, Scott G., ed. *Memories and Reflections: The Autobiography of E. E. Ericksen.* Salt Lake City: Signature, 1987.

————. *Wilford Woodruff's Journal.* 11 vols. Salt Lake City: Signature, 1983.

Kimball, Stanley B., ed. *On the Potter's Wheel: The Diaries of Heber C. Kimball.* Salt Lake City: Signature, 1987.

Krenkal, John H., ed. *The Life and Times of Joseph Fish, Mormon Pioneer.* Danville, Ill.: Interstate, 1970.

Larson, A. Karl, and Katharine Miles Larson, eds. *Diary of Charles Lowell Walker.* 2 vols. Logan: Utah State University Press, 1980.

Larson, Stan, ed. *A Ministry of Meetings: Diaries of Rudger Clawson.* Salt Lake City: Signature, 1993.

————. *Prisoner for Polygamy: The Memoirs and Letters of Rudger Clawson at the Utah Territorial Penitentiary, 1884–87.* Urbana: University of Illinois Press, 1993.

Lee, George P. *Silent Courage, an Indian Story: The Autobiography of George P. Lee, a Navajo.* Salt Lake City: Deseret Book, 1987.

McIntyre, Myron W., and Noel R. Barton, eds. *Christopher Layton: Colonizer, Statesman, Leader.* Salt Lake City: Christopher Layton Family Organization, 1966.

Madsen, Carol Cornall, ed. *Journey to Zion: Voices from the Mormon Trail.* Salt Lake City: Deseret Book, 1997.

Martins, Helvecio. *The Autobiography of Elder Helvecio Martins.* Salt Lake City: Aspen, 1994.

Nixon, Loretta D., and L. Douglas Smoot. *Abraham Owen Smoot: A Testament of His Life.* Provo, Utah: Brigham Young University Press, 1994.

Olpin, Robert S., ed. *A Basket of Chips: An Autobiography by James Taylor Harwood.* Salt Lake City: Tanner Trust Fund, 1985.

Pratt, Parley P., ed. *Autobiography of Parley Parker Pratt.* Salt Lake City: Deseret Book, 1961. (lst pub., 1874.)

Robertson, Frank C. *A Ram in the Thicket: The Story of a Roaming Homesteader Family on the Mormon Frontier.* Moscow: University of Idaho Press, 1994.

Sessions, Gene A., ed. *Mormon Democrat: The Religious and Political Memoirs of James Henry Moyle.* Salt Lake City: James Moyle Genealogical and Historical Association, 1975.

Shipps, Jan, and John W. Welch, eds. *The Journals of William E. McLellan, 1831–1836.* Provo, Utah: BYU Studies, 1994.

Smart, Donna Toland, ed. *Mormon Midwife: The 1846–1888 Diaries of Patty Bartlett Sessions.* Vol. 2 of *Life Writings of Frontier Women.* Logan: Utah State University Press, 1997.

Smith, George D., ed. *An Intimate Chronicle: The Journals of William Clayton.* Salt Lake City: Signature, 1991.

Smith, Oliver R., ed. *Six Decades in the Early West: The Journal of Jesse Nathaniel Smith, 1834–1906.* Provo, Utah: Jesse N. Smith Family Association, 1970.

Staker, Susan, ed. *Waiting for World's End: Diaries of Wilford Woodruff.* Salt Lake City: Signature, 1993.

Tanner, Annie Clark. *A Mormon Mother: An Autobiography.* Salt Lake City: Tanner Trust Fund, University of Utah Library, 1973.

Walker, Ronald W., ed. "Lucy Mack Smith Speaks to the Nauvoo Saints." *Brigham Young University Studies* 32 (Winter/Spring 1992): 276–84.

Ward, Maurine Carr, ed. *Winter Quarters: The 1846–1848 Life Writings of Mary Haskin Parker Richards.* Logan: Utah State University Press, 1996.

Watson, Elden J., ed. *The Orson Pratt Journals.* Salt Lake City: Elden J. Watson, 1975.

Whitcomb, Elias W. "Reminiscences of a Pioneer: An Excerpt from the Diary of Elias W. Whitcomb." *Annals of Wyoming* 57 (Fall 1985): 21–32.

White, Jean Bickmore, ed. *Church, State, and Politics: The Diaries of John Henry Smith.* Salt Lake City: Signature, 1990.

BIOGRAPHIES

Alexander, Thomas G. *Things in Heaven and Earth: The Life and Times of Wilford Woodruff, a Mormon Prophet.* Salt Lake City: Signature, 1991.

Allen, James B. *Trials of Discipleship: The Story of William Clayton, a Mormon.* Urbana: University of Illinois Press, 1987.

Anderson, Lavina Fielding. "A Ministry of Blessing: Nicholas Groesbeck Smith." *Dialogue: A Journal of Mormon Thought* 31 (Fall 1998): 59–78.

Anderson, Paul L. "William Henry Folsom: Pioneer Architect." *Utah Historical Quarterly* 43 (Summer 1975): 240–59.

Arrington, Harriet Horne. "Alice Merrill Horne, Art Promoter and Early Utah Legislator." *Utah Historical Quarterly* 58 (Summer 1990): 261–76.

Arrington, J. Earl. "William Weeks, Architect of the Nauvoo Temple." *Brigham Young University Studies* 19 (Spring 1979): 337–59.

Arrington, Leonard J. *Brigham Young: American Moses.* New York: Knopf, 1985.

———. *Charles C. Rich: Mormon General and Western Frontiersman.* Provo, Utah: Brigham Young University Press, 1974.

———. *David Eccles: Pioneer Western Industrialist.* Logan: Utah State University Press, 1975.

———. *From Quaker to Latter-day Saint: Bishop Edwin D. Woolley.* Salt Lake City: Deseret Book, 1976.

———. *Madelyn Cannon Stewart Silver: Poet, Teacher, Homemaker.* Salt Lake City: Publishers Press, 1998.

Arrington, Leonard J., and Davis Bitton. *Saints without Halos: The Human Side of Mormon History.* Salt Lake City: Signature, 1982.

Arrington, Leonard J., and John R. Alley Jr. *Harold F. Silver: Western Inventor, Businessman, and Civic Leader.* Logan: Utah State University Press, 1992.

Arrington, Leonard J., and Susan Arrington Madsen. *Mothers of the Prophets.* Salt Lake City: Deseret Book, 1987.

———. *Sunbonnet Sisters: The Stories of Mormon Women and Frontier Life.* Salt Lake City: Bookcraft, 1984.

Arrington, Leonard J., ed. *The Presidents of the Church.* Salt Lake City: Deseret Book, 1986.

Arrington, Leonard J., and Richard Jensen. "Pioneer Portraits: Lorenzo Hill Hatch." *Idaho Yesterdays* 17 (Summer 1973): 2–8.

Avery, Valeen Tippets. *From Mission to Madness: Last Son of the Mormon Prophet.* Urbana: University of Illinois Press, 1998.

———. "Sketches of the Sweet Singer: David Hyrum Smith, 1844–1904." *John Whitmer Historical Association Journal* 5 (1985): 3–15.

Avery, Valeen Tippetts, and Linda King Newell. "Lewis C. Bidamon, Stepchild of Mormondom." *Brigham Young University Studies* 19 (Spring 1979): 375–88.

————. "The Lion and the Lady: Brigham Young and Emma Smith." *Utah Historical Quarterly* 48 (Winter 1980): 81–97.

Backman, Milton V. Jr. *A Profile of Latter-day Saints of Kirtland, Ohio, and Members of Zion's Camp, 1830–1839.* Provo, Utah: Brigham Young University Department of Church History and Doctrine, 1982.

Backus, Anna Jean. *Mountain Meadows Witness: The Life and Times of Bishop Philip Klingensmith.* Spokane, Wash.: Arthur H. Clark, 1995.

Barron, Howard H. *Orson Hyde: Missionary, Apostle, Colonizer.* Bountiful, Utah: Horizon, 1977.

Barton, Peggy Petersen. *Mark E. Petersen: A Biography.* Salt Lake City: Deseret Book, 1985.

Bates, Irene M. "Uncle John Smith, 1781–1854: Patriarchal Bridge." *Dialogue: A Journal of Mormon Thought* 20 (Fall 1987): 79–89.

Beecher, Maureen Ursenbach. "Each in Her Own Time: Four Zinas." *Dialogue: A Journal of Mormon Thought* 26 (Summer 1993): 119–35.

————. *Eliza and Her Sisters.* Salt Lake City: Aspen, 1991.

Bennion, Sherilyn Cox. "Lula Greene Richards: Utah's First Woman Editor." *Brigham Young University Studies* 21 (Spring 1981): 155–74.

Bergman, Ray L. *The Children Sang: The Life and Music of Evan Stephen.* Salt Lake City: Northwest, 1992.

Bishop, M. Guy. "After Sutter's Mill: The Life of Henry Bigler, 1848–1900." *Dialogue: A Journal of Mormon Thought* 20 (Spring 1987): 125–35.

————. "'A Great Little Saint': A Brief Look at the Life of Henry William Bigler." *Brigham Young University Studies* 30 (Fall 1990): 27–38.

————. *Henry William Bigler: Soldier, Gold Miner, Missionary, Chronicler, 1815–1900.* Logan: Utah State University Press, 1998.

Bitton, Davis. "Claude T. Barnes, Utah Naturalist." *Utah Historical Quarterly* 49 (Fall 1981): 316–30.

————. *George Q. Cannon: A Biography.* Salt Lake City: Deseret Book, 1999.

————. *Images of the Prophet Joseph Smith.* Salt Lake City: Aspen, 1996.

————. *The Martyrdom Remembered.* Salt Lake City: Aspen, 1994.

————. *The Redoubtable John Pack.* Salt Lake City: Eden Hill, 1982.

Black, Susan Easton, and Larry C. Porter, eds. *Lion of the Lord: Essays on the Life and Service of Brigham Young.* Salt Lake City: Deseret Book, 1995.

Black, Susan Easton, and Charles D. Tate Jr., eds. *Joseph Smith: The Prophet, the Man.* Provo, Utah: Religious Studies Center, Brigham Young University, 1993.

Bradford, Mary Lythgoe. *Lowell L. Bennion: Teacher, Counselor, Humanitarian*. Salt Lake City: Dialogue Foundation, 1995.

Bringhurst, Newell G. *Brigham Young and the Expanding American Frontier*. Boston: Little, Brown, 1986.

———. "The Private versus the Public David O. McKay: Profile of a Complex Personality." *Dialogue: A Journal of Mormon Thought* 31 (Fall 1998): 11–32.

Brodie, Fawn M. *No Man Knows My History: The Life of Joseph Smith, The Mormon Prophet*. New York: Knopf, 1945.

Brooks, Juanita. *John D. Lee: Zealot, Pioneer Builder, Scapegoat*. Rev. ed. Glendale, Calif.: Arthur H. Clark, 1972.

Buchanan, Frederick S. "Robert Lang Campbell: 'A Wise Scribe in Israel' and Schoolman to the Saints." *Brigham Young University Studies* 19 (Summer 1989): 5–27.

Burgess-Olson, Vicky D., ed. *Sister Saints*. Provo, Utah: Brigham Young University Press, 1978.

Bushman, Claudia, ed. *Mormon Sisters: Women in Early Utah*. Cambridge, Mass.: Emeline Press, 1976. Rev. ed. Logan: Utah State University Press, 1997.

Bushman, Richard L. *Joseph Smith and the Beginnings of Mormonism*. Urbana: University of Illinois Press, 1984.

Campbell, Eugene E., and Richard D. Poll. *Brown: His Life and Thought*. Salt Lake City: Bookcraft, 1975.

Cannon, Kenneth L. II. "Brigham Bicknell Young, Musical Christian Scientist." *Utah Historical Quarterly* 50 (Spring 1982): 124–38.

Carmack, Noel A. "The Seven Ages of Thomas Lyne: A Tragedian among the Mormons." *John Whitmer Historical Association Journal* 14 (1994): 53–72.

Cheney, Thomas E. *The Golden Legacy: A Folk History of J. Golden Kimball*. Santa Barbara: Peregrine Smith, 1974.

Corbett, Pearson H. *Hyrum Smith, Patriarch*. Salt Lake City: Deseret Book, 1963.

Cook, Lyndon W. "Isaac Galland—Mormon Benefactor." *Brigham Young University Studies* 19 (Spring 1979): 261–84.

———. *Joseph C. Kingsbury: A Biography*. Provo, Utah: Grandin, 1985.

———. *William Law*. Orem, Utah: Grandin, 1994.

———. "William Law, Nauvoo Dissenter." *Brigham Young University Studies* 22 (Winter 1982): 47–72.

Crawley, Peter. "Parley P. Pratt: Father of Mormon Pamphleteering." *Dialogue: A Journal of Mormon Thought* 15 (Fall 1982): 13–26.

Davies, J. Kenneth. "Thomas Rhoads, Forgotten Mormon Pioneer of 1846." *Nebraska History* 64 (Spring 1983): 81–95.

Day, Kimberly. "Frederick Kesler, Utah Craftsman." *Utah Historical Quarterly* 56 (Winter 1988): 54–74.

Dew, Sheri L. *Ezra Taft Benson: A Biography.* Salt Lake City: Deseret Book, 1987.

———. *Go Forward with Faith: The Biography of Gordon B. Hinckley.* Salt Lake City: Deseret Book, 1996.

Durham, G. Homer. *N. Eldon Tanner: His Life and Service.* Salt Lake City: Deseret Book, 1982.

Edwards, Paul M. *The Chief: An Administrative Biography of Fred M. Smith.* Independence, Mo.: Herald, 1988.

Ellsworth, S. George. *Samuel Claridge: Pioneering the Outposts of Zion.* Logan, Utah: S. George Ellsworth, 1987.

England, Breck. *The Life and Thought of Orson Pratt.* Salt Lake City: University of Utah Press, 1985.

England, Eugene. *Brother Brigham.* Salt Lake City: Bookcraft, 1980.

Erekson, Arthur B. *A History of John Benbow.* Provo, Utah: Arthur B. Erekson, 1987.

Evans, Richard L. Jr. *Richard L. Evans: The Man and the Message.* Salt Lake City: Bookcraft, 1973.

Flake, Lawrence R. *Mighty Men of Zion: General Authorities of the Last Dispensation.* Salt Lake City: Karl D. Butler, 1974.

Foster, Craig L. "From Temple Mormon to Anti-Mormon: The Ambivalent Odyssey of Increase Van Deusen." *Dialogue: A Journal of Mormon Thought* 27(3) (Fall 1994): 275–86.

Fox, Frank W. *J. Reuben Clark: The Public Years.* Provo, Utah: Brigham Young University Press, 1980.

Gibbons, Francis M. *Brigham Young: Modern Moses, Prophet of God.* Salt Lake City: Deseret Book, 1981.

———. *George Albert Smith: Kind and Caring Christian, Prophet of God.* Salt Lake City: Deseret Book, 1990.

———. *Harold B. Lee: Man of Vision, Prophet of God.* Salt Lake City, Deseret Book, 1993.

———. *Heber J. Grant: Man of Steel, Prophet of God.* Salt Lake City: Deseret Book, 1979.

———. *John Taylor: Mormon Philosopher, Prophet of God.* Salt Lake City: Deseret Book, 1985.

———. *Joseph Smith: Martyr, Prophet of God.* Salt Lake City: Deseret Book, 1977.

————. *Joseph F. Smith: Patriarch and Preacher, Prophet of God*. Salt Lake City: Deseret Book, 1984.

————. *Lorenzo Snow: Spiritual Giant, Prophet of God*. Salt Lake City: Deseret Book, 1982.

————. *Spencer W. Kimball: Resolute Disciple, Prophet of God*. Salt Lake City: Deseret Book, 1995.

————. *Wilford Woodruff: Wondrous Worker, Prophet of God*. Salt Lake City: Deseret Book, 1988.

Goates, L. Brent. *Harold B. Lee: Prophet and Seer*. Salt Lake City: Bookcraft, 1985.

Godfrey, Donald G. "Zina Prescendia Young Williams Card: Brigham's Daughter, Cardston's First Lady." *Journal of Mormon History* 23 (Fall 1997): 107–27.

Gregory, Thomas J. "Sidney Rigdon: Post Nauvoo." *Brigham Young University Studies* 21 (Winter 1981): 51–67.

Gunn, Stanley R. *Oliver Cowdery: Second Elder and Scribe*. Salt Lake City: Bookcraft, 1962.

Harris, Lynda W. "The Legend of Jessie Evans Smith." *Utah Historical Quarterly* 44 (Fall 1976): 351–64.

Hartley, William G. *Kindred Saints: The Mormon Immigrant Heritage of Alvin and Kathryne Christensen*. Salt Lake City: Eden Hill, 1982.

————. *These Are My Friends: A History of the Joseph Knight Family, 1825–1850*. Provo, Utah: Grandin, 1986.

Hatch, Jo Ann F. *Willing Hands: A Biography of Lorenzo Hill Hatch, 1826–1910*. Pinedale, Ariz.: Kymera, 1996.

Hefner, Loretta L. "From Apostle to Apostate: The Personal Struggle of Amasa Mason Lyman." *Dialogue: A Journal of Mormon Thought* 16 (Spring 1983): 90–104.

Hickman, Martin B. *David Matthew Kennedy: Banker, Statesman, Churchman*. Salt Lake City: Deseret Book, 1987.

Hiles, Norma Derry. *Gentle Monarch: The Presidency of Israel A. Smith*. Independence, Mo.: Herald, 1991.

Hill, Donna. *Joseph Smith, The First Mormon*. Garden City, N.Y.: Doubleday, 1977.

Hoopes, David S., and Roy Hoopes. *The Making of a Mormon Apostle: The Story of Rudger Clawson*. Lanham, Md.: Madison Books, 1990.

Howard, F. Burton. *Marion G. Romney: His Life and Faith*. Salt Lake City: Bookcraft, 1988.

Hunt, Larry E. *Fred M. Smith: Saint as Reformer*. Independence, Mo.: Herald, 1982.

Hunter, Milton R. *Brigham Young the Colonizer.* 4th ed. rev. Santa Barbara, Calif.: Peregrine Smith, 1973.

Hyde, Myrtle Stevens, and Everett L. Cooley. *The Life of Andrew Wood Cooley: A Story of Conviction.* Provo, Utah: Andrew Wood Cooley Family Association, 1991.

Jenson, Andrew. *Latter-day Saint Biographical Encyclopedia.* 4 vols. Salt Lake City: Deseret News, 1901–36.

Jessee, Dean C. "Brigham Young's Family: The Wilderness Years." *Brigham Young University Studies* 19 (Summer 1979): 474–500.

Johnson, Catherine M. "Emma Lucy Gates Bowen: Singer, Musician, Teacher." *Utah Historical Quarterly* 64 (Fall 1996): 344–55.

Kimball, Edward L., and Andrew E. Kimball Jr. *Spencer W. Kimball.* Salt Lake City: Bookcraft, 1977.

———. *The Story of Spencer W. Kimball: A Short Man, A Long Stride.* Salt Lake City: Bookcraft, 1985.

Kimball, Edward L., and Caroline Eyring Miner. *Camilla: A Biography of Camilla Eyring Kimball.* Salt Lake City: Deseret Book, 1980.

Kimball, Stanley B. *Heber C. Kimball: Mormon Patriarch and Pioneer.* Urbana: University of Illinois Press, 1981.

Knowles, Eleanor. *Howard W. Hunter.* Salt Lake City: Deseret Book, 1994.

Larson, Andrew Karl. *Erastus Snow: The Life of a Missionary and Pioneer for the Early Mormon Church.* Salt Lake City: University of Utah Press, 1971.

Legg, Phillip R. *Oliver Cowdery: The Elusive Second Elder of the Restoration.* Independence, Mo.: Herald, 1989.

Lyman, Edward Leo. "The Alienation of an Apostle from His Quorum: The Moses Thatcher Case." *Dialogue: A Journal of Mormon Thought* 18 (Summer 1985): 67–91.

Lyon, T. Edgar Jr. *John Lyon: The Life of a Pioneer Poet.* Provo, Utah: Brigham Young University, Religious Studies Center, 1989.

McCloud, Susan Evans. *Not in Vain: The Inspiring Story of Ellis Shipp, Pioneer Woman Doctor.* Salt Lake City: Bookcraft, 1984.

McConkie, Joseph F. *True and Faithful: The Life Story of Joseph Fielding Smith.* Salt Lake City: Bookcraft, 1971.

McCue, Robert J. "Anthony Maitland Stenhouse, Bachelor 'Polygamist.'" *Dialogue: A Journal of Mormon Thought* 23 (Spring 1990): 108–25.

Macfarlane, L. W., M.D. *Yours Sincerely, John M. Macfarlane.* Salt Lake City: privately published, 1980.

McKiernan, F. Mark. *The Voice of One Crying in the Wilderness: Sidney Rigdon, Religious Reformer, 1793–1876.* Lawrence, Kans.: Coronado, 1971.

Madsen, Carol Cornwall. "Emmeline B. Wells: 'Am I Not a Woman and a Sister?'" *Brigham Young University Studies* 22 (Spring 1982): 161–78.
———. "Emmeline B. Wells: A Voice for Mormon Women." *John Whitmer Historical Association Journal* 2 (1982): 11–21.
Madsen, Truman G. *Defender of the Faith: The B. H. Roberts Story.* Salt Lake City: Bookcraft, 1980.
Maxwell, Bruce David. "George Careless, Pioneer Musician." *Utah Historical Quarterly* 53 (Spring 1985): 131–43.
Merrill, Milton R. *Reed Smoot: Apostle in Politics.* Logan: Utah State University Press, 1990.
Mullikin, Frances Hartman. *First Ladies of the Restoration.* Independence, Mo.: Herald, 1985.
Newell, Linda King, and Valeen Tippetts Avery. *Mormon Enigma: Emma Hale Smith.* Garden City, N.Y.: Doubleday, 1984.
Newton, Marjorie. *Hero or Traitor: A Biographical Study of Charles Wesley Wandell.* John Whitmer Association Monograph Series. Independence, Mo.: Independence Press, 1992.
Noord, Roger Van. *King of Beaver Island: The Life and Assassination of James Jesse Strang.* Urbana: University of Illinois Press, 1988.
Oman, Richard G., and Richard L. Jensen. *C.C.A. Christensen, 1831–1912: Mormon Immigrant Artist.* Salt Lake City: Church of Jesus Christ of Latter-day Saints, 1984.
Parkinson, Benson Young. *S. Dilworth Young: General Authority, Scouter, Poet.* American Fork, Utah: Covenant, 1994.
Peterson, Charles S. "'A Mighty Man Was Brother Lot': A Portrait of Lot Smith, Mormon Frontiersman." *Western Historical Quarterly* 1 (October 1970): 393–414.
Peterson, Janet, and LaRene Gaunt. *Elect Ladies: Presidents of the Relief Society.* Salt Lake City: Deseret Book, 1990.
———. *Keepers of the Flame: Presidents of the Young Women.* Salt Lake City: Deseret Book, 1993.
Peterson, Levi. *Juanita Brooks: Mormon Woman Historian.* Salt Lake City: University of Utah Press, 1988.
Peterson, Richard H. "Jesse Knight, Utah's Mormon Mining Mogul." *Utah Historical Quarterly* 57 (Summer 1989): 240–53.
Poll, Richard D. *Working the Divine Miracle: The Life of Apostle Henry D. Moyle.* Salt Lake City: Signature, 1999.
Porter, Larry C. "Reverend George Lane—Good 'Gifts,' Much 'Grace,' and Marked 'Usefulness.'" *Brigham Young University Studies* 9 (1970): 321–40.

Porter, Larry C., and Susan Easton Black, eds. *The Prophet Joseph: Essays on the Life and Meaning of Joseph Smith.* Salt Lake City: Deseret Book, 1988.

Pratt, Steven F. "Parley P. Pratt in Winter Quarters and the Trail West." *Brigham Young University Studies* 24 (Summer 1984): 373–88.

Pusey, Merlo J. *Builders of the Kingdom: George A. Smith, John Henry Smith, George Albert Smith.* Provo, Utah: Brigham Young University Press, 1981.

Quinn, D. Michael. "Jesse Gause: Joseph Smith's Little-Known Counselor." *Brigham Young University Studies* 17 (Summer 1984): 9–34.

————. *J. Reuben Clark: The Church Years.* Provo, Utah: Brigham Young University Press, 1983.

Rodriguez, Derin Head. *From Every Nation.* Salt Lake City: Deseret Book, 1990.

Rollmann, Hans. "The Early Baptist Career of Sidney Rigdon in Warren, Ohio." *Brigham Young University Studies* 21 (Winter 1981): 37–50.

Romney, Thomas C. *Life Story of Miles Park Romney.* Salt Lake City: Zions, 1948.

Rowley, Dennis. "Fishing on the Kennet: The Victorian Boyhood of James E. Talmage, 1862–1876." *Brigham Young University Studies* 33 (Fall 1993): 480–520.

Schindler, Harold. *Orrin Porter Rockwell: Man of God, Son of Thunder.* Salt Lake City: University of Utah Press, 1966.

Schlup, Leonard. "Utah Maverick: Frank J. Cannon and the Politics of Conscience in 1896." *Utah Historical Quarterly* 62, 4 (Fall 1994): 335–48.

Schnibbe, Karl-Heinz, Alan F. Keele, and Douglas F. Tobler. *The Price: The True Story of a Mormon Who Defied Hitler.* Salt Lake City: Bookcraft, 1984.

Seegmiller, Janet Burton. *"Be Kind to the Poor": The Life Story of Robert Taylor Burton.* N.p.: Robert Taylor Burton Family Organization, 1988.

Seifrit, William C. "Charles Henry Wilcken, an Undervalued Saint." *Utah Historical Quarterly* 55 (Fall 1987): 308–21.

————. "The Prison Experience of Abraham H. Cannon." *Utah Historical Quarterly* 53 (Summer 1985): 223–36.

Sessions, Gene A. *Latter-day Patriots: Nine Mormon Families and Their Revolutionary War Heritage.* Salt Lake City: Deseret Book, 1975.

————. *Mormon Thunder: A Documentary History of Jedediah Morgan Grant.* Urbana: University of Illinois Press, 1982.

Smart, William B. "William H. Smart, Builder in the Basin." *Utah Historical Quarterly* 50 (Winter 1982): 59–67.

Smith, Andrew F. *The Saintly Scoundrel: The Life and Times of John C. Bennett*. Urbana: University of Illinois Press, 1997.

Smith, Henry A. *Matthew Cowley: Man of Faith*. Salt Lake City: Bookcraft, 1954.

Smith, Joseph Fielding. *Life of Joseph F. Smith*. Salt Lake City: Deseret Book, 1938.

Smith, Joseph Fielding Jr., and John J. Stewart. *The Life of Joseph Fielding Smith, Tenth President of the Church*. Salt Lake City: Deseret Book, 1972.

Smith, Lucy Mack. *History of Joseph Smith by His Mother, Lucy Mack Smith*. Salt Lake City: Bookcraft, 1958. (1st pub., 1853.)

Sonne, Conway B. *Knight of the Kingdom: The Story of Richard Ballantyne*. Salt Lake City: Deseret Book, 1949.

———. *A Man Named Alma: The World of Alma Sonne*. Bountiful, Utah: Horizon, 1988.

Stott, G. St. John. "John Taylor's Religious Preparation." *Dialogue: A Journal of Mormon Thought* 19 (Spring 1986): 94–104.

Swetnam, Susan Hendricks. *Lives of the Saints in Southeast Idaho: An Introduction to Mormon Pioneer Life Story Writing*. Moscow: University of Idaho Press, 1991.

Talmage, John R. *The Talmage Story: Life of James E. Talmage–Educator, Scientist, Apostle*. Salt Lake City: Bookcraft, 1972.

Tate, Lucile C. *Andrew B. Christenson: Mormon Educational Pioneer*. Provo, Utah: Brigham Young University Press, 1981.

———. *David B. Haight: The Life of a Disciple*. Salt Lake City: Bookcraft, 1987.

———. *LeGrand Richards: Beloved Apostle*. Salt Lake City: Bookcraft, 1982.

Taylor, Samuel W. *The Kingdom or Nothing: The Life of John Taylor, Militant Mormon*. New York: Macmillan, 1976.

Taylor, Samuel W., and Raymond W. Taylor. *The John Taylor Papers: Records of the Last Utah Pioneer*. 2 vols. Redwood City, Calif.: Taylor Trust, 1984–85.

Van Orden, Bruce A. *Prisoner for Conscience' Sake: The Life Story of George Reynolds*. Salt Lake City: Deseret Book, 1992.

Van Wagoner, Richard S. *Sidney Rigdon: A Portrait of Religious Excess*. Salt Lake City: Signature, 1994.

Van Wagoner, Richard S., and Mary C. Van Wagoner. "Orson Pratt, Jr.: Gifted Son of an Apostle and an Apostate." *Dialogue: A Journal of Mormon Thought* 21 (Spring 1988): 84–94.

Van Wagoner, Richard S., and Steven C. Walker. *A Book of Mormons*. Salt Lake City: Signature, 1982.

Walgren, Kent L. "James Adams: Early Springfield Mormon and Freemason." *Journal of the Illinois State Historical Society* 75 (Summer 1982): 121–36.

Walker, Ronald W. "Crisis in Zion: Heber J. Grant and the Panic of 1893." *Arizona and the West* 21 (Fall 1979): 257–78. Abridged and reprinted in *Sunstone* 10 (May 1985): 70–8.

———. "Heber J. Grant's European Mission, 1903–1906." *Journal of Mormon History* 14 (1988): 17–34.

———. "Martin Harris: Mormonism's Early Convert." *Dialogue: A Journal of Mormon Thought* 19 (Winter 1986): 29–43.

———. "Mesquite and Sage: Spencer W. Kimball's Early Years." *Brigham Young University Studies* 25 (Fall 1985): 19–41.

———. "Rachel R. Grant: The Continuing Legacy of the Feminine Ideal." *Dialogue: A Journal of Mormon Thought* 15 (Fall 1982): 105–21.

———. "Young Heber J. Grant's Years of Passage." *Brigham Young University Studies* 24 (Spring 1984): 131–49.

Ward, Margery W. *A Life Divided: The Biography of Joseph Marion Tanner, 1859–1927*. Salt Lake City: Publishers Press, 1980.

West, Franklin L. *Life of Franklin D. Richards*. Salt Lake City: Deseret News, 1924.

Widtsoe, John A. *Joseph Smith: Seeker after Truth, Prophet of God*. Salt Lake City: Deseret News, 1951.

Wight, Jeremy Benton. *The Wild Ram of the Mountains: The Story of Lyman Wight*. Star Valley, Wyo.: Afton Thrifty Print, 1996.

Williams, Frederick G. III. "Frederick Granger Williams of the First Presidency of the Church." *Brigham Young University Studies* 12 (Spring 1972): 243–61.

Wilson, Marian Robertson. *Leroy Robertson: Music Giant from the Rockies*. Salt Lake City: Blue Ribbon, 1996.

Winder, Michael K. *John R. Winder: Member of the First Presidency, Pioneer, Temple Builder, Dairyman*. Salt Lake City: Horizon, 1999.

Wirthlin, LeRoy S. "Joseph Smith's Boyhood Operation: An 1831 Surgical Success." *Brigham Young University Studies* 21 (Spring 1981): 131–54.

Wixom, Hartt. *Edward Partridge: The First Bishop of the Church of Jesus Christ of Latter-day Saints*. Springville, Utah: Cedar Fort, 1998.

Zobell, Albert L. *Sentinel in the East: A Biography of Thomas L. Kane*. Salt Lake City: Nicholas G. Morgan, 1965.

HISTORIES

General

Alexander, Thomas G., ed. *The Mormon People: Their Character and Traditions*. Provo, Utah: Brigham Young University Press, 1980.

Alexander, Thomas G., and Jessie L. Embry, eds. *After 150 Years: The Latter-day Saints in Sesquicentennial Perspective*. Provo, Utah: Charles Redd Center for Western Studies, 1983.

Allen, James B., and Glen M. Leonard. *The Story of the Latter-day Saints*. 2nd ed., rev. Salt Lake City: Deseret Book, 1992.

Andrew, Laurel B. *The Early Temples of the Mormons*. Albany: State University of New York Press, 1978.

Arrington, Leonard J., and Davis Bitton. *The Mormon Experience: A History of the Latter-day Saints*. New York: Knopf, 1979. 2nd ed. Urbana: University of Illinois Press, 1992.

Barlow, Philip L. *Mormons and the Bible*. New York: Oxford University Press, 1990.

Barrett, Ivan J. *Joseph Smith and the Restoration: A History of the LDS Church to 1846*. Provo, Utah: Brigham Young University Press, 1973.

Bartholomew, Rebecca. *Audacious Women: Early British Mormon Immigrants*. Salt Lake City: Signature, 1995.

Bates, Irene M., and E. Gary Smith. *Lost Legacy: The Mormon Office of Presiding Patriarch*. Urbana: University of Illinois Press, 1996.

Beecher, Maureen Ursenbach, and Lavina Fielding Anderson, eds. *Sisters in Spirit: Mormon Women in Historical and Cultural Perspective*. Urbana: University of Illinois Press, 1987.

Bergera, Gary James, and Ronald Priddis. *Brigham Young University: A House of Faith*. Salt Lake City: Signature, 1985.

Berrett, William E. *The Latter-day Saints: A Contemporary History of the Church of Jesus Christ of Latter-day Saints*. Salt Lake City: Deseret Book, 1985.

Bitton, Davis. *The Ritualization of Mormon History and Other Essays*. Urbana: University of Illinois Press, 1994.

Bitton, Davis, and Leonard J. Arrington. *Mormons and Their Historians*. Salt Lake City: University of Utah Press, 1988.

Bitton, Davis, and Maureen Ursenbach, eds. *New Views of Mormon History: Essays in Honor of Leonard J. Arrington*. Salt Lake City: University of Utah Press, 1987.

Bradley, Martha Sonntag. "Seizing Sacred Space: Women's Engagement in Early Mormonism." *Dialogue: A Journal of Mormon Thought* 27 (Summer 1994): 57–70.

Bringhurst, Newell G. *Saints, Slaves, and Blacks: The Changing Place of Black People within Mormonism.* Westport, Conn.: Greenwood, 1981.

Britsch, R. Lanier. *Unto the Islands of the Sea: A History of the Latter-day Saints in the Pacific.* Salt Lake City: Deseret Book, 1986.

Brooke, John L. *The Refiner's Fire: The Making of Mormon Cosmology, 1644–1844.* Cambridge: Cambridge University Press, 1994.

Brunson, L. Madelon. *A History of the RLDS Women's Organizations, 1842–1983.* Independence, Mo.: Herald, 1985.

Buerger, David John. *The Mysteries of Godliness: A History of Mormon Temple Worship.* Salt Lake City: Signature, 1994.

Bunker, Gary L., and Davis Bitton. *The Mormon Graphic Image, 1834–1914.* Salt Lake City: University of Utah Press, 1983.

Bush, Lester E. Jr. *Health and Medicine among the Latter-day Saints.* New York: Crossroad, 1993.

Carter, Kate B. *Denominations That Base Their Beliefs on the Teachings of Joseph Smith.* Salt Lake City: Daughters of Utah Pioneers, 1969.

Cook, Lyndon W. *Joseph Smith and the Law of Consecration.* Provo, Utah: Grandin, 1985.

Cook, Lyndon W., and Donald Q. Cannon, eds. *A New Light Breaks Forth: Essays in Mormon History.* Salt Lake City: Hawkes, 1980.

———. *The Exodus and Beyond: Essays in Mormon History.* Salt Lake City: Hawkes, 1980.

Cooper, Rex Eugene. *Promises Made to the Fathers: Mormon Covenant Organization.* Salt Lake City: University of Utah Press, 1990.

Davis, David Brion. "The New England Origins of Mormonism." *New England Quarterly* 27 (June 1953): 148–53.

———. "Some Themes of Counter-Subversion: An Analysis of Anti-Masonic, Anti-Catholic, and Anti-Mormon Literature." *Mississippi Valley Historical Review* 47 (September 1970): 205–24.

De Pillis, Mario. "The Quest for Religious Authority and the Rise of Mormonism." *Dialogue: A Journal of Mormon Thought* 1 (Spring 1966): 68–88.

———. "The Social Forces of Mormonism." *Church History* 37 (March 1968): 50–79.

Derr, Jill Mulvay, Janath Russell Cannon, and Maureen Ursenbach Beecher. *Women of Covenant: The Story of Relief Society.* Salt Lake City: Deseret Book, 1992.

Divett, Robert J. *Medicine and the Mormons: An Introduction to the History of Latter-day Saint Health Care.* Bountiful, Utah: Horizon, 1981.

Durham, Reed C., and Steven H. Heath. *Succession in the Church.* Salt Lake City: Bookcraft, 1970.

Edwards, Paul M. *Our Legacy of Faith: A Brief History of the Reorganized Church of Jesus Christ of Latter Day Saints.* Independence, Mo.: Herald, 1991.

Embry, Jessie L. *Black Saints in a White Church: Contemporary African-American Mormons.* Salt Lake City: Signature, 1994.

Epperson, Steven. *Mormons and Jews: Early Mormon Theologies of Israel.* Salt Lake City: Signature, 1992.

Erickson, Dan. *As a Thief in the Night: The Mormon Quest for Millennial Deliverance.* Salt Lake City: Signature, 1998.

Firmage, Edwin Brown, and Richard Colling Mangrum. *Zion in the Courts: A Legal History of the Church of Jesus Christ of Latter-day Saints, 1830–1900.* Urbana: University of Illinois Press, 1988.

Foster, Lawrence. "New Paradigms for Understanding Mormonism and Mormon History." *Dialogue: A Journal of Mormon Thought* 27 (Spring 1994): 91–105.

———. *Religion and Sexuality: The Shakers, the Mormons, and the Oneida Community.* Urbana: University of Illinois Press, 1984.

———. "Sex and Prophetic Power: A Comparison of John Humphrey Noyes, Founder of the Oneida Community, with Joseph Smith, the Mormon Prophet." *Dialogue: A Journal of Mormon Thought* 31 (Winter 1998): 65–83.

———. "Women and Utopia: Life among the Shakers, Oneidans, and Mormons." *Communities: Journal of Cooperative Living* 82 (Spring 1994): 53–6.

———. *Women, Family, and Utopia: Communal Experiments of the Shakers, the Oneida Community, and the Mormons.* Syracuse, N.Y.: Syracuse University Press, 1992.

Givens, Terryl L. *The Viper on the Hearth: Mormons, Myths, and the Construction of Heresy.* New York: Oxford University Press, 1997.

Hanks, Maxine, ed. *Women and Authority: Re-emerging Mormon Feminism.* Salt Lake City: Signature, 1992.

Hansen, Klaus J. *Mormonism and the American Experience.* Chicago: University of Chicago Press, 1981.

———. *Quest for Empire: The Political Kingdom of God and the Council of Fifty in Mormon History.* East Lansing: Michigan State University Press, 1967.

Hardy, B. Carmon. *Solemn Covenant: The Mormon Polygamous Passage.* Urbana: University of Illinois Press, 1992.

Hicks, Michael. *Mormonism and Music: A History.* Urbana: University of Illinois Press, 1989.

Hill, Marvin S. *Quest for Refuge: The Mormon Flight from American Pluralism.* Salt Lake City: Signature, 1989.

———. "The Shaping of the Mormon Mind in New England and New York." *Brigham Young University Studies* 9 (Spring 1969): 351–72.

Hill, Marvin S., and James B. Allen, eds. *Mormonism and American Culture.* New York: Harper & Row, 1972.

Hinckley, Gordon B. *Truth Restored: A Short History of the Church of Jesus Christ of Latter-day Saints.* Salt Lake City: Church of Jesus Christ of Latter-day Saints, 1979.

Holzapfel, Richard N., and T. Jeffrey Cottle. *Old Mormon Kirtland and Missouri.* Santa Ana, Calif.: Fieldbook Productions, 1991.

Howard, Richard L. *The Church through the Years. Vol. 1. RLDS Beginnings to 1860.* Independence, Mo.: Herald, 1992.

———. *The Church through the Years. Vol. 2. The Reorganization Comes of Age, 1860–1992.* Independence, Mo.: Herald, 1993.

———. *Restoration Scriptures: A Study of Their Textual Development.* Independence, Mo.: Herald, 1969.

Hughes, Dean. *The Mormon Church: A Basic History.* Salt Lake City: Deseret Book, 1986.

Launius, Roger D., and Linda Thatcher, eds. *Differing Visions: Dissenters in Mormon History.* Urbana: University of Illinois Press, 1994.

McKiernan, F. Mark, Alma Blair, and Paul M. Edwards, eds. *The Restoration Movement: Essays in Mormon History.* Lawrence, Kans.: Coronado Press, 1973.

Mangum, Garth L., and Bruce D. Blumell. *The Mormons' War on Poverty: A History of LDS Welfare, 1830–1990.* Salt Lake City: University of Utah Press, 1993.

Matthews, Robert J. *"A Plainer Translation": Joseph Smith's Translation of the Bible.* Provo, Utah: Brigham Young University Press, 1975.

Paul, Erich Robert. *Science, Religion, and Mormon Cosmology.* Urbana: University of Illinois Press, 1992.

Poll, Richard D., Thomas G. Alexander, Eugene E. Campbell, and David E. Miller, eds. *Utah's History.* Provo, Utah: Brigham Young University Press, 1978; Reprinted, Logan: Utah State University Press, 1989.

Priddis, Ron, and Gary James Bergera. *The Lord's University: Inside BYU.* Salt Lake City: Signature, 1994.

Quinn, D. Michael. *Early Mormonism and the Magic World View.* Salt Lake City: Signature, 1987.

————. "LDS Church Finances from the 1830s to the 1990s." *Sunstone* 19 (June 1996): 17–29.

————. *The Mormon Hierarchy: Extensions of Power.* Salt Lake City: Signature, 1997.

————. *The Mormon Hierarchy: Origins of Power.* Salt Lake City: Signature, 1994.

Quinn, D. Micahel, ed. *The New Mormon History: Revisionist Essays on the Past.* Salt Lake City: Signature, 1992.

Rich, Russell R. *Ensign to the Nations: A History of the Church from 1846 to the Present.* Provo, Utah: Brigham Young University Publications, 1972.

Roberts, B. H. *A Comprehensive History of the Church of Jesus Christ of Latter-day Saints.* 6 vols. Salt Lake City: The Church of Jesus Christ of Latter-day Saints, 1930.

Shepherd, Gordon, and Gary Shepherd. *A Kingdom Transformed: Themes in the Development of Mormonism.* Salt Lake City: University of Utah Press, 1984.

Shields, Steven L. *Divergent Paths of the Restoration: A History of the Latter Day Saint Movement.* Bountiful, Utah: Restoration Research, 1982.

Shipps, Jan. *Mormonism: The Story of a New Religious Tradition.* Urbana: University of Illinois Press, 1985.

Smith, George D., ed. *Faithful History: Essays in Writing Mormon History.* Salt Lake City: Signature, 1992.

Talbot, Wilburn D. *The Acts of the Modern Apostles.* Salt Lake City: Randall Books, 1985.

Tobler, Douglas F., and Nelson B. Wadsworth. *The History of the Mormons in Photographs and Text, 1830 to Present.* New York: Saint Martin's Press, 1987.

Todd, Jay M. *The Saga of the Book of Abraham.* Salt Lake City: Deseret Book, 1969.

Underwood, Grant. *The Millenarian World of Early Mormonism.* Urbana: University of Illinois Press, 1993.

Van Wagoner, Richard S. *Mormon Polygamy: A History.* Salt Lake City: Signature, 1989.

Walker, Ronald W. "Golden Memories: Remembering Life in a Mormon Village." *Brigham Young University Studies* 37 (1997–98): 191–218.

————. "Seeking the 'Remnant': The Native American during the Joseph Smith Period." *Journal of Mormon History* 19 (Spring 1993): 1–33.

Wilcox, Pearl. *Roots of the Reorganized Latter Day Saints in Southern Iowa*. Independence, Mo.: n.p., 1989.

Wilkinson, Ernest L., et al. *Brigham Young University: The First One Hundred Years*. 4 vols. Provo, Utah: Brigham Young University Press, 1975–76.

Wilkinson, Ernest L., and Cleon W. Skousen. *Brigham Young University: A School of Destiny*. Provo, Utah: Brigham Young University Press, 1976.

Winn, Kenneth H. *Exiles in a Land of Liberty: Mormons in America, 1830–1846*. Chapel Hill: University of North Carolina Press, 1989.

Yorgason, Laurence M. "Preview on a Study of the Social and Geographical Origins of Early Mormon Converts, 1830–1845." *Brigham Young University Studies* 10 (Spring 1970): 279–82.

New York Period

Anderson, Richard Lloyd. *Investigating the Book of Mormon Witnesses*. Salt Lake City: Deseret Book, 1980.

———. *Joseph Smith's New England Heritage: Influences of Grandfathers Solomon Mack and Asael Smith*. Salt Lake City: Deseret Book, 1971.

———. "The Mature Joseph Smith and Treasure Searching." *Brigham Young University Studies* 24 (Fall 1984): 489–560.

Arrington, Leonard J. "Mormonism: From Its New York Beginnings." *New York History* 61 (October 1980): 387–410.

Backman, Milton V. Jr. *American Religions and the Rise of Mormonism*. Rev. ed. Salt Lake City: Deseret Book, 1970.

———. *Eyewitness Accounts of the Restoration*. Salt Lake City: Deseret Book, 1986.

———. *Joseph Smith's First Vision: Confirming Evidences and Contemporary Accounts*. 2nd ed. Salt Lake City: Bookcraft, 1980.

Hill, Marvin S. "Money-Digging Folklore and the Beginnings of Mormonism: An Interpretive Suggestion." *Brigham Young University Studies* 24 (Fall 1984): 473–88.

———. "The Rise of Mormonism in the Burned-Over District: Another View." *New York History* 61 (October 1980): 411–30.

Madsen, Gordon A. "Joseph Smith's 1826 Trial: The Legal Setting." *Brigham Young University Studies* 30 (Spring 1990): 91–108.

Marquadt, H. Michael, and Wesley P. Walters. *Inventing Mormonism: Tradition and the Historical Record*. Salt Lake City: Signature, 1994.

Paul, Robert. "Joseph Smith and the Manchester Library." *Brigham Young University Studies* 22 (Summer 1982): 333–56.

Perciaccante, Marianne. "Backlash against Formalism: Early Mormonism's Appeal in Jefferson County." *Journal of Mormon History* 19 (Fall 1993): 35–63.

Prince, Gregory A. *Having Authority: The Origins and Development of Priesthood during the Ministry of Joseph Smith.* Independence, Mo.: Independence Press, 1993.

———. *Power from on High: The Development of Mormon Priesthood.* Salt Lake City: Signature, 1995.

Quinn, D. Michael. "The First Months of Mormonism: A Contemporary View by Rev. Diedrich Willers." *New York History* 54 (July 1973): 317–33.

Underwood, Grant. "Early Mormon Millenarianism: Another Look." *Church History* 54 (June 1985): 215–29.

Vogel, Dan. "The Locations of Joseph Smith's Early Treasure Quests." *Dialogue: A Journal of Mormon Thought* 27 (Fall 1994): 197–231.

Walker, Ronald W. "Joseph Smith: The Palmyra Seer." *Brigham Young University Studies* 24 (Fall 1984): 461–72.

OHIO PERIOD

Adams, Dale W. "Chartering the Kirtland Bank." *Brigham Young University Studies* 23 (Fall 1983): 467–82.

Anderson, Karl R. *Joseph Smith's Kirtland: Eyewitness Accounts.* Salt Lake City: Deseret Book, 1989.

Backman, Milton V. Jr. *The Heavens Resound: A History of the Latter-day Saints in Ohio, 1830–1838.* Salt Lake City: Deseret Book, 1983.

———. "The Quest for a Restoration: The Birth of Mormonism in Ohio." *Brigham Young University Studies* 12 (Summer 1972): 346–64.

Bitton, Davis. "Kirtland as a Center of Missionary Activity, 1830–1838." *Brigham Young University Studies* 11 (Summer 1971): 497–516.

Grandstaff, Mark R., and Milton V. Backman Jr. "The Social Origins of the Kirtland Mormons." *Brigham Young University Studies* 30 (Spring 1990): 47–66.

Hill, Marvin S. "Cultural Crisis in the Mormon Kingdom: A Reconsideration of the Causes of Kirtland Dissent." *Church History* 49 (September 1980): 286–97.

Hill, Marvin S., Keith C. Rooker, and Larry T. Wimmer. *The Kirtland Economy Revisited.* Provo, Utah: Brigham Young University Press, 1977.

Launius, Roger D. "The Dream Shattered: The Abandonment of the Kirtland Temple, 1837–1862." *Restoration Studies* 5 (April 1986): 13–19.

————. *The Kirtland Temple: A Historical Narrative.* Independence, Mo.: Herald, 1986.

————. "The Latter Day Saints in Ohio: Writing the History of Mormonism's Middle Period." *John Whitmer Historical Association Journal* 16 (1996): 31–56.

Layton, Robert L. "Kirtland: A Perspective on Time and Place." *Brigham Young University Studies* 11 (Summer 1971): 423–38.

McKiernan, F. Mark. "The Conversion of Sidney Rigdon to Mormonism." *Dialogue: A Journal of Mormon Thought* 5 (Summer 1970): 71–8.

Matthews, Robert J. "The 'New Translation' of the Bible, 1830–33: Doctrinal Development during the Kirtland Era." *Brigham Young University Studies* 11 (Summer 1971): 400–23.

Newell, Linda King, and Valeen Tippetts Avery. "Sweet Counsel and Seas of Tribulation: The Religious Life of the Women in Kirtland." *Brigham Young University Studies* 20 (Winter 1980): 151–62.

Parkin, Max H. "Mormon Political Involvement in Ohio." *Brigham Young University Studies* 9 (Summer 1969): 484–502.

Robison, Elwin C. *The First Mormon Temple: Design, Construction, and Historic Context of the Kirtland Temple.* Provo, Utah: Brigham Young University Press, 1997.

Missouri Period

Anderson, Richard Lloyd. "Atchison's Letters and the Causes of Mormon Expulsion from Missouri." *Brigham Young University Studies* 26 (Summer 1986): 3–47.

————. "Jackson County in Early Mormon Descriptions." *Missouri Historical Review* 65 (April 1971): 270–93.

Arrington, Leonard J. "Early Mormon Communitarianism: The Law of Consecration and Stewardship." *Western Humanities Review* 7 (Fall 1953): 341–69.

Baugh, Alexander L. "Missouri Governor Lilburn W. Boggs and the Mormons." *John Whitmer Historical Association Journal* 16 (1998): 111–32.

Blair, Alma. "The Haun's Mill Massacre." *Brigham Young University Studies* 13 (Fall 1972): 62–7.

Bushman, Richard L. "Mormon Persecution in Missouri, 1833." *Brigham Young University Studies* 3 (Fall 1960): 11–20.

Crawley, Peter, and Richard L. Anderson. "The Political and Social Realities of Zion's Camp." *Brigham Young University Studies* 14 (Summer 1974): 406–20.

Durham, Reed C. Jr. "The Election Day Battle at Gallatin." *Brigham Young University Studies* 13 (Fall 1972): 36–61.

Gentry, Leland H. "The Danite Band of 1838." *Brigham Young University Studies* 14 (Summer 1974): 421–50.

Hartley, William G. "'Almost Too Intolerable a Burthen': The Winter Exodus from Missouri, 1838–39." *Journal of Mormon History* 18 (Fall 1992): 6–40.

Jennings, Warren A. "The Army of Israel Marches into Missouri." *Missouri Historical Review* 62 (January 1968): 107–35.

————. "The Expulsion of the Mormons from Jackson County, Missouri." *Missouri Historical Review* 64 (October 1969): 41–63.

————. "Factors in the Destruction of the Mormon Press in Missouri, 1833." *Utah Historical Quarterly* 35 (Winter 1967): 56–76.

Johnson, Clark V. "The Missouri Redress Petitions: A Reappraisal of Mormon Persecutions in Missouri." *Brigham Young University Studies* 26 (Spring 1986): 31–44.

Launius, Roger. *Zion's Camp: Expedition to Missouri, 1834.* Independence, Mo.: Herald, 1984.

LeSueur, Stephen C. *The 1838 Mormon War in Missouri.* Columbia: University of Missouri Press, 1987.

————. "The Danites Reconsidered: Were They Vigilantes or Just the Mormons' Version of the Elks Club?" *John Whitmer Historical Association Journal* 14 (1994): 35–51.

————. "High Treason and Murder: The Examination of Mormon Prisoners at Richmond, Missouri, in November 1838." *Brigham Young University Studies* 26 (Spring 1986): 3–30.

Lyon, T. Edgar. "Independence, Missouri, and the Mormons, 1827–1833." *Brigham Young University Studies* 13 (Fall 1972): 10–19.

McKiernan, F. Mark. "Sidney Rigdon's Missouri Speeches." *Brigham Young University Studies* 11 (Fall 1970): 90–2.

McLaws, Monte B. "The Attempted Assassination of Missouri's Ex-Governor, Lilburn W. Boggs." *Missouri Historical Review* 60 (October 1965): 50–62.

Maynard, Gregory. "Alexander Doniphan: Man of Justice." *Brigham Young University Studies* 13 (Summer 1973): 462–72.

Richards, Paul C. "Missouri Persecutions: Petitions for Redress." *Brigham Young University Studies* 13 (Summer 1973): 520–43.

Roberts, B. H. *The Missouri Persecutions.* Salt Lake City: Bookcraft, 1965.

Illinois Period

Allen, James B., Ronald K. Esplin, and David J. Whittaker. *Men with a Mission: The Quorum of the Twelve Apostles in the British Isles, 1837–1841.* Salt Lake City: Deseret Book, 1992.

Bishop, M. Guy. "Sex Roles, Marriage and Childrearing at Mormon Nauvoo." *Western Illinois Regional Studies* 11 (Fall 1988): 30–45.

———. "'What Has Become of Our Fathers?': Baptism for the Dead at Nauvoo." *Dialogue: A Journal of Mormon Thought* 23 (Summer 1990): 85–97.

Bishop, M. Guy, Vincent Lacey, and Richard Wixon. "Death at Mormon Nauvoo, 1843–1845." *Western Illinois Regional Studies* 9 (Fall 1986): 70–83.

Bitton, Davis. "The Martyrdom of Joseph Smith in Early Mormon Writings." *John Whitmer Historical Association Journal* 3 (1983): 29–39. Revised and divided as two chapters in Bitton, *The Martyrdom Remembered* (1994), 1–36.

Black, Susan Easton. "How Large Was the Population of Nauvoo?" *Brigham Young University Studies* 35 (1995): 91–4.

Cannon, Janath. *Nauvoo Panorama: Views of Nauvoo before, during, and after Its Rise, Fall, and Restoration.* Salt Lake City: Nauvoo Restoration, 1991.

Clark, David L. "The Mormons of the Wisconsin Territory, 1835–1848." *Brigham Young University Studies* 37 (1997–98): 57–85.

Compton, Todd. *In Sacred Loneliness: The Plural Wives of Joseph Smith.* Salt Lake City: Signature, 1997.

Daynes, Kathryn M. "Family Ties: Belief and Practice in Nauvoo." *John Whitmer Historical Association Journal* 8 (1988): 63–75.

Ehat, Andrew F. "'It Seems Like Heaven Began on Earth': Joseph Smith and the Constitution of the Kingdom of God." *Brigham Young University Studies* 20 (Spring 1980): 253–79.

Ellsworth, Paul. "Mobocracy and the Rule of Law: American Press Reaction to the Murder of Joseph Smith." *Brigham Young University Studies* 20 (Fall 1979): 71–82.

Flanders, Robert B. *Nauvoo: Kingdom on the Mississippi.* Urbana: University of Illinois Press, 1965.

Gardner, Hamilton. "The Nauvoo Legion, 1840–1845: A Unique Military Organization." *Journal of the Illinois State Historical Society* 65 (Summer 1961): 181–97.

Gayler, George R. "The 'Expositor' Affair, Prelude to the Downfall of Joseph Smith." *Northwest Missouri State College Studies* 25 (February 1961): 3–15.

———. "Governor Ford and the Death of Joseph and Hyrum Smith." *Journal of the Illinois State Historical Society* 50 (Winter 1957): 391–411.

———. "The Mormons and Politics in Illinois: 1839–1844." *Journal of the Illinois State Historical Society* 49 (Spring 1956): 48–66.

Givens, George W. *Old Nauvoo: Everyday Life in the City of Joseph.* Salt Lake City: Deseret Book, 1990.

Godfrey, Kenneth W. "Crime and Punishment in Mormon Nauvoo, 1839–1846." *Brigham Young University Studies* 32 (Winter/Spring 1992): 195–227.

———. "Non-Mormon Views of the Martyrdom: A Look at Some Early Published Accounts." *John Whitmer Historical Association Journal* 7 (1987): 12–20.

Hallwas, John E., and Roger D. Launius. *Cultures in Conflict: A Documentary History of the Mormon War in Illinois.* Logan: Utah State University Press, 1999.

Hamilton, Marshall. "From Assassination to Expulsion: Two Years of Distrust, Hostility, and Violence." *Brigham Young University Studies* 32 (Winter/Spring 1992): 229–48.

Hampshire, Annette P. *Mormonism in Conflict: The Nauvoo Years.* New York: Edwin Mellen Press, 1985.

———. "The Triumph of Mobocracy in Hancock County, 1844–1845." *Western Illinois Regional Studies* 5 (Spring 1982): 17–37.

Harrington, Virginia S. *Rediscovery of the Nauvoo Temple.* Salt Lake City: Nauvoo Restoration, 1971.

Hartley, William G. "Nauvoo Stake, Priesthood Quorums, and the Church's First Wards." *Brigham Young University Studies* 32 (Winter/Spring 1992): 57–80.

Holzapfel, Richard Neitzel, and Jeffery T. Cottle. "The City of Joseph in Focus: The Use and Abuse of Historic Photographs." *Brigham Young University Studies* 32 (Winter/Spring 1992): 249–68.

———. *Old Mormon Nauvoo and Southeastern Iowa, 1839–1846.* 2nd ed. Santa Ana, Calif.: Fieldbrook Productions, 1991.

Holzapfel, Richard Netzel, and Jeni Broberg Holzapfel. *Women of Nauvoo.* Salt Lake City: Bookcraft, 1992.

Homer, Michael W. "'Similarity of Priesthood in Masonry': The Relationship between Freemasonry and Mormonism." *Dialogue: A Journal of Mormon Thought* 27 (Fall 1994): 1–113.

Jeffress, Melinda Evans. "Mapping Historic Nauvoo." *Brigham Young University Studies* 32 (Winter/Spring 1992): 269–75.

Jensen, Richard L. "Transplanted Zion: The Impact of British Latter-day Saint Immigration upon Nauvoo." *Brigham Young University Studies* 31 (Winter 1991): 76–87.

Jolley, Jerry C. "The Sting of the Wasp: Early Nauvoo Newspaper—April 1842 to April 1843." *Brigham Young University Studies* 22 (Fall 1982): 487–96.

Jorgensen, Lynne Watkins, and BYU Studies staff. "The Mantle of the Prophet Joseph Passes to Brother Brigham: A Collective Spiritual Witness." *Brigham Young University Studies* 36 (1996–97): 125–204.

Kimball, James L. Jr. "The Nauvoo Charter: A Reinterpretation." *Journal of the Illinois State Historical Society* 64 (Spring 1971): 66–78.

———. "A Wall to Defend Zion: The Nauvoo Charter." *Brigham Young University Studies* 15 (Summer 1975): 491–7.

Kimball, Stanley B. "Heber C. Kimball and Family: The Nauvoo Years." *Brigham Young University Studies* 15 (Summer 1975): 447–79.

———. "The Mormons in Illinois, 1838–1846: A Special Introduction." *Journal of the Illinois State Historical Society* 64 (Spring 1971): 4–21.

Launius, Roger D. "The Murders in Carthage: Non-Mormon Reports of the Assassination of the Smith Brothers." *John Whitmer Historical Association Journal* 15 (1995): 17–34.

Launius, Roger D., and John E. Hallwas, eds. *Kingdom on the Mississippi Revisited: Nauvoo in Mormon History*. Urbana: University of Illinois Press, 1996.

LeBaron, E. Dale. "Benjamin Franklin Johnson in Nauvoo: Friend, Confidant, and Defender of the Prophet." *Brigham Young University Studies* 32 (Winter/Spring 1992): 175–94.

Leonard, Glen M. "Letters Home: The Immigrant View from Nauvoo." *Brigham Young University Studies* 31 (Winter 1991): 89–100.

———. "Picturing the Nauvoo Legion." *Brigham Young University Studies* 35 (1995): 95–135.

Lyon, T. Edgar. "Doctrinal Development of the Church during the Nauvoo Sojourn, 1839–1846." *Brigham Young University Studies* 15 (Summer 1975): 435–46.

Miller, David E., and Della S. Miller. *Nauvoo: The City of Joseph*. Salt Lake City: Peregrine Smith, 1974.

Mulder, William. "Nauvoo Observed." *Brigham Young University Studies* 32 (Winter/Spring 1992): 95–118.

Oaks, Dallin H. "The Suppression of the Nauvoo Expositor." *Utah Law Review* 9 (Winter 1965): 862–903.

Oaks, Dallin H., and Marvin S. Hill. *Carthage Conspiracy: The Trial of the Accused Assassins of Joseph Smith.* Urbana: University of Illinois Press, 1975.

Poll, Richard D. "Joseph Smith and the Presidency, 1844." *Dialogue: A Journal of Mormon Thought* 3 (Fall 1968): 17–21.

Porter, Larry C., and Milton V. Backman Jr. "Doctrine and the Temple in Nauvoo." *Brigham Young University Studies* 32 (Winter/Spring 1992): 41–56.

Quinn, D. Michael. "The Council of Fifty and Its Members, 1844 to 1945." *Brigham Young University Studies* 20 (Winter 1980): 163–97.

Rowley, Dennis. "The Mormon Experience in the Wisconsin Pineries, 1841–1845." *Brigham Young University Studies* 32 (Winter/Spring 1992): 119–48.

Rugh, Susan Sessions. "Conflict in the Countryside: The Mormon Settlement at Macedonia, Illinois." *Brigham Young University Studies* 32 (Winter/Spring 1992): 149–74.

Saunders, Richard L. "Officers and Arms: The 1843 General Return of the Nauvoo Legion's Second Cohort." *Brigham Young University Studies* 35 (1995): 138–51.

Smith, George D. "Nauvoo Roots of Mormon Polygamy, 1841–46: A Preliminary Demographic Report." *Dialogue: A Journal of Mormon Thought* 27 (Spring 1994): 1–72.

Tanner, Terence A. "The Mormon Press in Nauvoo, 1839–1846." *Western Illinois Regional Studies* 11 (Fall 1988): 5–29.

Van Orden, Bruce A. "William W. Phelps' Service in Nauvoo as Joseph Smith's Political Clerk." *Brigham Young University Studies* 32 (Winter/Spring 1992): 81–94.

Van Wagoner, Richard S. "The Making of a Mormon Myth: The 1844 Transfiguration of Brigham Young." *Dialogue: A Journal of Mormon Thought* 28 (Winter 1995): 1–24.

The Exodus

Bashore, Melvin L. "On the Heels of the Handcart Tragedy: Mormondom's Forgotten 1856 Wagon Companies." *Annals of Wyoming* 68 (Summer 1996): 38–49.

Beecher, Maureen Ursenbach. "Women in Winter Quarters." *Sunstone* 8 (July–August 1983): 11–19.

Bennett, Richard E. "Cousin Laman in the Wilderness: The Beginnings of Brigham Young's Indian Policy." *Nebraska History* 67 (Spring 1986): 68–82.

———. "Eastward to Eden: The Nauvoo Rescue Missions." *Dialogue: A Journal of Mormon Thought* 19 (Winter 1986): 100–8.

———. "Lamanism, Lymanism, and Cornfields." *Journal of Mormon History* 13 (1986–1987): 45–59.

———. *Mormons at the Missouri, 1846–52: "And Should We Die."* Norman: University of Oklahoma Press, 1987.

———. *We'll Find the Place: The Mormon Exodus, 1846–1848.* Salt Lake City: Deseret Book, 1997.

Bitton, Davis. "Mormons in Texas: The Ill-fated Lyman Wight Colony, 1844–1858." *Arizona and the West* 11 (Spring 1969): 5–26.

Black, Susan Easton, and William G. Hartley, eds. *The Iowa Mormon Trail: Legacy of Faith and Courage.* Orem, Utah: Helix, 1997.

Brown, Joseph E. *The Mormon Trek West: The Journey of American Exiles.* Garden City, N.Y.: Doubleday, 1980.

Bryson, Conrey. *Winter Quarters.* Salt Lake City: Deseret Book, 1986.

Campbell, Eugene. "Authority Conflicts in the Mormon Battalion." *Brigham Young University Studies* 8 (Winter 1968): 127–42.

Carter, Lyndia. "The Mormon Handcart Companies." *Overland Journal* 13 (1995): 2–18.

Christian, Lewis Clark. "Mormon Foreknowledge of the West." *Brigham Young University Studies* 21 (Fall 1981): 403–15.

Coates, Lawrence. "Cultural Conflict: Mormons and Indians in Nebraska." *Brigham Young University Studies* 24 (Summer 1983): 275–300.

———. "Refugees Meet: The Mormons and Indians in Iowa." *Brigham Young University Studies* 21 (Fall 1981): 491–514.

Crockett, David R. *Saints in Exile: A Day by Day Pioneer Experience, Nauvoo to Council Bluffs.* Tucson, Ariz.: LDS-Gems Press, 1996.

Gardner, Hamilton. "The Command and Staff of the Mormon Battalion in the Mexican War." *Utah Historical Quarterly* 29 (October 1952): 331–52.

Homer, Michael W. "After Winter Quarters and Council Bluffs: The Mormons in Nebraska Territory, 1854–1867." *Nebraska History* 65 (Winter 1984): 467–83.

Kimball, Stanley B. *Historic Sites and Markers along the Mormon and Other Great Western Trails.* Urbana: University of Illinois Press, 1988.

———. "Mormon Trail Network in Nebraska, 1846–1868." *Brigham Young University Studies* 24 (Summer 1984): 321–36.

Kimball, Stanley B., and Hal Knight. *111 Days to Zion*. Salt Lake City: Deseret News, 1978.

King, Robert R. "The Enduring Significance of the Mormon Trek." *Dialogue: A Journal of Mormon Thought* 13 (Summer 1980): 102–7.

Melville, J. Keith. *Conflict and Compromise: The Mormons in Mid-Nineteenth-Century American Politics*. Provo, Utah: Brigham Young University Press, 1975.

Powell, A. Kent. *Mormon Battalion Trail Guide*. Salt Lake City: Utah State Historical Society, 1972.

Ricketts, Norma Baldwin. *The Mormon Battalion: United States Army of the West, 1846–1848*. Logan: Utah State University Press, 1996.

Stegner, Wallace. *The Gathering of Zion: The Story of the Mormon Trail*. Salt Lake City: Westwater, 1981.

Tyler, Daniel. *A Concise History of the Mormon Battalion in the Mexican War, 1846–47*. N.p., 1881; reprint, Chicago: Rio Grande Press, 1964.

Utah Period

Alexander, Thomas G. "Charles S. Zane, Apostle of the New Era." *Utah Historical Quarterly* 34 (Fall 1966): 290–314.

———. "Cooperation, Conflict, and Compromise: Women, Men, and the Environment in Salt Lake City, 1890–1930." *Brigham Young University Studies* 35 (1995): 7–39.

———. "An Experiment in Progressive Legislation: The Granting of Woman Suffrage in Utah in 1870." *Utah Historical Quarterly* 38 (Winter 1970): 20–30.

———. "Federal Authority versus Polygamic Theocracy: James B. McKean and the Mormons, 1870–1875." *Dialogue: A Journal of Mormon Thought* 1 (Fall 1966): 85–100.

———. "Some Meanings of Utah History." *Utah Historical Quarterly* 64 (Spring 1996): 155–67.

———. *Utah: The Right Place*. Salt Lake City: Gibbs Smith, 1995.

———. "Utah's Constitution: A Reflection of the Territorial Experience." *Utah Historical Quarterly* 64 (Summer 1996): 264–281.

———. "Wilford Woodruff, Intellectual Progress, and the Growth of an Amateur Scientific and Technological Tradition in Early Territorial Utah." *Utah Historical Quarterly* 59 (Spring 1991): 164–88.

Anderson, Nels. *Desert Saints: The Mormon Frontier in Utah*. Chicago: University of Chicago Press, 1942.

Arrington, Leonard J. *Great Basin Kingdom: An Economic History of the Latter-day Saints*. Cambridge, Mass.: Harvard University Press, 1958.

————. "Rural Life among Nineteenth-Century Mormons: The Woman's Experience." *Agricultural History* 58 (July 1984): 239–46.

Arrington, Leonard J., and Dean May. "'A Different Mode of Life': Irrigation and Society in Nineteenth-Century Utah." *Agricultural History* 49 (January 1975): 3–20.

Arrington, Leonard J., and Linda Wilcox. "From Subsistence to Golden Age: Cache Valley Agriculture, 1859–1900." *Utah Historical Quarterly* 57 (Fall 1989): 340–69.

Arrington, Leonard J., Dean May, and Feramorz Fox. *Building the City of God: Community and Cooperation among the Mormons*. Salt Lake City: Deseret Book, 1976.

Ashton, Wendell J. *Voice in the West: Biography of a Pioneer Newspaper*. New York: Duell, Sloan, & Pearce, 1950.

Beecher, Maureen Ursenbach. "Women's Work on the Mormon Frontier." *Utah Historical Quarterly* 49 (Summer 1981): 276–90.

Bigler, David L. *Forgotten Kingdom: The Mormon Theocracy in the American West, 1847–1896*. Spokane, Wash.: Arthur H. Clark, 1998.

Bitton, Davis. "B. H. Roberts at the World Parliament of Religions." *Sunstone* 7 (January–February 1982): 46–51.

————. "The B. H. Roberts Case of 1898–1900." *Utah Historical Quarterly* 25 (January 1957): 27–46. Revised and reprinted in Bitton, *The Ritualization of Mormon History and Other Essays*. Urbana: University of Illinois Press, 1994, 150–70.

————. "Zion's Rowdies: Growing up on the Mormon Frontier." *Utah Historical Quarterly* 50 (Spring 1982): 182–95. Reprinted in Bitton, *The Ritualization of Mormon History and Other Essays,* 54–68.

Bitton, Davis, and Linda P. Wilcox. "The Transformation of Utah's Agriculture, 1847–1900." In Thomas G. Alexander and John F. Bluth, eds., *The Twentieth Century American West*. Provo, Utah: Charles Redd Center for Western Studies, 1983, 57–83.

Brooks, Juanita. *The Mountain Meadows Massacre*. Norman: University of Oklahoma Press, 1962.

Buchanan, Frederick S. "Education among the Mormons: Brigham Young and the Schools of Utah." *History of Education Quarterly* 22 (Winter 1982): 435–59.

Buerger, David John. "The Development of the Mormon Temple Endowment Ceremony." *Dialogue: A Journal of Mormon Thought* 20 (Winter 1987): 33–76.

Campbell, Eugene E. *Establishing Zion: The Mormon Church in the American West, 1847–69*. Salt Lake City: Signature, 1988.

Cannon, Kenneth L. II. "After the Manifesto: Mormon Polygamy, 1890–1906." *Sunstone* 8 (January-April 1983): 27–35.

———. "Mountain Common Law: The Extralegal Punishment of Seducers in Early Utah." *Utah Historical Quarterly* 51 (Fall 1983): 308–27.

Clayton, James L. "The Supreme Court, Polygamy and the Enforcement of Morals in Nineteenth Century America: An Analysis of *Reynolds v. United States.*" *Dialogue: A Journal of Mormon Thought* 12 (Winter 1979): 46–61.

Cornwall, J. Spencer. *A Century of Singing: The Salt Lake Mormon Tabernacle Choir.* Salt Lake City: Deseret Book, 1958.

Cornwall, Rebecca, and Leonard J. Arrington. *Rescue of the 1856 Handcart Companies.* Provo, Utah: Charles H. Redd Monographs in Western History, 1981.

Cowan, Richard O. "The Mormon Battalion and the Gadsden Purchase." *Brigham Young University Studies* 37 (1997–98): 48–64.

Davies, J. Kenneth. *Mormon Gold: The Story of California's Mormon Argonauts.* Salt Lake City: Olympus Publishing, 1984.

Daynes, Kathryn M. "Single Men in a Polygamous Society: Male Marriage Patterns in Manti, Utah." *Journal of Mormon History* 24 (Spring 1998): 89–111.

Dwyer, Robert Joseph. *The Gentile Comes to Utah: A Study in Religious and Social Conflict, 1862–1890.* 2nd ed. rev. Salt Lake City: Western Epics, 1971.

Embry, Jessie L. "Burden or Pleasure? A Profile of LDS Polygamous Husbands." *Dialogue: A Journal of Mormon Thought* 20 (Winter 1987): 158–66.

———. "Effects of Polygamy on Mormon Women." *Frontiers* 7(3) (1984): 56–61.

———. "Little Berlin: Swiss Saints of the Logan Tenth Ward." *Utah Historical Quarterly* 56 (Summer 1988): 222–35.

———. *Mormon Polygamous Families: Life in the Principle.* Salt Lake City: University of Utah Press, 1987.

———. "Mormon Polygamy: Unconventional Practice or Adaptation to American Values?" *Journal of Unconventional History* 3 (1992): 42–56.

Embry, Jessie L., and Martha S. Bradley. "Mothers and Daughters in Polygamy." *Dialogue: A Journal of Mormon Thought* 18 (Fall 1985): 99–107.

Furniss, Norman. *The Mormon Conflict, 1850–1859.* New Haven, Conn.: Yale University Press, 1960.

Godfrey, Kenneth W. "Charles W. Penrose and His Contributions to Utah Statehood." *Utah Historical Quarterly* 64 (Fall 1996): 356–71.

———. "Moses Thatcher in the Dock: His Trials, the Aftermath and His Last Days." *Journal of Mormon History* 24 (Spring 1998): 54–88.

Grow, Stewart L. *A Tabernacle in the Desert.* Salt Lake City: Deseret Book, 1958.

Hafen, LeRoy R., and Ann W. Hafen. "Handcarts to Utah, 1856–1860." *Utah Historical Quarterly* 24 (October 1956): 309–17.

———. *Handcarts to Zion: The Story of a Unique Western Migration, 1856–1860.* Glendale, Calif.: Arthur H. Clark, 1960.

Hartley, William G. "The Priesthood Reorganization of 1877: Brigham Young's Last Achievement." *Brigham Young University Studies* 20 (Fall 1979): 3–36.

———. "The Seventies in the 1880s: Revelations and Reorganizing." *Dialogue: A Journal of Mormon Thought* 16 (Spring 1983): 62–88.

Heinerman, Joseph. "The Old Folks Day: A Unique Utah Tradition." *Utah Historical Quarterly* 53 (Spring 1985): 157–69.

Homer, Michael W. "The Judiciary and the Common Law in Utah Territory, 1850–61." *Dialogue: A Journal of Mormon Thought* 21 (Spring 1988): 97–108.

Howard, Richard P. "The Changing RLDS Response to Mormon Polygamy: A Preliminary Analysis." *John Whitmer Historical Association Journal* 3 (1983): 14–29.

Iversen, Joan Smyth. "A Debate on the American Home: The Antipolygamy Controversy, 1880–1890." *Journal of the History of Sexuality* 1,4 (April 1991): 585–602.

Johnson, Jeffery Ogden. "Determining and Defining 'Wife': The Brigham Young Households." *Dialogue: A Journal of Mormon Thought* 20 (Fall 1987): 57–70.

Larson, Gustive O. *The "Americanization" of Utah for Statehood.* San Marino, Calif.: Huntington Library, 1971.

———. "The Mormon Reformation." *Utah Historical Quarterly* 26 (January 1958): 45–63.

———. *Prelude to the Kingdom: Mormon Desert Conquest, A Chapter in American Cooperative Experience.* Francestown, N.Y.: Marshall Jones, 1947.

Leonard, Glen M. "The Mormon Boundary Question in the 1849–50 Statehood Debates." *Journal of Mormon History* 18 (Spring 1992): 114–36.

———. "William Allen's Clients: A Socioeconomic Inquiry." *Utah Historical Quarterly* 54 (Winter 1986): 74–87.

Logue, Larry. "Tabernacles for Waiting Spirits: Monogamous and Polygamous Fertility in a Mormon Town." *Journal of Family History* 10 (Spring
1985): 60–74.

Long, E. B. *The Saints and the Union: Utah Territory during the Civil War.*
Champaign: University of Illinois Press, 1981.

Lyman, E. Leo. "The Political Background of the Woodruff Manifesto."
Dialogue: A Journal of Mormon Thought 24 (Fall 1991): 21–39.

———. *Political Deliverance: The Mormon Quest for Utah Statehood.*
Urbana: University of Illinois Press, 1986.

McLaws, Monte B. *Spokesman for the Kingdom: Early Mormon Journalism
and the Deseret News, 1830–1898.* Provo, Utah: Brigham Young University Press, 1977.

Madsen, Carol Cornwall. "'At Their Peril': Utah Law and the Case of Plural
Wives, 1850–1900." *Western Historical Quarterly* 21 (November 1990):
425–43.

———. "Mormon Women and the Struggle for Definition: The Nineteenth-
Century Church." *Sunstone* 6 (November–December 1981): 7–11.

Madsen, Carol Cornwall, and Susan Staker Oman. *Sisters and Little Saints:
One Hundred Years of Primary.* Salt Lake City: Deseret Book, 1979.

May, Dean L. "People on the Mormon Frontier: Kanab's Families of 1874."
Journal of Family History 1 (December 1976): 169–92.

———. *Utah: A People's History.* Salt Lake City: University of Utah Press,
1987.

———. "Utah Writ Small: Challenge and Change in Kane County's Past."
Utah Historical Quarterly 53 (Spring 1985): 170–83.

Mehr, Kahlile. "Women's Response to Plural Marriage." *Dialogue: A Journal of Mormon Thought* 18 (Fall 1985): 84–97.

Miller, David S. *Hole-in-the-Rock: An Epic in the Colonization of the Great
American West.* Salt Lake City: University of Utah Press, 1959.

Miller, Jeremy M. "A Critique of the Reynolds Decision." *Western State
University Law Review* 11 (Spring 1984): 165–98.

Moorman, Donald R., and Gene A. Sessions. *Camp Floyd and the Mormons: The Utah War.* Salt Lake City: University of Utah Press, 1992.

Nelson, Lowry. *The Mormon Village: A Pattern and Techniques of Land
Settlement.* Salt Lake City: University of Utah Press, 1952.

Pace, D. Gene. "Changing Patterns of Mormon Financial Administration:
Traveling Bishops, Regional Bishops, and Bishop's Agents, 1851–88."
Brigham Young University Studies 23 (Spring 1983): 183–95.

Peterson, Charles S. "Jacob Hamblin, Apostle to the Lamanites, and the
Indian Mission." *Journal of Mormon History* 2 (1975): 21–34.

———. "The Hopis and the Mormons, 1858–1873." *Utah Historical Quarterly* 39 (Spring 1971): 179–93.

Poll, Richard D. "The Legislative Antipolygamy Campaign." *Brigham Young University Studies* 26 (Fall 1986): 107–21.

———. "The Mormon Question Enters National Politics, 1850–1856." *Utah Historical Quarterly* 25 (April 1957): 117–31.

———. "The Move South." *Brigham Young University Studies* 29 (Fall 1989): 65–88.

———. *Quixotic Mediator: Thomas L. Kane and the Utah War.* Ogden, Utah: Weber State College, 1985.

Poll, Richard D., and William P. MacKinnon. "Causes of the Utah War Reconsidered." *Journal of Mormon History* 20 (Fall 1994): 16–44.

Polson, D. Michol. "The Swedes in Grantsville, Utah, 1860–1900." *Utah Historical Quarterly* 56 (Summer 1988): 208–21.

Quinn, D. Michael. "LDS Church Authority and New Plural Marriages, 1890–1904." *Dialogue: A Journal of Mormon Thought* 18 (Spring 1985): 9–105.

Ricks, Joel E. *Forms and Methods of Early Mormon Settlement in Utah and Surrounding Regions, 1847 to 1877.* Logan: Utah State University Press, 1974.

Sherlock, Richard. "Mormon Migration and Settlement after 1875." *Journal of Mormon History* 2 (1975): 53–68.

Simmonds, A. J. *The Gentile Comes to Cache Valley: A Study of the Logan Apostasies of 1874 and the Establishment of Non-Mormon Churches in Cache Valley, 1873–1913.* Logan: Utah State University Press, 1976.

Smart, Donna T. "Over the Rim to Red Rock Country: The Parley P. Pratt Exploring Company of 1849." *Utah Historical Quarterly* 62 (Spring 1994): 171–90.

Smart, William B., and Donna T. Smart, eds. *Over the Rim: The Parley P. Pratt Exploring Expedition to Southern Utah, 1849–50.* Logan: Utah State University Press, 1999.

Smith, Craig S. "The Curious Meet the Mormons: Images from Travel Narratives, 1850s and 1860s." *Journal of Mormon History* 24 (Fall 1998): 155–81.

Smith, E. Gary. "The Office of Presiding Patriarch: The Primacy Problem." *Journal of Mormon History* 14 (1988): 35–48.

Snow, Edwina Jo. "British Travelers View the Saints." *Brigham Young University Studies* 31 (Spring 1991): 63–81.

Stott, Clifford L. *Search for Sanctuary: Brigham Young and the White Mountain Expedition.* Salt Lake City: University of Utah Press, 1984.

Van Wagenen, Lola. "In Their Behalf: The Politicization of Mormon Women and the 1870 Franchise." *Dialogue: A Journal of Mormon Thought* 24 (Winter 1991): 31–43.

Walker, Ronald W. "B. H. Roberts and the Woodruff Manifesto." *Brigham Young University Studies* 22 (Summer 1982): 363–6.

————. "Brigham Young on the Social Order." *Brigham Young University Studies* 28 (Summer 1988): 37–52.

————. "Growing up in Early Utah: The Wasatch Literary Association, 1874–1878." *Sunstone* 6 (November–December 1981): 44–51.

————. "Toward a Reconstruction of Mormon and Indian Relations, 1847-1877." *Brigham Young University Studies* 19 (Fall 1989): 23–42.

————. *Wayward Saints: The Godbeites and Brigham Young.* Urbana: University of Illinois Press, 1998.

————. "When the Spirits Did Abound: Nineteenth-Century Utah's Encounter with Free-Thought Radicalism." *Utah Historical Quarterly* 50 (Fall 1982): 304–24.

West, Ray B. *Kingdom of the Saints: The Story of Brigham Young and the Mormons.* New York: Viking, 1957.

Whittaker, David J. "The Bone in the Throat: Orson Pratt and the Public Announcement of Plural Marriage." *Western Historical Quarterly* 18 (July 1987): 293–314.

TWENTIETH CENTURY

Alexander, Thomas G. *Mormonism in Transition: A History of the Latter-day Saints, 1890–1930.* Urbana: University of Illinois Press, 1986.

————. "The Reconstruction of Mormon Doctrine: From Joseph Smith to Progressive Theology." *Sunstone* 5 (July–August 1980): 24–33.

————. "Reed Smoot, the LDS Church, and Progressive Legislation, 1903–1933." *Dialogue: A Journal of Mormon Thought* 7 (Spring 1972): 47–56.

Allen, James B. "'Good Guys' vs. 'Good Guys': Rudger Clawson, John Sharp, and Civil Disobedience in Nineteenth-Century Utah." *Utah Historical Quarterly* 48 (Spring 1980): 148–74.

————. "On Becoming a Universal Church: Some Historical Perspectives." *Dialogue: A Journal of Mormon Thought* 25 (March 1992): 13–36.

Allen, James B., Jessie L. Embry, and Kahlile B. Mehr. *Hearts Turned to the Fathers: A History of the Genealogical Society of Utah, 1894–1994.* Provo, Utah: BYU Studies, 1995.

Anderson, Paul. "Heroic Nostalgia: Enshrining the Mormon Past." *Sunstone* 5 (July–August 1980): 47–55.

Arrington, Leonard J. "The Founding of the LDS Institutes of Religion." *Dialogue: A Journal of Mormon Thought* 2 (Summer 1967): 137–47.

———. "Origin of the Welfare Plan of the Church." *Brigham Young University Studies* 5 (Winter 1964): 67–85.

Bennion, Lowell C. "Ben," and Lawrence A. Young. "The Uncertain Dynamics of LDS Expansion, 1950–2020." *Dialogue: A Journal of Mormon Thought* 29 (Spring 1996): 8–32.

Calman, Charles Jeffrey, and William I. Kaufman. *The Mormon Tabernacle Choir*. New York: Harper & Row, 1979.

Christianson, James R., and Richard Cowan. *The International Church*. Provo, Utah: Brigham Young University Publications, 1982.

Cowan, Richard O. *The Church in the Twentieth Century*. Salt Lake City: Bookcraft, 1985.

———. *Temples to Dot the Earth*. Salt Lake City: Bookcraft, 1989.

De Pillis, Mario S. "The Persistence of Mormon Community into the 1990s." *Sunstone* 15(4) (September 1991): 28–49.

Driggs, Ken. "Twentieth-Century Polygamy and Fundamentalist Mormons in Southern Utah." *Dialogue: A Journal of Mormon Thought* 24 (Winter 1991): 44–58.

Hartley, William G. "The Priesthood Reform Movement, 1908–1922." *Brigham Young University Studies* 13 (Winter 1973): 137–56.

Holsinger, M. Paul. "For God and the American Home: The Attempt to Unseat Senator Reed Smoot, 1903–1907." *Pacific Northwest Quarterly* 60 (July 1969): 154–60.

Jacobson, Cardell K. "Black Mormons in the 1980s: Pioneers in a White Church." *Review of Religious Research* 33 (December 1991): 146–52.

Mauss, Armand L. *The Angel and the Beehive: The Mormon Struggle with Assimilation*. Urbana: University of Illinois Press, 1994.

Ostling, Richard N., and Joan K. Ostling. *Mormon America: The Power and the Promise*. San Francisco: Harper San Francisco, 1999.

Palmer, Spencer J., ed. *The Expanding Church*. Salt Lake City: Deseret Book, 1978.

———. *Mormons and Muslims*. Provo, Utah: Brigham Young University Press, 1983.

Petersen, Gerald A. *More Than Music: The Mormon Tabernacle Choir*. Provo, Utah: Brigham Young University Press, 1979.

Peterson, Charles S. "Life in a Village Society, 1877–1920." *Utah Historical Quarterly* 49 (Winter 1981): 78–96.

Sillitoe, Linda, and Allen D. Roberts. *Salamander: The Story of the Mormon Forgery Murders*. Salt Lake City: Signature, 1988.

Taber, Susan Buhler. *Mormon Lives: A Year in the Elkton Ward*. Urbana: University of Illinois Press, 1993.

Thorp, Malcolm R. "The British Government and the Mormon Question, 1910–1922." *Journal of Church and State* 21 (Spring 1979): 305–23.

Tullis, F. Lamond. *Mormonism: A Faith for All Cultures*. Provo, Utah: Brigham Young University Press, 1978.

Turley, Richard E. Jr. *Victims: The LDS Church and the Mark Hoffman Case*. Urbana: University of Illinois Press, 1992.

Local and Regional U.S.

Anderson, Lavina Fielding, ed. *Chesterfield: Mormon Outpost in Idaho*. Bancroft, Idaho: The Chesterfield Foundation, 1982.

Arrington, Leonard J. "A Mormon Apostle Visits the Umatilla and Nez Perce in 1885." *Idaho Yesterdays* 31 (Spring/Summer 1987): 47–54.

———. "The Mormon Settlement of Cassia County, Idaho, 1873–1921." *Idaho Yesterdays* 23 (Summer 1979): 36–46.

———. *The Mormons in Nevada*. Las Vegas, Nev.: Las Vegas Sun, 1979.

———. "The Promise of Eagle Rock: Idaho Falls, Idaho, 1863–1980." *Rendezvous* 18 (Spring 1983): 2–17.

Bagley, Will. "'Every Thing Is Favourable! And God Is on Our Side': Samuel Brannan and the Conquest of California." *Journal of Mormon History* 23 (Fall 1997): 185–209.

Bitton, Davis. "Peopling the Upper Snake: The Second Wave of Mormon Settlement in Idaho." *Idaho Yesterdays* 23 (Summer 1979): 47–52.

Boyce, Ronald R. "The Mormon Invasion and Settlement of the Upper Snake River Plain in the 1880s: The Case of Lewisville, Idaho." *Pacific Northwest Quarterly* 78 (January–April 1987): 50–8.

Britsch, R. Lanier. *Moramona: The Mormons in Hawaii*. Laie, Hawaii: Institute for Polynesian Studies, 1989.

Buice, David. "When the Saints Come Marching In: The Mormon Experience in Antebellum New Orleans, 1840–1855." *Louisiana History* 23 (Summer 1982): 221–37.

Coates, Lawrence G., Peter G. Boag, Ronald L. Hatzenbuehler, and Merwin R. Swanson. "The Mormon Settlement of Southeastern Idaho, 1845–1900." *Journal of Mormon History* 20 (Fall 1994): 45–62.

Cowan, Richard, and William E. Homer. *California Saints: A 150-year Legacy in the Golden State*. Provo, Utah: Religious Studies Center, Brigham Young University, 1996.

Durham, Michael S. *Deseret between the Mountains: Mormons, Miners, Padres, Mountain Men, and the Opening of the Great Basin, 1772–1869.* New York: Henry Holt, 1997.

Ellsworth, S. George. *Mormon Settlement on the Muddy.* Ogden, Utah: Weber State College Press, 1987.

Grattan-Aiello, Carolyn. "New St. Joseph, Nevada: The Muddy Mission Experience Revisited." *Nevada Historical Society Quarterly* 29 (Spring 1986): 31–52.

Hatch, William Whitridge. *There Is No Law: A History of Mormon Civil Relations in the Southern States, 1865–1905.* New York: Vantage, 1968.

Kimball, Monique E. "A Matter of Faith: A Study of the Muddy Mission." *Nevada Historical Society Quarterly* 30 (Winter 1987): 291–303.

Larson, Andrew Karl. *"I Was Called to Dixie": The Virgin River Basin, Unique Experiences in Mormon Pioneering.* Salt Lake City: Deseret News, 1961.

Logue, Larry M. *A Sermon in the Desert: Belief and Behavior in Early St. George, Utah.* Urbana: University of Illinois Press, 1988.

Lyman, Edward Leo. *San Bernardino: The Rise and Fall of a California Community.* Salt Lake City: Signature, 1996.

May, Dean L. "Star Valley in the Context of Western Settlement." *Snake River Echoes* 14 (Autumn 1985): 103–10.

Miller, Mark E. "St. Johns's Saints: Interethnic Conflict in Northeastern Arizona, 1880–85." *Journal of Mormon History* 23 (Spring 1997): 66–99.

O'Brien, Robert. *Hands across the Water: The Story of the Polynesian Cultural Center.* Laie, Hawaii: Institute for Polynesian Studies, 1983.

Orton, Chad M. *More Faith than Fear: The Los Angeles Stake Story.* Salt Lake City: Bookcraft, 1987.

Peterson, Charles S. *Take up Your Mission: Mormon Colonizing along the Little Colorado River, 1870–1900.* Tucson, Ariz.: University of Arizona Press, 1973.

Rich, Russell R. *Land of the Sky-Blue Water: A History of the LDS Settlement of the Bear Lake Valley.* Provo, Utah: Brigham Young University Press, 1963.

Ricks, Joel E., ed. *The History of a Valley: Cache Valley, Utah-Idaho.* Logan: Utah State University Press, 1956.

Simmonds, A. J. "Southeast Idaho as a Pioneer Mormon Safety Valve." *Idaho Yesterdays* 23 (Winter 1980): 20–30.

Tullis, F. LaMond. "California and Chile in 1851 as Experienced by the Mormon Apostle Parley P. Pratt." *Southern California Quarterly* 67 (Fall 1985): 291–307.

Vogt, Evan Z., and Ethel M. Albert, eds. *People of Rimrock: A Study of Values in Five Cultures.* Cambridge, Mass.: Harvard University Press, 1966.

Wells, Merle W. *Anti-Mormonism in Idaho, 1872–1892.* Provo, Utah: Brigham Young University Press, 1978.

Countries outside the United States and Immigration

Acevedo A., Rodolfo. *Los Mormones en Chile.* Santiago, Chile: Impresos y Publicaciones Cumora, 1990.

Arrington, Leonard J. "Mormon Women in Nineteenth-Century Britain." *Brigham Young University Studies* 27 (Winter 1987): 67–83.

Baldridge, Steven W., and Marilyn M. Rona. *Grafting In: A History of the Latter-day Saints in the Holy Land.* Murray, Utah: Roylance Publishing, 1989.

Bartholomew, Rebecca. *Audacious Women: Early British Mormon Immigrants.* Salt Lake City: Signature, 1995.

Beecher, Dale F. "Rey L. Pratt and the Mexican Mission." *Brigham Young University Studies* 15 (Spring 1975): 293–307.

Biddulph, Howard L. *The Morning Breaks: Stories of Conversion and Faith in the Former Soviet Union.* Salt Lake City: Deseret Book, 1996.

Bloxham, V. Ben, James R. Moss, and Larry C. Porter, eds. *Truth Will Prevail: The Rise of the Church of Jesus Christ of Latter-day Saints in the British Isles, 1837–1987.* Solihull, Engl.: The Church of Jesus Christ of Latter-day Saints, 1987.

Britsch, R. Lanier. "Church Beginnings in China." *Brigham Young University Studies* 10 (Winter 1970): 161–72.

———. "The Closing of the Early Japan Mission." *Brigham Young University Studies* 15 (Winter 1975): 171–90.

———. *From the East: The History of the Latter-day Saints in Asia, 1851–1996.* Salt Lake City: Deseret Book, 1998.

———. "The Latter-day Mission to India, 1851–1856." *Brigham Young University Studies* 12 (Spring 1972): 262–77.

———. *Unto the Islands of the Sea: A History of the Latter-day Saints in the Pacific.* Salt Lake City: Deseret Book, 1986.

Browning, Gary L. "Out of Obscurity: The Emergence of the Church of Jesus Christ of Latter-day Saints in 'That Vast Empire' of Russia." *Brigham Young University Studies* 33 (1993): 674–89.

———. *Russia and the Restored Gospel.* Salt Lake City: Deseret Book, 1997.

Buchanan, Frederick S. "The Ebb and Flow of Mormonism in Scotland, 1840–1900." *Brigham Young University Studies* 17 (Spring 1987): 27–52.

Cannon, Donald Q. "George Q. Cannon and the British Mission." *Brigham Young University Studies* 27 (Winter 1987): 97–112.

Card, Brigham Y. "The Canadian Mormon Settlements, 1886–1925: A North-American Perspective." *Canadian Ethnic Studies* 26 (1994): 19–38.

Card, Brigham Young, Herbert C. Northcott, John E. Foster, Howard Palmer, and George K. Jarvis, eds. *The Mormon Presence in Canada.* Logan: Utah State University Press, 1990.

Conkling, J. Christopher. "Members without a Church: Japanese Mormons in Japan from 1924 to 1948." *Brigham Young University Studies* 15 (Winter 1975): 191–214.

Cuthbert, Derek A. "Church Growth in the British Isles, 1937–1987." *Brigham Young University Studies* 27 (Spring 1987): 13–26.

———. *The Second Century: The Latter-day Saints in Great Britain, 1937–1987.* Cambridge: Cambridge University Press, 1987.

Davies, Douglas J. *Mormon Spirituality: Latter-day Saints in Wales and Zion.* Nottingham, Engl.: University of Nottingham, 1987.

Davis, Garold N., and Norma S. Davis. "Behind the Iron Curtain: Recollections of Latter-day Saints in East Germany, 1945–1989." *Brigham Young University Studies* 35 (1995): 47–79.

Dennis, Ronald D. *The Call of Zion: The Story of the First Welsh Mormon Emigration.* Provo, Utah: Religious Studies Center, Brigham Young University, 1987.

Dixon, Joseph F. "Mormons in the Third Reich, 1933–1945." *Dialogue: A Journal of Mormon Thought* 7 (Fall/Winter 1971): 70–78.

Ellsworth, S. George, and Kathleen C. Perrin. *Seasons of Faith and Courage: The Church of Jesus Christ of Latter-day Saints in French Polynesia, 1843–1993.* Sandy, Utah: Yves Perrin, 1994.

Evans, Richard L. *A Century of Mormonism in Great Britain.* Salt Lake City: Deseret News, 1937.

Folsom, Marjorie Wall. *Golden Harvest in Ghana.* Bountiful, Utah: Horizon Publishers, 1989.

Geddes, Ross. "'A Storm in the Camp of Brighamism': LDS-RLDS Relations in Brisbane, Australia, 1901–1918." *John Whitmer Historical Association Journal* 11 (1991): 47–59.

———. "Before Stakehood: The Mission Years in Brisbane, Australia." *Journal of Mormon History* 22 (Fall 1996): 92–119.

Grover, Mark L. "Migration, Social Change, and Mormonism in Portugal." *Journal of Mormon History* 21 (Spring 1995): 65–79.

Harris, Claudia W. "Mormons on the Warfront: The Protestant Mormons and Catholic Mormons of Northern Ireland." *Brigham Young University Studies* 30 (Fall 1990): 7–19.

Harris, Jan G. "Mormons in Victorian Manchester." *Brigham Young University Studies* 17 (Winter 1987): 46–56.

Haslam, Gerald M. *Clash of Cultures: The Norwegian Experience with Mormonism, 1842–1920.* New York: Peter Lang, 1984.

Hatch, Nelle Spillsbury. *Colonia Juarez.* Salt Lake City: Deseret Book, 1954.

Heaton, Tim B., Stan B. Albrecht, and J. Randal Johnson. "The Making of British Saints in Historical Perspective." *Brigham Young University Studies* 27 (Spring 1987): 119–35.

Jensen, Richard L., and Malcolm R. Thorp, eds. *Mormons in Early Victorian Britain.* Salt Lake City: University of Utah Press, 1989.

Jenson, Andrew. *History of the Scandinavian Mission.* Salt Lake City: Deseret News Press, 1927.

Katanuma, Seiji. "The Church in Japan." *Brigham Young University Studies* 14 (Fall 1973): 16–28.

Knowlton, David Clark. "Mormonism in Latin America: Towards the Twenty-First Century." *Dialogue: A Journal of Mormon Thought* 29 (Spring 1996): 159–76.

LeBaron, Dale E. *All Are Alike Unto God.* Salt Lake City: Bookcraft, 1990.

Lemble, Jean. *Dieu et les Francais: Les saints des derniers jours francophones.* Paris: Editions Liahona, 1986.

Louder, Dean R. "Canadian Mormons in Their North American Context: A Portrait." *Social Compass* 40 (1993): 271–90.

Lozano, Agricol. *Historia de la iglesia en Mexico.* Mexico: D.F., 1980.

Mabey, Rendell N., and Gordon T. Allred. *Brother to Brother: The Story of Latter-day Saint Missionaries Who Took the Gospel to Black Africa.* Salt Lake City: Bookcraft, 1984

Marsh, Don W., comp. *"The Light of the Sun": Japan and the Saints.* Tokyo, Japan: Japan Mission, 1968.

Mehr, Kahlile. "Enduring Believers: Czechoslovakia and the LDS Church, 1884–1990." *Journal of Mormon History* 18 (Fall 1992): 111–54.

———. "Keeping Promises: The LDS Church Enters Bulgaria, 1990–1994." *Brigham Young University Studies* 36 (1996–97): 69–106.

Morrison, Alexander B. *The Dawning of a Brighter Day: The Church in Black Africa.* Salt Lake City: Deseret Book, 1990.

Moss, James R., R. Lanier Britsch, James R. Christiansen, and Richard O. Cowab. *The International Church*. Provo, Utah: Brigham Young University Publishing, 1982.

Mulder, William. *Homeward to Zion: The Mormon Migration from Scandinavia*. Minneapolis: University of Minnesota Press, 1957.

Newton, Marjorie. "The Gathering of the Australian Saints in the 1850s." *Brigham Young University Studies* 27 (Spring 1987): 67–78.

———. *Southern Cross Saints: The Mormons in Australia*. Laie, Hawaii: Institute for Polynesian Studies, 1991.

Palmer, Spencer J., and Shirley H. Palmer, eds. *The Korean Saints: Personal Stories of Trial and Triumph, 1950–1980*. Provo, Utah: Religious Studies Center, Brigham Young University, 1995.

Palmer, Spencer W. *The Church Encounters Asia*. Salt Lake City: Deseret Book, 1970.

Phillips, Andrew. "Mormons in Essex, 1850–1870." *Essex Journal* 18 (Winter 1983–84): 57–65.

Romney, Thomas C. *The Mormon Colonies in Mexico*. Salt Lake City: Deseret Book, 1938.

Scharffs, Gilbert W. *Mormonism in Germany*. Salt Lake City: Deseret Book, 1970.

Sonne, Conway B. *Saints on the Seas*. Salt Lake City: University of Utah Press, 1983.

———. *Ships, Saints and Mariners: A Maritime Encyclopedia of Mormon Migration, 1830–1890*. Salt Lake City: University of Utah Press, 1987.

Sorenson, John L. "Mormon World View and American Culture." *Dialogue: A Journal of Mormon Thought* 8 (Summer 1973): 17–29.

Tagg, Melvin S. *A History of the Mormon Church in Canada*. Lethbridge, Alberta: Lethbridge Herald, 1968.

Taylor, P. A. M. *Expectations Westward: The Mormons and the Emigration of Their British Converts in the Nineteenth Century*. Edinburgh: Oliver & Boyd, 1965; Ithaca, N.Y.: Cornell University Press, 1966.

Thorp, Malcolm R. "Sectarian Violence in Early Victorian Britain: The Mormon Experience, 1837–1860." *Bulletin of the John Rylands University Library* 70 (Fall 1988): 135–47.

Tullis, F. LaMond. "Early Mormon Exploration and Missionary Activities in Mexico." *Brigham Young University Studies* 22 (Summer 1982): 289–310.

———. *Mormons in Mexico: The Dynamics of Faith and Culture*. Logan: Utah State University Press, 1987.

———. "Reopening the Mexican Mission in 1901." *Brigham Young University Studies* 22 (Fall 1982): 441–53.

———. "Three Myths about Mormons in Latin America." *Dialogue: A Journal of Mormon Thought* 7 (Spring 1972): 79–87.

Van Orden, Bruce A. "The Decline in Convert Baptisms and Member Emigration from the British Mission after 1870." *Brigham Young University Studies* 27 (Spring 1987): 97–105.

Walker, Ronald W. "Cradling Mormonism: The Rise of the Gospel in Early Victorian England." *Brigham Young University Studies* 17 (Winter 1987): 25–36.

Williams, Frederick S., and Frederick G. Williams. *From Acorn to Oak Tree: A Personal History of the Establishment and First Quarter Development of the South American Missions.* Fullerton, Calif.: Etcetera, 1987.

Zobell, Albert L. Jr. *Under the Midnight Sun: Centennial History of the Scandinavian Missions.* Salt Lake City: Deseret Book, 1950.

SOCIAL SCIENCE

Albrecht, Stan L., and Tim B. Heaton. "Secularization, Higher Education, and Religiosity." *Review of Religious Research* 26 (September 1984): 43–58.

Alston, Jon P., and David Johnson. "A Cross-Cultural Analysis of Mormon Missionary Success." *Measuring Mormonism* 5 (Fall 1979): 1–17.

Bahr, Howard M., and Renata Tonks Forste. "Towards a Social Science of Contemporary Mormonism." *Brigham Young University Studies* 26 (1986): 73–121.

Bush, Lester E. "Birth Control among the Mormons: Introduction to an Insistent Question." *Dialogue: A Journal of Mormon Thought* 10 (Fall 1976): 12–44.

Christensen, Harold T. "Mormon Sexuality in Cross-Cultural Perspective." *Dialogue: A Journal of Mormon Thought* 10 (Fall 1976): 62–75.

———. "The Persistence of Chastity: A Built-in Resistance within Mormon Culture to Secular Trends." *Sunstone* 7 (March–April 1982): 7–14.

Corcoran, Brent, ed. *Multiply and Replenish: Mormon Essays on Sex and Family.* Salt Lake City: Signature, 1994.

Cornwall, Marie, Tim B. Heaton, and Lawrence A. Young, eds. *Contemporary Mormonism: Social Science Perspectives.* Urbana: University of Illinois Press, 1994.

Leone, Mark P. *Roots of Modern Mormonism.* Cambridge, Mass.: Harvard University Press, 1979.

Mauss, Armand L. "The Mormon Struggle with Assimilation and Identity: Trends and Developments since Midcentury." *Dialogue: A Journal of Mormon Thought* 27 (Spring 1994): 129–49.

—————. "Sociological Perspectives on the Mormon Subculture." *Annual Review of Sociology* 10 (1984): 437–60.

O'Dea, Thomas F. *The Mormons*. Chicago: University of Chicago Press, 1957.

Peck, Granger C. "The Religiosity of Mormon Academicians." *Measuring Mormonism* 5 (Fall 1979): 18–41.

Schow, Ron, Wayne Schow, and Marybeth Raines, eds. *Peculiar People: Mormons and Same-Sex Orientation*. Salt Lake City: Signature, 1995.

Shepherd, Gary, and Gordon Shepherd. *Mormon Passage: A Missionary Chronicle*. Urbana: University of Illinois Press, 1998.

Sorenson, John L. *Mormon Culture: Four Decades of Essays on Mormon Society and Personality*. Salt Lake City: New Sage Books, 1997.

Toney, Michael B., Carol McKewan-Stinner, and Stephen H. Kan. "Mormon and Non-Mormon Migration in and out of Utah." *Review of Religious Research* 25 (December 1983): 114–26.

Vernon, Glenn M. *Research on Mormonism: A Collection of Readings*. Salt Lake City: Association for the Study of Religion, 1974.

—————. *Sociology of Mormonism: A Preliminary Analysis*. Salt Lake City: Glenn M. Vernon, 1975.

Vernon, Glenn M., and Charles E. Waddell. "Dying as Social Behavior: Mormon Behavior through Half a Century." *Omega* 5 (Fall 1974): 199–206.

PHILOSOPHY

Edwards, Paul M. *Preface to Faith: A Philosophical Inquiry into RLDS Beliefs*. Midvale, Utah: Signature, 1984.

McMurrin, Sterling M. *The Theological Foundations of the Mormon Religion*. Salt Lake City: University of Utah Press, 1965.

FOLKLORE

Cheney, Thomas E., ed. *Lore of Faith and Folly*. Salt Lake City: University of Utah Press, 1971.

Eliason, Eric A. "Toward the Folkloristic Study of Latter-day Saint Conversion Narratives." *Brigham Young University Studies* 38 (1999): 137–50.

Fife, Austin, and Alta Fife. *Saints of Sage and Saddle: Folklore among the Mormons*. Bloomington: Indiana University Press, 1956.

Wilson, William A. "Mormon Folklore: Cut from the Marrow of Everyday Experience." *Brigham Young University Studies* 33 (1993): 521–40.

———. "Mormon Folklore: Faith or Folly?" *Brigham Young Magazine* 49 (May 1995): 47–54.

PERSONAL ESSAYS

Barlow, Philip L., ed. *A Thoughtful Faith: Essays on Belief by Mormon Scholars*. Centerville, Utah: Canon Press, 1986.

Black, Susan Easton, ed. *Expressions of Faith: Testimonies of Latter-day Saint Scholars*. Salt Lake City: Deseret Book Company, and Provo, Utah: FARMS, 1996.

Bradford, Mary Lythgoe, ed. *Mormon Women Speak: A Collection of Essays*. Salt Lake City: Olympus, 1982.

Cannon, D. James. *Mormon Essays*. Salt Lake City: Deseret Book, 1970.

Christensen, Parley A. *All in a Teacher's Day: Essays of a Mormon Professor*. Salt Lake City: Parley A. Christensen, 1948.

———. *Of a Number of Things*. Salt Lake City: University of Utah Press, 1962.

England, Eugene. *Dialogues with Myself: Personal Essays on Mormon Experience*. Salt Lake City: Orion, 1984.

———. *The Quality of Mercy: Personal Essays on Mormon Experience*. Salt Lake City: Bookcraft, 1992.

———. *Why the Church Is As True As the Gospel: Personal Essays on Mormon Experience*. Salt Lake City: Bookcraft, 1986.

Geary, Edward A. *Goodbye to Poplarhaven: Recollections of a Utah Boyhood*. Salt Lake City: University of Utah Press, 1985.

King, Arthur Henry. *The Abundance of the Heart*. Salt Lake City: Bookcraft, 1986. Revised, expanded edition entitled *Arm the Children: Faith's Response to a Violent World*. Provo, Utah: Brigham Young University Studies, 1998.

Poll, Richard D. *History and Faith: Reflections of a Mormon Historian*. Salt Lake City: Signature, 1989.

Rasmussen, Dennis. *The Lord's Question: Thoughts on the Life of Response*. Provo, Utah: Keter Foundation, 1985.

DOCTRINAL AND APOLOGETIC

Barker, James L. *Apostasy from the Divine Church*. Salt Lake City: Bookcraft, 1984.

Bennion, Lowell L. *The Religion of the Latter-day Saints*. Salt Lake City: LDS Department of Education, 1940.

———. *Religion and the Pursuit of Truth*. Salt Lake City: Deseret Book, 1968.

———. *Understanding the Scriptures*. Salt Lake City: Deseret Book, 1981.

Blombert, Craig L., and Stephen E. Robinson. *How Wide the Divide?: A Mormon and an Evangelical in Conversation*. Downers Grove, Ill.: InterVarsity Press, 1997.

Derrick, Royden G. *Temples in the Last Days*. Salt Lake City: Bookcraft, 1987.

Edmunds, John K. *Through Temple Doors*. Salt Lake City: Bookcraft, 1978.

England, Eugene, ed. *Converted to Christ through the Book of Mormon*. Salt Lake City: Deseret Book, 1989.

Eyring, Henry. *The Faith of a Scientist*. Salt Lake City: Bookcraft, 1967.

Hafen, Bruce C. *The Believing Heart: Nourishing the Seed of Faith*. 2nd ed. Salt Lake City: Deseret Book, 1986.

———. *The Broken Heart: Applying the Atonement to Life's Experiences*. Salt Lake City: Deseret Book, 1989.

Jackson, Kent P., et al., eds. *Studies in Scripture*. 8 vols. Salt Lake City: Randall Book, 1984–85; Deseret Book, 1986–89.

Keller, Roger R. *Reformed Christians and Mormon Christians: Let's Talk*. N.p.: Pryor Pettengill, 1986.

Lee, Rex E. *What Do Mormons Believe?* Salt Lake City: Deseret Book, 1992.

Ludlow, Daniel H., ed. *Latter-day Prophets Speak*. Salt Lake City, Bookcraft: 1948.

Ludlow, Victor L. *Principles and Practices of the Restored Gospel*. Salt Lake City: Deseret Book, 1992.

McConkie, Bruce R. *A New Witness for the Articles of Faith*. Salt Lake City: Deseret Book, 1985.

———. *Mormon Doctrine*. 2nd ed. Salt Lake City: Bookcraft, 1966.

McConkie, Mark L., ed. *Doctrines of the Restoration: Sermons and Writings of Bruce R. McConkie*. Salt Lake City: Bookcraft, 1989.

Madsen, Truman G., ed. *Reflections on Mormonism: Judaeo-Christian Parallels*. Provo, Utah: Brigham Young University, Religious Studies Center, 1978.

Matthews, Robert J. *"A Plainer Translation": Joseph Smith's Translation of the Bible*. Provo, Utah: Brigham Young University Press, 1975.

Millet, Robert L. *Alive in Christ: The Miracle of Spiritual Rebirth*. Salt Lake City: Deseret Book, 1997.

———. *By Grace Are We Saved*. Salt Lake City: Deseret Book, 1989.

———. *An Eye Single to the Glory of God*. Salt Lake City: Deseret Book, 1991.

———. *The Mormon Faith: A New Look at Christianity*. Salt Lake City: Shadow Mountain, 1998.

———. *The Power of the Word: Saving Doctrines from the Book of Mormon*. Salt Lake City: Deseret Book, 1994.

Nibley, Hugh. *The Collected Works of Hugh Nibley*. 14 vols. Salt Lake City: Deseret Book, 1986–2000. This multivolume work by Mormonism's most erudite, prolific defender of the late 20th century includes studies of the Old Testament, ancient history, the Pearl of Great Price, early Christianity, the Book of Mormon, and early Mormon history.

Packer, Boyd K. *The Holy Temple*. Salt Lake City: Bookcraft, 1980.

Palmer, Spencer J., and Roger R. Keller. *Religions of the World: A Latter-day Saint View*. Provo, Utah: Brigham Young University, 1989.

Peterson, Daniel C., and Stephen D. Ricks. *Offenders for a Word: How Anti-Mormons Play Word Games to Attack the Latter-day Saints*. Salt Lake City: Aspen, 1992.

Peterson, H. Donl. *The Pearl of Great Price: A History and Commentary*. Salt Lake City: Deseret Book, 1987.

Principles of the Gospel. Salt Lake City: Church of Jesus Christ of Latter-day Saints, 1976.

Rector, Hartman, and Connie Rector. *No More Strangers*. 4 vols. Salt Lake City: Bookcraft, 1971–90.

Reynolds, Noel, ed. *Book of Mormon Authorship Revisited: The Evidence for Ancient Origins*. Provo, Utah: FARMS, 1997.

Rich, Wendell O. *Distinctive Teachings of the Restoration*. Salt Lake City: Deseret News, 1962.

Richards, LeGrand. *A Marvelous Work and a Wonder*. Salt Lake City: Deseret Book, 1950.

Roberts, B. H. *The Falling Away*. Salt Lake City: Deseret Book, 1931.

———. *The Truth, The Way, The Life: An Elementary Treatise on Theology*. Ed. John W. Welch. Provo, Utah: BYU Studies, 1994; *The Truth, The Way, The Life, an Elementary Treatise on Theology: The Masterwork of B. H. Roberts*. Ed. Stan Larson. San Francisco: Smith Research Associates, 1994. These two editions, published simultaneously, follow different but defensible editorial procedures. The former edition has the advantage of 12 essays by different scholars analyzing and evaluating different aspects of Roberts's work.

Robinson, Stephen E. *Are Mormons Christians?* Salt Lake City: Bookcraft, 1991.

Sessions, Gene A., and Craig J. Oberg, eds. *The Search for Harmony: Essays on Science and Mormonism.* Salt Lake City: Signature, 1993.

Shipps, Jan. "Is Mormonism Christian? Reflections on a Complicated Question." *Brigham Young University Studies* 33 (1993): 438–65.

Smith, Joseph Fielding. *Answers to Gospel Questions.* 5 vols. Salt Lake City: Deseret Book, 1957–66.

———. *Doctrines of Salvation.* 3 vols. Salt Lake City: Deseret Book, 1954–56.

Sorenson, John L. *An Ancient American Setting for the Book of Mormon.* Salt Lake City: Deseret Book, 1985.

———. *Images of Ancient America: Visualizing Book of Mormon Life.* Provo, Utah: Research Press, FARMS, 1998.

Sorenson, John L., and Melvin J. Thorne, eds. *Rediscovering the Book of Mormon.* Salt Lake City: Deseret Book, 1991.

A Sure Foundation: Answers to Difficult Gospel Questions. Salt Lake City: Deseret Book, 1988.

Talmage, James E. *The Articles of Faith.* Salt Lake City: Deseret News, 1899.

———. *The Great Apostasy.* Salt Lake City: Deseret News, 1909.

———. *The House of the Lord: A Study of Holy Sanctuaries, Ancient and Modern.* Salt Lake City: Deseret News, 1912.

———. *Jesus the Christ: A Study of the Messiah and His Mission according to Holy Scriptures both Ancient and Modern.* Salt Lake City: Deseret Book, 1915.

Taylor, John. *The Mediation and Atonement of Our Lord and Savior Jesus Christ.* Salt Lake City: Deseret News, 1882.

Welch, John W. *The Sermon at the Temple and the Sermon on the Mount.* Salt Lake City: Deseret Book, 1990.

Welch, John W., ed. *Reexploring the Book of* Mormon. Salt Lake City: Deseret Book, 1992.

Widtsoe, John A. *Evidences and Reconciliations.* Salt Lake City: Bookcraft, 1960.

———. *Priesthood and Church Government.* rev. ed. Salt Lake City: Deseret Book, 1939.

————. *A Rational Theology.* Salt Lake City: General Priesthood Committee, 1915.

Widtsoe, John A., and Leah D. Widtsoe. *The Word of Wisdom: A Modern Interpretation.* Salt Lake City: Deseret Book, 1937.

LITERATURE AND ART

Anderson, Lavina Fielding, and Eugene England, eds. *Tending the Garden: Essays on Mormon Literature.* Salt Lake City: Signature, 1996.

Bell, Shane, ed. *Washed by a Wave of Wind: Science Fiction from the Corridor.* Salt Lake City: Signature, 1993.

Card, Orson Scott. *A Storyteller in Zion: Essays and Speeches.* Salt Lake City: Bookcraft, 1993.

England, Eugene, ed. *Bright Angels and Familiars: Contemporary Mormon Stories.* Salt Lake City: Signature, 1992.

Mulder, William. "Telling It Slant: Aiming for Truth in Contemporary Mormon Literature." *Dialogue: A Journal of Mormon Thought* 26 (Summer 1993): 155–69.

Oman, Richard G., and Robert O. Davis. *Images of Faith: Art of the Latter-day Saints.* Salt Lake City: Deseret Book, 1995.

About the Author

Davis Bitton was born in Blackfoot, Idaho, in 1930. After graduating from Brigham Young University, he earned M.A. and Ph.D. degrees at Princeton University. He had faculty appointments at the University of Texas, the University of California at Santa Barbara, and since 1966, the University of Utah, where he was professor of Renaissance and Reformation history. In 1995 he retired and became an emeritus professor.

Always interested in Mormon history, Bitton was among the charter members of the Mormon History Association and served as its president. Starting in 1972, he served as assistant church historian for 10 years. Compiler of a massive reference work summarizing 2,800 diaries and autobiographies, he has also authored or coauthored several books, including *Images of the Prophet Joseph Smith, George Q. Cannon: A Biography*, and (with Leonard J. Arrington) *The Mormon Experience: A History of the Latter-day Saints*.

Residing in Salt Lake City with his wife, JoAn, Bitton continues his historical research and enjoys his hobby of classical piano.